*The Languages
of Criticism
and the Sciences
of Man*

The Languages
of Criticism and
the Sciences of Man

The Structuralist Controversy

edited by
Richard Macksey
and Eugenio Donato

The Johns Hopkins Press
Baltimore and London

To the memory of Jean Hyppolite—
scholar, teacher, and friend of scholars

. . . Seit ein Gespräch wir sind
Und hören können voneinander.

—Hölderlin

Contents

Preface

*Les théories et les écoles,
comme les microbes et les
globules, s'entre-dévorent
et assurent par leur lutte la
continuité de la vie.*
—Marcel Proust

The papers and discussions collected in this volume constitute the proceedings of the international symposium entitled "The Languages of Criticism and the Sciences of Man," ["Les Langages Critiques et les Sciences de l'Homme"] enabled by a grant from the Ford Foundation. The sessions were convened under the auspices of the Johns Hopkins Humanities Center, during the week of October 18–21, 1966, when over one hundred humanists and social scientists from the United States and eight other countries gathered in Baltimore. The symposium inaugurated a two-year program of seminars and colloquia which sought to explore the impact of contemporary "structuralist" thought on critical methods in humanistic and social studies. The general title emphasized both the pluralism of the existing modes of discourse and the interaction of disciplines not entirely limited to the conventional rubric of the "humanities."

By focusing the discussions on the structuralist phenomenon, the organizers were not seeking to promote a manifesto nor even to arrive at a fixed and unambiguous definition of structuralism itself. To many observers there seemed already to be too many manifestos, while satisfactory definitions of such polymorphic activities, or cultural events, are generally only achieved after the principals are safely dead. The danger was clearly that of deforming a method or a "family of methods" into a doctrine. The purpose of the meetings, rather, was to bring into an active and not uncritical contact leading European proponents of structural studies in a variety of disciplines with a wide spectrum of American scholars. It was hoped that this contact could, in turn, stimulate innovations both in the received scholarship and in the training of scholars.

As this was the first time in the United States that structuralist thought had been considered as a cross-disciplinary phenomenon, the organizers of the program sought to identify certain basic problems and concerns common to every field of study: the status of the subject, the general theory of signs and language systems, the use and abuse of models, homologies and transformations as analytic techniques, synchronic (vs.) diachronic descriptions, the question of "mediations" between objective and subjective judgments, and the possible relationship between microcosmic and macrocosmic social or symbolic dimensions. In addition to affording a common ground for the discussions, the same questions seemed to be paradigmatic to any critical analysis of the prospects for interdisciplinary co-operation.

With these aims and questions in view, the organizers felt that it was important to guarantee that both the symposium and the program of continuing seminars which it generated would include representatives of alien, if not hostile, viewpoints. Certain of the European visitors were more closely identified with "thematic" approaches or with traditional phenomenology, while many of the American delegates to the symposium and participants in the seminars were representatives of archetypal, Gestaltist, contextualist, communication-theory, or transformationalist persuasions. Further, to introduce many of the latter to the European context of structuralist debate, it was decided to try to maintain a balance between more or less theoretical papers and a number of historical or applied topics. In addition, the continuing seminars attempted to explore a number of inter-relationships and complementarities between specifically American and European problems and methods in the sciences of man. Finally, another sort of balance was sought between representation of senior men in the field and a number of younger scholars who had not yet achieved an international reputation. Thus, at the symposium the youngest active participant was under the fateful age of thirty, while the eldest was over eighty. The presence of such younger scholars was a local stimulation to those Hopkins students who worked closely with the visitors on the details of the program and who were able to renew these contacts during study abroad under a program which was initiated at the same time.

The composition of the symposium program, which presented fifteen communications and eleven discussions, included representatives from the following disciplines: anthropology, classical studies, comparative literature, linguistics, literary criticism, history, philosophy, psychoanalysis, semiology, and sociology. It also reflected the active participation at all stages in the planning of colleagues from the Sixième Section of the Ecole Pratique des Hautes Etudes. In addition to those colleagues present at the sessions, the organizers also owe a debt of gratitude to MM Fernand Braudel and Claude Lévi-Strauss for counsel and encouragement. The American colloquists, who were charged with initiating the discussions, were drawn from disciplines complementary to those of the European visitors. In all, there were fifteen colloquists. Although two of the original panel, Professors David Schneider and Roman Jakobson, were prevented (in the first instance by illness, in the latter by obligations in Europe) from participating in the debates, their advice was appreciated even as their presence was missed.

The balance in both the communications and the discussions gave the sessions a distinctly Gallic flavor. (One journalist described the symposium as "a ninety-six-gun French dispute.") The dominance of French as the natural language of the meetings was not unexpected, given the differing life-styles of American and European scholars, but it placed a considerable burden on those who generously supplied consecutive summary translations of the interventions, Bernard Vannier of Hopkins and Gerald Kamber of Bowdoin. Any review of the transcriptions reminds one of the wit and economy with which they courageously negotiated the bridge between the two languages.

The present volume represents an edited version of some thirty hours of tapes. Inevitably, some comments have been omitted or severely edited; others perhaps less germane have been included in the interests of suggesting important transitions in the discussions. The discussions in some cases escaped the transcription entirely, continuing informally at the luncheons and dinners which were served on the Homewood campus or spilling over into the corridors of the hotel where most of the guests were lodged. Further, most of the communications were intended for oral presentation, but were supported by papers distributed to the delegates in advance of the sessions. In a number of cases, as indicated in the notes, an attempt has been made in this volume to conflate the two texts, or alternately to publish the "position paper" as an appendix.

The symposium was followed by a series of continuing seminars conceived as a means of exploring in greater depth over a two-year period certain topics raised initially at the symposium. Twenty-six scholars visited Hopkins to conduct the forty seminars in series and were joined by other visitors who participated in the discussions. A number of the original participants in the symposium also offered seminars, but the program also afforded an opportunity for visits by scholars who were unable to attend the opening sessions. The series was concluded by

Hans-Georg Gadamer and Gérard Genette speaking from European corners and Northrop Frye as a representative of North American criticism.

The continuing seminars also sponsored a series of four small colloquia on contemporary problems of structural analysis in the arts, concentrating in turn on the drama, the novel, the film, and some aspects of contemporary music. In addition, there were a number of related events: a group of undergraduate students, who had been following the colloquia and the questions of interpretation through performance, secured funds and conducted their own seminars under the general title "The Person of the Maker"; another group was organized as an informal arena in which to discuss topics raised by the symposium and seminars and as a forum for work-in-progress by the post-doctoral fellows and faculty; this latter, The First Draft Club, was modeled on the interdisciplinary *Kneipe* convened in the first years of the University by Peirce and Royce and met informally in a faculty home. Finally, the range and resources of the continuing seminars were enhanced by other activities of the Humanities Center, notably the series of seminars on hermeneutical problems offered during 1967–68 and subsequently published by The Johns Hopkins Press as *Interpretation: Theory and Practice* and a colloquium in Zürich devoted to congruent problems of literary interpretation. (The papers of the Swiss colloquium are eventually scheduled for joint publication by The Johns Hopkins Press and Franke Verlag.) The symposium and seminars also initiated a series of student and faculty exchange programs, a series of interdisciplinary courses, and the publication of a number of other texts which have all had their effect on the local intellectual climate.

As in any venture so programmatically international and interdisciplinary, the success of "The Languages of Criticism and the Sciences of Man" depended vitally on the co-operation of many scholars, both on the Hopkins campus and in the larger community to which the meetings were addressed. In addition, a group of students performed many crucial roles during the symposium and the seminars which followed, helping with problems of logistics, translation, and distribution of texts. In the same sense, the present volume has incurred for its editors debts well beyond those which can be recorded here. Some mention, however, should be made of Tom Bray and the students who assisted him with the original transcription; of John Blegen, who worked closely with M. Ruwet on the revision of his paper for publication and whose version of the text, with only minor revisions, appears here; of Anthony Wilden, who worked with Dr. Lacan as well as on two drafts of symposium papers; and of Mme Janine Sommer, who brought a native ear to some of the more obscure Gallic noises on the tapes. During a six-week period in 1968 Gracia Holt gave a witty and intelligent impulse to the problems of transcribing the tapes without which the present text would never have been completed. George Boas generously agreed to review the final draft of Jean Hyppolite's lecture after the latter's untimely death. Sally Donato and Catherine Macksey have perhaps the most invested in this volume, including a leaven of skepticism and impatience. Finally, Nancy Gallienne of The Johns Hopkins Press succeeded, after many delays and indirections on the part of the editors, in submitting the manuscript to the rites of passage with a steady interest and untarnished good humor which should be the model for all critics.

For the infelicities or the inaccuracies of the translations, which account for about eighty per cent of the text, the editors must take full responsibility, though they received help from many quarters in trying to make out passages in the transcription or in trying to carry over the sense of an argument. Except where indicated, the apparatus has been supplied by the editors. It was judged that the proceedings could most fully realize the original aims of the symposium if the volume were published entirely in English, however ungracefully this ideal may have been realized. Consequently, some of the participants in the discussions may have difficulty in recognizing themselves in another language. Unfortunately, the written text is also an inadequate gauge of the liveliness of that community of discussion into which the contributors willingly entered and to which they gave the weight of their critical experience.

Finally, the organizers of the program are grateful to the Ford Foundation for the freedom in which the symposium and seminars were allowed to develop; for the intelligently critical interest which was evidenced by the active presence of a Ford representative, Dr. Sigmund Koch, at the symposium; and for the timely opportunity to bring together under this aegis a range of scholars and critical perspectives which would have been impossible within a conventional institutional or disciplinary frame. Many scholars, students, and citizens contributed to whatever success the entire program may have achieved, but, in hopes that this volume is not unworthy of his own humane inspiration, the editors wish to dedicate these proceedings to the memory of the man whose generous critical spirit so vitally presided at the original sessions, Jean Hyppolite.

Lions and Squares:
Opening Remarks

Richard Macksey

The Johns Hopkins
University

On behalf of my colleagues, of the newly instituted Humanities Center, and of The Johns Hopkins University, it is my privilege to welcome you to the first session of the symposium "The Languages of Criticism and the Sciences of Man." We are especially grateful to those of you who have traveled such a long distance, ideologically as well as geographically, to attend these meetings. There are representatives among us from eight countries and at least as many formal disciplines, who by their presence have expressed a willingness to submit, provisionally, to the, perhaps, tendentiously pluralistic topic suggested by our dual title of convention. Some of our initial difficulties are clearly indicated by the fact that the symmetrical English and French titles are not, on close examination, identical. More significantly, many here would reject, even for the rhetoric of symposia programs, the seductive allure which the word "Sciences" borrows from fields alien to our endeavor. Further, I realize that others, in the wake of Foucault and Heideggerian revisionism, would question the legitimacy for this time of the word "Man" and the metaphysical pathos attached to it by *humanistic* conventions and titular sponsors such as a *Humanities* Center (however loosely defined operationally both its virtual center and effective circumference may be).

Traditionally, international symposia such as this are convened in response to some real or alleged crisis. We do not have to search far to find at least the symptoms and the rhetoric of crisis in our professional journals or scholastic in-fighting. Clearly, recent polemics, especially in Europe, has raised serious and generalizable questions about the privileged status of our disciplinary languages and, behind the linguistic issue, of the status of the subject and the so-called "subject matter." But symposia and crises must also find their definition in the perspective of history, a perspective which is itself, for many of us, highly problematic. As an overture to any methodological discussion some sea-mark [*amer*] or historical point of repair may be valuable. In the longest view, and recognizing the distinctively Gallic character of the present gathering, I am thus reminded that an encounter such as ours has ample precedent in earlier Anglo-French confrontations; indeed, we are celebrating (or quietly mourning) this month the nine-hundredth anniversary of a spirited event which has had profound linguistic and cultural consequences for all of us, the Battle of Hastings. More painfully though, I know that both guests and hosts may find the present moment of our national history an unhappy and inauspicious one which casts a shadow, making this difficult ground on which to meet. Although I cannot annul the dark presence of recent history, I would rather turn to a more local historical perspective to find that shred of encouragement which custom demands at the opening of ventures such as this.

I am thinking of the history of our University and of certain concerns which presided over its inception. The foundations of the Johns Hopkins as a community of scholars rest firmly on the ideal of an international exchange, on a transatlantic dialogue. Someone suggested, almost a century ago, that Daniel Coit Gilman, at the time he was planning and staffing this University, was trying to say that for the intellectual life "il n'y a plus d'Atlantique." Though he may later have encountered at least some of the economic problems and disillusionments which beset his Bourbon predecessor, he clearly did, in the early years, vitally and fruitfully achieve what had been too long absent from the American scene: a continuing exchange of creative men and ideas between Europe and America. This alone was enough to revolutionize what Veblen somewhat ironically called the Higher Learning. Hopkins began in the idea of transatlantic dialogue and has, in the best of times, prospered in it. Indeed, many of us feel that this institution's future may well depend upon it. But this has been, I would emphasize, part of a *continuing* dialogue beyond parochial or institutional borders and interests, part of a larger community. Thus, while for some of our visitors today these sessions mark a return long awaited here by friends, for others, coming for the first time, the trip itself merely punctuates discussions, critical exchanges, begun at Cerisy or Royaumont or Coppet. This is a stop along the way. But the common concern, I think, which binds us all together here today and makes the hope of dialogue possible, however diverse or even irreconcilable our critical languages may be, is the attempt to interpret our beleaguered culture and ultimately to understand our own act of interpretation. And this, in turn, means a common interest in method.

Now this common interest brings me back to the origins of the University, where we may find an emblem and a warning. The emblem is to be found in the career and ambition of an exemplary man, that ornament and gadfly of the new University, Charles Sanders Peirce. He was but one of that extraordinary galaxy of seminal minds which Gilman managed to gather around a new idea (new at least for this country): Sylvester, Gildersleeve, Rowland, Remsen, Martin, H. B. Adams, Hall—a nucleus supplemented by visitors such as Lord Kelvin, Arthur Cayley, E. A. Freeman, Lord Bryce, William James, and J. W. Gibbs. The fellows, associates, and students with whom Peirce had contact, either in his seminars or through the Metaphysical Club which he founded, were hardly less remarkable, including names which were to define American intellectual life for another fifty years—among them Josiah Royce, W. E. Story, Christine Ladd, Oscar Mitchell, Thomas Craig, John Dewey, Thorstein Veblen, and Lester Ward (to be followed in a few years by F. J. Turner and Woodrow Wilson). Ideally at least, this was a community in which ideas moved freely, both horizontally across disciplinary lines and vertically between master and student. Tokens, at least, of this movement would be the career of Royce, who arrived as one of the first Fellows in literature before turning to philosophy, and the *Johns Hopkins Studies in Logic* of 1883, which gathered the contributions of Peirce and his students into what was probably the most important book in its field published in America during the nineteenth century.

Many of the most original minds among those just named went on to leave their mark on other institutions and another generation of students. Peirce, however, held only one formal academic appointment, and that too briefly, during a long and frustrating career. But the major contribution which he and his extraordinary students made during the Hopkins years to the logic of relations, to the foundations of modern logic, and to the pragmatism which these logical developments suggested to Peirce are no doubt still his most familiar achievements.[1]

[1] For what still remains the best survey of Peirce's logical contributions, see Clarence I. Lewis, *A Survey of Symbolic Logic* (Berkeley, 1918), chap. 1, sec. 7. For an intellectual biography of unusual coherence and detail, see Murray G. Murphey, *The Development of Peirce's Philosophy* (Cambridge, Mass.,

Yet he also worked extensively and with great originality in many other fields: epistemology, physics, scientific method, semiotics, metaphysics, psychology, cosmology, ontology, and pure mathematics—as well as more tangentially in ethics, aesthetics, phenomenology, history, and religion. (The one book published during his lifetime, *Photometric Researches*, with pioneer work in mensurational problems, has an important place in the history of astrophysics, while his professional training was in chemistry.)

Yet it is not as one of the last polymaths in a century of increasing specialization that I would appeal to Peirce as our historical precedent. It would be tempting to see in his lifelong quest, through successive revisions necessitated by his own discoveries, for an architectonic system, the precise origins of much that obsesses modern critical speculation in the so-called sciences of man. The emphases shifted and the actual discoveries were diverse, but a few themes constantly reappear in his efforts at systematic consolidation, among them themes which have returned to haunt most current discussion of theory in our disciplines: the need for a generalized study of methods, a comprehensive theory of signs, the semiotic status of the person and the interpretant, the use of "existential graphs," the relationship of chance to purpose, the movement from diachronic to synchronic description. Pre-eminently, for Peirce man was a "signifying animal." Thus, Roman Jakobson has traced his own elaboration of "shifters" to Peirce's work on the indexical sign, while others might see in his speculations on the homologies between thought and language (say in the unpublished popular lecture on "Language and Consciousness") the anticipation of certain metapsychic models and their consequences which will undoubtedly concern us here at these meetings. Again, his search for a logic of invention or of the creative process—through concepts such as abduction, hypothesis, retroduction, and presumption—has anticipated controversial theories about the generation of "plausible hypotheses" such as that of N. R. Hanson and, latterly, has anticipated the provocative topic with which M. Morazé will formally open these sessions.[2]

1961). Among Peirce's contributions to symbolic logic are his development of the free variable and the rheme or propositional function, the elaboration of the logic of relatives or calculus of relative rhemes, the introduction of the class-inclusion relation into Boolean algebra, the generalization of the algebra to apply to propositions, an anticipation of the modern distinction of material implication, and contributions to the logistic thesis.

[2] N. R. Hanson, "Is There a Logic of Discovery?" in H. Feigl and G. Maxwell (eds.), *Current Issues in the Philosophy of Science* (New York, 1961); the contrast with the situation in deductive logic with respect to discovery and justifi-

And, finally, throughout our discussions here this week of the use of models and conjectural method in our various disciplines, we might well attend to Peirce's rehabilitation of the traditional trivium—speculative grammar and speculative rhetoric, as well as the new logic.

Yet all this wealth of wide-ranging speculation and original apparatus, much of which strikes us as so modern in its address, was to be subordinated to the systematic edifice which was framed by what he styled "synechism." On this notion of universal continuity and *haecceity* Peirce grounded his most basic assumptions: logical realism, objective idealism, and evolutionary tychism. The grand design, of course, foundered. He recognized the central position which the new field of topology was to play in sustaining his concept of the continuum as the keystone of his philosophic model. And yet he had to work with tools inadequate to the task—the low-level Listing theorem, his own extension of it, and the clear recognition that the original combinatorial topology must be reconciled with a set-theoretic foundation. In his controversy with Cantor on the theory of continuity he turned, in fact, precisely *away* from the direction in which Brouwer was ultimately to resolve the impasse and create the topology which Peirce's system required. (It is bitter to speculate that had Peirce remained in an active university community he would before his death probably have had access to Brouwer's Cantorian reconstruction, however unpalatable he would have found the topologist's extreme intuitionism.) Though the edifice was not, in fact could not have been, completed, the relevance of much that Peirce did accomplish clearly remains. He sowed widely and, as Paul Weiss has observed, often wildly, but the crops are still being harvested.

But if I may search for a single brief statement to relate the historical burden of Peirce's career at the Hopkins to our present undertaking and to a preoccupation which might unite us, I would turn to the year 1882 and to a public lecture which he gave at the beginning of the new term. Peirce is describing the course which he hopes to offer at Hopkins and a new direction for future study: "This is the age of methods; and the university which is to be the exponent of the living

---

cation is discussed pointedly in R. Carnap, *Logical Foundations of Probability* (2nd ed., Chicago, 1962), sec. 43; on the impossibility of a decision method for the whole of the lower functional calculus (as opposed to the decision method for the propositional calculus in the truth tables), see Alonzo Church, *Introduction to Mathematical Logic* (Princeton, 1956), sec. 46; on an attempt to circumvent the induction problem, see Karl Popper, *The Logic of Scientific Discovery* (New York, 1959).

Richard Macksey

condition of the mind, must be *the university of methods.*" [3] He quickly adds, "Now I grant you that to say that this is the age of the development of new methods of research is so far from saying that it is the age of the theory of methods, that it is almost to say the reverse." And later, Peirce, who was himself a noted pendulum-swinger, argues, "The scientific specialists—pendulum-swingers and the like—are doing a great work; each one very little, but altogether something vast. But the higher places . . . in the coming years are for those who succeed in adapting the methods of one science to the investigation of another." Elsewhere he cites the familiar example of the way the logic of probable inference had been applied fruitfully and successively to resolve long-standing problems in various disciplines. But this plea and the proposed series of courses constitute a warning as well as a challenge. Perhaps Johns Hopkins was the only university then (or now) which could entertain the idea of a chair in the method of methods, this in a century of which Whitehead remarked that its greatest invention was the *method* of invention. I said that we might find an emblem and a warning, for in the year following Peirce's modest proposal, when his work with his students in logic was bearing richest fruit, G. Stanley Hall received appointment to the professorship for which he and his brilliant colleague had been in probation, and Charles Peirce's contract was summarily terminated under obscure circumstances.[4]

[3] Quoted in Max H. Fisch and Jackson I. Cope, "Peirce at the Johns Hopkins University," in P. P. Wiener and F. H. Young (eds.), *Studies in the Philosophy of Charles Sanders Peirce* (Cambridge, Mass., 1952), p. 289. The article makes use of circular and unpublished material in the Hopkins archives.

[4] For a discussion of one possible contributing factor, Peirce's dispute with his eminent and irascible colleague, J. J. Sylvester, about the priority of work on nonions (analogues of Hamiltonian quarternions), see Fisch and Cope, "Peirce at the Johns Hopkins." Although both Peirce and Sylvester finally achieved some degree of ironic detachment about the controversy, Peirce left an amusing account of an earlier interview touching on his decision to suppress his pamphlet of 1882 on the algebra of relatives:

When it was done and I was correcting the last proof, it suddenly occurred to me that it was after all nothing but Cayley's theory of matrices which appeared when I was a boy. However, I took a copy of it to the great algebraist Sylvester. He read it, and said very disdainfully—Why it is nothing but my umbral notation. I felt squelched and never sent out the copies. But I was a little comforted later by finding that what Sylvester called "my umbral notation" had first been published in 1693 by another man of some talent named Godfrey William Leibniz.

The quotation may stand as a commentary on the over-heated "community of scholars" which contained in uneasy proximity mathematicians of the caliber of

Having situated our sessions here this week in the somewhat ironical *temporal* perspective of this University's history, we might conclude and so begin by suggesting some image representative of the metaphoric *space* which will define our meetings. At such interdisciplinary gatherings we have often invoked hortatory images of walls being razed, windows being thrown open, new corridors or prospects being opened up. In the face of such aggressive architectural rhetoric I am tempted to propose a rather ambitious or desperate model. The progressive configurations of symposia have often reminded me of the paradigmatic dynamics of certain board games, games which may provoke the most uncompromising struggle, but which are still governed by an elaborate set of conventions and "moves" which formally abstract the conflict. The comparison with the ideal, arbitrary space of the chess board may have been suggested to me by the intriguing title of M. Derrida's paper, but I suppose that these preliminary remarks themselves could be likened to a commonplace but prescribed pawn move in an opening gambit. Further, our sessions here resemble a board game not only in the demarcation of this arbitrary space, the "squares" we shall each occupy in the days ahead, but in the equally arbitrary ordering of time, which we must accept in order to complete the play, and in that delicate equilibrium between randomness and repetition which would seem to govern our moves. There are, however, both precedents and limitations to our metaphor, as well as considerable ambiguity about the question of "rules" and relevance.[5]

It is probably unnecessary to remind our visitors that in the Anglo-American world games can be a deadly serious business. You may have learned from native informants that Baltimore, by virtue of having "slaughtered Los Angeles in four straight," has just become the [temporary] world capital of baseball. But if one reflects for a moment on the pervasive role which the "game metaphor" has played when extended to recent model-building in the humane sciences, the full force and mixed consequences of such a comparison to our present under-

---

Sylvester and Cayley ("the invariant twins") and younger men such as Peirce and Story.

[5] The questions concerned with rule-formulation and operative sense of the word are complex. Consider, for instance, the differences between the following statements or "rules": (1) In chess, one may not castle if the king has been in check; (2) In chess, one castles to protect the king; (3) In chess, control of the center board is the key to the game; (4) In chess, a knight always moves to a square of a color different from the one it is occupying at the start of the move. For a therapeutic discussion of rules and their relation to language, see Max Black, *Models and Metaphors* (Ithaca, 1962), pp. 95–139.

taking can be briefly assayed. (For our present purpose, I should like to moot the question of whether the metaphor serves as a theoretical model, i.e., a set of assumptions about a formal system structurally maintained, or whether it simply functions as a general, context-bound analogy.) By far the most famous of recent applications of games to human behavior is, I suppose, the work of John von Neumann and his colleagues on formal decision theory in economics and strategic conflict situations.[6] The burgeoning popularity of this mode of analysis among many policy-makers needs little emphasis and serves as a reminder, if one is needed, that even models may have profound consequences. Our fate may even now lie in the balance on the playing tables of Princeton. Although the mathematical elaboration of the theory is complex, the assumptions are quite simple as far as definitions are concerned. The "game" is conceived as involving two or more players, a succession of choices or moves by certain rules of play which result in successive "situations"; the choices by each player may or may not be known to the others, though most board games are classified as "games of perfect information"; the play is governed by a termination rule which results in the adjudication of certain "pay-offs." So far, the basic description would seem to apply to the proprieties of our symposium game, which could further be analyzed in terms of its "zero-sum" (but negotiable) character, its "saddle-points" (which imply optimal pure strategy), the application of "minimax" or "maximin," and so on. If the "moves" could, hypothetically, be reduced to sufficient simplicity, we could even take the first step toward analysis—reduction from the *extensive* (or diachronic) *form* of the "game-tree" to its *normal form* as a synchronic matrix. At about this point, however, the analogy begins to crack, since formal game theory assumes (as did the Chevalier de Méré in his letter to Pascal which provoked modern probability theory) that the players are entirely governed by rational interests. There is no room in the theory

---

[6] John von Neumann and Oskar Morgenstern, *The Theory of Games and Economic Behavior* (Princeton, 1947). See also, R. D. Luce and Howard Raiffa, *Games and Decisions* (New York, 1957) and Martin Shubik (ed.), *Game Theory and Related Approaches to Social Behavior* (New York, 1964). For a lively consideration of some of the paradoxes and problems in the formal theory, see R. B. Braithwaite, *Theory of Games as a Tool for the Moral Philosopher* (Cambridge, 1955). Thanks to his presence at the Symposium, I have since come upon Richard Schechner's suggestive essay "Approaches to Theory/Criticism," in *Tulane Drama Review*, 10, 6 (1966): 20–53, which considers the use of models to delimit the presentational characteristics of such quasi-dramatic events as sports, rituals, and happenings.

for the vagaries of individual psychology or style—precisely what, for some of us, makes certain games and other human activities interesting. Further, game theoretical analysis can only commence after the utilities are given and the goals accepted; it can never, despite the sophistication of its apparatus, inquire into the genesis of the conflict nor question the rationality of the pay-off. As such, it offers one more vivid commentary on the apparent limitations of rational analysis, but also affords us one more reminder of the extraordinary complexity of actual human choices on even the most restricted board.

A second effluence of the game model may be found in the social sciences and psychiatry, where it seems to function more as an aid to the understanding than as a decision calculus. I am thinking here of such appeals to rule-dominated games as have informed the theories of R. S. Peters and Erving Goffman about paradigms of social motivation and encounter.[7] Peters would in fact argue that "man is a chess player writ large," while Goffman (who seems to have drawn from many sources, including Kenneth Burke's "dramatistic" analysis of literary texts) would examine human behavior in terms of role-playing, teams, ceremonial rules, and staging. One of the difficulties of both theories is precisely the difficulty of defining the limits of the metaphor, of telling when the action is on the board (or boards) and when it is authentic and unmediated by the game.

The same difficulties of untrimmed metaphor can be seen in some of the imaginative applications of the game model to psychiatric situations. Thus Eric Berne, starting perhaps with some notions of Freudian demystification which Harry Stack Sullivan elaborated in his interpersonal approach while at Hopkins, has tried to interpret his transactional theory of behavior in terms of an inventive budget of "the games that people play" (an inventory which has itself become an important ploy for domestic in-fighting).[8] Thomas Szasz, in *The Myth of Mental Illness*, has used the game metaphor to argue against prevalent mechanical models and to present the hysteric (and by extension other "clinical cases") as engaged in playing games, in "putting on an act." He recognizes, of course, that some people play

[7] R. S. Peters, *The Concept of Motivation* (London, 1958) and Erving Goffman, *The Presentation of Self in Everyday Life* (New York, 1959); *Encounters* (Indianapolis, 1961); *Behavior in Public Places* (Glencoe, 1963).

[8] Eric Berne, *Transactional Analysis in Psychotherapy* (New York, 1961); *The Games People Play* (New York, 1964). For an introduction to the theoretical and clinical conceptions of Harry Stack Sullivan, see *The Interpersonal Theory of Psychiatry* (New York, 1953); *The Fusion of Psychiatry and Social Science* (New York, 1964); and *Schizophrenia as a Human Process* (New York, 1962).

9

undeclared games with secret rules, where the moves are to the un-
initiated ambiguous or unintelligible, rather than the stereotyped
dramas of Berne's "adapted" players. Like R. D. Laing, who shows a
certain sympathy for the game idiom, Szasz sees neurotic and psychotic games as no more absurd in their pay-offs than the hollow
rewards of so-called civilized and socially conventional games.[9] In
addition to the limitations circumscribing formal game theory, however, these social and psychic extrapolations introduce new difficulties.
There seems to be, as noted, considerable ambiguity about when the
game is serving as an explanatory metaphor and when it functions as
a theoretical model for interpersonal relations. Further, there can be
some confusion between a mode of explanation which says *what*
people do and one which also suggests *why*. There is the final difficulty, not binding perhaps on symposia, that the more complex forms
of human encounter seem to involve the intersection and meshing of
a number of different game situations, conflicting rules, and strategic
demands.

This cursory review brings us finally to perhaps the most seminal
and probably the most relevant appeal to the game analogy in our
time, namely, Wittgenstein's notion of *Sprachspiel* in *The Philosophical Investigations* and other posthumous papers.[10] If we, in fact, are
about to play games here, they are pre-eminently language-games, and
the dominant image in Wittgenstein's development of the comparison
is most often that of a board game such as chess. (His *trouvaille* has
been localized, with the usual pious precision of his students, to a

[9] Thomas Szasz, *The Myth of Mental Illness* (New York, 1961). Also, R. D.
Laing, *The Divided Self* (Baltimore, 1965).

[10] Ludwig Wittgenstein, *Philosophical Investigations* [*Philosophische Unter-
suchungen*] (New York, 1953), paragraph 7 and thence throughout the volume
["Ich werde auch das Ganze: der Sprache und der Tätigkeiten, mit denen sie
verwoben ist, das 'Sprachspiel' nennen."] See also, related passages in the "preliminary studies," *The Blue and Brown Notebooks* (Oxford, 1958), pp. 77ff. Interpreters of Wittgenstein, such as David Pole, who would try to derive a rule-
dominated notion of language have received the hostile attention of Stanley
Cavell in "The Availability of Wittgenstein's Later Philosophy," *The Philosophical Review*, 71 (1962), an essay which includes some timely warnings
against assuming the "obviousness" of the language-game and other ideas in the
Investigations. One brief quote from the *Notebooks*, however, will suffice to
warn us here of the danger of imputing to our "critical languages" the purity
of an exact calculus: "Our ordinary use of language conforms to this [mathe-
matical] standard of exactness only in rare cases. Why then do we in philosophizing constantly compare our use of words with one following exact rules?
The answer is that the puzzles which we are trying to remove always spring
from just this attitude toward language" (pp. 25–26).

walk past a Cambridge playing field, but the origins could no doubt also be traced back to the eighteenth century in the linguistic inventions and gaming aphorisms of one of his favorite authors and stylistic affinities, C. G. Lichtenberg. It is interesting to note, however, that the model of a chess game had served another "language-haunted" man, Ferdinand de Saussure, to conceptualize the functioning of a language when one element, or "piece," effects the passage of the system from one synchrony to the next.) [11] The comparison of game and language, which is a theme running throughout the *Investigations*, interacting with other related themes such as "family resemblance" and "form of life," generates a whole metaphorics of speaking-gaming in Wittgenstein's later thought. It has also generated considerable commentary and variant if not conflicting interpretations, themselves critical games of some little ingenuity. In the hands of some of his interpreters, Wittgenstein's insistence on the plurality of games has been lost; in the hands of others, the person of the player has been submerged, despite Wittgenstein's emphasis of the improvisatory character of many language-games, in the rigid interpretation of prescriptive rules governing play.

Despite the mischief which the language-game analogy has provoked in some literalist circles, the comparison has several immediate advantages for our purposes here: it emphasizes the diversity of language uses and contexts; it defines both the language and its users in terms of an activity (and not a substance); it reminds us that demarcations of the "neighborhood" or "environment" or "region" of a specific linguistic topography, like the gaming board, may help to determine meaning. Conversely, the same "board" or "field" may be used to play different games with different counters, but each game can still be constituted, as in chess, by local rules of association, articulations of similar and dissimilar moves, paradigmatic alternatives, and so on.

[11] Ferdinand de Saussure, *Cours de Linguistique Générale* (Paris, 1916), pp. 125–27. See also, p. 43 and p. 153. Saussure recognizes an inexactness in the comparison: the chess player *intends* through his action to effect a change in the system, while the linguistic synchrony undergoes an *unpremeditated* displacement. It is interesting to compare Saussure's comments here on language as a game-like structure with his fascination with another kind of language-game, the anagrams (or "hypogrammes") which occupied so much of his speculation about poetic composition; for examples of his almost Nabokovian ingenuity, see Jean Starobinski, "Les Anagrammes de Ferdinand de Saussure: textes inédits," *Mercure de France* (February 1964): 243–62, Emile Benveniste (ed.), "Lettres de Ferdinand de Saussure à Antoine Meillet," *Cahiers Ferdinand de Saussure*, 21 (1964): 89–135.

Richard Macksey

It would be foolish, however, to read into Wittgenstein's examples, which after all share only their notorious "family resemblance," an insistence on rules as the determining characteristic of language. Quite the reverse, he tends to use the analogy to reinforce a notion of rules which bend in play, which are sometimes improvised or even forgotten. Further, contrary to some of his exegetes who argue the discrete, hermetic character of each game or "language stratum," he speaks of the "blurred edges" of each "game-bound" situation, allowing for the overlapping and interaction of different games. Languages like games can be "impure" or "mixed." Finally, in the observation of different games and the ways in which local meanings derive from each, he constantly recalls that each game demands players and that each player, by extension, brings to the game his own "form of life" and usages learned from preceding game contexts. Language like chess, for Wittgenstein, seemed to leave room for the idiosyncrasies of personal style, even though the resolution of a given game could be comprehended within the harmonic totality of parts and the general rules governing their interaction.

Chess had also, of course, been the favorite analogy of the mathematical formalists in their savage battle with Brouwer, Weyl, and the other intuitionists, a battle which made the first third of this century an especially bloody period in the history of mathematical philosophy. In the formalist reduction, as in the extreme position of some of Wittgenstein's disciples, people play chess, accept supremely arbitrary rules, but do not inquire into what a game *means;* nor, on any count, do they consider possible interpretations of their actions based on the historic evolution of the game, national characteristics of play, aesthetics, psychiatry, and so on. (The formalist position would correspond to a view of the chess model which Saussure cites to illustrate what he calls *"linguistique interne"* and the latter alternatives, roughly, to what he calls *"linguistique externe."*) These alternative ways of viewing chess—as a paradigm convention and as a means of expressing often hidden personal and social impulses, historical evolution, and other meanings not immanent in the play—could perhaps be used to represent one basic division which may separate us here: the two incompatible views of language implicit in *semiotic formalism* and *hermeneutic geneticism.* In the first case there is the risk of divorcing understanding from the contingency of the individual experience in its depth, while in the latter there is the risk, through the implication of the sign in the hermeneutic process (whether psychoanalytical, social, or historical), of sinking into an infinite regression in search of origins of meaning.

Now, if we can finally press the analogy of language-games just a bit further, Wittgenstein's generous examples clearly suggest that individual "moves" can be conceived of not merely as statements but rather as speech acts, judged not in terms of truth but rather of propriety, felicity, success. Without trying to conflate two very different philosophic minds and styles, it is just a step (though a long one) from Wittgenstein's assertion, "Words are also deeds," to John Austin's *How to Do Things with Words* and the illocutionary force of language.[12] This is a development, however, which could emphasize the quasi-moral character of the utterance (or game) as an action, opening a new and difficult perspective on our roles here as players. An awareness, however, of the moral dimension of language-games was already present, before any of our examples, in the traditional discipline of rhetoric, with the *Phaedrus* itself as a prime and ironic gloss to our activities.

I would close, however, with a curious sentence from Wittgenstein as a cautious counter-weight to Peirce's optimistic program. He is speaking about games we can't play: "If a lion could talk, we could not understand him." ["Wenn ein Löwe sprechen könnte, wir könnten ihn nicht verstehen."] [13] The philosopher is clearly not talking about "cracking the code" of lions or dolphins, but of the impossibility of apprehending any language unless we have some access to the speaker's *Lebensform*. Clearly, what is in question here is not the "form of life" peculiar to zoologists or lion-tamers, who might be expected to know

---

[12] John Austin, *How to Do Things with Words* (Cambridge, Mass., 1962). Cf. Wittgenstein's remark in the *Investigations*: "Words can be *hard* to say: such, for example, as are used to effect a renunciation, or to confess a weakness. (*Words are also deeds*)" (paragraph 546).

[13] *Philosophical Investigations*, p. 223. Cf. G. C. Lichtenberg's speculation about a language where the law of contrarieties does not operate: "Wenn uns ein Engel einmal aus seiner Philosophie erzählte, ich glaube es müßten wohl manche Sätze so klingen als wie 2 mal 2 ist 13," in *G. C. Lichtenbergs Aphorismen*, I, ed. A. Leitzmann (Berlin, 1902), #B238. Lichtenberg, in turn, may well have known Leibniz's comment in his *Méditation sur la Notion Commune de Justice*: "auroit-on raison de soutenir que ce n'est pas ainsi [i.e., $1^2 = 1$; $2^2 = 4$; $3^2 = 9$; ...] chez Dieu et chez les anges, et qu'ils voyent ou trouvent dans les nombres tout le contraire de ce que nous y trouvons?" in *Rechtsphilosophisches aus Leibnizens ungedruckten Schriften*, ed. G. Mollat (Leipzig, 1885), p. 60. From the *mathesis universalis seu divina* through Lichtenberg's optimistic calculus of the mind to Wittgenstein's linguistic skepticism is, however, a very long way.

Richard Macksey

something about lions, but of the form of life defined by a lion's view of the world. And, further, Wittgenstein construed "understand" as meaning "know how to go on" or "get on." And that is what I now must try to do, pausing only to remark that the sessions ahead may reveal a few lions among us. More likely, however, I think that they may reveal a little of the lion in each of us. Wittgenstein, after all, had to conceive of the possibility of the speaking lion before he could posit our incomprehension, and that initial conception is something like the act of sympathetic imagination we may need to understand each other from opposite corners of the room; in short, Wallace Stevens's artist—

> Being the lion in the lute
> Before the lion locked in stone.

Tiresias and the Critic

René Girard
The Johns Hopkins
University

An American author has defined our age as an age of criticism. To many of us, here, it looks more and more like the age of the symposium. And I refer to all those who have dedicated their talent, time, and resources to the success of this meeting. First, I want to thank the Ford Foundation and its representative among us, Dr. Sigmund Koch, whose generosity and understanding are beyond praise. I want to thank Dr. Eisenhower, who has encouraged and aided this enterprise in many ways. I also thank Dr. Charles Singleton, the Director of the Humanities Center, without whose sympathy and help nothing would have been possible. I thank the staff of this university and all our friends on the campus, notably in the natural and biological sciences. I thank all those who interrupted their work to join us here today. And I thank, of course, all members of our *Section on Language, Culture, and Literature* which is publicly born with this event and which will prosper, we hope, in the future. Of all those who helped, I will name only Eugenio Donato and Richard Macksey, the Chairman of the Section and the Chairman of this first meeting. Donato and Macksey are both responsible for much of the form and substance of what we are doing here. During the last two months, Richard Macksey has worked tirelessly, almost alone at times, in the face of many difficulties.

As I survey this room, I feel awed at the thought that I contributed, however modestly, to the presence here of such a distinguished and numerous company, from many a distant shore, intellectual as well as geographical. I am comforted, somewhat, by the thought that very few groups such

René Girard

as this ever had so many good and even urgent reasons to assemble as we have today.

Quite a few disciplines are represented here. Our philosophical backgrounds are different; so are the methodologies in which we trust. We do not speak the same languages or, worse still, we use the same words but they do not mean the same things to all of us. Yet, we all have one thing in common. We do not like the distance between us, we do not like the indifference; we do not like the division of what we still have to call Knowledge, in the singular form, as if it were one.

As we all know, in a limited number of areas and of institutions, notably at the Ecole Pratique des Hautes Etudes in Paris, this centrifugal tendency appears interrupted and even reversed. *Les Sciences de l'Homme*, the Sciences of Man, is the current label for the new area of convergence, or at least of dialogue. The *Sciences de l'Homme* cut across what we still generally call the Humanities and the Social Sciences. The very idea of *Sciences de l'Homme* is a direct challenge to this distinction. In order to engage in a fruitful dialogue we must grasp some of the basic assumptions in which the present dichotomies are rooted. As long as we talk in terms of "bridging the gap" between the so-called two cultures, we remain the prisoners of this duality. From the perspective of the *Sciences de l'Homme*, there is no gap to bridge. The sciences of man have altered, for the first time perhaps, a distinction between subject and object which we have inherited from the nineteenth century.

In the formulation of this important methodological and philosophical change abstractions should be avoided, because abstractions mean nothing, except to those who are already convinced. I will try to suggest this change, in a very tentative and imperfect fashion to be sure, through metaphor and myth.

If we believe, contrary to the perspective I will attempt to define, that the observer poses no more of a problem in human phenomena than he does, or rather than he formerly did, in the natural sciences, we refuse to descend, whether we know it or not, from an imaginary pedestal, high above humanity, from which all truth is deployed at our feet, transparent and readily available, free from the limitations of time and space. To this almost invincible (because invisible) illusion, I find a counterpart, as I do to almost every great human situation, in the Oedipus myth and, more specifically, in the beginning of Sophocles' tragedy.

King Oedipus thinks of himself as a man unattached to the city over which he reigns, a perfect stranger to this obscure past which he plans to investigate. Oedipus, the first Western hero of Knowledge, the researcher par excellence, neglects none of the formalities and precautions which a religious or scientific ritual demand. What more could be asked of him?

If, not unlike Tiresias, we suggest to our investigator that his relationship to the object of his investigation is a little more intricate, perhaps, and a little less distant than he thinks, Oedipus, I am afraid, will not understand this advice. A very conscientious scientist, he will question our own dedication to knowledge. He will read in us a preference for the ethical and the metaphysical over the intellectual. He will suspect a propensity to the irrational and a secret desire to reintroduce what he calls the "subjective element" into the deadly seriousness of his objectivity. And yet, what is urged on him is not a return to a Self whose abstraction and vacuity are predetermined by his own oversimplified definition of objectivity. What is urged on him is not old-fashioned introspection or that verbal debauchery sometimes called existential autoanalysis. Don't we all know that Oedipus is an avid practitioner of introspection and that he receives no light from it? What Oedipus needs is to do away with both his *Self* and his *Other* —equally imaginary, at least in part—through an abandonment of their sterilizing interplay in the constantly reforming structure of his relationships: first to Laios, then to Creon, then to Tiresias himself.

If we try to attract Oedipus's attention to the ambiguous signs from which this structure may finally reveal its outline, he will certainly accuse us of a morbid preference for the vague and the esoteric over our long cherished clear and distinct ideas. He will accuse us of neglecting the *facts* patiently gathered by him in the course of his investigation, unaware that these facts are rendered, if not totally useless, at least not immediately useful, by his false assumption of absolute autonomy, an assumption which predetermines the arrangement, the *découpage* of all possible reality.

The interpretation which Tiresias gives of Oedipus is really a response to the interpretation first given of Tiresias by Oedipus himself. In order to reply to Oedipus in kind, Tiresias cannot simply say: "You are such and such." Oedipus has already located that same being outside of himself, thereby implying that it is not his own. Tiresias must point out the opposition between the real being of Oedipus and Oedipus's opinion of himself. Oedipus, to Tiresias, is a man who, at all times, is what he thinks he is not and is not what he thinks he is. Tiresias must do more than reveal this contradiction; he must put it at the center of his interpretation. In order to be effective he must make it the core of his reply to his adversary. The words of Oedipus are far from forgotten, therefore; they are rearranged into a new structure within which they mean, ultimately, the very reverse of what Oedipus intended. Knowledge of man—knowledge of other men, that is—has become demystification or, should we say, demythification. Let us note, at this point, that the Oedipus myth is the only one which suggests—mythically perhaps, but still indisputably—its own destruction as myth.

I see Tiresias as a striking symbol of the changes which have occurred in our disciplines over the last decades, an allegory of the types of interpretation which will be under scrutiny at this symposium, a cipher more enigmatic, perhaps, and less one-sided than it appears at the present.

The similarity is indeed remarkable between the approach of Tiresias and these modern disciplines, notably psychoanalysis and sociology, which maintain that language signifies beyond and against the explicit and even implicit intentions of the speaker. At the other end of the epistemological ladder, the neo-Positivists refuse to enter into the linguistic maze which the endless debate between Oedipus and Tiresias is about to create. We can well understand their misgivings even if we deplore their defection.

Interpretation in depth will lead the sociologists to socioeconomic causes and it will lead the psychoanalyst to sexual causes, but this difference looks less significant, in the light of contemporary research, than the identical structure of interpretation. This structure of interpretation is that of the *Sciences de l'Homme* and it was very well defined by Michel Foucault in *Les Mots et les Choses*. When I point to Tiresias as a symbol of this approach I am fully aware that the implications are quite different from anything Michel Foucault had intended.

The *Sciences de l'Homme* are the redoubling of interpretation upon itself. They necessarily include in their significant structures and they contradict, since they reinterpret it, a first and more spontaneous interpretation more closely related to the original phenomenon.

Thus, Claude Lévi-Strauss tells us that the real structure of a cultural phenomenon cannot coincide with the spontaneous account given by the subjects themselves. Thus, the application of structural linguistics to phenomena which are extra-linguistic, at least in the narrow sense, necessarily empties these of their original value, destroying the grip on being itself which they appeared to have within their original context. Thus, we have a literary criticism, nowadays, which seeks to define not the unity of the work and the organization consciously designed by the author, or at least acceptable to him, but a more comprehensive structure in which the intentions of this author and the generally accepted interpretation of his audiences are viewed not as absolute yardsticks or impassable barriers beyond which the interpreter should not go, but as no more than elements in a total picture, and these elements can always be reinterpreted according to the requirements of the totalization.

At this point, the Humanists are concerned. They have been concerned, perhaps, for quite a while. Do not these interpretations destroy whatever faith we still have in the great creations of our Humanistic past? Do they not hasten the advent of a nihilism which it is our duty to fight? Before answering this question we must be sure we are not mistaking words for realities. The pieties of commencement speeches should not delude us into thinking that nihilism is something we are free to do battle with because it affects other people only. Thus, thinking himself free of the ills that befall this city, Oedipus wants freely to commit himself, and he offers his help to the plague-ridden fellows about him; but Oedipus will soon be disabused. The only way, perhaps, to stop the progress of nihilism is to recognize its presence and its significance within us. If we fear that the great works of Western civilization are threatened as they are submitted to a more searching and ruthless method of analysis, we unwittingly reveal the depth of our nihilism.

This fear—we are now ready to see it—is unfounded. If one point should emerge from the preceding and very fumbling remarks, this point is really not mine: it belongs to the myth and it belongs to Sophocles. I do not know whether Humanism is represented in the myth, I do not know whether Humanism is represented in Sophocles, but I sense the presence, here, of something truly essential to the existence and to the maintenance of Western civilization. As I try to manipulate my Oedipus metaphor and as it manipulates me, I realize how inadequate I am to the task of suggesting the infinite perspective which it opens to us. Far from undermining the relevance of the myth —and of Greek tragedy, as Freud himself, with all his genius, still unfortunately did—by calling it a dream (and Freud saw infinitely more in Oedipus than all Rationalists combined, beginning with Aristotle), the present orientation of research confirms the power of myth and the relevance of early Greek thought to our own experience. We can begin to unveil in the myth more than a coherent structure, a real matrix of diachronically ordered structures whose suggestiveness as metaphors of our individual and collective predicament—or should I say as *structural models?*—appears almost unlimited.

I am personally convinced that truly great works of art, literature, and thought stem, like Oedipus's own reinterpretation of the past, from a genius's ability to undertake and carry out a radically destructive reinterpretation of his former intellectual and spiritual structures. Unlike lesser works, perhaps, these masterpieces will pass the test of the most radical structural interpretation because they partake of the same essence, to a higher degree, no doubt, than our most searching analyses.

If the myth, and Sophocles, can accompany and illustrate the present changes in modes of interpretation; if the myth still understands us as well and better than even Freud understood it; we have not deviated from the main road of Western thought, we have only moved ahead an inch or two. Apollo's oracle still controls our destiny. The real dangers of the present lie elsewhere and it is the myth, once more, which should be consulted to ascertain their nature.

Our Tiresias symbol seems to settle once and for all the question of the truth. Truth is on the side of Tiresias and of that interpretation in depth which turns the tables on a former interpreter. Are we so sure that this is the end of the road? The truth of Tiresias, in Oedipus, remains a stillborn child, a dead letter which cannot get through to the hero or to anyone else. The blind prophet may well take such pride in having uncovered the illusions of his fellowmen, the demystificator may be so satisfied with his demystification that he, himself, may fall, ultimately, into an illusion almost identical to that of his adversary. At this point, everything Oedipus says of Tiresias will become as true as Tiresias's interpretation of Oedipus. Reciprocity is perfect; reciprocity, in the myth, is always perfect. Tiresias, losing sight of the fact that no God, really, speaks through him; forgetting that his truth, partial and limited, bears the imprint of its true origin which is the heated debates and battles of men as well as the imbrication of converging desires; Tiresias will think he incarnates the truth and he will abandon himself to oracular vaticinations. He, too, will believe that all riddles are solved, that all pitfalls are in the past. That is why Tiresias, too, can be obtuse. Having read the signs of others, at least up to a point, he neglects his own, which are beckoning him, more urgently, more desperately than ever.

This is the failure of Tiresias and it might be our own. It is this failure which drags Tiresias into a painful, sterile, interminable debate with Oedipus. This, of course, should not be a model for us in the discussions to come. Perhaps it is not fitting even to mention such a deplorable precedent. But, in matters intellectual as well as in matters financial, danger and profit always run together. Whenever a real profit is in sight, and it is in sight, we hope, in the days ahead, there is a risk to be run. We will run this risk, in order to reach the true intellectual challenge which is our common joy.

Literary Invention

Charles Morazé
Ecole Pratique
des Hautes Etudes

Mr. Chairman, I am very grateful to be invited to a Symposium of a sort that we would very much like to be able to hold in France itself. I cannot say, however, that I am particularly happy to have to open a conference that is undoubtedly going to prove so fertile and yet so difficult that in all likelihood what I am about to say will appear much less invigorating and less profound than the discussions which are to follow. But this will not be the first time that Frenchmen have been called on to leave their country in order to become better acquainted with each other, and sometimes to better understand each other. Let me add that I am most grateful that you have consented to our addressing you in French. For myself in particular, I would have considerable difficulty in maintaining the high intellectual level of discussion which you have encouraged had I to express myself in another language.

My subject this evening is "Literary Invention," [1] or more precisely, since I am not a specialist in either language or literature, the relationships of literary invention to invention in general.

In rereading the summary of this paper as I was giving it to be mimeographed, I noticed that it contained relatively little about literature and a great deal about other things. I must make my excuse for this the hope that you will not find it uncongenial to have the problem of literary invention and of all the discussions which will take

---

[1] "L'Invention littéraire": "literary inventiveness, discovery." The text which follows is a translation and in some instances a paraphrase of the tape-recording of M. Morazé's lecture. The footnotes have been supplied by the translator.

place here placed in a wider context. After all, since you are going to discuss not only the question of the language of criticism but also that of its place in the sciences of man, it is in this perspective that the generalizations which I shall make, even if some of them may appear somewhat obvious, will find their place.

Thus I find myself led by my own interests into speaking to you first of all about invention in mathematics. This is undoubtedly the result of the fact that as I have tried for years to discover what invention was, it has seemed to me that the authors who spoke of it in the clearest way were mathematicians. It is not that mathematicians are more gifted than other people in matters of introspection, but simply, it seems to me, that in mathematics invention appears in a system simple enough to be more easily recognizable.

Let me therefore recall that celebrated lecture by Henri Poincaré, sixty years or so ago, when he was asked by a number of Parisian psychologists to explain what in his personal experience invention was. What he said—and it has been quoted a hundred times since—was that the solution of a problem does not necessarily come about at the conclusion of a lucid and conscious effort, but that, on the contrary— especially for the really difficult problems which led him to propose entirely new formulas, creative formulas one might say—the solution had surged forth when he least expected it, at times when he was doing something quite different. The role of what he then called the unconscious is even more remarkable, since, as he says, he was led to address himself without knowing why to a certain element of the problem, or to a difficulty which seemed to be without any relationship to the general problem with which he was struggling, as if for relaxation. Then, after days or weeks, he realized that what he had thought was a contingent phenomenon was in fact precisely an element of the process of discovery which was to lead him to the final solution. The importance of the work of the unconscious in mathematical invention was thus emphasized by Poincaré, and the question was taken up again by Jacques Hadamard, who employed part of the time he spent in this country in exile during the war, in New York in fact, in extending the quest begun by Poincaré.[2] But the inquiry sheds light on other reflections which had long seemed incomprehensible—such as those to be found in Newton, or perhaps more precisely in Gauss, who, speaking of his *Disquisitiones arithmeticae* (1801), said: "I know that I discover things, but I don't know *how* I discover them,

[2] Jacques Hadamard, *The Psychology of Invention in the Mathematical Field* (Princeton, 1945).

Charles Morazé

and when I reflect on it, I think that it can only be a gift from God, since things come to me all of a sudden without my having done anything, apparently, to merit them." The philosophers of invention have attacked the problem in all sorts of ways, and it has been possible to find in the works of musicians, Chopin or Mozart for instance, and in the works of men of letters like Valéry, expressions which seem to indicate that the unconscious processes had in fields other than mathematics the same importance as that indicated by Poincaré. But let us restrict ourselves at this point to the general recognition that the operation of the mind can and does transpire apart from periods of [conscious] invention. Were we to comment on this assertion, which I shall provisionally enlist as a valid postulate, we could refer to a number of studies made by physiologists who, notably since Nicolle,[3] have long sought to reconcile the notion of invention with that of chance, as if lucky accidents had brought together extremely diverse notions, as in the case of Poincaré's discovery of Fuchsian groups and functions, belonging to mathematical domains which had never before been related and which were brought together for the first time by him in his discovery. Thus, according to this view, a chance phenomenon would account for the construction of a new idea out of the juxtaposition of diverse ideas.

In fact, however, everything we know about the process of invention contradicts this reflection of Nicolle's. It is not a pure and general act of chance which admits of inventive creation. And no invention can be wholly accounted for by the theory of probability. If Poincaré invents, or if Chopin finds the theme of a melody, or if Mozart tells us that he discovered a quartet while he was traveling through Italy in a carriage, it is not so spontaneously that the discovery appears, but rather (doubtless after an interruption) as the result of a preliminary effort of preparation, which comes about through a series of stages. First of all the thinker must be familiar with mathematics, then within this area of familiarization he must further familiarize himself with the specific problem, or more precisely with the particular fields of mathematics necessary to the elucidation of the problem in question.

But one can go beyond this way of dealing with the stages of the preliminary preparation. If we analyze closely the testimony of a whole series of scientists, poets, and inventors—musical or mechanical—we can recognize three general phases in the process of invention. In order to elucidate each of these phases, it happens that reference to Latin is particularly suitable, as the French mathematician Hadamard sug-

[3] Charles Nicolle, *Biologie de l'invention* (Paris [1932]), pp. 5-7.

24

gested. The first phase would correspond to the meaning of the Latin *informare*. As I have just pointed out, the author or creator of the invention must familiarize himself with the use of signs and methods, he must deepen his general knowledge and pick out in this general area those particular areas which are especially suited to him. At this stage we must emphasize the importance of all the collective contributions of society. A mind alone is not capable of forming itself or of *in*forming itself. It is society as a whole which has offered the inventor all the books which he has had the opportunity to read. (It happens that Gauss was the son of a gardener, whereas Poincaré came from a much more bourgeois family. Both had been able to familiarize themselves with a certain number of texts which were more or less recent products of society.) What is more, since all reasoning processes are both a function of and in relationship with all sorts of actions in daily life, I would note at this point, without going into detail, that the framework of civilization in which one lives has an exceptional importance for the inventor. It is certainly true, for instance, that Newton would not have thought of gravitation if the idea of a globe suspended in space had not become a familiar one in his century. And it is probably not without relation to the taste which architects developed at this time for the construction of cupolas like that of the Pantheon where Foucault's pendulum was to be suspended, the pendulum which was to permit an entirely new precision in measuring the speed of the earth's rotation. At this stage then, the inventor is part of a group whose products he assimilates. These products are not of course simply those directly useful to his invention, but all those which are capable of orienting his meditation in the direction of a discovery to be made.

The second moment is that in which the brain must be put to work, not simply abandoned to the contemplation of works of art or the works of civilization, not simply allowed to indulge in a passive reading, but a moment in which the brain must be put into a state of activity. Many of our contemporary authors employ stimulants at this stage. Poincaré tells us that he used to drink quantities of strong black coffee. But such things are no more than catalysts acting on the nervous system; they are insignificant in relation to the extreme concentration of attention which actually starts a mechanism. Referring once again to a Latin expression, I would say that here the word is *cogitare*, in the sense of *coagitare*. It is a question of making a whole series of notions act together, notions that one will choose from the areas which seem as close as possible to the goal in view. But these notions are assembled and made to act together without one's knowing where one is going, since obviously the invention has not yet been accomplished. Thus an interior process begins to operate, guided by consciousness and often quite clear to consciousness, but a process which goes on even when one's attention is relaxed during periods of sleep, or while one is on vacation. As many inventors have replied when asked about it, this process as often as not is all the more successful in proportion as one's attentiveness allows it to develop freely and does not attempt to force it into a path which might be too particular and preconceived for the new idea to be produced.

Obviously the material which is put to work in this way (Poincaré used to speak of "atomes agités") is derived from the productions of society of which I was speaking a moment ago.

And then, at a certain moment of this activity of co-agitation or meditation, a light breaks through. This—as Chopin, or Valéry, or Poincaré have told us—is a "sudden illumination." A sudden illumination which forces us to insist upon the neurological character which is already implied by the fact that, outside attention or attentiveness, the process is, if not actually begun, at least continued. This is a sudden illumination which everyone agrees gives a feeling of marvelous liberation, a feeling of a sudden internal happiness. To speak in a very concrete way and without referring to experiments concerning microelectronics, which are not yet very far developed in physiology, one might say that this feeling probably corresponds to a sort of better organization of our cerebral cells: a mass of cells which had been blocked by a problem suddenly finds itself liberated because a better organization of what I shall call later on formulas or vectors of thoughts corresponds to an improved economy of our cerebral process, liberating an energy which had been blocked, and thus giving that joyous satisfaction which is doubtless the phenomenon which reawakens the attention. For an example one might cite the joy of Poincaré when he was going for an outing in the countryside around Caen and suddenly found the solution of his problem as he was stepping onto a bus.

But if the solution to a mathematical problem, like the solution to a poetical one, is actually discovered in this way, it is one possible combination amongst many other possible combinations which have been tried in thousands of ways in the work of cogitation. This phenomenon or experience of choice in fact corresponds to the Latin word *intellegere*. I choose in the midst of a set of possibilities. On this point, Valéry, who in studying the problems of poetry tried to take up again the problem of invention, emphasizes that when he finds something, or more exactly when he is in the process of seeking and finding at one and the same time the solution to a poetic problem, he feels himself to be two persons.[4] He becomes double. Preceding him, without having had the same preoccupations with explicating the internal nature of invention, Renan had already said (at the beginning of his *Philosophical Dialogues*): "When I reflect, I have the impression of being the author of a dialogue between the two lobes of my brain." [5] This anatomical metaphor would no longer be accepted by physiologists, but the doubling corresponds to the effort of bringing into action all sorts of propositions and positions and to the choice of a particular conjunction amongst many others which could have presented themselves.

But we must not visualize the operation of cogitation or meditation and the operation of intellection as two rigorously distinct operations, the one characterizing a phase precisely defined within one duration and the other, another completely distinct phase in a later duration. In reality, intellection intervenes, either consciously or unconsciously, at every moment in cogitation in order to relieve the machine of the work which is useless to it and in order to add to it what is necessary to it—just as the mathematical and arithmetical experiences of Poincaré were necessary to the solution of the problem of the Fuchsian function, which had originally appeared to him as of a purely geometrical nature. Consequently, at every instant of the process there is a simultaneous duality of interacting possible formulas and of choices which are as yet only provisional but nevertheless active and which will eventually blossom into a perfect intellection. Obviously one must beware of the great satisfaction felt as a result of finding a solution, for it alone is no guarantor of the authenticity of that solution. Hadamard once remarked to me on the number of students who would come to see him and say, "I've found a marvelous formula for resolving this form of integral." They would be so enchanted that they had no suspicion that they were not right, but a precise proof would show that they were mistaken. They would have simply forgotten an essential element. We are all aware of this, whether in our writing or in our teaching. Many students who are absolutely sure that they have

[4] Valéry develops this idea in "L'Infini esthétique," *Oeuvres*, II (Pléiade), pp. 1342–44. See also "L'Invention esthétique," *Oeuvres*, I (Pléiade), pp. 1412–15, and the text discussed by Hadamard entitled "La Création artistique," originally read to the *Société française de philosophie* (28 January 1928) which is reprinted in *Vues* (Paris, 1948), pp. 285–303.

[5] Ernest Renan, *Dialogues et fragments philosophiques* (Paris, 1876).

produced a magnificent essay are very surprised when we show them that, while their essay included a sudden illumination in the sense that I have already used the term, it did not amount to a discovery of authenticity.

There is authenticity only when the process of intellection has been conducted with all the desirable controls. That is to say, in the case of mathematics, all the mathematical knowledge which *must* be at the disposal of the inventor, who will verify what was produced in illumination and cogitation, will enable him to judge that it is valid. If he is a very good mathematician whose power of intellection has operated throughout the process of cogitation, then of course verification will be a mere formality. If he is not, on the other hand, then a defective piece of work will result. And in any case, apart from the verification by the man himself, there is still the verification of other mathematicians, just as you verify what I say while I am speaking. Thus there follows an effort which gives intellection its true meaning: the effort of a collective control by means of all the products of the same order elaborated by the collectivity. So that if we attempt to distinguish between the exact part played by co-agitation or cogitation in information, which comes entirely from the social, and an intellection, which is only valid if it brings into play all that is suitable in the social, we see that the phenomenon proper to cogitation depends on a kind of surface or line without thickness, or on a kind of point without any essential dimension, but which ultimately reduces considerably the part played by the personal element in invention. Is this to say that the author must be considered as not existing at all? Certainly not. If there were no men, there would be no inventions. And it is certainly in the brain of an author that the phenomenon is produced. But it is produced there insofar as the author does what? In the first place, he has put himself in a certain situation, in a certain state; he has at his disposal his cerebral cells, his body, his eyes. He has been situated in a certain social environment, as in a certain universe of signs, in a universe of information, and in the same way he has been placed in this universe in order to be able to be intelligent, that is to say in order to be able to choose with good reason the correct solution among the possible solutions available. In this function the author obviously has an essential importance.

I would say that he has an equivalent importance on a second level, which I shall dwell on at much greater length. The author supplies a certain energy, an energy which can perhaps be measured only quantitatively. This is a central problem which I don't think is one to be discussed here, but which will be the main object of the preoccupations of physiologists and psycho-physiologists of the brain in the years to come. Whether it is a question of a quantitative energy or not, it is certainly a question of genuine energy. It is precisely on the way that this energy fixes itself to ideas, signs, and images in order to direct them toward the creation of new ideas, signs, and images that I want to insist. Not on its nature—I don't know that its nature is known—but on the manner in which it treats the problems which it animates.

The difference between mathematical and literary invention is evident in the fact that the mathematician works with signs—unhappily called symbols by most mathematicians—which mean nothing to anybody not initiated into the science of mathematics. Mathematical signs are completely devoid of any specific energy, whereas the signs presented in a book of reproductions—a painting by Ingres or Michelangelo for instance—strike us immediately without our being particularly informed on the subject. The mathematical sign is therefore a sign which by itself is devoid of energy. Consequently the work of information in mathematics consists of an operation of conditioning. These signs have nothing to say, they mean nothing, they do not by themselves strike our imagination, nor our profoundest organisms, nor our emotions. They bring about no modification in our glands, nor in the constitution of our blood, nor in the circulation of the humors, but these alien signs are then charged with signification and force, and it is after this artificial charging of neutral signs that the process of invention takes place. At the end of the process, what is produced is retranslated into signs and the signs are left in their neutrality until they are charged again, and so forth.

Signs belonging to the aesthetic universe are, however, directly charged with emotions. Without our even having to make a specific effort, these signs set off an emotional energy process within us. This or that pleases or displeases us, it inspires us with desire or disgust, but the sign paints, sculpts, or speaks directly, insofar as it carries an image which recalls something to us, which strikes our senses indirectly, or which awakens a sensation. The process which creates and orients the energy I speak of is set off by the sign. I would say that the most powerful action of poetry or aesthetics is that which lends signs—or more exactly symbols in this case—the maximum amount of force.

This is when, in spite of ourselves, after reading the first three words of a poem, we continue to read the rest; it is when, after perceiving the vague gleam emanating from a painting, we wish to look at it and contemplate it longer. It is from the moment that a certain energy develops with great force from a work of art or from an aesthetic experience that we find ourselves facing a great phenomenon, a great poem or a great aesthetic response. This aesthetic process operates on symbols, and it is not unrelated to the disincarnated mathematical sign, precisely because it is its opposite and therefore its necessary complement. For in the work of what I would broadly call poetics, when signs or symbols are offered us, and when they are offered us less in isolation than in a sort of confrontation with each other, they wear out, they become exhausted. And when, after a long historical process, certain signs or symbols are situated in a totally exhausted terrain, they then become pure articulations, without meaning. These are the most useful words for mathematical invention, which then recharges them.

In poetry therefore there is a double quest, or rather double labor which will erode a certain number of signs. And since all signs cannot be eroded, since one cannot live in a universe of signs reduced to the state of pure articulation, the poetic effort of painting and the arts recharges other signs.

It happens that in studying these problems of linguistic economy, the economy of words or of the letters of the alphabet, or the economy of language, there has been a great deal of talk, from Saussure and all his imitators, about the example of the word "boeuf." It is certain that the word "boeuf" can lend itself to all sorts of different emotive charges. More precisely, in the temples of Egypt it was charged with a superpowerful emotivity. Many of the words which for us have become ordinary words—and "boeuf" for a biologist is no more than a sign almost as disincarnated as a mathematical sign—must have been at the origin, when they came forth from an imagination full of symbolism, carriers of a charge which invited the faithful not to an effort of abstraction but to an effort of adoration. Thus the ultimate action of poetry is both to choose among the signs with which it deals those most apt for the pure articulation of a supposedly perfect logic and, from period to period when a mode of diction or an aesthetic meaning becomes exhausted, to try to recharge it with emotions so that the process of invention may go on.

Obviously in this recharging with emotion, images play a very important role. The value of words is not in their design alone; this is especially true of pictographic writing. The pure design of writing may have value, as certain French poets have tried to show in playing with the arrangement of lines, words, and syllables. But ultimately words derive their value from the images which they bear. And here, to evoke one of the most difficult problems of literary (or even scientific) comprehension, one could say that these images themselves or these articulations of images have value as representations of acts. Actions act on things, which images do not. Words act on images—and we find ourselves involved in a complex structure: words acting by means of images on men who act on things. We are in a sort of structure that I might call triangular, but which I think would be more complete if we called it a tetrahedral structure with four faces. But however this may be, the essential point is to note that literary production does not work with signs which are pure articulations, but with words bearing images which seek to establish between images the same type of inter-relation and inter-connection as the man of science or the mathematician tries to establish between signs devoid of emotion. Literary invention lives by discharging and recharging symbolic signs.

In every case, of course, the Social intervenes with considerable force. Mathematical, literary, poetic, or aesthetic invention is situated in a wider framework: the entire universe of action. When the President of the United States or the President of France wishes to launch a new policy, he uses words. Men of action like men of the business world begin with words. But there is a great difference between the universe of action and the universe of literary or other works, in the sense that when a man of action or a businessman or a statesman wishes to succeed in an undertaking, he may begin with words, but he must nevertheless wait days, weeks, or months while a whole series of inter-relations is established, often through the use of words, of course. When these inter-relations have brought together in the appropriate conditions a sufficient number of human beings or interests or nations, as the case may be, the man of action has then provided himself with the power to bring about an *event*. But this event is not always—in fact, is rarely—the one which the hero who began it actually desired, since all the time that he was trying to bring it off he was being forced to modify his plan in order to accommodate all the other people essential to the success of this event. The same thing will be found—but at a purely abstract level—repeated in mathematical invention, which, in its own way, is an event. And between the pure sign of mathematics on the one hand and the largely social phenomenon of action on the other, the same thing will be found in the domain of the aesthetic and, more precisely, of the literary work. The same phenomenon is involved, the same way of creating an event. But the words of literature and the images which they evoke are, as Catherine the Great once said to

Diderot, much easier to manipulate than are human groups. The easiest of all to manipulate is probably the mathematical sign. All this is not to say that words and images are less "social" than human groups. But unlike the action whose event is not achieved in its initial utterance, but only after an extensive reference to the "real world" has modified the words themselves sufficiently for them to become part of a movement or policy in history, the literary work, once it is written, comes into existence all at once, whole and entire. The literary work needs no public in order to exist. The task of the public is to judge the work and although its first judgment may be inaccurate, as in the case of Stendhal, communication is eventually established between the work and the public, and at that moment, it is the feeling the public has toward it that indicates the quality of the work. In other words, one can find in the social processes of political action, as in literary history or mathematical judgment, the very same set of phases which I spoke of at the beginning of this paper: information, cogitation, and intellection.

It is these three broad evolutionary phases of the work of the mind which give it, whether in the order of action or of pure science, its force, color, and savor, in fact its whole content and supreme justification. We find ourselves facing either a refinement of effort (in science) or, on the other hand, a materialization of effort (in action), and the work of art is situated between these two poles. The artfully successful sentence is perhaps, after all—since man is also a physiological organism in action—the highest product of human genius. It is sustained by its own logic. But this logic, a totally abstract articulation, could not possibly satisfy the needs which our taste for life, our feeling for life, our hope of life instill in us. If, therefore, the syllogism reduces abstract articulation as much as possible in the rigorous work, it is nothing by itself. On the contrary, the work affords a certain means for men to situate themselves in the midst of society in such a way that society itself is located in the universe of things that it creates or that is offered to it by nature. Thus, in the reduction of the literary work, the creator or his hero (who represents either the creator himself or his antithesis) stands in relationship to other men, so creating logical articulations and, at the same time, lending to the political, scientific, or literary event its *mass*. The articulation is what makes the event comprehensible; the mass is what gives it its weight, its force of impact, its real power—or to use a vague but evocative word: its *beauty*. Thus, if we wish to sum up in an approximate word or two all that invention represents as integrated into larger structures—the object invented or discovered at the very end of the creative process: we could say that the beautiful work is situated at the crossroads where what is accomplished comes forth from the possible and where certitude is offered as a reward for chances taken.

Discussion

JAMES EDIE: I want to ask a question; I would like to ask one that is very simple-minded. It struck me while listening to your very interesting discourse which attempted essentially to bring together, if not to identify, creativity, whether in mathematics, let's say, or in the realm of literary invention. Now, this is a very simple question and no doubt it hardly belongs here, but it might be interesting for us to have your reflections on it. It seems to me that in the realm of mathematics, for instance, in algebra or nearly any realm of mathematics, once the data of a problem are *set*, the structure, the *answer*, is also *set*; there's only one correct solution to a mathematical problem. Now, this may require a great deal of creativity, but there's really only one solution normally. This will not be true, I take it, in a problem that we can say is a work of literary invention. There seems to me to be a fundamental, essential difference.

CHARLES MORAZÉ: You say that there is only one reply to a mathematical question. It is very difficult to accept your assertion. I think that this is the ideal conception which we have of mathematics, but it is certain that the history of mathematics presents many crossroads; crossroads which suggest, at least for a particular period, which of several alternatives is the right or wrong answer.

The postulates go without saying. Men have made a whole mathematics, a whole Euclidian geometry, only to see, after all, that there were other possible off-shoots. Men thought there was only one solution while, in fact, the solutions were more numerous.

I would say that it is likely, it is very likely, but is not certain, that the invention of symbols—like the symbol "the root of minus one," for example, which is completely irrational—would have been the only solution to problems which were [then] posed. But, let's admit it, we see nevertheless that mathematics cuts across itself, from time to time, with irrational periods; that is to say that mathematics is a flow of inventions much more restricted certainly (and there you are entirely right) than aesthetic invention; but it is not absolutely a straight and rigid line. So, your observation is entirely right, but we should not push it to the point at which all comparison between mathematical invention and the invention of action, or aesthetic invention, is made impossible.

Let us say that mathematics is what is closest to a rational continuity, but that it is not identical with it. Mathematics goes through irrational periods, or zones, in which, suddenly, attitudes toward what might have been taken for certain before, change, and, consequently, there is that slight opening which is indispensable to mathematical invention; which means, once again, that one can discuss aesthetic and literary invention by following the same mental procedures and with the same models, which one must adapt (but which are really the same). I insist on this because you must not think that mathematics is entirely logical. That's not true; mathematics is full of illogical things which must be accepted as such.

Having said this, I think that it is clear that the mathematical universe in a given period, at a given moment, is more easily exhausted, and is enclosed by much more rigorous limits, than the poetic or aesthetic universe of which we never know if all the works of a period, all the authors of a period, have given a quarter, a third, or a thousandth of the possibilities offered.

RENÉ GIRARD: I will ask a question starting from the one just asked. If mathematical invention opens diverse possibilities, from another point of view, it seems to me that literary invention is perhaps *less* complex than is said; many great writers in fact (I am thinking particularly of novelists—of men like Proust) have said that the novel [has] absolutely no invention in it; and perhaps starting from certain personal and social contradictions, the possibilities of literary expression are I won't say only at one level, but perhaps very limited and not as vague and complex as the idea of imagination suggests.

MORAZÉ: I was trying to give some "spice" to the discussion, but it goes without saying that it is almost as difficult to invent a literature different from that which existed during a period, as to invent a mathematics different from the existing one at a certain time.

But I must simply say that there are, nevertheless, periods in the history of aesthetic production—you are going to say that I am straying a bit from the question, I confess, but I think it is important to draw attention to this—there are periods which lend themselves to many expressions; others, on the contrary, which are enclosed by unique expressions; and still others which cannot be expressed. They are *inexpressible*. There are *periods* in literature.

JEAN HYPPOLITE: Just a word; I wonder if great invention is not the invention of problems rather than the invention of solutions.

MORAZÉ: Certainly.

HYPPOLITE: According to Bachelard, we must reverse the question, "A problem well posed is always resolved"; we must say, "It is when it is three-quarters solved that the question is posed." The path of invention goes toward the "overture" of the field of problems and not toward the solutions. And it is this extraordinary opening which is, in retrospect, understandable, which is as profound in the mathematical domain as in the domain of the invention of literary structures; because the novel of Marcel Proust is entirely different from the novel of Balzac, and the "new novel" is something else again. There are, therefore, openings in history which are openings of a domain or of a problem. And consequently that is the invention of a problem. This said, I am not making anything clearer!

MORAZÉ: No, but I thank you for saying it because you emphasize what I was trying to say, too briefly and probably badly, in saying that the work itself emerges from the field of the possible and it's the exploration of the possible which is important, just as the work is, as I have already said, a recompense for risk. That's what Poincaré, I think, said: "The important thing, if you want to find the correct idea is to begin by thinking off-center [*penser à côté*]." (I'm not sure whether that's not a good symbol for this colloquium!)

LUCIEN GOLDMANN: M. Hyppolite has already touched on half of what I want to say, but I will just add a few words. I agree entirely with what M. Morazé has just said; well, I agree with almost all; but just one remark: cogitation (and information), cogitation, perception in the domain of science is found in the context of a posed question, as M. Hyppolite has just said. And this problem, the posing of the problem, is not an entirely intelligible phenomenon. It is obvious that the posing of a problem is closely allied to the state of scientific thought, to practical experience, to the social context, and it is within these contexts that the possibility of finding an answer is to be found; whether there be one or two, or a single correct answer depends on the precise institution. Now, I would like to ask the question, "What is the equivalent of this problem in the domain of artistic or literary imagination?", because it is not enough, perhaps, to say that the symbols are worn out; we must prove, first, that the symbols are *recognized* as worn out—and no one can tell us whether it is after ten years, or twenty, or thirty or seventy years that symbols appear to be exhausted—and secondly, that one must say something new. And it's to say this that one legislates certain symbols, certain forms, and that invention is born. Literary invention also comes out of this setting, and I will say here—I am replying to Girard—that it is not true, it's clear, that, say in the seventeenth century in France, there were innumerable possibilities to create a worth-while, coherent literary work. There were innumerable attempts—the history of literature, with today's methods, preserves a few—but the *society* decided which were the valid solutions. I think that perhaps—I present this for discussion —the difference, for the moment, resides above all in the fact that the history of the sciences has already been, for quite a while, cumulative. There are certain problems in the history of science which arise—I would say for almost all the members of the scientific society of America or of France—for entire countries study the same physics today, and even if we put ourselves in the seventeenth or in the eighteenth century there would be a very large common ground; whereas the problems, or the equivalent of the problems, which arise in literary creation are plural to the degree that it is a question of the common life of men, and in which, let us say—to take a concrete example— in the seventeenth century one didn't have the same thing to say at the Court that one had to say in the environment of Rome or that one had to say among people or among the bourgeoisie. But this much said, the number of solutions is limited for the questions posed, or for the equivalent of the questions, and for the functions to be fulfilled in the social life; they are much more limited, and probably, except for this difference which exists also between the natural sciences and the sciences of man—because the natural sciences are already cumulative, while with the sciences of man we know to what an extent particular values and particular problems intervene—the situation is analogous and M. Morazé was entirely right about that.

ROGER KEMPF: I think, as Goldmann does, that it would be fascinating to do a history of literary wear-and-tear someday, or of the creation of symbols and also of their aesthetic disqualification—the history of the passage of a symbol from a creative symbol to a platitude, for example. But perhaps we must distinguish also between poetry and novel; that is, that a metaphor can be perfectly dead poetically and still be viable in a novel. For example, Proust is very critical of certain metaphors of Flaubert which he considers deplorable from the standpoint of poetry. He is very hard on them, he finds them unpoetical precisely because he refuses to accept the romantic style of Flaubert, just as he rejects the romantic system of Balzac. There, I think, it is necessary to distinguish.

MORAZÉ: We certainly must distinguish between poetic procedures and novelistic procedures, as between novelistic procedures and dramatic ones.

HYPPOLITE: That is why my question is not so different. I wonder if you haven't given us an enigma in choosing your examples; an enigma simpler, in a way, or more complicated in another, because you have chosen, as domains of invention, mathematics and poetry, and you have opposed "action" to them. I am simplifying your presentation, but you have not spoken to us about invention in physics, in the laboratory, or of invention in natural history. Between the poetic and the mathematical, it is enough to think of Mallarmé in order to imagine that there can be "rapports" in a field which is self-sufficient and that the contrast with "action" is just as strong because the man of action is using dialectical argument without knowing it, while the mathematician speculates and ends his speculation in himself, or ends his speculation in the history of mathematicians, and the poet does likewise. And perhaps if we had taken the problem of invention at the level of the laboratory and if we had taken the problem of literary invention on the level of the novel rather than on that of poetry, perhaps we would have entirely simplified, or complicated, the problem. I think that this is perhaps not too far from what you call the problem of symbols.

KEMPF: I am afraid today that in structuralist activity the novel is being sacrificed a bit. People will prefer Mallarmé and Lautréamont to Balzac or Flaubert.

RICHARD MACKSEY: Although Todorov and his colleagues, who are studying the calibrations of narrative structures, would seem to be redressing this balance. My aside, however, would simply be that your opposition of action and poetry may be too schematic, since the constitutive ambivalence of literature as against other modes of discourse seems to be that it is at once both a free, unmediated act itself and the interpretative process which follows on that act. I would contrast this former immediacy with the distance which you, as a historian, can maintain between your language and the collective acts which it records. Put another way, a poetic invention may have the linguistic force of both a constatory, and, in some etiolated sense, a performative utterance—with all the consequences such an act implies.

MORAZÉ: I think that you are entirely right, and preferring discussions, which are always more enlightening than personal expositions, I passed very quickly over certain evocations of triangles and quadrangles . . . which were not of the clearest; but you have posed the problem, both of you [Goldmann and Hyppolite], in very clear terms. And you are thereby going to allow me to be more precise about something. . . .

I took mathematics because that is the simplest phenomenon. I evoked action because it is the most complex phenomenon, since it stretches over the greatest amount of time, and since it best brings into the question the way in which time can introduce variables at every stage of the process.

Literary invention is situated between the two. I evoked poetics because in the domain of the use of the word (it would have been painting in the use of colors), we are also at two extremes: the sign in mathematics and the sign in poetics. The invention of the physicist, like that of the biologist, is an invention which allies itself to action to the extent that it needs tools, it needs material, it begins an experiment, sometimes—and more and more these days—there are collaborators, the way a general of the army has soldiers. Anyway, it allies itself to the system of action. And as for the novel (Goldmann would not be satisfied to say that it has been sacrificed), it is found at the center of this triangle, in the ensemble of this figure, to the degree, I would say, that the figure is situated relative to positions that the line mathematics-poetry or the bond poetry-action or the bond action-invention describe. Each has its place and it tries to fill the voids which are effective between a certain way of using up words, and a certain way, on the contrary, of making them forceful, a certain way of representing an action or of denying it. But that is found, if you like, between the three poles. And surely this is a very schematic reduction.

I am not much clearer than I was a moment ago, but we have four days. It wouldn't do to exhaust all the obscurities at once!

JOSEPH DONNAY: My name is Donnay and I am professor of crystallography at this university. In following our distinguished visitor, I must admit, and we all admit it at Hopkins, that mathematics is a part of the humanities, so that you were not giving up your humanity in speaking of mathematics! As a teacher of the physical sciences, I would like to confirm what you said by quoting the opinion of a great French savant, Georges Friedel. . . . Georges Friedel was a crystallographer who had discovered, among other things, a very intriguing law called the Law of Mean Index. I won't inflict the explanation of this Law on you; it concerns the "point symmetry" revealed by crystals under X-ray diffraction. Someone asked Georges Friedel: "M. Friedel, how on earth could you think of such a thing?" And Friedel, with characteristic modesty, replied: "But, my dear sir, after you have manipulated thousands of rectangular planes, as I have, it's a perfectly natural intuition." He called "intuition" what you call "the gift of God," but certainly Friedel was trying to underline the first phase of invention, and we know of a lot of these "perfectly natural intuitions" which are the result of long work, and long, strict, hard discipline. In fact, "the gift of God" is analogous because the monks in medieval monasteries begin their prayer by saying: "Let us put ourselves in God's presence." They also needed this long preparation. So, to sum up, I would like to confirm that the three phases, which you gave, are all three found in our work in the physical sciences.

MORAZÉ: First I want to render unto Caesar that which is Caesar's and unto Gauss that which is Gauss's. It is Gauss who spoke of "the gift of God" . . . and it is striking because that poses a particularly delicate problem (which is also the problem of Stendhal and "Stendhalisme," in some ways); that is, that the success of *Disquisitiones arithmeticae* by Gauss came extraordinarily late. By simplifying a great deal—I should like at this point to evoke great perspectives and depths—we say that at the certain moment a problem is posed, a public exists for that problem, and there is a solution to the problem. In Gauss's case, strangely enough, his *Disquisitiones arithmeticae*—which he attributed to an "invention of God" and of which people have *sometimes* understood not only the importance, but the meaning (so badly did he write in his little notebooks)—was only appreciated twenty or thirty years later. But that doesn't prevent this process from showing just how difficult these genetic problems are to study; these [problems] which arise from the ensemble or center of what you kindly confirmed —and I thank you for that confirmation.

MACKSEY: I would like to clear up something which is still bothering me because it seems to me that there are at least two quite different sorts of invention, and that the distinction between these inventions is perhaps not terribly clear in the minds of some among us—including me. There is the invention which corresponds to the solution of a problem; as an example, you yourself used the invention of imaginary numbers: one day someone decided that the symbol "i" had to be invented, and that the symbol would be defined: "i^2 equals -1" and that solved all kinds of problems. That is one kind of invention. The corresponding invention in literature might be the invention of bourgeois drama (at least in a vague and general sort of way), and I think that it is here that M. Goldmann's remarks take on all their meaning. On the other hand, there are inventions which are much more limited, like that, which you cited, of the mathematics professor who was posing a certain problem, it was a question of deciding the curve of a certain complicated equation, and there were certain tests which allowed him to say, "No, you were wrong, it's not that curve," and so on. To this might correspond the invention of certain tragedies, peculiar to the classical or the neo-classical period, which in turn correspond to particular tests, to certain social (and other) exigencies. And, within this second kind of invention, we must further distinguish, it seems to me, between the invention we all call "traditional"—for this reason I used the example of classical tragedies—and "contemporary," which perhaps takes in, a bit more, the idea of chance (which you put aside at the beginning [of this discussion]) and perhaps some other ideas too, because there are certainly ideas which are dead today, and [yet] certain concepts of invention seem to be based on them.

MORAZÉ: The essence of what you have said would be a kind of typology of invention which it would be interesting to make. I don't feel myself qualified to do this. I think that perhaps we could take up this theme in the colloquium, and we might see that, in fact, it is desirable to consider a sort of typology of inventions. Obviously, for my part, I would be very pleased if we could make some finds of the so-called rational kind correspond with some types of invention in the aesthetic realm. Well, I think we should consider this, but I cannot reply to the question, which is beyond me for the moment.

But, by the way, there are two details in what you said which caught my attention, and which I would like to correct. When I heard you say that someone one day decided that "i" should be the root of minus one . . . I said to myself "Goodness, what a simplification!" Just think what a drama that was, not only within the Italian who perhaps discovered it first, but it was the object of an exchange of letters, of disputes, of discussions, of obscure writings (voluntarily obscure!), of internal dramas and external dramas. Let's not discuss this rather complicated affair; but everyone knows, because I think it is in all the classical courses of study, the disputes which envenomed the life of Newton and of Leibniz. It's not "one day" that one decides. . . . I said that it's extremely simple; it is *relatively* simple, but let's recognize that all this happened, after all, in a rather dramatic atmosphere; that all the myths, tensions, and personal circumstances come into it—Who is the inventor? Who is the inventor's father? Who is the son?—I mean, all kinds of dramas.

HYPPOLITE: And it might not even have turned out.

MORAZÉ: And it might not even have turned out, at any rate at that time.

HYPPOLITE: And it is because (a + b) is susceptible to commutative, distributive, and applicative operations, because you can treat an imaginary number like any number; but if you go off into other dimensions it does not work anymore. It is because those who had this intuition succeeded in the course of history (a kind of rational happenstance), in opening a possible field—and all fields are not possible, as Leibniz said (the greatest theoretician of invention and of the "system-ness" of systems, is surely Leibniz). If you will allow me to add one more remark, namely that Einstein is perhaps the last "individual brain" (since you used the word brain) and perhaps today there will be only "collective brains."

MORAZÉ: That's what I wanted to say about this "chance" you were speaking of. We are not going to examine the axiomatic of chance, but I want to say that we must give a place to spontaneity in invention; precisely because, before the event, we cannot avoid leaving all that to what we *call* spontaneity (about which we will have much to say, and about what goes on inside the brain). During the classical period it is likely that [thought] took place only in a group; which means that what seemed to be chance for "Nicolle" is not chance for someone who would expect not a thinker (*savant*), but a scientific society. What I am trying to say is that it would not be a question of the same "chance," of the same opening of possibilities. We would be more at the center of the curve of certainties; this is itself a probability.

JACQUES LACAN: It is rare for a discussion to bring forward so quickly what could have remained unsettled after a presentation. Much of what there is [to discuss] has been put in its proper place. A minute ago, for example, when you were saying that as to the question of the "imaginary root," things had been resolved very simply. You yourself brought the necessary corrective, *viz.*, that it was a terrible drama. What it seemed to me was the essence of your communication, what it centered about, what gave it its essential character, was that you touched on the question of invention, namely: Who invents? There would be no question of invention if *that* were not the question. You consider this question resolved. In any case, you were very anxious to be precise about the fact that whatever the constellation, the configuration, in which you place the phenomenon we call "invention" (and which you brought into the discussion in an admirably cogent and primary way): one invents to the degree that he puts a number of signs in relationship to each other. I do not advance this argument; it is you who have restated the problem in this way. (Parenthetically I am leaving aside here something that it seems useful to me to recall concerning the use of the term "symbol," which you seem to regret [coming from] the mouth of mathematicians, and which means only this: symbols are the relations between signs.)

But I want to keep to the heart of the matter, which is something you evidently took to be resolved from the beginning—that the man who invents is he whom you were speaking of when you spoke, a moment ago, of *saveur de vivre, goût de vivre, espoir de vivre* [zest for life, love of life, anticipation]. It is a question of the living being, it is the individual, the living individual. But there must still have been a question in the back of your mind, since throughout your exposé that point seemed so obvious that it was almost surprising to hear you emphasize it. You explained that, in spite of all you had said about the context of the invention, it was after all the inventor who invented, who was the author of the invention, and your phrases *saveur de vivre, goût de vivre, espoir de vivre,* actually implied the flesh-and-blood individual. The term "disincarnated" you used, not in connection with this inventor, but in connection with the *sign,* the mathematical sign; which goes to show that the question of incarnation was there present in your mind, although we don't, of course, both give it equal value. It is certain that in this domain of mathematics, which you have aptly chosen in introducing the question of invention, inventions are produced, we may say, at exactly the same time, or within a few months of each other, by *subjects* (I must pronounce the word sooner or later) who are at great distances (geographic or otherwise) from one another. The same phenomenon is no less observable in other fields of invention and especially in the field of literature, although here it does not evoke the same property of astonishment as in mathematics. So, here is where the question lies. In proposing the term *subject* in this connection, and asking that we distinguish it from your living being with all his animation (your conception of which you have clearly expressed since it is a question of that *charge* which does or does not attach itself to the manipulation of the signs, and which you have presented to us on the whole as an emotional charge), you have shown us that this can go even further where the apprehension of signs is involved, for example pictorial signs, whose intuitive connotations you have rightly accepted: the picturesque element counts for something in the way in which they move us more than other signs.

But, leaving the elements in this sort of relationship in which you have left them, are we not ourselves losing something essential, an approach which we must adopt in posing the question? I mean the one which might appear if we focused on the most paradoxical points. I seemed to understand you to say that it was necessary for these mathematical signs to be *recharged* at times. But with what? You certainly emphasized what Russell had said, after all, that in mathematics one knows neither if what one is saying is true, nor precisely of what one is speaking. In this sense, of course, and only in this sense, one can talk of a certain *emptiness* of the sign. In any case, one thing seemed to me certain: that the sign is not recharged with this emotional quality. This I believe is the same thing you suggested when you talked of a purely "quantitative" energy. That must have been what you were thinking of—that it wasn't a—let's not call it "quantitative," which would be really awkward, but a, shall we say, "qualified," energy.

So, if it's not that which periodically presents us with a certain crisis in mathematics, if it is no re-charging of this kind, then the question comes up: What accounts for the passion of this mathematical crisis? What is this passion which is internal, in your admirable demonstration, to this crisis of the signs? To use your vocabulary (at least one I think you can accept, even if you are not the one who associated these exact words): What is the order of the passions around which this event will or will not occur, whatever it may be, this alogarithm, invention of a new sign or of a new alogarithm or a different organization of some logical system? Asked in this way the question seems to show a close connection with the question posed by the introduction of the term *subject* as [something] distinct from the function of individuality you introduced—and it is quite normal to have done so—as essential to the question of the inventor. Is the inventor the physical person that each of us is here, facing the other, being looked at, capturing and being captured, more or less, within a play of gestures? Is it something else? Or is it to the extent that we are both caught up in the system of signs which is creeping into our debate with a sort of effort at approximation, but in which all the same there is a necessary internal coherence, a logical necessity—as someone here recalled just a little while ago. It is after all true that a *collective agreement* does not bring about the triumph or the failure of a theory in formal mathematics. There is another sort of necessity which obtains. Only this other necessity transfers a certain charge which plays, may I say, the same role as that which we call roughly the "affective charge" [*charge affective*]. This seems to me very close to my immediate concern and what it seeks to elucidate: to know in what sense it is, properly speaking, concerned with the *status of the subject,* in so far as it is the same question as the question of the "passion of signs." If one goes a little further in this line, one very quickly, it seems to me, comes to what could seem mysterious to M. Hyppolite in the announcement of the title of my own communication here. I am thinking of the word "inmixing" [*inmiction*]. I think that the first time I introduced this word was precisely in respect to subjects. Subjects (even the *Natural History* of Buflon was not so "natural" as that, may I add) are not as isolated as we think. But, on the other hand, they are not collective. They have a certain structural form, precisely "inmixing," which is, properly speaking, that to which a discussion such as that today can introduce us, and I think uniquely in so far as we are not so sure that he who invents is exactly he who is designated by a certain proper name.

MORAZÉ: Yes, here is a very important problem which I will certainly not exhaust either, but here, too, I invoke the rest of the colloquium which, after all, goes on for several days. But I am grateful to you for several things, large and small. First, for having pronounced the name Russell; it is unthinkable that a discussion of invention should not pronounce this name, and you have done well to introduce it here. Then, for having evoked—this was not central to your remarks, but I note it—the possibility that an invention manifests itself in several places, almost in the same way, almost at the same instant. Let us note, however, that these places are not, after all, as random as one might think; it wouldn't do that, in the minds of our listeners, these places should be considered as just any places. I freely admit that Leibniz and Newton, or a Venetian and a Florentine, were on the track of the same subject, or on the path of the same solution. But one does not imagine that the same solution appears on the banks of the Congo, or even on the banks of the Yangtze Kiang, at these moments. There is consequently a certain fan of possibilities which makes the two inventions, the two phenomena of the same invention (the two manifestations of the invention) contemporary. But this fan does reach over the whole universe or to the whole of humanity.

(But I must say once again that we must always think in terms of what is more or less probable, and not think that invention can happen—that Newtonian or Leibnizian invention could have happened in India or with the Indians in America, that's obvious. But I think that this error is not in *your* minds.)

So, what does this mean? It means that, in fact, a certain number of problems—because in general, men had read the same authors, they were fascinated by the same problems—that roughly speaking, certain problems are, in themselves, ready for solution. This is not to say that the problems are living and that if humanity disappeared they would continue by themselves, it means simply that at a certain moment certain problems are so close to their maturation that perhaps one mind can seize them before another, but that several minds can (also) reach them together.

There is certainly, then, a phenomenon of the maturation of a problem which means, simply, that the problem having been considered before by a large number of minds has arrived at the point that a mind, or a group of minds together, can grasp it effectively. But since you are on the subject of mathematics, it is enough to read the first introductions of Newton to show how much he owes to a great number of contemporaries, or men who worked in earlier years, to see that it was a matter, there, of an "offering" which could have been seized just as easily by another as by himself. (But I think that this is not, either, what matters most to you.)

It remains to be seen, then, whether the "structuration" which appears at the heart of invention is a purely social phenomenon. I want to say: no, it is not a purely social phenomenon; I would say, however, that it is a phenomenon which takes place only to the degree that a human collectivity exists; but if it is purely social I don't quite see what meaning you could give it. . . . If ideas are brought together in the heart of a tragedy, if colors are brought together in a painting, if two ideas are brought together in a mathematical system, it is because they could be brought together, they had that quality in themselves.

I told you (I think, but perhaps I didn't insist on it enough) that that which is pure articulation is probably what the psycho-physiologists will have to study in the years ahead—this is to admit that I don't know what it is—[this pure articulation] can be traced to a cerebral phenomenon; that is to say that in this pure articulation the collective plays less of a part than the natural—I don't know how to say it— let's say, the biological.

I also said that I have a tendency to consider that the energy which was involved here was purely quantitative. But I didn't know if this energy was—not qualitative—but as you said yourself [Lacan], "qualified." I don't know, it's possible. And I think that it's a question which I will leave open.

One last word: You said, "what is the [kind of] energy which draws one's interest? What is this energy, this re-charge of something which draws the interest?" I would say to you: "Define for me what you mean by 'interest' and you can immediately get from that my definition of energy! If you don't define for me your word, 'interest,' don't ask me to define my word, 'energy'!" I say for the moment, let us keep our two ways of naming, [and] of considering a reality which are probably the same in both cases, but which we see differently. This is purely a working hypothesis, but I ask you to consider it as such.

As for this "energy charge" of ideas, I believe quite willingly—I have used a figure of speech here and I apologize because, in addition, this image is borrowed unhappily from what it is most modern to claim—that the sciences of man borrow from the exact sciences all their hypothetical images. First, one more nuance—there are the German linguistics, and on the other side, a spirit perhaps too French-Cartesian, concerned with what happens within the mathematical sign. (Is it with signs that one works? Hadamard formally says, "No, I work with something like vague ideas, which underlie signs.") But this risks being a quarrel over words because these are the ideas which are the most immediately subjacent to any sign whatever. But it is not, after all, about signs that we are talking; it is something, it is the idea to which the sign clings as closely as it can. So that if one simplifies one should say, the sign. But still it must be known that it is not the sign itself, but an idea to which it clings very directly.

LACAN: As close as it may be. It is so difficult to . . .

MORAZÉ: [As close] as you wish; let's recognize this nuance. It won't do anything for us maybe, but I think it must be introduced. Now, what strikes me—I am going to speak in a very rough manner —in an invention (in other words in an event, since for me it's the same thing) is its transformation from a gross form to an articulated one. When the event, or the need to invent, shows up in us, it is a kind of indistinct mass, and if it becomes charged with energy, or if (to use your expression) it attracts interest, it is probably because of numerous internal articulations that we don't know about and that we want to discover. And then, when the articulations are discovered, they fall into their places. And at that moment, occurs what I have called the "re-structuration" which gives us a feeling of liberty, of opening out.

I don't believe I have replied to all your questions, but I think I have made specific, in terms of my vocabulary—as one of my former masters, Nabert, used to say, naïve and rough—that which you said with the fineness of a razor blade. And I think that we should take up this question again in the days to come.

CARROLL C. PRATT: I should like to make a few comments on the historical background to the question of invention and the creative mind raised by M. Morazé. In recent years this topic has come to occupy a foremost position in the work of several groups of psychologists. The most intensive and extensive studies have been made by the psychologists at IPAR (Institute for Personality Assessment and Research) at Berkeley, California. Large groups of top-ranking writers, scientists, architects, and mathematicians were cajoled into spending a week or more at IPAR in close association with members of the staff who conducted interviews, administered all manner of tests of intellectual and creative ability, and then wrote up their reports regarding the salient characteristics of the creative mind.

Of outstanding significance are various lines of evidence to the effect that there is no real difference between scientific and artistic imagination. The mental processes of a Milton and a Newton are much alike, i.e., the IPAR inventories show that writers and scientists perceive and grasp new and unusual relationships in their respective materials in much the same manner and in such a way that the strange is made familiar and the familiar strange.

Creativity of all kinds involves aesthetic sensitivity. Artists and scientists, when tested in this respect, both score way above average and also show a preference for a complexity-asymmetry dimension as against a simplicity-symmetry dimension.

Various tests indicate that highly inventive persons are above average in a number of neurotic tendencies: hypochondria, depression, hysteria, paranoia, and schizophrenia. These results are at variance with Terman's findings many years ago, that brilliant children (those with very high

I.Q.s) are well above average in mental and physical health. But it may be reasonable to assume that in respect of emotional stability older people whose promise has already been fulfilled do not belong in the same category with children whose promise still lies in the future. In any event, it may well be asked how creative adults with all sorts of neurotic traits manage to achieve so much. The answer seems to be that they are markedly above average in ego-strength. They have what it takes to get things done, especially when those things involve putting their flights of imagination into some sort of permanent record. Their ego-strength may be related to W. H. Sheldon's evidence that great geniuses are more mesomorphic than ectomorphic in their constitutional make-up, i.e., they possess hard muscular strength combined with great ambition and drive. The ectomorphic introverts have vivid imaginations and are perpetually on the verge of important accomplishments, whereas the mesomorphic extroverts with creative minds are successful in their tireless search for ways of giving expression to their imagination.

RICHARD SCHECHNER: It seems to me that perhaps I ought to raise a basic question. In your paper, there seemed to be a confusion of projecting onto the artist the methods of the critic. In other words, you proposed that art—the creativity of the artist—and the creativity of the scientist were parallel. But I wonder if it isn't the creativity of the critic and the creativity of the scientist that are parallel; that what the scientist treats of nature and discovers from nature and develops as a methodology, and the critic treats of the work of art are in a parallel relationship; that criticism and scientific method are in a parallel relationship, and that when you try to suggest that the methods of the artist are parallel to the methods of the scientist there is perhaps a cross-transaction, and those methods really are not similar. Because it seems to me that the criticism of a scientific hypothesis is another hypothesis; while the criticism of a work of art is an analysis of that art work and if we try to figure out what a scientific hypothesis is, it is an analysis of nature and it seems to me that the parallel is between the scientific hypothesis and the critical analysis. And I'd like to know your feelings on this.

MORAZÉ: Ah, you mean that it is in criticism that the analogy . . . Well, I'll tell you, my perplexity with this question is that, first of all, the words "nature" and "art" bother me. What is Nature, for us who are closed in this room? It is the walls, the seats, the faces . . . , but after all many works of art are nature for us. You understand, we live, for example, here in a whole set-up which is nature for us, in which we are, but which is a work of art. (My reference is very rough, but I stress the difficulty which I have in distinguishing clearly between nature and a work of art). . . . As for science, it is said that it works on nature. Ah, it is very difficult— What is the nature of mathematics? And what happens in a cyclotron? Is this "nature"? Is it not also a work of art?—in a way.

Thus science doesn't work only on nature, it works on a complex combination to which we attribute all the virtues of nature, but which is a complex melange of nature and art. When you say that criticism works on the work of art, you are no doubt right. What bothers me, is that while you have done well to say, that when science criticizes itself, it transforms one hypothesis by another, as I put the question to you, criticism of art does not create a work of art. But probably Barthes will give us an answer (rather, he will give us *his* answer to a question which perhaps has none). There are perhaps some forms of criticism which are works of art, but is this, then, criticism which can be validly compared to the criticism which is of a scientific hypothesis? In other words, to compare the criticism of art to a scientific hypothesis, is this not to condemn oneself not to know how art replaces art?—You see what I am trying to say?

In other words, I think that your distinction between "nature" and "art" should be considered with precaution and that it is really very difficult when one speaks, whether of a painting or of a poet, or of a play, or of a scientific object, to say exactly what "nature" and "art" are.

Second, I think that we must not limit to criticism only, the valid comparison with the *processus* of invention. Real invention in science is indeed what replaces one hypothesis by another, but true invention in art is, in fact, that which replaces one system of representation by another.

CHARLES SINGLETON: To break the English ice and to join Mr. Schnechner, I'll speak in English to say what I didn't know I was going to say a moment before. But if I understood M. Morazé just now, he suggested that there is little distinction between the work of art and nature. This troubles me very much and might, it seems to me, form a fundamental question. (Incidentally, just as he said, "What is nature? Here we are in this room . . ." I happened to see that it was just beginning to rain outside. And I think that the fact that, in this line of thought, we can suddenly see an analogy between nature and *this* room and *these* walls, suggests a postulate or a focus of thought which perhaps we are not trying to analyze, or explore.) Now, predictably I'm going to speak about a certain Italian poet. I'm known to think of nothing else or read nothing else. I'm going to hold to my old habit, use Dante as a touchstone, and test some of the speculations and assertions made today, including collectivity, social classes, and possibly —though I still have to understand M. Lacan—in-mixing, and so forth. But as far as invention goes, it is in a sense safe to say that Dante invented nothing . . . in the sense of a problem. And yet he invented everything. What did he invent? An experience. An experience that the mathematical symbol does not offer. He says *"sensibile," "sensibile-mente."* It is a vivid, incarnate experience delivered through words. Why? Now, to test some of the hypotheses and to use Dante in this sense. *Why*, since he invents nothing in terms of doctrine, philosophy, ideas out of his social milieu, and so forth, why do we wait a thousand years to get the poet to invent, in the sense I've just said? What explains his coming at just that time? I hope someone will tell me that. When the dissolution or crumbling is threatening sense, there the poetic vision comes forth in its totality. I think that this question was excellently launched today in terms of invention. The experience is there to be had by all who can read the language and prepare themselves to have it. It is repeatable, and keeps on repeating itself. But in terms of "charge" and "recharge" it went a long time through Renaissance and Enlightenment "uncharged"—no battery was ever more so—and then in our time, perhaps we could explain that, it takes on a charge. So that a lecture on Dante by *"qui que ce soit"* attracted crowds. What's happening? What's happening to recharge this decharged battery of Dante? I don't know whether it's any good as a touchstone or not, but it certainly is a case. My colleague went further back in time to Oedipus, but it is a case of going back to a time in history when there was no confusion between nature and art. Dante knows nature is a work of art, God's work, and so forth. I grant you that. *But,* he makes a firm distinction between nature and man's work. Now this isn't coming close at all to "signe," and "invention de problème," it's just suggesting that we are already operating here in terms of *modern problems,* and just let a plodding medievalist suggest that there are other historical horizons in which it might be interesting to situate our thoughts occasionally, as René Girard did in terms of Oedipus.

MORAZÉ: I think that the problem of nature and of art, as you have just re-posed it, is going to be so important in all this discussion that

I won't say anything more about it at the moment; it is, really, a problem which for my part I find very delicate to define. I have not said that they should be mixed together or that they should be opposed to one another; it's just that I am very much perplexed before this difficult problem and words often fail me. On the other hand, I think that this will be the subject of the colloquium—to manage to arrive at this definition. Yet I am very grateful to you for having insisted on an aspect that I didn't discuss at all, which is that we are ourselves inventors, in a way, when we read of the inventions of others and when the admiration which we have for great authors or great poets of the past, in a way, resuscitates in us their invention. And I think—if this is, in fact, what you meant to say—that this is an essential aspect, because when we consider the work of art, or the invention of the work of art, we place ourselves always in the position of the one to whom we attribute it, by coupling it with a name while evoking those who give it a justification—that is, those who are the readers, those who are the admirers; in other words, in sum, the users and those who re-make something in themselves in this regard. For your having called this to our attention, I am very grateful. I think that this is going to give to our coming debates a breadth which perhaps my report alone had not envisaged.

JAN KOTT: I think that this drawing together of mathematical invention and poetic invention is fairly easy. We have, first, the *ensembles* which are limited and *elements* in the ensemble which are limited. And then, there is always the rule of transformation. But if we make some observations in another field; for instance, if a mouse finding itself in a closed circuit, finds the opening and gets out, is it possible to say that the mouse made an invention? Even in the domain of fictional invention in which there is no symbol, the novelistic invention [after all] is fairly difficult to treat at the level of sentences, at the level of words; we are always having to do something similar to what the mouse did—in other words, find the opening, but not in the sign.

If we take another example, for instance the invention of the director of a play. The director's invention consists in fixing a gesture among an innumerable number of gestures. Well, I think that perhaps the greatest division is between the invention in which the number of ensembles and the number of elements is limited (even if it is quite large), and the invention, where one can say the elements are infinite and where it is quite difficult to say what the definition of the ensemble may be, where the rule of the game, the rule of transformation, is not defined. In other words, I think that if there is a large division between invention in the poetic domain and that in mathematics—I do not say an invention in the literary domain, which is much larger (let us say that the novelist doesn't invent with words, doesn't invent with sentences, but invents with the context or even the action)—well, here there is something which is quite perplexing to me, which really poses the problem of invention in which the greatest drawing together in the invention of action equals the invention in the domain of the sciences.

MORAZÉ: What you say interests me very much and reminds me first that I was wrong to suppress a paragraph of my paper which was a necessary definition of the distinction we must often make between invention [*invention*] and discovery [*discovery*]. The latter is the bringing to light or the lucky find [*trouvaille*] of something which already existed, like the exit for your mouse. While invention is the creation of something that did not formerly exist.

Your mouse does not make an invention. It does not create the exit. But it does make a discovery. It finds the exit.

The second point, for which I am grateful to you, is precisely to have evoked these mice, since they have done us such yeoman service in all our psychological laboratories. We torment and frustrate them; we slam doors in their faces. And then they work out the problem. Now, why do we do this? In order to find the basic constitutive elements in the operation of the intelligence. When we refer to the mouse in its labyrinth we are referring to attitudes which may help us to understand our own. If we refused to postulate that operational identity, we would have to do away with a great many laboratories [but we are still talking about the most basic kinds of problem solving and not of isolated cases of invention].

And finally, whereas the number of combinations in mathematical invention may be very limited, it is obviously very great in what the director of a play might do. You are quite right there, but I must set aside that awesome problem of almost innumerable variables in a sequence of solutions as beyond my competence and adhere to the model case of mathematical invention.

HYPPOLITE: Isn't an invention simply what is called in rhetoric an *ellipsis*. From the point of view of logic, one would examine one by one all possible combinations and eventually find the solution, but one can take a short cut. Invention is often the short cut.

MORAZÉ: I welcome the recovery of the principle of *economy*, the abandoning of sequential development for the shortest path.

MACKSEY: But must we not distinguish an inspired short-cut in the initial solution of a problem from economy in the demonstration of the solution? In other words, can't we distinguish psychological from logical processes? And then further distinguish those problems where there is a routine procedure of solution, an algorithm, from those where there is not. To take a simple mathematical case, differentiation answers to the former instance and integration to the latter. I assume that M. Kott's mouse should solve his labyrinth according to what the experimenter might call a "routine decision method" if he is an intelligent mouse (anthropomorphically conceived); but if the experimenter has been careless and left some extraneous clues or crumbs, the mouse may be able to short-circuit the decision method.

HYPPOLITE: I was finding in invention a sort of rhetorical figure, like ellipsis, because logicians must follow their logical steps; they won't skip anything. While the mathematician, who is often an imperfect logician, does skip, and he goes faster.

Apropos of Leibniz and Newton, it is not often enough pointed out that they did not discover *exactly* the same thing. If Newton alone had existed, we would have been headed toward a very different calculus out of his fluxions.

The community of invention is a community in a possible dialogue which takes on meaning only when a third man (such as Lagrange in the history of the calculus) comes along to rethink the dialogue and to see what had not been seen by either of the other two. And only then is there a recurrent history of invention—a fundamental, continuing problem which is, itself, an invention.

MACKSEY: You are certainly right to emphasize, in the case of the famous coincidence of the calculus, both the genuine divergence between the achievements of Newton and Leibniz and also the vital continuity of the *problem* in the next generation. But I am also struck by a number of other aspects of the example: the approximate coincidence of solution, given the diversity of the approach—Newton's being basically cinemetical and Leibniz's geometrical; the fact that the dialogue had some antecedents known to both men, such as the "characteristic triangle" (dx, dy, ds) of Pascal and Isaac Barrow; and, finally, the way in which certain more general assumptions and aims clearly predisposed each mathematician to his particular line of attack—thus, Leibniz was

53

led by his "scientia generalis" to his search for a "lingua universalis" and thereby to the special case of change and motion. I suppose that few minds have ever been so heroically "structuralist" as Leibniz's, but even Lagrange, to take the later instance, was led to his particular line of approach through his algebraic bias and his obvious distaste for Newton's theory of limits. Even though he could not finally sustain his algebraic foundation of the calculus, the abstract treatment of a function was certainly a great invention.

PUCCI: I think that the problem which we posed just now—whether the replacement of one mathematical hypothesis by another can have some parallel with the work of art—might have some answer in the sense that each part in the literary invention tries to correspond to a story, to a truth, to a structure, which has already been *told*. I believe that from Homer to the tragedians to Dante, there is always this reflexive character. The invention of the poet turns toward the possibility of telling the truth in a manner different from the way in which it had been told before, of telling a story better, that is to say, of discovering something which had escaped the earlier poets. Dante actually criticizes some of his predecessors; Homer, in the case of Achilles, criticizes the poets who had told his story without the dimension of pity.

Now, in a sense, one could say that literary invention always leads to the *replacement* of a preceding invention; but there is here, I believe, a central problem: since a law of the structure of reality does not change because another is added, one could also see in the case of literary experience something parallel. Namely, a story. A literary invention preserves some truth if it has been able in some way to grasp the totality or a part of that totality of the society in which the work was conceived; and thus, in the historical process, this work preserves this validity precisely because it was able to apprehend this social totality in which resides the fundamental and essential determination of consciousness itself. But I believe that it is important to see in this case that the poet is more attentive to what we could call the *sub-structure*—the ideas, passions, feelings—than to the real structure of the concrete society. He relates a myth which he always intends to tell better than other poets; he intends to tell something which draws closer to the truth. Although we could find an analogue in this to the replacement of hypotheses, there is also a very great difference.

MORAZÉ: Your observation is certainly to the point and touches certain considerations, about the "renewal" of poetic inventions, which were noted by Professor Singleton. It is certainly true that a succession of poets have sought historically to treat the same theme in order each time to "do it better," each in his own time. The question is then to know if there are not moments when they are exhausted or when, having been exhausted, they suddenly recover their value because there are readers who rediscover their beauties, their validity, after centuries of neglect.

MACKSEY: If there is an evolution of forms, and an evolution within forms, there is obviously an evolution of problems and of modes of inference or invention which they evoke. We are all grateful to M. Morazé for having advanced this evolution and for having thereby opened so many points of entry to the sessions which will follow this meeting.

Criticism and the Experience of Interiority

Georges Poulet
Universität Zurich

At the beginning of Mallarmé's unfinished story *Igitur* there is the description of an empty room, in the middle of which, on a table, there is an open book. This seems to me the situation of every book, until someone comes and begins to read it. Books are objects. On a table, on shelves, in store windows, they wait for someone to come and deliver them from their materiality, from their immobility. When I see them on display, I look at them as I would at animals for sale, kept in little cages, and so obviously hoping for a buyer. For—there is no doubting it—animals do know that their fate depends on a human intervention, thanks to which they will be delivered from the shame of being treated as objects. Isn't the same true of books? Made of paper and ink, they lie where they are put until the moment someone shows an interest in them. They wait. Are they aware that an act of man might suddenly transform their existence? They appear to be lit up with that hope. Read me, they seem to say. I find it hard to resist their appeal. No, books are not just objects among others.

This feeling they give me—I sometimes have it with other objects. I have it, for example, with vases and statues. It would never occur to me to walk around a sewing machine or to look at the under side of a plate. I am quite satisfied with the face they present to me. But statues make me want to circle around them, vases make me want to turn them in my hands. I wonder why. Isn't it because they give me the illusion that there is something in them which, from a different angle, I might be able to see? Neither vase nor statue seems fully revealed by the unbroken perimeter of its surfaces. In addition to its surfaces it must have an interior. What this interior might be, that is what intrigues me and makes me circle around them, as though looking for the entrance to a secret chamber. But there is no such entrance (save for the mouth of the vase, which is not a true entrance since it gives access only to a little space to put flowers in). So the vase and the statue are closed. They oblige me to remain outside. We can have no true rapport—whence my sense of uneasiness.

So much for statues and vases. I hope books are not like them. Buy a vase, take it home, put it on your table or your mantel, and, after a while, it will allow itself to be made a part of your household. But it will be no less a vase, for that. On the other hand, take a book, and you will find it offering, opening itself. It is this openness of the book which I find so moving. A book is not shut in by its contours, is not walled-up as in a fortress. It asks nothing better than to exist outside itself, or to let you exist in it. In short, the extraordinary fact in the case of a book is the falling away of the barriers between you and it. You are inside it; it is inside you; there is no longer either outside or inside.

Such is the initial phenomenon produced whenever I take up a book, and begin to read it. At the precise moment that I see, surging out of the object I hold open before me, a quantity of significations which my mind grasps, I realize that what I hold in my hands is no longer just an object, or even simply a living thing. I am aware of a rational being, of a consciousness; the consciousness of another, no different from the one I automatically assume in every human being I encounter, except that in this case the consciousness is open to me, welcomes me, lets me look deep inside itself, and even allows me, with unheard-of license, to think what it thinks and feel what it feels.

Unheard of, I say. Unheard of, first, is the disappearance of the "object." Where is the book I held in my hands? It is still there, and at the same time it is there no longer, it is nowhere. That object wholly object, that thing made of paper, as there are things made of metal or porcelaine, that object is no more, or at least it is as if it no longer existed, as long as I read the book. For the book is no longer a material reality. It has become a series of words, of images, of ideas which in their turn begin to exist. And where is this new existence? Surely not in the paper object. Nor, surely, in external space. There is only one place left for this new existence: my innermost self.

How has this come about? By what means, through whose intercession? How can I have opened my own mind so completely to what is usually shut out of it? I do not know. I know only that, while reading, I perceive in my mind a number of significations which have made themselves at home there. Doubtless they are still objects: images, ideas, words, objects of my thought. And yet, from this point of view, there is an enormous difference. For the book, like the vase, like the statue, like the table, was an object among others, residing in the external world: the world which objects ordinarily inhabit exclusively in their own society or each on its own, in no need of being thought by my thought; whereas, in this interior world where, like fish in an aquarium, words, images, and ideas disport themselves, these mental entities, in order to exist, need the shelter which I provide; they are dependent on my consciousness.

This dependence is at once a disadvantage and an advantage. As I have just observed, it is the privilege of exterior objects to dispense with any interference from the mind. All they ask is to be let alone. They manage by themselves. But the same is surely not true of interior objects. By definition they are condemned to change their very nature, condemned to lose their materiality. They become images, ideas, words, that is to say purely mental entities. In sum, in order to exist as mental objects they must relinquish their existence as real objects. On the one hand, this is cause for regret. As soon as I replace my direct perception of reality by the words of a book, I deliver myself, bound hand and foot, to the omnipotence of fiction. I say farewell to what is, in order to feign belief in what is not. I surround myself with fictitious beings; I become the prey of language. There is no escaping this takeover. Language surrounds me with its unreality. On the other hand, the transmutation through language of reality into a fictional equivalent, has undeniable advantages. The universe of fiction is infinitely more elastic than the world of objective reality. It lends itself to any use: it yields with little resistance to the importunities of the mind. Moreover —and of all its benefits I find this the most appealing—this interior universe constituted by language does not seem radically opposed to the *me* who thinks it. Doubtless what I glimpse through the words, are mental forms not divested of an appearance of objectivity. But they do not seem to be of another nature than my mind which thinks them. They are objects, but subjectified objects. In short, since everything has become part of my mind thanks to the intervention of language, the opposition between the subject and its objects has been considerably attenuated. And thus the greatest advantage of literature is that I am persuaded by it that I am free from my usual sense of incompatibility between my consciousness and its objects.

This is the remarkable transformation wrought in me through the act of reading. Not only does it cause the physical objects around me to disappear, including the very book I am reading, but it replaces those external objects with a congeries of mental objects in close *rapport* with my own consciousness. And yet the very intimacy in which I now live with my objects is going to present me with new problems. The most curious of these is the following: I am someone who happens to have as objects of his own thought, thoughts which are part of a book I am reading, and which are therefore the cogitations of another. They are the thoughts of another, and yet it is I who am their subject. The situation is even more astonishing than the one noted above. I am thinking the thoughts of another. Of course, there would be no cause for astonishment if I were thinking it as the thought of another. But I think it as my very own. Ordinarily there is the *I* which thinks, which recognizes itself (when it takes its bearings) in thoughts which may have come from elsewhere but which it takes upon itself as its own in the moment it thinks them. This is how we must take Diderot's declaration "Mes pensées sont *mes* catins" ("My thoughts are *my* whores"). That is, they sleep with everybody without ceasing to belong to their author. Now, in the present case things are quite different. Because of the strange invasion of my person by the thoughts of another, I am a self who is granted the experience of thinking thoughts foreign to him. I am the subject of thoughts other than my own. My consciousness behaves as though it were the consciousness of another.

This merits reflection. In a certain sense I must recognize that no idea really belongs to me. Ideas belong to no one. They pass from one mind to another as coins pass from hand to hand. Consequently, nothing could be more misleading than the attempt to define a consciousness by the ideas which it utters or entertains. But whatever these ideas may be, however strong the tie which binds them to their source, however transitory may be their sojourn in my own mind, so long as I entertain them I assert myself as subject of these ideas; I am the subjective principle for whom the ideas serve for the time being as the predications. Furthermore, this subjective principle can in no wise be conceived as a predication, as something which is discussed, referred to. It is I who think, who contemplate, who am engaged in speaking. In short it is never a *he* but an *I*.

Now what happens when I read a book? Am I then the subject of a series of predications which are not *my* predications? That is impossible, perhaps even a contradiction in terms. I feel sure that as soon as I think something, that something becomes in some indefinable way my own. Whatever I think is a part of *my* mental world. And yet here I am thinking a thought which manifestly belongs to another mental world, which is being thought in me just as though I did not exist. Already the notion is inconceivable and seems even more so if I reflect that, since every thought must have a subject to think it, this *thought* which is alien to me and yet in me, must also have in me a *subject* which is alien to me. It all happens, then, as though reading were the act by which a thought managed to bestow itself within me with a subject not myself. Whenever I read, I mentally pronounce an *I*, and yet the *I* which I pronounce is not myself. This is true even when the hero of a novel is presented in the third person, and even when there is no hero and nothing but reflections or propositions: for as soon as something is presented as *thought*, there has to be a thinking subject with whom, at least for the time being, I identify, forgetting myself, alienated from myself. "Je est un autre," said Rimbaud. Another *I*, who has replaced my own, and who will continue to do so as long as I read. Reading is just that: a way of giving way not only to a host of alien words, images, ideas, but also to the very alien principle which utters them and shelters them.

The phenomenon is indeed hard to explain, even to conceive, and yet, once admitted, it explains to me what might otherwise seem even more inexplicable. For how could I explain, without such take-over of my innermost subjective being, the astonishing facility with which I not only understand but even *feel* what I read. When I read as I ought —that is without mental reservation, without any desire to preserve my independence of judgment, and with the total commitment required of any reader—my comprehension becomes intuitive and any feeling proposed to me is immediately assumed by me. In other words, the kind of comprehension in question here is not a movement from the unknown to the known, from the strange to the familiar, from outside to inside. It might rather be called a phenomenon by which mental objects rise up from the depths of consciousness into the light of recognition. On the other hand—and without contradiction—reading implies something resembling the apperception I have of myself, the action by which I grasp straightway what I think as being thought by a subject (who, in this case, is not I). Whatever sort of alienation I may endure, reading does not interrupt my activity as subject.

Reading, then, is the act in which the subjective principle which I call *I*, is modified in such a way that I no longer have the right, strictly speaking, to consider it as my *I*. I am on loan to another, and this other thinks, feels, suffers, and acts within me. The phenomenon appears in its most obvious and even naïvest form in the sort of spell brought about by certain cheap kinds of reading, such as thrillers, of which I say, "It gripped me." Now it is important to note that this possession of myself by another takes place not only on the level of objective thought, that is with regard to images, sensations, ideas which reading affords me, but also on the level of my very subjectivity.

When I am absorbed in reading, a second self takes over, a self which thinks and feels for me. Withdrawn in some recess of myself, do I then silently witness this dispossession? Do I derive from it some comfort, or, on the contrary, a kind of anguish? However that may be, someone else holds the center of the stage, and the question which imposes itself, which I am absolutely obliged to ask myself, is this: "Who is the usurper who occupies the forefront? Who is this mind who alone all by himself fills my consciousness and who, when I say *I*, is indeed that *I?*"

There is an immediate answer to this question, perhaps too easy an answer. This *I* who "thinks in me" when I read a book, is the *I* of the one who writes the book. When I read Baudelaire or Racine, it is really Baudelaire or Racine who thinks, feels, allows himself to be read within me. Thus a book is not only a book, it is the means by which an author actually preserves his ideas, his feelings, his modes of dreaming and living. It is his means of saving his identity from death. Such an interpretation of reading is not false. It seems to justify what is commonly called the biographical explication of literary texts. Indeed every word of literature is impregnated with the mind of the one who wrote it. As he makes us read it, he awakens in us the analogue of what he thought or felt. To understand a literary work, then, is to let the individual who wrote it reveal himself to us *in* us. It is not the biography which explicates the work, but rather the work which sometimes enables us to understand the biography.

But biographical interpretation is in part false and misleading. It is true that there is an analogy between the works of an author and the experiences of his life. The works may be seen as an incomplete translation of the life. And further, there is an even more significant analogy among all the works of a single author. Each of the works, however, while I am reading it, lives in me its own life. The subject who is revealed to me through my reading of it is not the author, either in the disordered totality of his outer experiences, or in the aggregate, better organized, and concentrated totality, which is the one of his writings. Yet the subject which presides over the work can exist only in the work. To be sure, nothing is unimportant for understanding the work, and a mass of biographical, bibliographical, textual, and general critical information is indispensable to me. And yet this knowledge does not coincide with the internal knowledge of the work. Whatever may be the sum of the information I acquire on Baudelaire or Racine, in whatever degree of intimacy I may live with their genius, I am aware that this contribution does not suffice to illuminate for me in its own inner meaning, in its formal perfection, and in the subjective principle which animates it, the particular work of Baudelaire or of Racine the reading of which now absorbs me. At this moment what matters to me is to live, from the inside, in a certain identity with the work and the work alone. It could hardly be otherwise. Nothing external to the work could possibly share the extraordinary claim which the work now exerts on me. It is there within me, not to send me back, outside itself, to its author, nor to his other writings, but on the contrary to keep my attention riveted on itself. It is the work which traces in me the very boundaries within which this consciousness will define itself. It is the work which forces on me a series of mental objects and creates in me a network of words, beyond which, for the time being, there will be no room for other mental objects or for other words. And it is the work, finally, which, not satisfied thus with defining the content of my consciousness, takes hold of it, appropriates it, and makes of it that *I* which, from one end of my reading to the other, presides over the unfolding of the work, of the single work which I am reading.

And so the work forms the temporary mental substance which fills my consciousness; and it is moreover that consciousness, the *I*-subject, the continued consciousness of what is, revealing iteIf within the interior of the work. Such is the characteristic condition of every work which I summon back into existence by placing my own consciousness at its disposal. I give it not only existence, but awareness of existence. And so I ought not to hesitate to recognize that so long as it is animated by this vital inbreathing inspired by the act of reading, a work of literature becomes at the expense of the reader whose own life it suspends a sort of human being, that it is a mind conscious of itself and constituting itself in me as the subject of its own objects.

II
The work lives its own life within me; in a certain sense, it thinks itself, and it even gives itself a meaning within me.

This strange displacement of myself by the work deserves to be examined even more closely.

If the work thinks itself in me, does this mean that, during a complete loss of consciousness on my part, another thinking entity invades me taking advantage of my unconsciousness in order to think itself without my being able to think it? Obviously not. The annexation of my consciousness by another (the other which is the work), in no way implies that I am the victim of any deprivation of consciousness. Everything happens, on the contrary, as though, from the moment I become a prey to what I read, I begin to share the use of my consciousness with this being whom I have tried to define and who is the conscious subject ensconced at the heart of the work. He and I, we start having a common consciousness. Doubtless, within this community of feeling, the parts played by each of us are not of equal importance. The consciousness inherent in the work is active and potent; it occupies the foreground; it is clearly related to its *own* world, to objects which are *its* objects. In opposition, I myself, although conscious of whatever it may be conscious of, play a much more humble role content to record passively all that is going on in me. A lag takes place, a sort of schizoid distinction between what I feel and what the other feels; a confused awareness of delay, so that the work seems first to think by itself, and then to inform me what it has thought. Thus I often have the impression, while reading, of simply witnessing an action which at the same time concerns and yet does not concern me. This provokes a certain feeling of surprise within me. I am a consciousness astonished by an existence which is not mine, but which I experience as though it were mine.

This astonished consciousness is, in fact, the consciousness of the critic: it is the consciousness of a being who is allowed to apprehend as its own what is happening in the consciousness of another being. Aware of a certain gap, disclosing a feeling of identity, but of identity within difference, critical consciousness does not necessarily imply the total disappearance of the critic's mind in the mind to be criticized. From the partial and hesitant approximation of Jacques Rivière to the exalted, digressive, and triumphant approximation of Charles Du Bos, criticism can pass through a whole series of nuances which we would be well-advised to study. That is what I now propose to do. By discovering the various forms of identification and non-identification to be found in French literature, I shall be able perhaps to give a better account of the variations of which this relationship—between criticizing subject and criticized object—is capable.

Let me take a first example. In the case of the critic of whom I shall speak first, this fusion of two consciousnesses is barely suggested. It is an uncertain movement of the mind toward an object which remains hidden. Whereas in the perfect identification of two consciousnesses, each sees itself reflected in the other, in this instance the critical consciousness can, at best, attempt but to draw closer to a reality which must remain forever veiled. In this attempt it uses the only mediators available to it in this quest, that is the senses. And since sight, the most intellectual of the five senses, seems in this particular case to come up against a basic opacity, the critical mind must approach its goal blindly, through the tactile exploration of surfaces, through a groping exploration of the material world which separates the critical mind from its object. Thus, despite the immense effort on the part of the sympathetic intelligence to lower itself to a level where it can, however lamely, make some progress in its quest toward the consciousness of the other, this enterprise is destined to failure. One senses that the unfortunate critic is condemned never to fulfill adequately his role as reader. He stumbles, he puzzles, he questions awkwardly a language which he is condemned never to read with ease; or rather, in trying to read the language, he uses a key which enables him to translate but a fraction of the text.

This critic is Jacques Rivière.

And yet it is from this failure that a much later critic will derive a more successful method of approaching a text. With this later critic, as with Rivière, the whole project begins with an attempt at identification on the most basic level. But this most primitive level is the one in which there flows, from mind to mind, a current which has only to be followed. To identify with the work means here, for the critic, to undergo the same experiences, beginning with the most elementary. On the level of indistinct thought, of sensations, emotions, images, and obsessions of preconscious life, it is possible for the critic to repeat, within himself, that life of which the work affords a first version, inexhaustibly revealing and suggestive. And yet such an imitation could not take place, in a domain so hard to define, without the aid of a powerful auxiliary. This auxiliary is language. There is no critical identification which is not prepared, realized, and incarnated through the agency of language. The deepest sentient life, hidden in the recesses of another's thoughts, could never be truly transposed, save for the mediation of words which allows a whole series of equivalences to arise. To describe this phenomenon as it takes place in the criticism I am speaking of now, I can no longer be content with the usual distinctions between the signifier (*signifiant*) and the signified (*signifié*); for what would it mean here to say that the language of the critic *signifies* the language of the literary work? There is not just equation, similitude. Words have attained a veritable power of recreation; they are a sort of material entity, solid and three-dimensional, thanks to which a certain life of the senses is reborn, finding in a network of verbal connotations the very conditions necessary for its replication. In other words, the language of criticism here dedicates itself to the business of mimicking physically the apperceptual world of the author. Strangely enough, the language of this sort of mimetic criticism becomes even more tangible, more tactile than the author's own; the poetry of the critic becomes more "poetic" than the poet's. This verbal *mimesis*, consciously exaggerated, is in no way servile, nor does it tend at all toward the pastiche. And yet it can reach its object only in so far as that object is deeply enmeshed in, almost confounded with, physical matter. This form of criticism is thus able to provide an admirable equivalent of the vital substratum which underlies all thought, and yet it seems incapable of attaining and expressing thought itself. This criticism is both helped and hindered by the language which it employs; helped, in so far as this language allows it to express the sensuous life in its original state, where it is still almost impossible to distinguish between subject and object; and yet hindered, too, because this language, too congealed and opaque, does not lend itself to analysis, and because the subjectivity which it evokes and describes is as though forever bogged in its objects. And so the activity of criticism in this case is somehow incomplete, in spite of its remarkable successes. Identification relative to objects is accomplished almost too well; relative to subjectivity it is barely sketched.

This, then, is the criticism of Jean-Pierre Richard.

In its extreme form, in the abolition of any subject whatsoever, this criticism seems to extract from a literary work a certain condensed matter, a material essence.

But what, then, would be a criticism which would be the reverse, which would abolish the object and extract from the texts their most subjective elements?

To conceive such a criticism, I must leap to the opposite extreme. I imagine a critical language which would attempt deliberately to strip the literary language of anything concrete. In such a criticism it would be the artful aim of every line, of every sentence, of every metaphor, of every word, to reduce to the near nothingness of abstraction the images of the real world reflected by literature. If literature, by definition, is already a transposition of the real into the unreality of verbal conception, then the critical act in this case will constitute a transposition of this transposition, thus raising to the second power the "derealization" of being through language. In this way, the mind puts the maximum distance between its thought and what *is*. Thanks to this withdrawal, and to the consequent dematerialization of every object thus pushed to the vanishing point, the universe represented in this criticism seems not so much the equivalent of the perceivable world, or of its literary representation, as rather its image crystallized through a process of rigorous intellectualization. Here criticism is no longer mimesis; it is the reduction of all literary forms to the same level of insignificance. In short, what survives this attempted annihilation of literature by the critical act? Nothing, perhaps, save a consciousness ceaselessly confronting the hollowness of mental objects, which yield without resistance, and an absolutely transparent language, which, by coating all objects with the same clear glaze, makes them, "like leaves seen far beneath the ice" ("comme des feuilles sous la glace au trou profond"), appear to be infinitely far away. Thus, the language of this criticism plays a role exactly opposite to the function it has in Jean-Pierre Richard's criticism. It does indeed bring about the unification of critical thought with the mental world revealed by the literary work; but it brings it about at the expense of the work. Everything is finally annexed by the dominion of a consciousness detached from any object, a *hyper*-critical consciousness, functioning all alone, somewhere in the void.

Is there any need to say that this hyper-criticism is the critical thought of Maurice Blanchot?

I have found it useful to compare the criticism of Richard to the criticism of Blanchot. I learn from this confrontation that the critic's linguistic apparatus can, just as he chooses, bring him closer to the work under consideration, or can remove him from it indefinitely. If he so wishes, he can approximate very closely the work in question, thanks to a verbal mimesis which transposes into the critic's language the sensuous themes of the work. Or else he can make language a pure crystallizing agent, an absolute transluscence, which, suffering no opacity to exist between subject and object, promotes the exercise of the cognitive power on the part of the subject, while at the same time accentuating in the object those characters which emphasize its infinite distance from the subject. In the first of the two cases, criticism achieves a remarkable *complicity*, but at the risk of losing its minimum lucidity; in the second case, it results in the most complete dissociation; the maximum lucidity thereby achieved only confirms a separation instead of a union.

Thus criticism seems to oscillate between two possibilities: a union without comprehension, and a comprehension without union. I may identify so completely with what I am reading that I lose consciousness not only of myself but also of that other consciousness which lives within the work. Its proximity blinds me by blocking my prospect. But I may, on the other hand, separate myself so completely from what I am contemplating that the thought thus removed to a distance assumes the aspect of a being with whom I may never establish any relationship whatsoever. In either case, the act of reading has delivered me from egocentricity. Another's thought inhabits me or haunts me, but in the first case I lose myself into that alien world, and in the other I keep my distance and refuse to identify. Extreme closeness and extreme detachment have then the same regrettable effect of making me fall short of the total critical act: that is to say, the exploration of that mysterious interrelationship which, through the mediation of reading and of language, is established to our mutual satisfaction between the work read and myself.

This extreme proximity and extreme separation each has grave disadvantages. And yet they have their privileges as well. Sensuous thought is privileged to move at once to the heart of the work and to share its own life; clear thought is privileged to confer on its objects the highest degree of intelligibility. Two sorts of insight are here distinguishable and mutually exclusive: there is penetration by the senses and penetration by the reflective consciousness. Now rather than contrasting these two forms of critical activity, would there not be some way, I wonder, not of practicing them simultaneously, which would be impossible, but at least of combining them through a kind of reciprocation and alternation?

Is not this perhaps the method used today by Jean Starobinski? For instance, it would not be difficult to find in his work a number of texts which relate him to Maurice Blanchot. Like Blanchot he displays exceptional lucidity and an acute awareness of distance. And yet he does not quite abandon himself to Blanchot's habitual pessimism. On the contrary, he seems inclined to optimism, even at times to a pleasant utopianism. Starobinski's intellect in this respect is analogous to that of Rousseau, yearning for an immediate transparence of all beings to each other, which would enable them to understand each other in an ecstatic happiness. From this point of view, is the ideal of criticism not precisely represented by the *fête citadine* (street celebration) or *fête champêtre* (rustic feast)? There is a milieu or a moment in the celebration in which everyone communicates with everyone else, in which hearts are open like books. On a more modest scale, doesn't the same

67

phenomenon occur in reading? Does not one being open its innermost self? Is not the other being enchanted by this opening? In the criticism of Starobinski we often find that crystalline tempo of music, that pure delight in understanding, that perfect sympathy between an intelligence which enters and that intelligence which welcomes it.

In such moments of harmony, there is no longer any exclusion, no inside or outside. Contrary to Blanchot's belief, perfect translucence does not result in separation. On the contrary, with Starobinski all is perfect agreement, joy shared, the pleasure of understanding and of being understood. Moreover, such pleasure, however intellectual it may be, is not here exclusively a pleasure of the mind. For the relationship established on this level between author and critic is not a relationship between pure minds. It is rather between incarnate beings, and the particularities of their physical existence constitute not obstacles to understanding, but rather a complex of supplementary signs, a veritable language which must be deciphered and which enhances mutual comprehension. Thus for Starobinski, as much physician as critic, there is a reading of *bodies* which is likened to the reading of *minds*. It is not of the same nature, nor does it bring the intelligence to bear on the same area of human knowledge. But for the critic who practices it, this criticism provides the opportunity for a reciprocating exchange between different types of learning which have, perhaps, different degrees of transparency.

Starobinski's criticism, then, displays great flexibility. Rising at times to the heights of metaphysics, it does not disdain the farthest reaches of the subconscious. It is sometimes intimate, sometimes detached; it assumes all the degrees of identification and nonidentification. But its final movement seems to consist in a sort of withdrawal by contradiction with its earlier accord. After an initial intimacy with the object under study, this criticism has finally to detach itself, to move on, but this time in solitude. Let us not see this withdrawal as failure of sympathy but rather as a way of avoiding the encumbrances of too prolonged a life in common. Above all we discern an acute need to establish bearings, to adopt the judicious perspective, to assess the fruits of proximity by examining them at a distance. Thus, Starobinski's criticism always ends with a view from afar, or rather from above, for while moving away it has also moved imperceptibly toward a dominating position. Does this mean that Starobinski's criticism like Blanchot's is doomed to end in a philosophy of separation? This, in a way, must be conceded, and it is no coincidence that Starobinski treats with special care the themes of melancholy and nostalgia. His criticism always concludes with a double farewell. But this farewell is exchanged by two beings who have begun by living together; and the one left behind continues to be illuminated by that critical intellect which moves on.

The sole fault with which I might reproach such criticism is the excessive ease with which it penetrates what it illuminates.

By dint of seeing in literary works only the thoughts which inhabit them, Starobinski's criticism somehow passes through their forms, not neglecting them, it is true, but without pausing on the way. Under its action literary works lose their opacity, their solidity, their objective dimension, like those palace walls which become transparent in certain fairy tales. And if it is true that the ideal act of criticism must seize (and reproduce) that certain relationship between an object and a mind which is the work itself, how could the act of criticism succeed when it suppresses one of the (polar) terms of this relationship?

My search must continue, then, for a criticism in which this relationship subsists. Could it perhaps be the criticism of Marcel Raymond and Jean Rousset, the two great masters of what has been called the School of Geneva? Raymond's criticism always recognizes the presence of a double reality, both mental and formal. It strives to comprehend almost simultaneously an inner experience and a perfected form. On the one hand, no one allows himself to be absorbed with such complete self-forgetfulness into the thought of another. But the other's thought is grasped not at its highest, but at its most obscure, at its cloudiest point, at the point at which it is reduced to being a mere self-awareness scarcely perceived by the being which entertains it, and which yet to the eyes of the critic seems the sole means of access by which he can penetrate within the precincts of the alien mind.

Raymond's criticism presents another aspect which is precisely the reverse of this confused identification of the critic's thought with the thought criticized. It is then the reflective contemplation of a formal reality which is the work itself. The work stands *before* the critical intelligence as a perfected object, which is in fact an enigma, an external thing existing in itself and with which there is no possibility of identification nor of inner knowledge.

Thus Raymond perceives sometimes a subject, sometimes an object. The subject is pure mind; it is a sheer indefinable presence, an almost inchoate entity, into which, by very virtue of its absence of form, it becomes possible for the critic's mind to penetrate. The work, on the contrary, exists only within a definite form, but this definition limits it, encloses it within its own contours, at the same time constraining the mind which studies it to remain on the outside. So that, if, on the one hand, the critical thought of Raymond tends to lose itself within an undefined subjectivity, on the other it tends to come to a stop before an impenetrable objectivity.

Admirably gifted to submit its own subjectivity to that of another, and thus to immerse itself in the obscurest depths of every mental entity, the mind of Raymond is less well-equipped to penetrate the obstacle presented by the objective surface of the works. He then finds himself marking time, or moving in circles around the work, as around the vase or the statue mentioned before. Does Raymond then establish an insurmountable partition between the two realities—subjective, objective—unified though they may be in the work? No, indeed, at least not in his best essays, since in them, by careful intuitive apprehension of the text and participation by the critic in the powers active in the poet's use of language, there appears some kind of link between the objective aspects of the work and the undefined subjectivity which sustains it. A link not to be confused with a pure relation of identity. The perception of the formal aspects of the work becomes somehow an analogical language by means of which it becomes possible for the critic to go within the work, beyond the formal aspects it presents. Nevertheless, this association is never presented by Raymond as a dialectical process. The usual state described by his method of criticism is one of plenitude, and even of a double plenitude. A certain fullness of experience detected in the poet and re-lived in the mind of the critic, is connected by the latter with a certain perfection of form; but why this is so, and how it does become so, is never clearly explained.

Now is it then possible to go one step further? This is what is attempted by Jean Rousset, a former student of Raymond and perhaps his closest friend. He also dedicates himself to the task of discerning the structure of a work, as well as the depth of an experience. Only what essentially matters to him is to establish a connection between the objective reality of the work and the organizing power which gives it shape. A work is not explained for him, as for the structuralists, by the exclusive interdependence of the objective elements which compose it. He does not see in it a fortuitous combination, interpreted *a posteriori* as if it were an *a priori* organization. There is not in his eyes any system of the work without a principle of systematization which operates in correlation with that work and which is even included in it. In short, there is no spider web without a center, which is the spider. On the other hand, it is not a question of going from the work to the psychology of the author, but of going back, within the sphere of the work, from the objective elements systematically arranged, to a certain power or organization inherent in the work itself, as if the latter showed itself to be an intentional consciousness determining its arrangements and solving its problems. So that it would scarcely be an abuse of terms to say that it speaks, by means of its structural elements, an authentic, a veritable language, thanks to which it discloses itself and means nothing but itself. Such then is the critical enterprise of Jean Rousset. It sets itself to use the objective elements of the work in order to attain, beyond them, a reality not formal, nor objective, written down however in forms and expressing itself by means of them. Thus the understanding of forms must not limit itself merely to the recording of their objective aspects. As Focillon demonstrated from the point of view of art history, there is a "life of forms" perceptible not only in the historic development which they display from epoch to epoch, but within each single work, in the movement by which forms tend therein sometimes to stabilize and become static, and sometimes to change into one another. Thus the two contradictory forces which are always at work in any literary writing, the will to stability and the protean impulse, help us to perceive by their interplay how much forms are dependent on what Coleridge called a shaping power which determines them, replaces them, and transcends them. The teaching of Raymond finds then its most satisfying success in the critical method of Jean Rousset, a method which leads the seeker from the continuously changing frontiers of form to what is beyond form.

It is fitting then to conclude here this inquiry, since it has achieved its goal, namely to describe, relying on a series of more or less adequate examples, a critical method having as guiding principle the relation between subject and object. Yet there remains one last difficulty. In order to establish the interrelationship between subject and object, which is the principle of all creative work and of the understanding of it, two ways, at least theoretically, are opened, one leading from the objects to the subject, the other from the subject to the objects. Thus we have seen Raymond and Rousset, through perception of the objective structures of a literary work, strive to attain the subjective principle which upholds it. But, in so doing, they seem to recognize the precedence of the subject over its objects. What Raymond and Rousset are searching for in the objective and formal aspects of the work is something which is previous to the work and on which the work depends for its very existence. So that the method which leads from the object to the subject does not differ radically from the one which leads from subject to object, since it does really consist of going from subject to subject through the object. Yet there is the risk of overlooking an important point. The aim of criticism is not achieved merely by the understanding of the part played by the subject in its interrelation with objects. When reading a literary work, there is a moment when it seems to me that the subject *present* in this work disengages itself from all that surrounds it, and stands alone. Had I not once the intuition of this, when visiting Scuola di San Rocco in Venice, one of the highest summits of art, where there are assembled so many paintings of the same painter, Tintoretto? When looking at all these masterpieces, brought there together and revealing so manifestly their unity of inspiration, I had suddenly the impression of having reached the common essence present in all the works of a great master, an essence which I was not able to perceive, except when emptying my mind of all the particular images created by the artist. I became aware of a subjective power at work in all these pictures, and yet never so clearly understood by my mind as when I had forgotten all their particular figurations.

One may ask oneself: What is this subject left standing in isolation after every examination of a literary work? Is it the individual genius of the artist, visibly present in his work, yet having an invisible life independent of the work? Or is it, as Valéry thinks, an anonymous and abstract consciousness presiding, in its aloofness, over the operations of all more concrete consciousnesses? Whatever it may be, I am constrained to acknowledge that all subjective activity present in a literary work is not entirely explained by its relationship with forms and objects within the work. There is in the work a mental activity profoundly engaged in objective forms; and there is, at another level, forsaking all forms, a subject which reveals itself to itself (and to me) in its transcendence relative to all which is reflected in it. At this point, no object can any longer express it; no structure can any longer define it; it is exposed in its ineffability and in its fundamental indeterminacy. Such is perhaps the reason why the critic, in his elucidation of works, is haunted by this transcendence of mind. It seems then that criticism, in order to accompany the mind in this effort of detachment from itself, needs to annihilate, or at least momentarily to forget, the objective elements of the work, and to elevate itself to the apprehension of a subjectivity without objectivity.

Discussion

JAN KOTT: Pardon me, M. Poulet, but the question which I should like to pose is very, very simple, in the manner of a Polish peasant. What is the difference between the process of reading and the process of understanding someone, another person who speaks, since, according to your analysis, the process of reading is the "interiorization" of an external object which becomes a mental object? Is it the same thing when we understand someone who speaks? Isn't it possible to make almost the same typology of auditions as the typology of possible critics which you have described? For example, in the process of understanding someone, could one not find or delimit a type which remains at the surface of the word, another which "interiorizes" the biography of the speaker, and a third opposing type which makes it possible to objectify this interior object which was originally an exterior object? That is to say, if this be the case, then there would not be any important difference between the task of the critic and the task of someone who comprehends a conversation; that is, there would not be a profound and fundamental difference between a reader and an auditor.

GEORGES POULET: The difference, Monsieur, is not in fact fundamental. You are quite right to remark on this point. The difference is not fundamental and yet it asserts itself, it stands out the moment that we engage in conversation. This is the case because in conversation the interlocutors not only are accustomed to listen to each other but are also accustomed to speak to each other; and when we speak, we don't listen. Thus, very often, conversation, instead of becoming an inquiry in which someone who listens (or who reads) strives to identify himself with the thought of someone who speaks (or writes), becomes instead, quite to the contrary, a sort of battle, a radical opposition, an insistence on *differentiation*. The act of reading, as I conceive it, is exactly the contrary of this differentiation. It is above all an acceding, even an adherence, provisionally at least, and without reserve.

RICHARD MACKSEY: I may be simply belaboring the point which you have already lucidly made about the division of interest in any conversation, but it seems to me that in dialogue (or more generally, in conversation) your equation of the ideal act of reading as the movement of subject to subject through an intermediate object is radically altered. That is to say, in dialogue there are two (or more) *independent* subjects erecting two *opposing* systems of objects, or linguistic configurations, each with its own intentional structure, each seeking to impose its own formal closure on the event. In conversation, then, there are two variables determining the tempi and the possible conclusion, and they are brought together in the instability of a unique and unreproducible moment. Your interpretative model of the reader might better suggest a third party to the conversation, standing aside from both egos and both juxtaposed discourses, while attempting, rather like Tristram listening to Walter and My Uncle Toby at linguistic cross-purposes, to be both a relationship and a description, to be, in short, a consciousness of divergent consciousnesses, just as the reader attends to several orders of *voices* in the act of reading.

Socrates seemed to be aware of the privileged or unilateral nature of reading in some of his ungenerous remarks about the Book, and yet the great middle dialogues often suffer, conversely, from the inconclusiveness of more than one scheme of "closure" or "totalization"; we seem to need the unifying cohesion of Plato's mind listening to the voices, or inventing them. We have only to look, though, at an ostensible dialogue where the unity of development is imposed from within by one of the participants, and I think that most of us will agree that we resent a little the one-sided hectoring by which Socrates himself refuses the existence, the personality, of poor Ion, for whom we itch to invent arguments; it may be a *tour de force*, but even as fiction it is hardly a convincing *dialogue*.

Now I seem to be begging that most difficult question which in your presentation seems to divide thought and language: the polarity of absolute expression and absolute communication. In other words, the way in which speech, especially in conversation, forces on us a dilemma of two opposing forms of alienation. In one set of familiar terms, this is the opposition of the message and the code, or to put it even more baldly: the more one communicates, the less one expresses oneself, and vice versa. The opposition could be couched in existential terms as a polarization between incomprehensibility and inauthenticity. Obviously the self, the subject or cogito, can be conceived as a simple function of expression, and one is close to Bergson's *ineffable* "profound self," or, conversely, located in the very act of communicating through signs, and then one is close to Durkheim's "collective self" which has no identity apart from its function in various forms of social communication. There is a kind of [artistic] personality which aims at reflecting the most intimate efflorescence of a speechless self —I think of authors dear to you, say Maine de Biran and Amiel—and there is a kind of persona which exists only as an integer in a larger linguistic code, an element of some supreme *marivaudage*. To put all this simplistic essay at antinomies in terms of *genre*, there is the *journal intime* and there is the complexly coded *drama;* the latter is much closer to the devices of the street-corner conversation (by which we often protect our subjectivity), however artfully these devices may in fact be deployed. In the former kind of writing we have access to that *knowledge* which you have described so eloquently, while in the latter performance we can participate in certain illocutionary *acts* of language which can only have an etiolated force when represented in writing. (I am not trying consciously to conflate the Aristotelian distinction between knowing, doing, and making.) The performance implies a special kind of presence; the writing a special kind of openness to interpretative participation. But the difficulty in the latter case is precisely in *distinguishing* the message from the code, a difficulty which, as my wife once observed, is especially difficult with very ancient or very contemporary writing. In writing the three essential elements of the *pacte de la parole*—the subject, the audience, and the moment—are all subtly altered.

As his contemporaries seem to have remarked, there was a profound gap between the rather venal, sharp-dealing Tintoretto who conversed with his rivals in Venice and the extraordinary "essence of Tintoretto" to which you had access in the luminosity and the movement of the San Rocco paintings. As is so often the case with "Visiting Writers," the presence of the former in the San Rocco could only have been an annoyance. To suggest these two "subjects," is, I suppose, simply to invoke once again the argument of the *Contre Sainte-Beuve*.

Finally, one can imagine your tentative typology of critics each in respect to what he might do in conversation: Jean-Pierre Richard entering, rather like Keats, with "negative capability" into the flow of things and Maurice Blanchot annihilating every conversational overture back to its origin and silence. But then this would be to confuse the two "subjects" at issue and to trivialize two critics.

POULET: You know my incapacities before dramatic performance well enough. My point about the critic's task is simply to insist on the primacy of adhesion, before any movement toward differentiation. The posture of the critic can adapt itself later on, as I noted for instance in the case of Jean Starobinski, to a detachment on the part of a reader who is no longer content simply to listen, but who begins to reflect independently while his interlocutor is speaking. It is possible to arrive at a detachment or withdrawal of this kind, but most of the time in the act of criticism, as I conceive it, there is first of all an initial stage which is necessarily one of absolute adherence. And you can style this absolute acceding to the other as the act of the reader or the act of the auditor, but it surely cannot be called a conversation.

JAMES EDIE: If I might be permitted to ask a rather simple-minded philosophical question, similar to the one I asked M. Morazé this afternoon, I think it might help some of us to have you comment on this, because it might make your point of view and your approach to structuralism, and the study of structure, somewhat more clear. Now, in listening to your very dense and concentrated exposition, I felt at the beginning that, in a sense, we were brought back almost to the Greeks with this radical opposition between subject and object and the desire to know, in discerning various types of criticism, whether the critic is going from the object to the subject or from the subject to the object, until we found, toward the end, that the proper route is to go from subject to subject to the object. Then I thought that you illustrated this very well at the very end when you recalled your visiting the Scuola di San Rocco surrounded by all those creations of Tintoretto, discovering there the very essence, one might say, of the creativity of Tintoretto. Now this seems to me to be a phenomenological discovery and I sense (and I think I understand) that notion of a structure, of the *signifié* which is transcendent to the experiencer and is experienced, not only transcendent to the experiencer but transcendent, in a sense, to the creator because it is in every one of his works and yet it is not completely in any one of them. It is a kind of eidetic structure. You emphasize the indeterminate character of this structure; it is pure subjectivity and you so emphasize the indeterminate character that it seems to me that in the end you lose all structure. In fact, you said that structure is disappearance of form and now I am lost again completely. I can understand the eidetic structure, let us say, of the discovery of the mind of a Tintoretto, but this is not *any* consciousness, and it is not the disappearance of consciousness; it is the consciousness of Tintoretto. Therefore, though it is sufficiently transcendent, I can at least attempt to understand a limited idea sufficiently transcendent that it is not incarnate completely in any one work. Nevertheless, it is the subjectivity of Tintoretto that you have discovered and not of Titian or of something else. Therefore it is not a lack of all determinacy; or otherwise, if it is, then I would like some elucidation about what you understand structure to be and what your position is on structuralism.

POULET: If I had to attempt some kind of explanation or conciliation of those different statements that I made which risk self-contradiction, I would say that speaking of Tintoretto and not of my experience at the School of Nice, what I had clearly in my mind at the time (but I am not so sure of that right now) was the fact that I was somehow in possession of the essence of, shall we say, Tintoretto; or, perhaps, of the genius of Tintoretto distinguished from Tintoretto the Man; or, better, of an essence which is only accessible when you have in mind the certain totality of the works of the same author. Probably because what becomes visible then, at that particular moment, and which is usually not so clearly visible in any particular work, are a certain number of habits, of images, of characteristics of the mind, of mental themes which, to my mind, are the very representation of another consciousness which is not necessarily, I fear, the consciousness of Tintoretto himself. Voilà! When I was speaking of arriving at the essence of Tintoretto, in using the word *essence* I had someone clearly in my mind. That someone was Marcel Proust. Marcel Proust in his young days, when he was translating Ruskin—a particular work of Ruskin, *The Bible of Amiens*—insisted on bringing a series of examples taken from all the other works of Ruskin, in order, he said, to make clear to the reader this fidelity of the consciousness of Ruskin to particular essences, to particular themes that, for him, seemed to be the very aim of consciousness.

And now, to arrive at something which is far more important and which was included in your question. Am I "for" or am I "against" structuralism? I simply do not know; it is not for me to say; it is for the structuralists themselves. For my own part, sometimes I feel rather alien to the abstract and to the voluntarily objective way in which these structuralists express their own discoveries, and sometimes I am even shocked by that position. Sometimes I am shocked especially by their air of objectivity (I think particularly of one of them whom I consider a friend). I am particularly shocked when he claims to arrive thereby at scientific attitudes. I must confess that, to my own mind, very clearly, very definitely, criticism has the character of knowledge, but it is not a kind of scientific knowledge, and I have to decline very strongly the name of *Scientist*. I am *not* a scientist and I do not think that any true critic when he is making an act of criticism can be a scientist. That is very clear and probably it puts me completely out of step with the structuralists, but sometimes also— very often (why should I not say their names?) with Roland Barthes or with Gérard Genette, for instance, and some of the Russian structuralists—I feel (I may be wrong) a close affinity and it seems to me that their claim to arrive at a kind of absolute objectivity is not very far from my hope of arriving at something which I call absolute subjectivity.

RICHARD SCHECHNER: This is a rather limited question and is to deal only with part of your paper. I also find your paper very dense and very interesting and I would like to read it. But I am concerned here only with that part of your paper which considers the subjectivity, that middle part we are talking about, the identification. It was all very familiar to me and I would like to suggest to you a model for that, and then some of the difficulties which I know from my own experience with that model; because when you suggest that the critic allows another consciousness to invade his consciousness and that his act is mimetic, and when you suggest an annexation, I think of an actor in possession of a play text whose whole rehearsal process is designed to do exactly what you described, almost in those terms, to allow that text not only to enter his consciousness literally and memorize it, but to find the gestures of that consciousness, to speak the voice of that consciousness, etc. So, my first question, and I will go on with an assumed answer (but if I am wrong I would like you to contradict me): Is not what you describe as a subjective mode of the critics, somewhat like or very close to what the actor does when he is in possession of someone's text and therefore tries to appropriate the consciousness of the playwright—at least one aspect of that consciousness? Now, if it is so that this is what you described the critic as doing at that point, that phase is close to what the actor should do, but there are several difficulties because the actor, even after weeks and months of work of appropriating this consciousness, never really appropriates it, never really enters into anything that is truly subjective. At best, he is able to imitate certain gestures; at best, he is able to somehow tune his mind into certain gestures and rhythms, but I think it is a mistake when you ended your answer to the last question claiming that one has approached an objective subjectivity. In other words, one has approached the consciousness of the author. It is true that the author grasps the mind, but I don't think that it is true that the resultant consciousness in the critic or in the actor is the consciousness that the author might have intended or might even be there in the work. Let me stop here, because I think I will have some later questions, but I really think that there is a difficulty involved in your basic structure.

POULET: Well, the sort of question that you ask me is very bad; I mean bad for me, because it exposes my essential weakness. My essential weakness is my near incapability of going to the theater to look at or listen to a play. For me that seems to be a spectacle absolutely unbearable, insufferable. I cannot do it; I never do it. The only possibility for me of tackling this play is to read it; that is what I do and then I have no difficulty whatever. It is a different experience for me from acting.

CHARLES SINGLETON: Two interlocutors have already told our speaker that he was very dense. I find to the contrary, that he was so lucid that he tended to disappear from this room as I followed his thought and he became part of me, and this was quite an experience. But it is not that to which I want to speak. I want to speak before the structuralists move in on you; I want to think that you had an experience in the Scuola di San Rocco that is ordinarily called mystical; that it quite transcends all sensible objects. I am not sure that anyone can follow you there any more than—well I won't mention that poem again, which we were talking about this afternoon—but it does seem to me that there is a touch in your finale which Christian theology does talk about in other terms. I am not preaching; I am just observing. But I want to ask the diabolical question, being, as I said, a lost man myself, and turn the screw just one more turn to see what you would do with the author, or creator, as reader of his own creation. What happens then, if you can imagine what happens? If the intentional power beyond the object, comes through the object to your "je," if you are replaced in that situation by the author of the object, what must we think the author, as reader, experiences?

POULET: Is your question related to the intentionality of the author himself, or to something else?

SINGLETON: But now his intention, his intentionality is objectified in this work in such a way that you, not the author, but the reader, can be in communication with it and we follow you there. Now replace that *I* with the authorial *I*.

POULET: I would not replace the *I* within the work by an *I* which would be outside the work, and if we put the name of Dante for instance as the name of the author in question, I would say that the only Dante with whom I would be preoccupied would be the Dante within the work, who is there in two ways. He is there as the hero of the poem; he is there also as the very intentionality present in the poem,

79

present in the poem in such a way that he cannot be distinguished from the poem itself. I have no need for this other Dante who, it is said, is the author of the *Divina Commedia.* He is said to be, but I am not sure of that, nor am I sure that William Shakespeare. . . .

SINGLETON: I did not mean to create a mystical or difficult situation. Let it be the simple act of reading on the part of an author who has just finished writing his work and is reading it over with a critical eye. Why does he change it here and there? What is he working with? An intentionality that is coming through to him. . . .

POULET: Let's not play on the word *"critical* eye." The expression should rather be *"uncritical* eye." When the author is looking at his work in such a particular way that he has to, that he wants to, see defects and to correct them, he is not making an act of criticism, he is doing just the contrary.

SINGLETON: Isn't he testing an identification?

POULET: He has to take his distance, he has to try, he has to continue the same act, which is the act of creation, and the act of creation is an unclean sort of act. . . .

SINGLETON: Then, can he ever be a reader of his own book?

POULET: Why not, why not! When he has forgotten that he has written it, there must be, I think, a way of perfect detachment in which the author can read his own stuff, having completely forgotten that he has written it.

HENRY AIKEN: I don't mean to be outdone by my old colleague, Professor Singleton, in my admiration for the splendid paper. I shall simply say that I found the remarks about Tintoretto at the Scuola also thoroughly and sublimely luminous. I mean now to make some remarks about your dialectic, Sir, and to query you about some implications of it. I want to begin by saying that I thoroughly share your feeling that the critic is not a scientist, and I hope it will be understood that the drift of my questioning is not intended to drive you, so to speak, into the arms of science, although there are worse arms I suppose; I want rather to suggest that you drew a set of distinctions in a way that it seems to me was not fully lucid. Now, let me begin in the following way: You began by distinguishing between the work of art (I suppose it was that we were talking about) and an object. The object there for all time and not to be "transgressed," as opposed to the literary work—the contrast being suggested that one was transgressible and the other was not. Then, unfortunately, you brought up the sewing machine, as I remember, and the sewing machine was now identified as an object, as something which reveals itself, I take it once for all, not subject to the interior transgressions of the critic. But at this point I began to fidget, for it seems to me that there was in some sense something that the artifacts—the sewing machine, and the poem—shared in common that distinguished them from the physical object; that both were in some sense products of the mind and both were identifiable by intentions other than those that are employed for the identification of physical objects. It seemed to me, therefore, that your distinction between the artifact and the work of art was not a hard distinction, or you had not made it hard. But, then, as we went along, as I saw your dialectic developing, it seemed to me perfectly plain that you were making now quite properly, and I thoroughly applaud it, a distinction between the work of art and my impression of the work of art, between the work of art and something that I impute to it or impose upon it; and it became gradually apparent to me that the transgressions which you forbade us in talking about the physical work also could be applied now to the work of art itself. And then it dawned on me, or seemed to, that the appearance-reality distinctions that you are now beginning to draw were applicable indeed to all of these things: to object, to artifact, and to work of art; further, that the indeterminacy that you properly ascribed to the work of art could also indeed be applied to the physical object and perhaps also, though I have not quite thought this through, to the artifact. And so it seemed to me that though I was following and applauding, I found in the end that, while I had thought I agreed with your dialectic in a way, you had left me unclear as to the distinction between the work of art with its interiority, the artifact with its, and now, so help me, the object also, if you follow me, with its. Correspondingly, I did not find myself clear about the objective difference between the physical object, the artifact, and the work of art. So, what I conclude is that, as much as I admired the development of your remarks when you finally approached criticism itself, I found that the idea of the work of art or the critical object, shall I say, had not been sufficiently differentiated yet from the artifact on the one side and from the physical object on the other, so that you had not quite earned the right, if I can put it this way, to your splendid remark that the critic is not a scientist.

PoULET: All right, Sir. You are quite right about the sewing machine. The sewing machine is something very dangerous; I should never have used it. I should have left it completely alone; but I used the sewing machine just as I would have used, for instance, a stone or a root of a chestnut tree, as Sartre did in *La Nausée*, you remember. That is to say that for me, at the moment that I used that unfortunate sewing machine, I was considering it not at all as the artifact that undoubtedly it is, but simply with that kind of rather stupid property that sewing machines have of being there before you and your being simply helpless before them, especially myself. But it is perfectly true that there is some sort of connection between the sewing machine and the work of art, since, in both cases, we obviously find the agency of Man. I do not like at all the expression "work of art," detest it in fact, and usually avoid it. I do not think that once in the text I read before you I used the expression "work of art." I used very often the expression "a mental work" or "a mental object" in contradistinction with that kind of external object which can be a sewing machine; but I freely confess that in a sewing machine we can obviously see the intervention of Man and this intervention can be constructed in a relationship within the object, a relationship which is of cause and effect. The sewing machine is created by Man and I consider the sewing machine as his creation. We can also consider another kind of cause which is the final cause; the sewing machine has been created in order to sew. All right. But that seems to me extremely different from that mental work which I now find myself suddenly trying to describe under the name of *reading*. There, the category of cause and effect, even the teleological idea of cause seems to me profoundly secondary, and what is extraordinarily important is simply the presence in an object of something which is not objective and something of which I cannot find an example in the sewing machine.

René Girard: I would like to ask a question about what Professor Poulet seems to assume to be the archetypal act of reading which is identification with the author, and this is what I would question. I think that the archetypal act of reading can sometimes be identification with the author, but in most instances the act of reading which is essential is one of fascination, I would say, and I am not the only one who says this. I feel all the great writers have been preoccupied with this problem. I mean, you can begin very far back. Paolo and Francesca, for instance, in Dante, are not interested in the author of Lancelot. They are not identifying with the author but they are identifying with the characters. Cervantes at the theater is not identifying with the author of the play; since he is fighting the puppets, he mistakes them for real beings. We have the same problem again in Mme.

Bovary and in many poets. I would think of Mallarmé's "Prose (pour des Esseintes)." I think of course of Proust and the theater posters, and the latest example which goes back to this problematic would be of Sartre and *Les Mots*. In each case the writer is terribly preoccupied with the fact that reading is essentially a loss, a dispossession of the individual who becomes possessed, not by an author, not identifying with another consciousness, but fascinated by a text, whatever the text means there. And in the case of a novel, it seems to me that the itinerary of the hero is always a shift from this fascination to a realization that the printed text, the work, is really a human act, a human action among others which may be replaced; in other words, a victory over this fascination. I would say the work is very ambiguous. A man like Cervantes is fully aware that a book written "against" the fascination of the book will become itself fascinating, and Don Quixote in the second part of the novel goes around with his book in his hand and Cervantes himself predicts the wrong interpretations, the identifications with his hero which the future will see. But essentially I feel the critical act cannot be *immediate*. It has to be mediated; it has to be the opposite of this fascination and it has to recover the situation of the work of art; or rather it has to span the whole distance between this fascination and this opposite which we call explication. Of course, all this implies an infinitely more complex relationship between the self and the other, the reader and the author, than the one we have in this dialectic.

POULET: My dear Girard, I see very clearly in your question your essential preoccupations, which are of very great importance, which have taught me many things; against which, however, I have defended myself with a certain energy. It is true—I say this with a certain "reluctance," I am speaking "franglais" now, I say it with a certain reluctance—it is true that in the act of reading there may be a kind of "deviation" (perhaps you will accept this term; I think that it is a good one). This is the kind of deviation which one finds provoked in reading "by the book" or, in any case, by even a part of the book, because in the essential episode which you cite, the episode of Paolo and Francesca, it is on the one hand a question of a book which is read by certain characters but, on the other hand, the book involved when we read is certainly the *Divine Comedy* itself. There is the *Divine Comedy* and there are the internal relations of the *Divine Comedy*. There is a part of the book which in a sense isolates itself in order to underline this deviation and which takes the form of a caricature or the obverse of the book. That is, in fact, something which you have taught us to see in literature and I am in complete agreement with your insight; the act of reading is not simply the innocent (or in any case, the simplistic) identification that I was suggesting initially, but is surely something infinitely more complex. Complex is the very word which you invoked. I think, then, that we are in accord on every point save one, namely, that of this secondary activity, this intervention of what is located between the Ego [*moi*] and the Other, this second Other which produces in respect to the first the *triangular* relationship (of which you are in a critical sense the king). I feel that in the last analysis this relationship must yield precedence to that of duality and even to that of fusion. It is true (if I may borrow a term from my correspondence with you) that there is something "devious" [*mesquin*] in the act of writing, something which will replicate itself with the same "deviousness" in the act of reading. But it is also true that we can move beyond this stage and that there is, then, a moment when we are in genuine fusion, when there are no longer *three*, when there are no longer *two*, when there is only *one*.

LUCIEN GOLDMANN: In order to understand the position of Poulet's criticism I should like to ask you a question. Obviously, between the "scientific" positions which I have tried to defend and what you have explicitly contrasted with science we are locating our criticism on different planes. It is not on this discrepancy of critical planes that I wish to speak, however. But you have defined your position as a form of knowledge which would not be science. I see very clearly what this type of activity which you have developed here in such a masterly manner and which you have outlined in a series of other critics of diverse modalities can contribute to our culture. As you yourself stated, this criticism is not located on the level of a science. But then, I would ask what is the criterion of falsity in this knowledge? To put it very simply and naively from an outsider, if a bad student of Poulet goes to the Scuola di San Rocco, has the impression that he is identifying, and finds what he takes to be an essence of Tintoretto—but he is mistaken. How could we in this case know that he is mistaken, while in another case, such as you have so magisterially analyzed, the identification has a creative, critical value? That would still not give the answer to the question whether a given work of art is valuable or not, but if an answer is possible it would give me considerable clarification of the status of your critical activity.

POULET: What would Poulet do with a bad student of Poulet? In reality, what I should try to do with any writer, or with Tintoretto in the case of painting—I would try to identify with my bad student, and I would not be able to do it; I would fail in this effort of identification. The sole criterion that I would have that Poulet's student was a bad student of Poulet would consist in the fact that Poulet could not identify with this student.

JAN MIEL: I would like to answer a question rather than ask one, if I may. I would like to return to Professor Singleton's question about the author reading himself. I think there is a very valid answer to that question which was not exactly given and that is, between the author writing his work and the author reading his work, even immediately afterward, and perhaps for the purpose of correcting his own work, something has intervened and, although I hesitate to say it, "c'est le temps humain." Now, the passage of time between these two acts clearly poses a problem of the identity of the subject through time. The author who reads his own work has passed through this intervening time and an important question is posed as to whether the "je" of the author "est un autre un moment après." I think this is an important question because I would see implied in your own manner of criticism that the consciousness of the author is total through all his works in spite of the fact that his consciousness has in fact crossed a considerable stretch of time, in many cases from the works of his youth to the works of his old age.

POULET: Yes, there is a problem there, a rather important problem. Considering the problem of reading oneself we could think of Sartre again. It was Sartre who said, I think it was somewhere in *L'être et le néant*, that as soon as the work was finished it becomes a kind of *en soi*; it is not a part of the *pour soi* of the artist. Therefore, it becomes something objective with which the author has no longer the close connection that he had for a time. And therefore the conclusion would be the fact that, as soon as an author has finished with a work, the only thing that he can do is to start another one. There is no possibility of re-establishing himself in a true, authentic relationship with his own work as soon as the work is finished. That is the position of Sartre; it would not certainly be my own. I would say rather the opposite; I would say that the only possibility for an author to establish himself in an authentic relationship with his work is precisely when that work is finished, and at the same time the intentional concentration with which the author has continuously gone at his work, trying to realize it, has stopped, then it is possible for the author to look at his work in a purely detached way, purely detached, but by detached I mean in a complete relaxation of mind, but at the same time it may be with an extreme lucidity, in such a way that it may be only at this exact moment that he can attain the complete knowledge of what he has done. That reminds me of a marvelous anecdote which I found in the American edition of the work of De Quincey. De Quincey relates that at the time of the French Revolution, being with Wordsworth somewhere in the Lake District, I think it was in Keswick, both of them went up the road which goes to Penrith in order to meet the mail post and hear the news of the war. And when neither of them heard anything at all, Wordsworth put his ear against the ground and listened intently. And then suddenly De Quincey says: "I looked at his face and I saw his face changing." Wordsworth explained afterward that his face had been changing because at the very moment when he relaxed, when he did not concentrate on listening to the noise of the wheels coming along the road, at that moment he had a new and marvelous view of the mountains around Keswick. Well, that new and marvelous view of one's own work is that same sort of thing.

NORMAN HOLLAND: I would like to introduce into all this Gallic logic and lucidity something dark and murky from psychoanalysis. I am a psychoanalytic critic and I find that most of my colleagues who are literary critics are unfamiliar with a very interesting experiment which was performed twenty-two, yes, twenty-two years ago, which bears on precisely this issue. It is called the Heider-Simmel experiment, so-called because it was performed by a gentleman named Heider and a lady named Simmel. It bears precisely on the point we are discussing, and it seems to me that it produces a kind of empirical confirmation and perhaps slight correction of your point. This was performed at Smith College. What they did was: they showed the Smith girls an animated cartoon detailing the adventures of a large black triangle, a small black triangle, and a small circle going into and out of a rectangle. Now, after seeing the movie, the Smith girls were asked to comment in various ways upon it and they concluded that the larger triangle was pugnacious, was ill-tempered, was belligerent and indeed 8 percent of the Smith girls concluded that the larger triangle had a lower I.Q. than the smaller triangle. Now, the point of all this is that, when we create characters, as Mr. Girard says, or when we identify with a work as you say, it seems to me we are creating this from *ourselves*. The work gives us something to create *with* but it is not nearly so active as you imply; and you also call it an *I*, a self, a subject, which again seems to me to suggest more activity than the experiment would indicate.

Again, if I may introduce another empirical version of this, hypnosis, which is very like our relationship with the work of literature. But the point is that in hypnosis, the subject—oh, excuse me, I'd better not use that word—the hypnotisand feels the personality of the hypnotist as though it is a part of himself; and when the hypnotist says: "Your hand feels cold": your hand does feel cold, which I think is rather like the way we respond to a book. And from this one comes to the conclusion that the term "identification" with all its implications of subject and object is much further along the developmental line than the psychoanalyst's term for our relationship with the book. The psychoanalyst would speak, I think, of incorporation, which is a much more primitive kind of mechanism; in fact related basically, ultimately to eating, as, for example, when we speak of a man as a voracious reader. The implication, I think, is when we can devour books but not sewing machines. Well, what I wanted to suggest ultimately, then, is a kind of correction, and I am not sure that to call the Other, the book, to call it an *I* having an impact on a passive or relatively passive *me* is an accurate description of what precisely goes on. There are many other models in this area that psychoanalysis would indicate. The model of the actor is an extremely interesting one in this case because his situation is very similar to that of the reader, but the relationship of the mother and the child is another one, and the relationship of two lovers. If you would care to explore this further, not the lovers, but the whole general topic, the opening chapter of *Civilization and Its Discontents* describes a great many things which bear on this relationship. That is where Freud talks about the oceanic experience. But anyway, it in many ways is a relationship like that between two lovers, which would get us into the other problem, namely how much to think when you are reading a book, and, I take it, it is like being in love. It is not good to think too much and it is not good not to think at all.

POULET: Yes . . . [laughter] First of all about the experiment, the Heider-Simmel experiment, considering that it is about triangles and that Professor Girard is a specialist on those, perhaps I could suggest that he answer, instead of me, this particular point. But, putting this joke aside and excusing myself for such an easy joke, I want to consider very seriously what you told me. What troubles me is the fact that in psychoanalysis you can find some kind of incorporation or identification in more than one example and in particular in the case of the identification of the patient with the doctor. Is there some kind of similarity between this kind of identification and the identification

I was speaking of? Probably at a certain level it is true, but at the level at which I want very carefully to place myself, I do not see any resemblance, considering that, in the case of the psychoanalytical identification, the best part at least of the identification is made at the subconscious level. What I was speaking of in the act of reading is something which is done at the fully conscious level. By fully conscious I do not mean that at any moment when we read we are in a kind of absolutely clear consciousness; there are a certain number of levels even in clear consciousness and it may be that in reading we are plunged into a kind of confused consciousness, a sort of cloudy consciousness, but what is definitely not the subconscious proper. There I see a difficulty, a difficulty which seems to me very great, since I need absolutely for my own kind of criticism what I would call with Descartes the *Cogito* and there is no kind of *cogito* in the subconscious identification.

HOLLAND: I would say, again talking on this purely empirical level, that you start with a conscious relationship with the book as you see it, sitting on the table, a separate object; then again consciously you become more involved with it, and then you begin to respond along a scale of a very primitive level at the bottom and then your *cogito* at the top.

POULET: At both times it is consciousness.

HOLLAND: Not at the bottom end . . .

POULET: Yes, at the bottom end also.

HOLLAND: Mr. Macksey says, "Would you believe *preconscious?*"

The Two Languages of Criticism

Eugenio Donato
The Johns Hopkins University

The works of Lévi-Strauss and Lacan have taken the place of the works of Sartre and Merleau-Ponty, and it is toward them that marginal disciplines, such as literary criticism, are turning in search of a methodological guide; in the same way as, a few years ago, they turned toward phenomenology and existentialism.

This sudden exemplary prominence of disciplines which not so long ago were defined exclusively in terms of particular methodologies suited to the study of the specific objects has brought forth the term "the Sciences of Man." Whether this expression is an apt one and whether we can talk of the "Sciences of Man" as we talk of the "Sciences of Nature" is not a problem which I wish to raise. Let us for the moment consider it simply as expressing a preoccupation for the unity of all disciplines dealing with the human phenomenon, independently of their particular methodologies.

With the advent of a style of thinking it is easy to forget precisely which question it answers. It tends to neglect its past and overlook the fact that its very advent represents an answer to the question raised by what preceded it and that the very ways it opened were predetermined by the dead ends of its predecessors. We may today be able to proceed without Sartre and Merleau-Ponty, yet without them I believe it would be impossible to understand the general acceptance that structuralism has had. Indeed, in spite of the divergences that may exist between, for instance, the anthropological theories of a Lévi-Strauss and the Freudian readings of a Lacan, one of the few undisputed points of agreement between them would be their common de-

nunciation of the notion of subject that had dominated phenomenological thought in general, and the works of Sartre and Merleau-Ponty
in particular. That is, a Cartesian subject rooted in the greater or lesser
presence that it affords to itself through consciousness.

Lévi-Strauss's statement in *Tristes tropiques*, dismissing phenomenology and existentialism, provides us with one of the most lucid explanations for such an avowed hostility to the notion of subject:

Phenomenology I found unacceptable, in so far as it postulated a continuity
between experience and reality. That the latter enveloped and explained
the former I was quite willing to agree, but I had learnt from my three mis-
tresses [Freud, Marx, Geology] that there is no continuity in the passage
between the two and that to reach reality we must first repudiate experience, even though we may later reintegrate it in an objective synthesis in
which sentimentality plays no part. As for the trend of thought which was
to find fulfilment in existentialism, it seemed to me to be the exact opposite
of true thought, by reason of its indulgent attitude towards the illusions
of subjectivity. To promote private preoccupations to the rank of philosophical problems is dangerous, and may end in a kind of shop-girl's philosophy—excusable as an element in teaching procedure, but perilous in the
extreme if it leads the philosopher to turn his back on his mission. That
mission [which he holds only until science is strong enough to take over
from philosophy] is to understand Being in relation to itself, and not in
relation to oneself. Phenomenology and existentialism did not abolish
metaphysics: they merely introduced new ways of finding alibis for metaphysics.[1]

The end of Lévi-Strauss's statement concerning the abolishment of
metaphysics gives us implicitly the philosophical tenor that anthropology, psychoanalysis, and linguistics have, since their scientific project is seen as the only alternative to a specific philosophical tradition
and the only way of providing a radical critique of it.

This scientific ambition, at least in the form given it by Lévi-Strauss
or Lacan, is, of course, completely foreign to phenomenology. Merleau-Ponty, for example, from his early *Phénoménologie de la perception* to his last published work *L'Oeil et l'esprit*, never stopped decry-
ing, in the name of a phenomenological description of the world, the
treatment that science sought for its objects.[2] To quote one of his

[1] Claude Lévi-Strauss, *Tristes tropiques*, Paris, 1955, p. 50. I have quoted from
John Russell's sensitive translation, published under the same title as the original
(New York, 1961).

[2] *Phénoménologie de la perception*, Paris, 1945 [English edition, London, 1962];
L'Oeil et l'esprit, Paris, 1964 [English translation in *The Primacy of Perception*,
James M. Edie, ed., Evanston, 1964].

most famous sentences "Science manipulates things but refuses to inhabit them."[3] For Merleau-Ponty then, the mode of understanding that we should strive for is one which remains as close as possible to the object we seek to understand: to use Lévi-Strauss's vocabulary, one that is *continuous* with the object it seeks to understand, and in fact Merleau-Ponty in his *Phenomenology of Perception* had contrasted description and analysis. His preference went to the former, because description as he understood it—and in as much as it differed from analysis—could hope to remain close to that original unity of world and subject given here in the form of a pre-reflective *cogito*. In later years he was to give up his former optimism, seeing in any linguistic description the impossibility of being completely adequate. Language has too much reality of its own to be a speechless accomplice to the philosopher. Hence Merleau-Ponty came to prefer the wordless silence of painting, which for him was closer to the unbroken continuity of subject and object in which being is grounded.

The merit of both Sartre and Merleau-Ponty will reside in their not having remained systematically faithful to their original project and the consciousness-centered subject that it implied. Having started within the broad context of the philosophy of the *cogito*, they succeeded in showing that its very *cogito* was incomprehensible outside intersubjectivity. To have gone beyond this would have required a set of new categories which would have scrapped the very modes of thought that brought them about. Merleau-Ponty came to denounce the solipsistic consciousness-centered subject that his phenomenological premises implied. As he put it: "Consciousnesses give themselves the ridiculous spectacle of a collective solipsism."[4]

Used as we are to the primacy of language in the very constitution of the subject, it is interesting to look back at the passages where Merleau-Ponty foresaw that it was in and through language that the individual constituted the ties that bind him to the world. We may ask what it was that prevented him from going further: it was certainly not lack of knowledge of either Saussure or the works of the linguists, but perhaps because he stubbornly refused to abandon the privileged position of consciousness which he had inherited from phenomenology and from which privileged position we can see better how the advent of linguistics, within the problem of language, corresponds to the possibility of treating the problem of the subject inde-

---

[3] *L'Oeil et l'esprit*, p. 9.
[4] *Phénoménologie de la perception*, p. 412.

Eugenio Donato

pendently from the level at which he became aware of himself as subject.

The case of Sartre is slightly different, since from the very beginning his subject is engaged in a deadly war with the Other. Yet this intersubjectivity remained far too simple for its very symmetry. Self and Other both doubled as subject and object. In its dualistic perspective there were always two distinct antithetic positions—the Other from the point of view of the Self, and the Self from the point of view of the Other—which somehow never acceded to a coherent synthesis, since Sartre claimed to salvage an autonomous subject yet subordinated him to the intersubjective relations binding him to the Other. After Sartre and Merleau-Ponty we were left with the necessary search for a system that would be able to treat the subject independently from the *cogito*.

In 1945 Lévi-Strauss in an article entitled "L'Analyse structurale en linguistique et en anthropologie" [5] advocated the use of models taken from structural phonetics to the description of the human phenomenon and in that particular case to kinship systems. This article contained in a nutshell the great developments of the elementary structure of kinships and delineated the main lines of a system that was to develop in a linear fashion from *Les Structures élémentaires de la parenté* to *Le Cru et le cuit*. The problem he faced was twofold for it implied on the one hand the Saussurian distinction between signifier and signified and on the other hand the more explicit reference to phonetics. The simultaneous translation of these linguistic categories to a nonlinguistic domain cannot but raise some methodological problems.

The phonetical dimension of language exists at a different level from the one in which words are apprehended as distinct units to which Saussure's analysis applies. The two orders, even if hierarchically subordinated, are discontinuous and the laws that govern each one of them are quite different.

An isolated phoneme by its very nature cannot exist in a relationship of sign. From that point of view it does not fall within the division of signifier and signified, but is only a consequence of its corresponding to a certain *découpage* of the former. Could the same be said of a kinship term? The question is rhetorical. To apply to the study of kinship systems patterns derived from structural phonetics—and we

[5] First published in *Word* I, 2 (August, 1945), 1–21; reprinted as "Structural Analysis in Linguistics and in Anthropology" in *Structural Anthropology*, New York, 1963 (translated by Claire Jacobson and Brooke Grundfest Schoepf), pp. 31–54.

must keep in mind that when Lévi-Strauss in his early works speaks of linguistics his reference is usually to the works of Jakobson in particular and to those of the school of Prague in general—implies two distinct operations which have rather different consequences. Once a kinship term is *reduced* to the status of a phoneme then one may go and search for rules of combination which remain constant in different systems and thus arrive at certain laws which could be said to be *similar* to those that prevail in phonetics. At this level the relationship of the linguist's enterprise and that of the ethnologist is purely analogical. However, as we suggested, this analogy is based on the first operation—namely, that which reduces the status of the kinship term to that of a phoneme—the status of which is more ambiguous and the consequences more radical.

The importance of the linguistic theory and of Saussure's treatment of the linguistic sign was that they permitted the introduction of the notion of discontinuity, which Lévi-Strauss claims to be essential for the rational understanding of any given phenomena. The value of Saussure's division of the linguistic sign into signifier and signified lies, I believe, within the unbridgeable gap that exists between the two orders.

This can be better appreciated if one were, for instance, to turn again to one of Merleau-Ponty's statements on language. Merleau-Ponty used the same vocabulary of signifier and signified and his later writings do show a knowledge of Saussure. However, for Merleau-Ponty the signifier was irrelevant, it was the mediating term that was to lead to the signified and the whole semantic dimension of language. In his words, "meaning devours signs," [6] yet if we are to listen to the linguists, the proposition would be reversed; the order of the signified is secondary to the order of the signifier, which constitutes language in its essence. It is because of the order of the signifier that, to use Foucault's expression, we have the order of "words" and the order of "things," and within this dualism it is the former and not the latter that holds the key to understanding.[7]

To return to Lévi-Strauss. If we were to look for a brief moment at, say, his treatment of kinship systems, in spite of his own vehement statements there is nothing in them that is quite similar to a signifier or a signified, and his treatment is not a simple, mechanical application of a linguistic model. What we do find, however, is his distinguishing

---

[6] *Phénoménologie de la perception*, p. 213.
[7] Michel Foucault, *Les mots et les choses*, Paris, 1966.

within his subject matter two distinct orders. One in which his object of study is apprehended as its own end, governed by its own laws constituting it a system, and the other order, namely, that through which an individual enters, perceives, and understands the system. The two are discontinuous and the anthropologist's task is to study the former and to discard the latter. The distinction between the two orders becomes even more apparent if one turns to problems of primitive classification, ritual, or myth, and it is in part this latter development which underscores the fact that what we are witnessing in a work such as that of Lévi-Strauss is not a simple application of a linguistic model but the use of Saussure's formula as what one may call, for want of a better term, an epistemological operator. It is the possibility of maintaining the discontinuity between the order of the signifier and the order of the signified that permits Lévi-Strauss to avoid dealing with the problem of an individual subject and makes for the extreme rigor of his work. Others are not so fortunate. Strangely enough, it is language that does not lend itself to such an absolute separation between the two orders. It is, of course, true that the Saussurian distinction permitted the methodological success of structural phonetics; yet we cannot be completely sure that even the phonetic level of language can be understood independently from all semantic considerations. Even if this were so, it is far from exhausting the linguistic phenomenon. The relationship that the order of the signifier maintains to the order of the signified, of words to their semantic content, or more simply stated, of words to things, is a paradoxical one, for it is a relationship that has to be defined simultaneously by two propositions which are contradictory: the word *is* the thing; the word is identical to that which it represents, and the space between the two is continuous. Yet, words are different from things, words do not merely represent things; the two orders are discontinuous, their relationship is one of difference. It is difficult to think of a better statement of this paradox than Mallarmé's famous phrase, rose "absente de tous bouquets." And as some critics, such as Barthes, have pointed out, it is this very paradox which constitutes in a way the essence of literature, since language is always communication, yet at the same time, in as much as it states its linguistic nature, it cannot but denounce its instrumental nature. Literature would be, and a poet such as Mallarmé would tend to confirm this, difference denouncing identity.

Lacan's theoretical contribution to this problem is worth mentioning in as much as it might help us understand the nature of some of the more extreme statements made about literature, such as those of Derrida.[8] Being a psychoanalyst who has to deal with the everyday speech of his patients, and through it with the discourse of their unconscious, Lacan cannot afford to take as extreme a position as Lévi-Strauss and to maintain himself in a system of absolute difference. Instead he has given a different formalization of the two contradictory exigencies that language imposes. On the one hand, language is identity based on a system of representation that is visual and not linguistic—the word as identical to the thing it represents, supported by a visual *imago* which constitutes the subject of consciousness. This subject implies presence of the self to the self inherited from the philosophical tradition that extends from Descartes to Merleau-Ponty, but which from Freud on has to be denounced as illusory, even if this illusion is a necessary ingredient of our everyday life. On the other hand, the subject of difference is given to us by langauge, in as much as language is difference, a subject that inhabits the order of the signifier, an off-centered subject which is not present to itself, but, is in internal exclusion of itself, or as Lacan puts it, in his famous parodic formula, "I think there where I am not, hence I am there where I think not." [9]

It should be possible to see, for literature, both the necessity and the dilemma of an enterprise such as that of Derrida, in as much as language in its being is difference, yet it cannot escape the tyranny of the linguistic sign; that is to say, identity and presence. It has the constant and interminable task of demystifying itself, but it can only do so from a position which it can never occupy. Grammatology, as the science of a language from which presence is banished, is a project which can never be accomplished yet one which has to be stated, since it is only from that virtual position of a future perfect that one can denounce the inevitable residue of metaphysical presence that language carries within itself. The nature of Derrida's enterprise shows how the literary act is at the same time always new and necessary yet inessential and derivative, since it is always parasitically dependent on a previous position.

Derrida's enterprise also reveals within our modern context the impossibility of drawing an essential line between literature and criticism. Literature can only be a denunciation of literature and is not therefore different in essence from criticism. Criticism, in as much as it is a denunciation of literature, is, itself, nothing but literature. Henceforth the distinction between the two types of discourse is blurred,

[8] "De la grammatologie," *Critique* (December, 1965–January, 1966): 223–24; reprinted as first part of *De la grammatologie*, Paris, 1967.
[9] *Ecrits*, p. 517. Paris, 1966.

and instead what we have is language and the single problematic it imposes, namely, that of interpretation. Something no doubt which we should have known since Nietzsche and Freud, but which we are barely beginning to understand.

If, as Derrida puts it, linguistic signs refer themselves only to other linguistic signs, if the linguistic reference of words is words, if texts refer to nothing but other texts, then, in Foucault's words, "If interpretation can never accomplish itself, it is simply because there is nothing to interpret." [10] There is nothing to interpret, for each sign is in itself not the thing that offers itself to interpretation but interpretation of other signs. There is never an *interpretandum* which is not already an *interpretans*, so that a relationship of both violence and elucidation establishes itself with interpretation. Interpretation does not shed light on a matter that asks to be interpreted, that offers itself passively to interpretation, but it can only seize violently an interpretation that is already there, one which it must overturn, overthrow, shatter with the blows of a hammer—the reference here is, of course, to Nietzsche. Interpretation then is nothing but sedimenting one layer of language upon another to produce an illusory depth which gives us the temporary spectacle of things beyond words. Yet this momentary fixation is dependent always on re-establishing that very subject which we had begun by denouncing. To quote Foucault again, "Interpretation will henceforth always be an interpretation by the 'who.' One does not interpret that which is in a signified but in the last analysis the one 'who' has laid down the interpretation. The principle of interpretation is nothing but the interpreter himself." [11] What begins by being the questioning of a subject inevitably turns out to be an indictment of him who questions in the first place.

It is by the name we give others that in the last analysis we identify ourselves, and at this juncture it is difficult not to mention the name of Freud, who was the first one to see that interpretation was not normative but, at best, that it uncovers a number of phantasms which are themselves already interpretations. The analytical dialogue between two subjects, through the establishment of those elusive relations which are transference and countertransference, is open ended. If analysis is interminable, if it never uncovers a founding origin, it is perhaps because analysis has carried to its extreme conclusion the implacable logic of interpretation. After Freud we must all come to recognize that, to use a formula coined

[10] *Nietzsche* (no ed.), Cahiers de Royaumont, Philosophie, no. 6, p. 189. Paris, 1967.
[11] *Ibid.*, p. 191.

by Jean Wahl, "Nous sommes tous malades d'interpretation." [12]

To return to our original statement of Lévi-Strauss, his reproach to phenomenology stemmed in part from postponing forever the project of a science and, in the last analysis, making it perhaps impossible. Science with respect to interpretation might be only a Pascalian *divertissement*. Yet the possibility of its existence is well worth considering, if only to give us a brief breathing space from the heavy demands of interpretation. As Foucault has shown in his *Les Mots et les choses*, analysis and interpretation are only two valid approaches to language. These two modes co-exist yet are fundamentally opposed to each other. If interpretation plays on the gap resulting from the interjection of the subject, analysis requires the elimination of that subject as a necessary prerequisite to the study of the formal properties which condition the unfolding of any particular type of discourse. More specifically for literature, as Barthes has eloquently argued, a science of literature hinges upon the possibility of being able to treat literary works as myth. The word myth may here be understood with the precise meaning that Lévi-Strauss gives it, namely, a type of discourse from which the subject of the enunciation has been eliminated. Whether such a science of literature will ever be possible remains to be seen.

I should like to finish by mentioning the paradox offered to us by such works as *Le Cru et le cuit* of Lévi-Strauss. Successful literary works seem to have the property either of indicting the ideology which provoked them in the first place, or else of achieving what would seem ideologically impossible; and to me a work such as *Le Cru et le cuit* falls into the latter category. It offers itself as an analytical study of South American myths and the material lends itself to the scientific treatment that Lévi-Strauss imposes upon it. The author succeeds by a set of transformations in showing the unity of the particular discourse constituted by South American myths. So well does he describe the laws of the grammar that govern them that it is not inconceivable for a reader to write himself what would qualify as a South American myth. Yet as Lévi-Strauss points out, his treatment of those myths is nothing but another version of those myths. It is as if through the language that he lends them the myths interpret themselves. I believe that it is impossible in a work such as *Le Cru et le cuit* to separate myth and literature, science and interpretation, and analysis and criticism, and I believe that it is in the attempt to understand such works that the future of literary criticism lies.

[12] *Ibid.*, p. 195.

97

Structure: Human Reality and Methodological Concept[1]

Lucien Goldmann

Ecole Pratique
des Hautes Etudes
and Institut de Sociologie,
Université de Bruxelles

First of all I would like to add a few things that I had left out of the text because they seemed so obvious.[2] I have tried to define the method of genetic structuralism using examples that could be easily understood: a cat hunting a mouse, two men lifting a table that would be too heavy for one man alone. These are events and it is a question of structure, but I am not saying that the behavior of these men or of this mouse, as such, constitutes a structure and that if the behavior were slightly changed we would have another structure. The problem of structure is also a problem of levels.

I have defined structure, as reality and as a concept of research, as originating from real behavior, but I must add that it originates from the solution of practical problems encountered by living beings. Man has a limited consciousness, a limited number of categories that can be combined in a limited number of ways, so that, facing hundreds of thousands of concrete situations, he is forced to create structures as patterns of behavior [comportements] which he retains for a long time to solve a whole series of similar problems, although he must adapt the structures a little each time and renounce the possibility of an ideal solution.

Between the two extremes of individual problems concerning particular events and the most general categories of the human mind—which are purely formal and do not

[1] "La Structure: Réalité humaine et concept méthodologique." The text which follows is a translation and, in some instances, a paraphrase of the tape-recording of M. Goldmann's lecture. The footnotes have been supplied by the translation.

[2] The reference is to a supporting essay (in French), distributed at the Symposium, which is printed as an appendix to this volume.

permit one to understand the difference say between a play of Racine and the *Iliad*—are situated all structures and structuralist analysis. It is impossible to situate them more precisely between these two extremes for two reasons. The first is that the transformation of a structure and the number of events that it can include depend on concrete situations: there are cases where social groups and individuals must change their mental structures very quickly in order to adapt to new situations. Next, on the level of research, it depends on the formulation of the problem and the type of solution that is sought. If I am studying the Jansenist group or the social context of a Pascal or Racine, I must—and this is the fundamental problem of all research—look for the group and circumscribe (*découper*) my object so that it can only be associated with a group which could solve a certain number of important practical problems with—and only with—a given set of mental structures, which, applied to the solution of imaginary problems, have resulted in the theater of Racine.

If I want to confront a much vaster problem such as foreign policy in the seventeenth century, I might have categories and structural patterns (*structuration*) which might include terms such as France or Holland or, inversely, at a much more limited level one might study segments of groups where a number of major structures would be involved. The *découpage* of the physicist's enterprise is different from the chemist's—the latter stops at molecules whereas the former goes all the way to atoms and particles. The important point is the thesis that structures are born from events and from the everyday behavior of individuals and that, except for the most formal characteristics, there is no permanence in these structures. If we want to study a human phenomenon we must circumscribe the object in a certain way and try to determine the essential questions: Who is the subject? In whose life and practical activities (*praxis*) did the mental structures and categories and the forms of thought and affectivity arise which determined the origin and behavior of the object studied? At the level of the event there is neither sociology nor structuralism; for example, if we look at a play by Racine simply as a localized event it is impossible to explain and understand it. Inversely, if we go to the level of the most general structures it is history and transformation that disappear—and this is what is happening today in one current of structuralism.[3] It is in this perspective that you must understand the two examples which I have taken as a point of departure.

[3] For a further methodological discussion, see M. Goldmann's essay "Le Structuralisme génétique en histoire de la littérature," *MLN,* 79, 3 (1964): 225–39.

Lucien Goldmann

The fundamental thesis of all genetic structuralist sociology is that all human behavior, and more generally the behavior of any living being of some complexity, is significant [*a un charactère significatif*]. That is, it is a question of a subject who, within a certain situation, will change this situation in a way that is favorable to his needs and, on the human level, to his affective needs and concepts. In very general terms, there is a disequilibrium and the behavior is significant to the degree that it tends to re-establish an equilibrium. In man significant behavior is of course always accompanied by consciousness which introduces a complexity that must be taken into account in speaking of literature and culture. However it isn't always necessary to suppose consciousness. For example, a cat hunting a mouse behaves in a way that we can translate, when we study it, into a problem. The problem is how to find food and catching the mouse is the solution to this problem. Of course neither problem nor solution exists for the cat, but we can study the analogy between this behavior and cultural or social behavior. There are significant structures on this level: the behavior of the cat is not merely a sum of elements but a real structural pattern. The cat adapts itself; if there is an obstacle it will go to the left and then come back to the right. There is a structure of behavior and a physiological organization [*montage*] created in order for the cat to adapt to the situations that it faces. There is no consciousness here. Structure is essentially defined by the necessity to fulfill a function in a certain situation. History is constituted by the fact that, in the changing situation created by the action of the subject and by exterior interventions, structures, which have been developed as being rational and having a chance to fulfill their function to allow a group or an individual to live in conditions that existed previously, are no longer rational, and must be modified to fulfill their function. To forget—as a whole school of sociology has done—that, since all human reality is made up of overlapping structures, every structure fulfills a function within a larger structure and that a structure is defined as rational only by its ability to solve a practical problem, incurs the risk of denying history and assuming that everything takes place within one particular structure. It is this dialectic of function and structure, which I will call significance [*signification*], that separates the two structuralist schools. It is within this dialectic that we find the separation of signifier and signified which, of course, is important only on the human level.

Here I would like to add a second, particularly important, distinction. Since psychoanalysis has familiarized us with the concept of the unconscious, we too often, in speaking of the psychical, see only the conscious and the unconscious. However, for our analysis it is essential to distinguish a third category. I think it is best to leave to the word unconscious its psychoanalytical meaning which supposes a repression of things that are not accepted by consciousness. In addition to the conscious and the unconscious, there is a domain which is very important in our research and which can be called the implicit or the non-conscious. This is obvious, for instance, where I talk of my physiology: I am not conscious of the physiological basis which determines the way I walk or run, but it is not unconscious. I have not repressed it and if a physiologist explains it to me, I will understand it and it will become conscious. The same situation exists on the psychical level; for example, I am not conscious of the structure of formal logic. We must strictly separate the repressed unconscious, the implicit non-conscious and the conscious.

I would now like to approach the extremely important problematic of the subject. When I say the cat catches a mouse, there is no problem: the cat is the subject of this behavior. However at the level where there is language and symbolic systems the situation is completely changed. A new element appears which makes it necessary to distinguish two different types of structures. This new element, which is made possible by communication, is the division of labor. Were one to take the subject in the very strict sense as the agent of the action, if this table is too heavy to be lifted by one person and if two people, say John and James, lift it, it is neither John nor James who lifts the table: it is John-and-James. This is very important, because when it becomes a question of transforming society, of modifying a whole combination of interior or exterior givens, there are no longer any individual subjects. Symbolic communication takes place between two configurations, which must be distinguished. In the case of moving the table, between John and James lifting the table communication takes place *within the subject;* it is intrasubjective. If there were another person who didn't want John and James to remove the table, he would be the subject of another action, and they would speak as one subject to another. There is the intersubjective on the level of the individual and on the level of groups; and there is the intrasubjective which is communication between individuals who are together the subject of the same action, and that is something quite different. Biological or libidinal behavior is transformed by communication; there is, for example, the interiorization of the other. But, however modified, there remains a domain of behavior in which, if one links consciousness and symbolization to *praxis*, the subject remains an individual, intersubjective but individual. But with the division of labor, with a production that is related to a whole series of different behaviors, the situation is very different. Can we distinguish between the two types of subjects? In the first case we have an individual subject—intersubjective if you wish—for whom the other can be only an object—of love, of repulsion, of indifference, etc.—but not a subject. In the second case, what we have is a transindividual subject, in which the subject is made up of several individuals—transindividual signifying that the subject is always a group. I propose the hypothesis that individual subjects—or individual consciousnesses—by acting within behavior patterns which in turn go through the division of labor—become transindividual. It is the group that is in charge of satisfying the need to appease hunger or to provide shelter and, at the other extreme of the scale, of building the Empire State building. All activities connected with technology, civilization, or culture depend on the group.

It is very important to add that in reality things are not separate. Taking our simple example again, let us say that there are six people lifting a table. It could happen that two of the six have complexes that will interfere with the action of moving the table or, inversely, individual intersubjective actions might be favorable to the moving of the table. The important point is that, in order to conduct a scientific study, I must first make distinctions. It is impossible to make an analysis of or to establish a dialectic from a mixture. Of course even at the transindividual level two groups which are opposed in one context might be united in another. Imagine for instance a conflict between workers and businessmen in a country which suddenly finds itself at war. A new solidarity between the two groups might arise. The overlapping is permanent and all individual consciousnesses are mixtures. However, the historian or the sociologist must always separate first the larger group from the individual and then the various sub-groups within the larger unit. If I am studying Jansenism, relating it to the *noblesse de robe*, I know very well that each individual Jansenist belongs to numerous other groups; but what interests me, in analyzing the Jansenist group, is whether what they have in common, in comparison to what separates them, will allow me to understand certain patterns of behavior which result precisely from the fact that they are together. What we have here is the conceptual necessity to divide our object of study and such a division is indispensable if our work is to be scientific.

Another very important problematic which I should like to take up is that of the relationships between Freudian psychoanalytic interpretation and genetic structuralist sociological explanation. Here the importance of the concept of the subject becomes obvious. First, is the question of the subject purely a conceptual game, a matter of ideological sympathy? No, the question is essential from a scientific standpoint. In relationship to what does the object that I propose to study—the theater of Racine or the French Revolution—become comprehensible and intelligible? I should also like to ask what may sound like a naïve question, but think about it and try to take it seriously. Why should it be inconceivable that Racine could write a play which might express his individual, unconscious, and biographical problems while using a formal pattern (*schema*) which does not manifest an unresolvable contradiction, where there might be a predominance or a preference for reasons as in the great Cornelian dramas? I don't think that at an individual level you could say this to be impossible. But if the mental categories, the fundamental structures of Racine's tragedies, stem from a concrete historical situation such as that of the French parliamentarians, who were dissatisfied with the monarchy's centralist politics but who could not oppose the monarchy because they were dependent on it, one can hardly conceive of Racine taking a positive position or displaying Cornelian *génerosité* at a time when his group was in a fundamentally unsatisfactory position in society.

The structural configuration of research is much different in the case of collective creation from that in dream analysis, where interpretation and explanation are inseparable. There are many common elements in psychoanalysis and genetic structuralism: the affirmation that all human behavior has a meaning; that to understand this meaning one must refer to a larger context—to the biography of the individual in one case or to history in the other—which goes beyond the level of the manifest. But there is a fundamental difference in that it is impossible in Freudian psychoanalysis to separate interpretation from explanation. That is, in interpreting a dream one must at the same time have recourse to the psychological category of the unconscious and to the whole totality in which the dream is inserted. I should like here to make a parenthesis. The two most important intellectual procedures in the scientific study of human facts are comprehension and explanation. Both are purely conceptual procedures in spite of the fact that comprehension is often thought of as being related to identification, empathy, sympathy, etc. Comprehension is the rigorous description of a significant structure in its relation to a function. Explanation is the comprehensive description of a larger structure in which the struc-

Lucien Goldmann

ture being studied has a function. For example, if I describe Jansenist mentality, thought, theology, I understand Jansenism; I am making an effort of comprehension; I am not explaining anything. But in understanding Jansenism I explain how the works of Racine and Pascal originated in Jansenism. I describe the relationships of the classes in seventeenth-century France; I am again in the process of describing a structure and making it comprehensible; but I am also explaining how Jansenism was born. Explanation is the insertion of the structure that we have described and understood into a larger structure in which it has its function and where I can understand the nature of its unity.

Let us note then that it is impossible to understand a dream or any phenomenon connected with the individual subject without explanation. Freud links interpretation to the unconscious, that is, psychological categories are necessary for interpretation. This may be because all forms of behavior of the individual subject originate in structures where consciousness enters only as an auxiliary element and has no autonomous structure.

In sociology the situation is very different. Here consciousness tends to create autonomous structures, structures that can be written, understood, and interpreted in themselves. I need sociology to see how they originated, but, for example, once I understand the genetic origin of French tragedy in the seventeenth century, I can explain the life of *Phèdre* without adding anything to or taking anything away from the text, which, by the way, gives us a quantitative criterion by which to judge an interpretation. An interpretation can be considered satisfactory only if it takes into account a high enough fraction of the text to be the only possible one—if one for instance is satisfied with accounting for only 60 per cent of the text, then there are at least six or seven interpretations.

I would say that all phenomena of consciousness are situated on a line with two extremities and that by understanding the two extremities we can understand what goes on between them. At one end we have the transindividaul behavior of the group in which the individual subject's behavior produces no distortion—the individual either having sufficiently repressed his personal needs and drives or being remarkably well adapted. In this case the text can be interpreted autonomously, without explanation or recourse to symbolism. There is no need to extricate the subject in order to determine the mental structure which has created it, but it is there and it has its meaning. For example, in *Brittanicus*, Narcissus is killed; Julie retires to the vestal virgins; Nero cannot enter. "Absolutely improbable!" the critics cried immediately.

One doesn't enter the vestal virgins at eighteen years of age, and Nero entered the temple whenever he wanted to. Of course, but that is not the point. Within the mental structures of the Jansenist group, to which Racine belonged, the King, the temporal power, does not enter the temple. This doesn't mean that the temple in the play symbolizes the Christian Church or heaven. It does mean that the mental categories of the tragedy originated in a certain group of *noblesse de robe* and were formulated more precisely by the Jansenist group from which Racine came. Great cultural works are those which can be interpreted without adding anything—and where the interpretation takes into account 80 or 90 per cent of the text, that is to say, the only reading possible. Inversely, at the other end of the line, individual, libidinal problems intervene so forcefully that they completely deform social logic; for example in the case of dreams. Although dreams have a meaning, it cannot be communicated or autonomously interpreted at the explicit level of the dream. It is by explaining it that one interprets it, and even then one cannot interpret a dream without having recourse to the symbolic order, the unconscious and other similar categories. Between these two extremes, the great cultural creation and the dream or neurosis, are situated the enormous majority of individual consciousnesses and behavior, which are mixtures and mixtures cannot be analyzed. Social reality is always a mixture. Any historian will tell us that pure capitalism or pure feudalism are nowhere to be found. But these essential instrumental concepts are based on the structure of reality and allow us to understand the mixture.

Roland Barthes's talk is entitled "To Write: An Intransitive Verb?" I believe he was right to raise the question but only at the individual level. As he once said, the writer writes for the sake of writing and as such he is different from the man of action who speaks or writes in order to act upon society. But if the question of writing is raised within the context of the logical structures of a collective subject, then the question as to whether "to write" is an intransitive verb is eliminated, for the problem of writing for its own sake is now raised in relationship to the collective subject of social life. Did Racine's works act upon society? For there is a division of labor and the problematic of literary history, like that of history, is to situate all human behavior in a framework within which it becomes necessary and comprehensible. And I remind you that this is only possible at the level of a transindividual subject. An analysis that remains on the personal level is equivalent, for instance, to the assertion that the workers that built The Johns Hopkins University worked only for their salary. This cannot be derived. They were not interested in Hopkins. Yet through a division of labor and the elimination from consciousness of certain factors this University, a society, and social concepts have been constructed, and these workers have participated in this construction. The Cartesian ego, the theory of autonomous thought, the psychology of intransitive writing cannot be understood unless we situate them within a structure through which we can comprehend them and see them as one part of a collective subject which must be related to all the rest.

I would like now to pose a series of methods—logical problems. First, there exist two distinct levels of form. Beyond the pure form spoken of by the linguist or the semiologist, there is what could be called the form of content. Some might call this content, but it *is* form; it is the significant structure of the universe created by the writer. In both *Théophile* and *Faust* we are told the story of a man who has sold his soul to the devil. In *Théophile* such an act should lead to hell, and it is only through the intervention of the Virgin that the man gets to heaven. Whereas in *Faust* this very same act is the only way to heaven—as the fact that Marguerite gets to heaven after Faust clearly shows. The difference between the two is essential and makes for distinct structures. For another concrete example of this problem, consider the two plays: *Haute Surveillance* and *Les Bonnes*, both by Genêt. In each case we have two groups of individuals composed of a superior who is absent and two subordinate characters, one of whom kills the other at the end which leads to a new configuration symmetrical with the first—i.e., two new groups are formed one absent the other present. However, there are also differences between these two plays. The characters are women in one case and men in the other. In *Les Bonnes* by killing one of the subordinate partners the maids arrive at a triumph, an apotheosis, while *Haute Surveillance* ends with a defeat. The universe of *Les Bonnes*, which does not exist in *Haute Surveillance*, can be exactly defined by the opposition between the dominated and the dominating, the impossibility of killing the dominating, and therefore the necessity—which did not exist in the other play—for the ritual murder of the absent mistress within an imaginary dimension (*dans l'imaginaire*).

It is the semantic material that we have analyzed, not the linguistic form of the message. The problem is whether one can analyze the structure of form, within a narrow linguistic or stylistic context, before knowing what the pure linguistic forms served to express, or what universe the writer wanted to convey. Personally, I have never been able to do it, even though it should be theoretically possible. But from the perspective in which I am working I can point to a few cases where problems that stylists had encountered in working with certain formal structures have become clear once the form—meaning, as I indicated, form of content or form of a particular universe—was extricated. My first example will be taken from Pascal and will deal with the nature of the fragment and the structure of "the wager"; my second will deal with a line from Racine's *Phèdre* which a whole series of French critics have considered either devoid of content or independent of the content of the play: *"la fille de Minos et de Pasiphaë"* [*the daughter of Minos and of Pasiphaë*]. You are familiar with all that was written about the "true outline" of the *Pensées,* until a structuralist analyst showed not only that the fragment as a literary form was necessary to Pascal but that—and this is far more important —he used it intentionally and that it was a Cartesian perspective that had prevented considering fragments as ends in themselves. For Pascal's message is that Man is great in that he searches for absolute values but small in that, without ever ceasing to search, he knows that he can never approach these values. The only form to express this content is, of course, one which does not prove the contrary: which doesn't show either a man who has abandoned the search or one who has approached the goal. The fragment is such a form. Let us not forget that in Jansenist literature there is a great deal of discussion about the relationship between content and form. What hasn't been written about the dialogue of the wager and the question as to who is the partner? There is supposed to be a partner who is a libertine, because it is said that Pascal couldn't bet with himself. Yet the text tells us that he does, for Pascal's faith is a wager that is a total commitment to God, with the permanent possibility of its not being kept—an uncertain certitude. The text itself must then show both aspects of total commitment and of the refusal of such a commitment by him who bets in the void. We can see why the form in which Pascal cast his "wager" is a necessary one and perfectly adapted to its content.[4]

Now let us briefly turn to Racine's line *"la fille de Minos et de Pasiphaë"* which has been considered by some to be pure sonority. In a sociological study of Racine I defined Phèdre as a being who does not seek her values in a world which is based on separation and compromise; Phèdre demands both extremes: Venus and the Sun, love

[4] For an extended discussion of "Le Pari de Pascal," see *Le Dieu caché* (Paris: Gallimard, 1955), pp. 315–37.

and glory, values which cannot be reconciled in Racine's universe. At this point the line *"la fille de Minos et de Pasiphaë"* suddenly becomes much clearer in its relationship to the play. Minos and Pasiphaë are opposites: not only is Pasiphaë in heaven and Minos in hell, but Minos is a judge in hell and Pasiphaë a sinner in heaven. These oppositions in turn correspond to the contrasting sonorities which characterize the composition of the verse. These examples were rather sketchy. I mentioned them only because I wanted to show that there was a possibility of bringing together abstract linguistic or stylistic forms with what I have chosen to call the form of content.

What I briefly tried to show in this analysis is that our research deals with intrasubjective structures with transindividual subjects. If I am asked, not why Racine's tragedies could be written from Port Royal but why it was Racine who wrote them, that is a problem for the psychoanalyst. Among twenty-five or fifty Jansenists it was Racine who found in this world-view the possibility of expressing his personal problems in a coherent manner. Another who might have arranged them a little less coherently would not have created a masterpiece. But the essential fact is that if I want to understand the meaning of Phèdre or of Genêt's plays, I must refer them not to the individual Racine or Genêt but to the social groups who worked out the structures with which the plays (which have no symbolic meaning) have created a rigorously coherent universe, the same structures which on the practical level facilitated the group's possibility for living. Therefore the important thing is to know with which *collective subject* one is dealing. To transfer problems with an individual subject to a collective social context—and vice versa—is absurd and dangerous even if the separation between the individual and the collective is clear only to the analyst.

I have already mentioned what I consider to be a fundamental contemporary problem: Can studies of the linguistic type be extended to the totality of signifieds, the thought or the universe that a work is intended to express? I doubt it very much. Valid and exciting as these studies may be in their own domain, my example related to the two plays of Genêt ought to show how they methodologically eliminate both the basic content and the subject. If from an infinite possibility of choices people choose only one particular structural configuration it is because of the need to express certain things and, inversely, what is expressed depends on the fact that it must be expressed in language. However, it should be obvious that the two are not identical. If applied to the meaning or content of a work, linguistic studies will surely fail to grasp the form of meaning.

Furthermore, I believe that any study which attempts to explain the literary work by an individual subject will always encounter at least two fundamental difficulties. Most often it will be able to deal only with a limited number of elements of the work, namely those in which the writer has expressed his individual problems, perhaps in a symbolized form, but the structural configuration of the universe of a literary work is transindividual and it is this unity which will be missed. Even admitting that such an analysis might succeed, in an exceptional case, it will never be able to explain the difference between a masterpiece and the work of a lunatic which has an analogous individual function. Aesthetic value belongs to the social order; it is related to a transindividual logic.

It is equally beside the point in the field of aesthetic sociology to do what nine-tenths of sociologists continue to do: to attempt to relate the content of a work with the content of the collective consciousness. It can be done. There is no writer who has not put in his work something of what he has seen or lived through, but the more mediocre a writer is, the less he has invented. This is why sociology has such extraordinary success with mediocre novels. On the level of structure, the content of a work can be treated neither as symbolizing something else nor as a sociological category. There are no sociological elements in a literary work; there are only imaginary individual characters and situations. There is no Jansenist theology or morality in *Phèdre*; there are only Phèdre, Hippolyte, and Bérénice. However, the structural configuration, the world view, the mental categories, good and evil, the absolute, marriage, etc., and the relationships which link them all together and make for the unity of the play were worked out on the social level.

Finally, even the most orthodox structuralist sociology is threatened by the danger of reductionism. It is of little interest if I say that Racine is a representative of the *noblesse de robe*. He is much more. Great literary works, such as those of Racine, originate from a certain social situation but, far from being the simple reflection of a collective consciousness, they are a particularly unified and coherent expression of the tendencies and aspirations of a given group. They express what the individual members of the group felt and thought without being conscious of it or without being able to formulate it so coherently. They are a meeting of the personal and the collective on the highest level of significant structuring. Their function is analogous to that of thought and action: to organize social structures so that life becomes more acceptable.

Discussion

ALBERT COOK: I think that the causal connection between John and James around the table is very simple, but the literary work transforms these meanings, even social meanings. Even if you account for Racine's work through genetic structures and even if your analysis maintains a perfect coherence between the individual and society, in any case, your question implies your answer. There are other questions as well, questions which, in fact, you have raised. For example, the question of Pascal. I am in perfect agreement that for Pascal the necessity of the fragment is clear. This question is independent of the social origins of Pascal's thought. Also your categories of closure and opening on Minos and Pasiphaë, with which I believe I am equally in agreement, are independent of your social analyses. What, then, is the necessity of sociology for such an analysis?

GOLDMANN: First allow me to make my thought a little more explicit. There is no causal connection between John and James. What there is, more exactly, is a common subject, a subject which is in the process of moving the table. Starting from there, if I want to understand what John is thinking and what James is thinking, there is a subject. There is no *we; we* is a pronoun which means *I* and *you.* In any case the relationship is not a causal one. This much is to specify and to eliminate a preliminary misunderstanding. But take the example of the daughter of Minos and Pasiphaë. Of course, I said myself, if I know that what is expressed in the work is a universe in which man must re-unite two opposite values or in which he must always search for absolute truths which he cannot find, then I don't need sociology. It remains to be seen, first of all, how I could have known this. For there is an enormous literature on both Racine and Pascal which has not known this. I don't believe there has been any coherent interpretation of Pascal. Now in order to know this, I would have had to ask myself first of all where the social group that thinks in a certain way is: it is in the *noblesse de robe* and in the Jansenist group that I found it. It is only within this group that this vision of the world came into being. It was a social group which, in translating its way of feeling and of thinking, worked out a theology and a morality, and then a genius arrived who gave it an imaginary form in a play. But as I said, this is one of the theses. Once I have it, I can very well interpret the play and explain the fragment and Racine's verse without sociology. There is no sociology in the play.

JEAN HYPPOLITE: I simply wanted to say that what I can't understand is the relationship between structure and function. It seems to me that M. Goldmann's whole analysis is oriented toward function, rather than toward structure. Personally, without solving the problem in the same way that he does, I look for the structure before looking for the function. For you, there is no function except when it applies to a structure and no structure except when the structure is made for a function. When I take structure in the algebraic sense of the term, there I know what it means: there are commutative and distributive properties which belong to certain wholes; these are structures. When I take Proust's work and I see the way in which the sentences are organized, climbing one out of the other in a sort of perpetual re-ascent toward the past, to stem the irreversibility of time, I analyze a structure. When I take Proust's admirable work, *Contre Sainte-Beuve*, and I see Proust imagining that he is speaking to his mother, I discover there a *structure* that exists elsewhere. But the discovery of the relationship of this structure in Proust to a general social function—I don't say that one is wrong to do it—I say that it is abusing the word *structure* to connect structure to function before analyzing the structure itself. That is what I want to say.

Homology between a social structure and a literary structure is a mathematical abuse, for I know what *homology* means in mathematics. I don't see what homology between a social and a literary structure means. That is why I don't contest what you are looking for; I look elsewhere. That is, I carry forward the analysis of structure before being predetermined by the notion of function. What I recognize as infinitely valuable in what you are doing is the sense of totality over or against any method which would consist in isolating the elements. The search for the totality in a structure is fundamental, but you abuse the word *structure* through a functionalism which is different from what we call analysis of structures, it seems to me. There you are; this is a remark rather than a criticism, strictly speaking.

GOLDMANN: Of course, it's not a matter of terminology. If we reserve the word *structure* for mathematical structures, then I will have to find another for literary structures. There is no doubt about that. But let's go beyond words and get to realities. What interests me is that in a social group certain relationships are found which have the peculiar property that a certain change—to maintain their meaning—carries with it a whole series of other changes, which may be indicated. I shall take an example from Genêt. When, in the combat between the dominated and the dominating, the dominating cannot be beaten, ritual appears. Whereas it disappears with Saïd [in *Les Paravents*], because Saïd isn't beaten by anybody. The necessity for the revolutionary [in *Le Balcon*] to go into the house of illusions and ask to play the chief of police appears after the defeat. Of course these transformations take place inside a structure—call it a structure or a totality—but I want to say that this totality is not vague.

Now let us come to the relationship between function and structure. In research, of course, I don't begin with function because I must have the situation. I begin with a work of art and I look for its structural analysis. But in concrete research I go very quickly: it suffices to compare two articles, one which I published previously on *Le Balcon* and one that I am publishing now, to see the progression. A whole series of problems appears together which are difficult to solve, unless one has extraordinary intuition or is exceptionally lucky. That happens, unless one asks where and for what reason this way of seeing things was born. If you like, this manner of seeing wasn't born, at least not arbitrarily. I am not going to understand it from the perspective of individual biography, but rather from a group situation, which could have happened only as it did. Genêt is incomprehensible without taking into account the situation of the Left in Europe, in which his behavior begins to have the value of ritual, precisely because, whether for the moment or for a foreseeable future, social transformation has become difficult.

I didn't say what you attributed to me. There is only one thing which is valid. I said that the vital functions of the individual or trans-individual subject in a world situation cannot be satisfied because one never succeeds in obtaining complete satisfaction of needs and aspirations except with the aid of global attitudes in which similar changes can be established, attitudes which I call structures. I didn't say that the structure searches out function or that there is no function before structure. There is function: there is the need for the cat to eat; but that depends on where it is, in a cage or a field, or elsewhere. Perhaps there are also biological transformations and I am not enough of a biologist to take on this problem. But in the social domain it is clear. At a certain time it is forbidden for Christians in the West to charge interest. Then, one fine day, it becomes normal and is introduced among the Protestants. This happens through modifications in European Christian thought, but I think that it is connected with a change in the situation. Previously loans were given to unfortunate and poor people during a strike, but now loans are given to rich people to carry on business affairs, because a certain economic structure has developed. Therefore it is inside this new situation that certain attitudes are changed. Without relation to function the transformation disappears. All writers have said the same thing, except at a very formal level, and if I find common structures and common elements in all stories, I don't know when there is a difference between Perrault's tales and Grimm's tales. However, it is very important to know. It is a matter of knowing why forms of thought are transformed. I must deal with groups which try to live, which must behave in a certain manner on the level of reality, of conception, of imagination, and that is all I said.

HYPPOLITE: It is not a retraction when I say that it is an effort; there is always a fundamental primacy in thought.

GOLDMANN: Ontologically yes; for research one begins with structure, because one doesn't have the thought.

HYPPOLITE: I am not sure of your ontological primacy. Yet, I am sure that research must start with structures. Everything is constructed from the beginning.

GOLDMANN: Most of my students will tell you that that is not what I teach them first.

HYPPOLITE: But I wanted to make you say that everything is ordered by you; yes, by an ontological investigation of functions. That is what is fundamental.

GOLDMANN: Yes, I can reply to you. What I want to say is very simple. When you are dealing with mathematical structures, you can define them, define their coherences precisely. They seem to be general forms for every human mind. And I am dealing with questions of this type. For example (let us suppose that it is well formulated—I haven't prepared my text), why is there no rigorous opposition for Montaigne between different forms of individualism, scepticism, stoicism, epicurianism, etc., while in the seventeenth century it would lead to total incoherence to mix them. It is a completely different world from that of Molière, Gassendi, Descartes, and Corneille. The answer is not immanent. It is not a unity; the unity is not of the logical type. The unity results from the existential situation. The essential problem was to find the forms of individualism at a certain moment in the seventeenth century when individualism is acquired by all the fundamental groups. It is a matter of finding out how. It is beginning from the situation and from the necessity of a functional reply that you have coherence at the cultural level which is not mathematical.

RICHARD MACKSEY: This is just an aside, but without engaging the larger question of immanent hermeneutics, I did want to suggest that your example of the identity of Grimm's tales and Perrault's tales will not wash with the history of folklore studies. It was precisely when, in the 1920s, the emphasis of ethnographic studies was shifted *away from* speculations about origins *toward* the synchronic, formal aspects of the folktale that the great morphological achievements we associate with the names of Propp and Shklovski (on the prose of the Russian fairy tale) were at last possible. Here in North America, Dundes, using both Propp's pioneer work and Kenneth Pike's structural model, has extended the method to native materials. Of course, the original studies were the result of an international co-operation in synchronic analysis, stemming from the Finnish–American ethnographers as well as from the Russian Formalists, but I'd readily admit that the subsequent assimilation of such elements as Pike's model introduces into questions of structure new functional considerations (if not quite in your sense of the term). Pace Lévi-Strauss.

PETER CAWS: I find myself in almost total agreement with Mr. Goldmann on the nature and even on the necessity of structural analysis. The thing that is perplexing me is the status of the transindividual subject, and I can see that the *we* is a linguistic device—we have to use it this way—or I can see it as part of a hypothetical reconstruction of human behavior, but I wonder if Mr. Goldmann wants to push it to an ontological status so as to say the transindividual subject is a real subject having in that case to revert to what he spoke of at the beginning, the possibility of a transindividual consciousness, a transindividual unconscious, a transindividual nonconscious perhaps?

GOLDMANN: I would like to specify that I did not use the term transindividual consciousness. There is no consciousness except in the individual. But I say that to understand the consciousness of the individual, his youth, his transformations, I must link them to behavior, not to his behavior, but to behavior in which he does not have the status of subject. I return to my elementary example, but it is valid for all. Who carries out the table? Does John? Does James? In behavior, in a thought, there is a subject side and an object side. Is John or James on the object side? In carrying out the table, does John think of the other end of the table as having the same status? Or does he know very well that his consciousness must take into account the fact that two men are carrying out the table? Inside the individual consciousness there are structurations in which every other is object—object of love, of desire, of hate—and elements in which there is no individual coherence because the coherence is situated on the level of the fact that the action is carried out by two. And I believe that that is a given, permanent reality. Then, when one tries to see the coherence of Racine's work in relationship to Racine, one doesn't succeed. But when one tries to see the coherence of Racine's work—and this is always valid for great works—in relationship to the group, then one finds coherences that Racine never even suspected, because he simply has the aesthetic need to construct a coherent universe, without knowing why. And coherence is achieved in relationship to the group. I said that all our knowledge implies a subject-pole and an object-pole. In my text I have three points concerning the subjective and the objective element of all knowledge. I'm sorry that I didn't read them because of the time.

RICHARD SCHECHNER: In regard to the theater, I wonder how you treat the real event of performance, including the audience, the theater building, and the entire environment of the theatrical event. What effect does this have on your analysis of the aesthetic event going on in that environment? Especially in regard to the modern theater, Genêt and Beckett and Ionesco, when the writer uses the mechanics of the theater, when the very fact of the theatrical event is introjected into the text, how does this affect your analysis?

GOLDMANN: All I can say about this is what I have already said, that this sort of thing can be done, but that I haven't done it. The problem is one of sufficient research. A whole series of research projects would be necessary, based on the total structure of the message and its relationship to all the modes of expression, not only language but the theatrical whole and the consciousness of the theater. That would assume a chair in the sociology of the theater in addition to another chair in the sociology of literature which would be concerned with the formal relationships between means of expression and that which is expressed. But here is a problem that I am dealing with in my own research. The problem is in regard to Sartre and Genêt: what they have to say and the questions that they ask are transformed at a given moment. And at this point both Sartre and Genêt change from prose writing to the theater. Sartre first tries to write a novel with the new problematic, *L'Âge de la Raison*, which everyone today agrees is not a masterpiece; it doesn't have the value of either *La Nausée* or *Les Séquestrés d'Altona*. He discovers very quickly that what he wants to say can only be said in a play. Genêt, who was a novelist, also changes suddenly to the theater in order to deal with a new problematic. Why? I don't know; but I think that an answer is possible, although it might require a year or two of work on the question.

EUGENIO DONATO: I would like to take up an old discussion in terms of what you have said today. It seems to me that your project can be defined as follows. I want to be scientific, therefore I must eliminate the problem of the observer. I must find a means of speaking of the object without taking into account the one who speaks of it. In this way, you end up confusing what I would call a distinction between the subject of the science and the science of the subject. For example, physics would amount to what is happening in this table. Whereas physics, as physics, is the knowledge that is being communicated, by means of certain signs and symbols, in a building near here, and which is independent of what is happening in this table. I think you are taking an absolutely empirical notion of structure. To begin with, you want to consider any situation as a structure and then to look for its functions. Personally, I don't see how we can define a structure without beginning with functions which put the terms of the structure into relationship. To return to the question of science, it is obvious that through the precise formulas of each scientific language one can give any element the status of subject. Let us say that in a certain formula the atom functions as subject. But the collective *we* can also be taken in that sense. It becomes a very different *we* from that which is spoken in communication through a subjectivity which thinks this science. You speak of physics and chemistry as if they spoke of the same subject, but they don't. And they constitute their subject through the different languages that they speak.

GOLDMANN: Do you mean subject or object?

DONATO: Object.

GOLDMANN: To indicate that I didn't intend to eliminate subjectivity and that everything that you have just said on science and the significant and subjective structure of science is an important problem, I will read a few passages in my talk that I skipped for purely temporal reasons. I begin by saying that scientific results obtained from human facts can be neither purely subjective nor purely objective for two reasons. The first reason is that which you have indicated: science is itself a significant structure. The second reason which reinforces the first is that the same collective subject studies objects which it has made by means of concepts which it has made. Furthermore, I said that the fundamental difference between the human sciences and the physico-chemical sciences is that the latter have values which, although not absolutely objective, are at least objective in the general sense that is valid for everybody today: mastery of nature. For the moment, however, it is absolutely impossible to conduct the human sciences in this perspective because the values of structures are still specific and particular. The three reasons you give for the impossibility of objectivity are, therefore, briefly outlined in my text. However, it is at this point that the problem begins. I also said that these elements do not mean that our efforts are purely arbitrary, and in spite of them we must attempt to conduct scientific research, for which the empirical fact is the only criterion. You know that I have dealt with this problem elsewhere and that it is very difficult to discuss it here in this short period of time. In order to conduct scientific research one must be perfectly conscious of the difficulties and try to overcome them. The objectivity that is not that of an object without a subject, but that of validity for all men, is what all science must try to approach as nearly as possible, while realizing that it can never really attain it. But this difficulty is different and much greater for the human sciences than for the natural sciences.

DONATO: How do you distinguish these three levels: the empirics of physics, physics as a language of signs, and physics as the control of nature?

GOLDMANN: I am quite willing to admit one thing which doesn't change my position at all. Today the relationship between empirical problems and theoretical problems in physics is very mediated because the science is made up of research apparatus and conceptual operations which, for the most part, are concerned with internal problems. But the science had its origins in the problems of life. On the level of research, it is obvious that every theory must be experimentally confirmed, even if we have to wait fifty to one hundred years to be able to conduct the experiment. Anyway, I think it is obvious that modern physics serves to control nature; you have only to take an airplane

Discussion

from here to Paris to see that, in spite of the fact that the physicist may be a pure theoretician who is not at all interested in the mastery of nature.

MACKSEY: This is just a qualifying aside on the relation of empirics to theory, but I think that those of us outside the natural sciences too readily assume, with Bacon, that confirmation is simply a matter of adequate quantification, instrumentation, and "crucial experiment." After all, within the hypothetico-deductive framework there has been, since Duhem, increasing scepticism about experiment as a means of establishing and, even more recently, disconfirming theory in the natural sciences. The shadow of Hume is a long one, despite even such modern ruses as using probability inference, and some would simply argue that the abandonment of any theory is really a problem for the sociology of knowledge and not empirics.

JEAN-PIERRE VERNANT: I would like to make three related points. The first is the necessity of separating, more than you do, the ideas of structure and meaning [*signification*]. You say, for example, that the behavior of a cat chasing a mouse is structured and consequently has a meaning. This behavior has a meaning for you, just as the structure of a crystal has meaning for a physicist, but this is obviously not *meaning* as the word is used in relation to human phenomena. In other words, what must be taken into consideration here is what certain psychologists call the symbolic function. This is the fact that man is set apart from animal conduct as well as physical facts by language, by the fact of meaning. This is the human reality which cannot be reduced to biological or physical elements.

My second point is that the notion of *subject*, which you have brought into the discussion, is a very confusing one. In the case of human phenomena we are dealing with a level of meaning rather than of subject. On the linguistic level, I know what *subject* means. It is a grammatical form in relationship with the verb. (Even here, there are languages which don't have this system.) But when you say *subject* there is a whole series of implicit contents. There is the notion of *subjectivity* which arose at a certain period in the western world when an interior dimension of man became the object of language in certain literary works. There is also the notion of the *individual* and the problem of recognizing the category of the individual when it appears. I think that instead of saying *subject* we should say the *human level*.

The third point is the relationship between structure and function.

118

In your discussion with M. Hyppolite you both seemed to use *structure* as the internal structure of the work, as a work, and *function* as something social. That doesn't seem to me to be exactly the nature of the problem. If you want to maintain, in opposition to certain structuralists, that structures cannot be stated independently of functions, then functions cannot be social, but as functions they must be linked to structures. It was the linguists who first emphasized structural studies, but certain linguists say that the structures of language cannot be analyzed apart from the function of language: communication, the need to decipher a message following binary rules. The function of mathematical signs is not communication but to permit definite operations through a language in which each word has an exact signification. In analyzing the structures of kinship, as Lévi-Strauss does, one might ask what, apart from communication, is the function of kinship. When you analyze the structures of myth you might ask if the function of these structures is communication or something else. And when you examine aesthetic structures the problem is, I believe, to determine their functions within the work, and not simply their social functions.

GOLDMANN: I think that we are entirely in agreement on the first point. I said very explicitly that the behavior of the animal is *translatable* in terms of problems to be resolved, but that there is no differentiation of signifier and signified and no communication. One of the central ideas of my talk was that, at the moment when communication appears, the nature of what I call the subject is transformed: in place of the individual subject we then see the transindividual subject in which subjectivity is only an internal element. Therefore I did make this distinction, although I also spoke of intersubjectivity. I also emphasized the fact that there is no consciousness. But I believe there is also a danger of forgetting that through language and the detours of civilization (division of labor) and technology (the transindividual subject at more and more complicated levels) all of this is still linked to praxis. The cat must live and, in spite of everything, men think and act, with all the complexity that that implies, in order to survive and solve their problems. I emphasized the difference just where you indicate it by saying that the problem does not exist for the cat, but only in my study of it. But I think we must also emphasize the relationship in order to avoid arriving at the idea that thought can be independent of praxis.

All I want to say about the subject is that in order to understand the cat's behavior I must relate it to a being who acts and brings about transformations. Every time I approach a human problem, at whatever level, I must—if I don't want to see it as a purely intellectual or aesthetic phenomenon—establish its intelligibility in relationship to behavior. A certain case of behavior, thought, or imagination becomes intelligible only when I relate it to a group situation. For the natural sciences this group situation may be mankind in nature, but in other cases it must be a much more specific group. In this sense I am speaking of a subject and a very mediated action because, finally, I believe that Racine's work is only immediately written by Racine. To write it he needed a whole world-view, a whole group of problems, and an orientation of solutions which had been worked out at various levels by 400 Jansenists and, before them, thousands of Parlementarians in France. That is what I refer to when I speak of the subject, not to the individual subject but to the subject with intelligible behavior. There is always a subject which is not an expression of individual subjectivity, but of a group with mental categories to conceive the world and to resolve aesthetic problems. Individual behavior does exist; it is primarily biological, eating for example. However, producing food is cultural behavior.

I think we should be in agreement on functions. I said that every human phenomenon is a structure in that it is found within a larger phenomenon and in a relationship which I can understand only in terms of functions. To be sure, there is a function of the element within the work, this element being a very reduced structure inside a global work. However, the work itself is inserted in a larger totality and I see no reason to stop at the last page of Racine's *Phèdre*. The larger structure in which *Phèdre* is inserted is multiple. First there is its meaning for the individual, which is studied by the psychologist or the psychoanalyst. There is also its meaning in the structure of the seventeenth century. Finally, it has another meaning at each later point in history. Each element in each structure has a function in each totality, and this continues indefinitely. Thus there is an internal function but also an external function.

JACQUES LACAN: M. Goldmann has just shown how difficult it will be for me to communicate to you tomorrow what I have, just this morning, with the kind help of my translator, begun to put into a form worthy of this present meeting. M. Goldmann is already well known to you, having taught here for several months. What I may have to contribute will be less familiar. I have tried to prepare something which will represent the first cutting-edge of my thought. Since this project is something I have been working on for fifteen years, you will understand that tomorrow's exposé cannot be exhaustive. However, in order to facilitate my task and to prepare your ear, I should like to say this: A few words concerning the *subject*. I feel that they are necessary since I interjected the term yesterday and since even M. Derrida here asked me at dinner, "Why do you call *this* the subject, this unconscious? What does the subject have to do with it?" In any case, it has nothing whatsoever to do with what M. Goldmann has talked about as *subject*. Of course it is only a question of terminology, and M. Goldmann can use the term *subject* to mean anything he likes. But what I should like to emphasize is the fact that what characterizes M. Goldmann's subject (which is very close to the commonplace definition) is the function of *unity*, of a unifying unity. His subject is the subject of knowledge, the support (false or not) of a whole world of objects. And M. Goldmann carries over this function of unity into fields other than that of knowledge, into the sphere of action for example, when he calls John and James carrying a table a single subject in so far as they are united in this common action.

But what prompts me to speak is the fact that I have had just this experience. I did not myself (although my name is "James" [*Jacques*]) move a table together with John, but I did not do so only for reasons of personal fatigue and not because I lacked the will to move it myself, as you will see. However what happened was quite different.

I was in a local hotel whose name I won't mention (known to all of you) and I wanted to have a table, which was against a wall, moved in front of the window, in the interest of working for this meeting. To the right of the window there was a chest of drawers which would have prevented this. I picked up the telephone and asked for some one to help me. There appeared a very dignified, white-haired character who had on his uniform the designation (which still has no very precise meaning for me, although things have since changed) "Bellman" To this name, which must mean "beautiful man," I did not pay attention right away. I said to the "Bellman" in my English (imperfect, as you will see tomorrow, but sufficient to communicate a request) that what I wanted was to put this table by the window, and the chest in the place of the table. Those here who belong to the American community will not be surprised at the simple gesture I got in reply. "See here. I'm the Bellman. Whom do you take me for? That's a job for the Housekeeper." I said "No matter. All I want is to get the job done. Please be kind enough to notify the housekeeper, so that it won't be too late." I must say that in an exceptionally short time for this hotel

I got the housekeeper and was then entitled to the service of two blacks (again without waiting too long, since I was able to explain myself on the subject of my wishes). They arrived and, apparently paying very little attention to my request (they even seemed to be listening to something else), they did what I asked. They did it, I would say, *almost* perfectly, for there remained a few little imperfections in the job, but such definite imperfections that they could not have been unintentional.

Now where is the *subject* of this little story? At first glance (but you will quickly see why I do not stop at this) the subject is obviously myself, in so far as I was found wanting in the whole situation, for the important point in the story is obviously not the fact that I was the one who gave the order and, finally, got satisfaction, but rather the way in which I failed altogether by not asking, in the first place, for the proper person among the reigning hotel hierarchy, in order to obtain this service without too great a delay. Anyway this gives me an opportunity to point up the difference between subject and subjectivity. I might assuredly be the subject if it were only a question of this *lack*. I am the subjectivity in as much as, undeniably, I evinced throughout the affair a certain impatience.

On the other hand what seems to me to be the subject is really something which is not *intra* nor *extra* nor *inter*subjective. The subject of this affair seems to me (and don't take it amiss; I say it without the slightest derogatory intention, but fully aware of the weight of what I will propose): What sort of subject characterizes a style of society in which everyone is theoretically as ready to help you as the question "May I help you?" implies? It's the question your seat-mate immediately asks you when you take a plane—an American plane, that is, with an American seat-mate. The last time I flew from Paris to New York, looking very tired for personal reasons, my seat-mate, like a mother bird, literally put food into my mouth throughout the trip. He took bits of meat from his own plate and slipped them between my lips! What is the nature of this subject, then, which is based on this first principle, and which, on the other hand, makes it impossible to get service? Such then is my question, and I believe, as regards my story, that it is here, on the level of this *gap*—which does not fit into *intra* or *inter* or *extra*subjectivity—that the question of the subject must be posed.

CARROLL PRATT: One final comment is perhaps relevant to Lucien Goldmann's paper and the lively discussion aroused by the ideas expressed in that paper, especially the insistence that a literary work, or for that matter any work of art, cannot be properly understood and criticized apart from the social, ethical, religious, and economic milieu in which it was created and produced. This argument is an extension and application of the doctrine of *Gestalttheorie*. The Gestalt psychologists maintain that the whole—the *Gestalt*—has a property that cannot be deduced from the parts, and that the parts are meaningless unless perceived in relation to the whole, e.g., a melody. The last three notes of *God Save the Queen* are the same as the first three notes of *Three Blind Mice*, provided the two melodies are sung or played in the same key. Yet it is highly unlikely that either melody has ever served as a reminder of the other, although the old law of association might lead one to suppose that the beginning of *Three Blind Mice* would immediately suggest the cadence of *God Save the Queen*, or vice versa, because of the presence in both melodies of identical elements arranged in a familiar sequence. The fact that such is not the case lends support to the Gestalt view that wholes and parts are inextricably interrelated in perception, and especially to the insistence that the parts of a perception acquire significance only when they are studied in relation to the total configuration.

It is questionable whether *Gestalttheorie* is applicable in this fashion to the analysis and criticism of works of art. The theory was formulated largely as a protest against the methods by which classical psychologists studied perception. *Sensations* were regarded as the elements of mind, and since perception was thought of as the sum of sensory elements, the way to study perception was to make a minute quantitative inventory of the elements and then find out how they were pieced together in perception. The Gestalt psychologists produced powerful evidence and arguments against this atomistic doctrine. But *Gestalttheorie* does not argue that a perception, which is itself a *Gestalt* or whole, can only be understood in relation to still larger wholes. If such were the case, nothing could be understood apart from the totality of human experience, which is obviously absurd. Every whole, even if part of a larger whole, has intrinsic, self-contained properties that can be fruitfully studied in their own right, which of course does not preclude the possibility that the appreciation of those properties may be enhanced by a knowledge of their context or setting. But the latter are not necessary conditions for appreciation. The symphonies of Mozart and the novels of Tolstoi are self-contained units that possess intrinsic miracles of creativity which do not depend for their existence on the context in which they were produced—a situation quite different from the individual notes of a melody which have little significance apart from their place in the melody. It is worthy of note that the Gestalt psychologists often speak of *segregated* wholes, as if to emphasize the independence of such units. A melody is a segregated and independent whole, whereas the notes that go to make up the melody are dependent elements. The same distinction does not apply with equal force, if indeed it applies at all, to the relation of a whole to still larger wholes. If it did, literary and artistic criticism would never be able to get under way.

Language and Literature[1]

Tzvetan Todorov
Ecole Pratique
des Hautes Etudes

My topic can be summarized in this sentence by Valéry, which I will attempt to clarify and elaborate: "Literature is, and can be nothing other than, a kind of extension and application of certain properties of Language."

What permits us to affirm the existence of this relationship? The very fact that the literary work is a "verbal work of art" has for a long time moved scholars to speak of the "great rôle" of language in a literary work. An entire academic discipline, stylistics, has been created at the borders of literary studies and linguistics, and many theses have been written on the "language" of this or that writer. Language is defined here as the medium of the poet or the work.

This obvious *rapprochement* is far from exhausting the multitudinous relationships between language and literature. In Valéry's sentence it is not so much a question of language as medium, but of language as model. Language fills this function in many areas foreign to literature. Man has made himself from the beginning through language—the philosophers of our century have repeated this often enough—and we rediscover the model of language in all social activity. Or, to repeat the words of Benveniste, "the configuration of language determines all semiotic systems." Since art is one of these semiotic systems, we can be certain of discovering in it the imprint of the abstract forms of language. Literature enjoys, as we know, a particularly privileged status among semiotic activities. Literature uses language both as point of de-

[1] "Langage et littérature." The text which follows is a translation of the tape-recording and of the paper distributed at the Symposium.

Tzvetan Todorov

parture and as point of arrival; language endows literature with its abstract configuration as well as its perceptible medium; language is simultaneously mediator and mediated. Consequently literature is not only the first field that can be studied starting from language but also the first field the knowledge of which can cast new light on the properties of language itself.

This particular situation of literature determines our relationship with respect to linguistics. It is evident that in treating language, we do not have the right to ignore the knowledge accumulated by this science, nor by any other investigation of language. However, as in all sciences, linguistics often proceeds by reduction and simplification of its object in order to be able to manipulate it more easily; it dismisses or provisionally ignores certain traits of language so as to establish the homogeneity of others and to allow their logic to become manifest. This is undoubtedly a procedure which is justified in the internal evolution of this science, but of which those who extrapolate the results and methods must be wary. The traits which are ignored may have the greatest importance in another "semiotic system." The unity of the human sciences resides less in the methods elaborated in linguistics, which are beginning to be used elsewhere, than in the object common to all, which is indeed language. The concept that we have of language today, which is derived from certain studies of linguistics, will have to be enriched from teachings taken from those other sciences.

If this perspective is adopted, it is obvious that all knowledge of literature will follow a path parallel to that of the knowledge of language; moreover, these two paths will tend to merge. An immense area is open to this investigation; only a relatively small part has been explored until now in the work of the brilliant pioneer, Roman Jakobson. These studies have concentrated on poetry, and have sought to demonstrate the existence of a structure formed by the distribution of linguistic elements within the poem. I propose to indicate here, this time apropos of literary prose, some points where the *rapprochement* between language and literature seems particularly easy.

It goes without saying that owing to the present state of our knowledge in this area, I will limit myself to remarks of a general character, without the least pretension of "exhausting the subject."

Actually an attempt has already been made in prose studies to bring about this *rapprochement* and to profit from it. The Russian Formalists, who have been pioneers in more than one area, have already attempted to exploit this analogy. They situated it, more precisely, between the devices of style and the devices of organization in the *récit;* one of

Shklovski's first articles was in fact entitled, "The link between devices of composition and stylistic devices in general." The author noted that "construction in echelons [*paliers*] was found to be in the same series as the repetitions of sounds, tautology, tautological parallelism, repetitions." [2] The three blows struck by Roland on the stone were for him of the same nature as ternary lexical repetitions in folkloric poetry.

I do not wish to attempt a historical study here, so I will be content to recall briefly a few other results of the studies of the Formalists, presenting them in a way which will be useful here. In his studies on the typology of the *récit*, Shklovski distinguished two major types of combination among stories. First there is an open form to which new adventures can always be added at the end, for example, the adventures of some hero—such as Rocambole; and second, a closed form beginning and ending by the same motif, but having other stories told within. Take for example the story of Oedipus: at the beginning there is a prediction, at the end its realization; between the two are the attempts to avoid it. However, Shklovski had not realized that these two forms represent the rigorous projection of the two fundamental syntactical devices by which two propositions may be combined: coordination and subordination. Note that in linguistics today, this second operation is called *enchâssement*, a term borrowed from ancient poetics.

The concern of the passage previously cited was with *parallelism:* this device is only one of those raised by Shklovski. Analyzing *War and Peace*,[3] he reveals, for example, the *anthithesis* formed by pairs of characters: "1. Napoleon-Koutouzov; 2. Pierre Bezoukov-André Bolkonski and at the same time Nicolas Rostov who serves as point of reference for both pairs." [4] *Gradation* is also found; several members of a family exhibit the same character traits but to different degrees. Thus in *Anna Karenina*, "Stiva is situated on a lower echelon in relation to his sister." [5]

But parallelism, antithesis, gradation, and repetition are only rhetorical devices. One can then formulate the thesis implicit in Shklovski's remarks. There are devices in the *récit* which are projections of rhetorical devices. Starting from this supposition, we could identify what

---

[2] *Théorie de la littérature* (Paris: Editions du Seuil, 1965), p. 48.
[3] Shklovski, as quoted in *Théorie de la littérature: textes des formalistes russes reunis*, ed. and trans. by Tzvetan Todorov (Paris, 1965).
[4] *Ibid.*, p. 187.
[5] *Ibid.*, p. 188.

forms are taken on by other less familiar rhetorical devices, at the level of the *récit*.

Take for example *association*, a rhetorical figure which refers to the use of an inadequate person of the verb. For a linguistic example, let us take this question a professor might ask his students: "What have we got for today?" You probably recall the demonstration on the use of this device in the philosophic essay given by Michel Butor on Descartes as well as the use he himself makes of it in his book *La Modification*.

Here is another rhetorical figure that could have been taken for a definition of a detective story, were it not borrowed from the rhetoric of Fontanier, written in the beginning of the nineteenth century. It is *sustentation;* it "consists in holding the reader or listener in suspense for a long time, and finally surprising him by something he was far from expecting." This device can therefore be transformed into a literary genre.

M. M. Bakhtin, a great Soviet literary critic, has shown the particular use that Dostoevski made of another rhetorical device, *occupation*, defined in this way by Fontanier: "it consists of anticipating or rejecting in advance an objection that might be raised." [6]

All the utterances [*paroles*] of Dostoevski's characters implicitly include those of their interlocutor, be he imaginary or real. The monologue is always a concealed dialogue, which is precisely the reason for the profound ambiguity of Dostoevski's characters.

Lastly I will mention some rhetorical devices founded on one of the essential properties of language: the absence of an unambiguous one-to-one relationship [*relation biunivoque*] between sound and meaning; it gives rise to two well-known linguistic phenomena, synonymy and polysemy. Synonymy, the basis of plays on words in linguistic usage, takes the form of a literary device that is called "recognition." The fact that the same person can have two appearances, that is the existence of two forms for one and the same content, is similar to the phenomenon which results from the *rapprochement* of two synonyms.

Polysemy gives rise to several rhetorical figures, only one of which I will mention: syllepsis. A famous example of syllepsis is embodied in this verse of Racine: "Je souffre . . . brûlé de plus de feux que je n'en allumai." [I suffer . . . burning with more fire than I could kindle.] What is the source of the rhetorical figure? The fact is that the word *feux* [fire], which is part of each proposition, is taken in

[6] Tr. note: M. M. Bakhtin, *Problemy tvorchestra Dostoevskogo* (Leningrad, 1926).

two different ways. The fire of the first proposition is imaginary; it burns the soul of the person, while the fire of the second proposition corresponds to real flames.

This figure has received wide use in the *récit;* we can see it for example in a novella by Boccaccio. We are told that a monk was visiting his mistress, the wife of a village bourgeois. Unexpectedly the husband returns home. What is the couple going to do? The monk and the woman, who are hidden in the baby's room, pretend they are caring for the baby who, they say, is sick. The husband is content and thanks them warmly. The movement of the *récit*, as we see, follows exactly the same form as syllepsis. A single incident, the monk and the woman in the bedroom, acquires one interpretation in the first part of the *récit* and another interpretation in the part which follows. This figure appears quite frequently in Boccaccio; recall the stories of the nightingale or of the barrel.

Thus far my comparison, following the Formalists from whom I took my point of departure, has juxtaposed manifestations of language with literary manifestations; in other words, we have only been observing forms. I would like to sketch here another possible approach which would investigate the underlying categories of these two worlds, the world of utterances [*parole*] and the world of literature. To do this, we must leave the level of forms and move to the level of structures. In doing so, we go farther away from literature to come closer to that discourse upon literature which is criticism.

It has been possible to approach the problems of signification in a way, which if not felicitious, is at least promising, as soon as the notion of "meaning" has been more closely examined. Linguistics has neglected these problems for a long time; hence it is not from linguistics that we obtain our categories, but from the logicians. We can take as a point of departure the tripartite division by Frege: a sign would have reference, a meaning, and a representation (*Bedeutung, Sinn, Vorstellung*). Only meaning can be grasped with the help of rigorous linguistic methods, for it alone depends only on language, and is controlled by the authority of usage, by linguistic habit. What is meaning? According to Benveniste, it is the capacity of a linguistic unit to integrate itself into a unit on a higher level. The meaning of a word is defined by the combinations in which it can accomplish its linguistic function. The meaning of a word is the entirety of its possible relationships with other words.

To isolate meaning from the entirety of significations is a procedure which could greatly help the task of description in literary studies.

Tzvetan Todorov

In literary discourse, as in daily speech, meaning can be isolated from a host of other significations which one could call interpretations. However, the problem of meaning is more complex here. While in speech the integration of units does not go beyond the level of the sentence, in literature sentences are integrated again as part of larger articulations [*énoncés*], and the latter in their turn into units of greater dimension, and so on until we have the entire work. The meaning of a monologue or of a description can be grasped and verified by its relation to the other elements of the work. This can be the characterization of a person, the preparation for a reversal in an intrigue, or a delay. On the other hand, the interpretations of each unit are innumerable, for their comprehension depends on the system in which the unit will be included. According to the type of discourse in which the element of the work is projected, we will be concerned with a sociological, psychoanalytical, or a philosophical criticism. But it will always be an interpretation of literature in another type of discourse, while the search for meaning does not lead us outside the literary discourse itself. It is there, perhaps, that we must attempt to go beyond the limits of these two related but nevertheless distinct activities: poetics and criticism.

Let us proceed now to another pair of fundamental categories, which have been definitively formulated by Emile Benveniste in his research on the tenses of verbs. Benveniste has shown the existence in language of two distinct levels of *énonciation:* discourse and story. These levels of *énonciation* refer to the integration of the subject of the *énonciation* into the *énoncé*. In the case of the story, he tells us, "it is a question of the presentation of facts having occurred at a certain moment in time without any intervention of the narrator in the *récit*." By contrast, the discourse is defined as "any *énonciation* supposing a narrator and a listener, and an intention on the narrator's part to influence the listener in some way." Each language possesses a certain number of elements destined to inform us only about the act and the subject of the *énonciation*, and which bring about the conversion of language into discourse; the other elements are destined only for the "presentation of facts having occurred."

Thus, we must make a first division within language as literary medium, according to the level of *énonciation* which is operative. Take these sentences by Proust. "Il prodigua pour moi une amabilité qui était aussi supérieure à celle de Saint-Loup que celle-ci à l'affabilité d'un petit bourgeois. A côté de celle d'un grand artiste l'amabilité d'un grand seigneur, si charmante soit-elle, a l'air d'un jeu d'acteur, d'une simulation." [He lavished on me a kindness which was as superior to that of Saint-Loup as was the latter's to the affability of a petit bourgeois. Compared to the kindness of a great artist, the kindness of a great lord, charming as it may be, seems like an actor's role, a pretence.] In this text, only the first proposition (up to *amabilité* [kindness]) relates to the level of story. That the comparison that follows, as well as the general reflection contained in the second sentence, belongs to the level of discourse is marked by precise linguistic indicators (for example, the change of tense). But the first proposition is also tied to discourse, for the subject of the *énonciation* is indicated there by the personal pronoun [*moi*]. There are, then, a combination of means to indicate discursive force [*l'appartenance au discours*]: either by the status of the utterance [*parole*] (direct or indirect style) or by its mood, that is, the situation where the utterance does not refer to an exterior reality. The degree of opacity in literary language is determined by the calibration of the levels of *énonciation*. Every *énoncé* which belongs to discourse has a superior autonomy because its meaning is self-determined, without the intermediary of an imaginary reference. The fact that Elstir has lavished his kindness refers to an exterior representation, that of the two fictional characters and of an act; but the comparison and the reflection which follows are representations in themselves. They refer only to the subject of the *énonciation* and they thus affirm the presence of language itself.

The interpenetration of these two categories is manifestly great and already poses, in itself, multiple problems which have not yet been broached. The situation is further complicated if we realize that this is not the only possible form under which these categories appear in literature. The possibility of considering all utterance [*parole*] as preeminently an account of reality or as a subjective *énonciation* leads us to another important consideration. These are not only characteristics of two types of utterance, they are also two complementary aspects of all utterance, whether literary or not. In every *énoncé* these two aspects can be provisionally isolated: on the one hand an act of the narrator, that is, a linguistic arrangement; on the other hand the evocation of a certain reality, and in the case of literature this has absolutely no other existence than that conferred on it by the *énoncé* itself.

The Russian Formalists had, there again, pointed out the opposition without being able to show its linguistic basis. In all *récits* they distinguished the *tale*, that is, the sequence of events represented, such as they would have occurred in life, from the *plot* [*sujet*], the particular relationship given to these events by the author. Temporal inversions were their pet examples; it is evident that the telling of a posterior event before a prior event betrays the intervention of the author, or rather the subject of the *énonciation*. One can now realize that that opposition does not correspond to a dichotomy between the book and the representation of life but to the two aspects of the *énoncé* which are always present: its double nature of *énoncé* and *énonciation*. These two aspects give life to two equally linguistic realities, that of the characters and that of the narrator-listener duality.

The distinction between discourse and story more readily allows us to situate another problem of literary theory, "vision" or "point of view." Actually, this deals with transformations which the idea of person undergoes in the literary *récit*. This problem, formerly raised by Henry James, has been treated several times since, in France, notably by Jean Pouillon, Claude-Edmonde Magny, and Georgs Blin. These studies, which did not take into account the linguistic nature of the phenomenon, have not succeeded in fully explaining its nature although they described its most important aspects.

The literary *récit*, which is a mediated and not an immediate utterance [*parole*], and which furthermore suffers the constraints of fiction, knows only a single "personal" category, the third person, that is— impersonality. The individual who says *I* in a novel is not the *I* of the discourse, otherwise called the subject of the *énonciation*. He is only a character and the status of his utterances (the direct style) gives to them a maximum objectivity, instead of bringing them closer to the subject of the actual *énonciation*. But there exists another *I*, an *I* for the most part invisible, which refers to the narrator, the "poetic personality," which we apprehend through the discourse. There is then, a dialectic of personality and impersonality between the (implicit) *I* of the narrator and the *he* (which can be an explicit *I*) of the character, between the discourse and the story. The entire problem of point of view is there in the degree of transparence of the impersonal *he*'s of the story in relation to the opaque *I* of the discourse.

It is easy to see, in this perspective, what classification of points of view we can adopt; it nearly corresponds to what Jean Pouillon has proposed in his book *Temps et roman*. 1) Either the *I* of the narrator appears constantly through the *he* of the hero, as in the case of the classic *récit*, with an omniscient narrator; here the discourse supplants the story; or, 2) the *I* of the narrator is entirely hidden behind the *he* of the hero; this situation is the famous "objective narration," the type of *récit* notably practiced by American authors between the two wars. In this case the narrator knows nothing whatever about his character; he simply sees his movements and gestures and hears his utterances; or, finally, 3) the *I* of the narrator is on the same footing with the *he* of the hero, both being informed in the same way about the development of action. This type of *récit*, which first appeared in the eighteenth century, presently dominates literary composition; the narrator sticks to one of the characters and observes everything through his eyes. In this particular type of *récit*, the *I* and the *he* are fused into a narrating *I*, which makes the presence of the actual *I*, the narrator, even more difficult to grasp.

The above is only a first crude division; all *récits* combine several points of view at a time. There exist, besides, a multiplicity of intermediary forms. The character can fool himself while relating the story just as he can confess all he knows about it. He can analyze it in the minutest detail or be satisfied with the appearance of things. We could be presented with a dissection of his consciousness (the interior monologue) or an articulated utterance. All these varieties are part of a single point of view: the one which equalizes the narrator and the character. Analyses founded on linguistic categories could doubtless better recognize the nuances.

I have tried to discern a few of the most evident operations of a linguistic category in the literary *récit*. Other categories wait their turn. We must discover someday what transformations time, person, aspect, and voice assume in literature, for they must be present, if literature is only, as Valéry believes, an extension and application of certain properties of language.

To Write: An Intransitive Verb?[1]

Roland Barthes
Ecole Pratique
des Hautes Etudes

For centuries Western culture conceived of literature not as we do today, through a study of works, authors, and schools, but through a genuine theory of language. This theory, whose name, *rhetoric*, came to it from antiquity, reigned in the Western world from Gorgias to the Renaissance— for nearly two thousand years. Threatened as early as the sixteenth century by the advent of modern rationalism, rhetoric was completely ruined when rationalism was transformed into positivism at the end of the nineteenth century. At that point there was no longer any common ground of thought between literature and language: literature no longer regarded itself as language except in the works of a few pioneers such as Mallarmé, and linguistics claimed very few rights over literature, these being [limited to] a secondary philological discipline of uncertain status—stylistics.

As we know, this situation is changing, and it seems to me that it is in part to take cognizance of this change that we are assembled here: literature and language are in the process of finding each other again. The factors of this *rapprochement* are diverse and complex; I shall cite the most obvious. On one hand, certain writers since Mallarmé, such as Proust and Joyce, have undertaken a radical exploration of writing, making of their work a search for the total Book. On the other hand, linguistics itself, principally following the impetus of Roman Jakobson, has developed to include

[1] "Ecrire: Verbe intransitif?" The translation which follows is a composite of the communication which M. Barthes distributed in advance to the Symposium participants and the actual transcription of his address. The footnotes have been supplied by the translator.

within its scope the poetic, or the order of effects linked to the message and not to its referent. Therefore, in my view, we have today a new perspective of consideration which, I would like to emphasize, is common to literature and linguistics, to the creator and the critic, whose tasks until now completely self-contained, are beginning to inter-relate, perhaps even to merge. This is at least true for certain writers whose work is becoming more and more a critique of language. It is in this perspective that I would like to place the following observations (of a prospective and not of a conclusive nature) indicating how the activity of writing can be expressed [*énoncée*] today with the help of certain linguistic categories.

This new union of literature and linguistics, of which I have just spoken, could be called, provisionally and for lack of a better name, *semio-criticism*, since it implies that writing is a system of signs. Semio-criticism is not to be identified with stylistics, even in a new form; it is much more than stylistics. It has a much broader perspective; its object is constituted not by simple accidents of form, but by the very relationships between the writer [*scripteur*, not *écrivain*] and language. This perspective does not imply a lack of interest in language but, on the contrary, a continual return to the "truths"—provisional though they may be—of linguistic anthropology. I will recall certain of these truths because they still have a power of challenge in respect to a certain current idea of literature.

One of the teachings of contemporary linguistics is that there is no archaic language, or at the very least that there is no connection between simplicity and the age of a language: ancient languages can be just as complete and as complex as recent languages; there is no progressive history of languages. Therefore, when we try to find certain fundamental categories of language in modern writing, we are not claiming to reveal a certain archaism of the "psyche"; we are not saying that the writer is returning to the origin of language, but that language is the origin for him.

A second principle, particularly important in regard to literature, is that language cannot be considered as a simple instrument, whether utilitarian or decorative, of thought. Man does not exist prior to language, either as a species or as an individual. We never find a state where man is separated from language, which he then creates in order to "express" what is taking place within him: it is language which teaches the definition of man, not the reverse.

Moreover, from a methodological point of view, linguistics accustoms us to a new type of objectivity. The objectivity that has been required

Roland Barthes

in the human sciences up until now is an objectivity of the given, a total acceptance of the given. Linguistics suggests, on the one hand, that we distinguish levels of analysis and that we describe the distinctive elements of each of these levels; in short, that we establish the distinctness of the fact and not the fact itself. On the other hand, linguistics asks us to recognize that unlike physical and biological facts, cultural facts are always double, that they refer us to something else. As Benveniste remarked, the discovery of the "duplicity" of language gives Saussure's reflection all its value.[2]

These few preliminaries are contained in one final proposition which justifies all semio-critical research. We see culture more and more as a general system of symbols, governed by the same operations. There is unity in this symbolic field: culture, in all its aspects, is a language. Therefore it is possible today to anticipate the creation of a single, unified science of culture, which will depend on diverse disciplines, all devoted to analyzing, on different levels of description, culture as language. Of course semio-criticism will be only a part of this science, or rather of this discourse on culture. I feel authorized by this unity of the human symbolic field to work on a postulate, which I shall call a postulate of *homology*: the structure of the sentence, the object of linguistics, is found again, homologically, in the structure of works. Discourse is not simply an adding together of sentences: it is, itself, one great sentence. In terms of this hypothesis I would like to confront certain categories of language with the situation of the writer in relation to his writing.

The first of these categories is *temporality*. I think we can all agree that there is a linguistic temporality. This specific time of language is equally different from physical time and from what Benveniste calls "chronicle time" [*temps chronique*], that is, calendar time.[3] Linguistic time finds quite different expression and *découpages* in various languages. For example, since we are going to be interested in the analysis of myths, many languages have a particular past tense of the verb to indicate the past time of myth. One thing is sure: linguistic time al-

<hr />

[2] Emile Benveniste, *Problèmes de la linguistique générale* (Paris, 1966), p. 40. "Qu'est-ce donc que cet objet, que Saussure érige sur une table rase de toutes les notions reçues? Nous touchons ici à ce qu'il y a de primordial dans la doctrine saussurienne, à un principe qui présume une intuition totale du langage, totale à la fois parce qu'elle embrasse la totalité de son objet. Ce principe est que *le langage*, sous quelque point de vue qu'on l'étudie, *est toujours un objet double*, formé de deux parties dont l'une ne vaut que par l'autre.

[3] Cf. Benveniste, "Les Relations de temps dans le verbe français," *ibid.*, pp. 237-50.

ways has its primary center [*centre générateur*] in the present of the statement [*énonciation*]. This leads us to ask whether there is, homological to linguistic time, a specific time of discourse. On this point we may take Benveniste's explanation that many languages, especially in the Indo-European group, have a double system of time. The first temporal system is that of the discourse itself, which is adapted to the temporality of the speaker [*énonciateur*] and for which the *énonciation* is always the point of origin [*moment générateur*]. The second is the system of history or of narrative, which is adapted to the recounting of past events without any intervention by the speaker and which is consequently deprived of present and future (except periphrastically). The specific tense of this second system is the aorist or its equivalent, such as our *passé simple* or the preterit. This tense (the aorist) is precisely the only one missing from the temporal system of discourse. Naturally the existence of this a-personal system does not contradict the essentially logocentric nature of linguistic time that I have just affirmed. The second system simply lacks the characteristics of the first.

Understood thus as the opposition of two radically different systems, temporality does not have the morphological mark of verbs for its only sign; it is marked by all the signs, often very indirect, which refer either to the a-personal tense of the event or to the personal tense of the locutor. The opposition in its fullness permits us first to account for some pure, or we might say classic, cases: a popular story and the history of France retold in our manuals are purely aoristic narratives; on the contrary, Camus' *L'Etranger*, written in the compound past, is not only a perfect form of autobiography (that of the narrator, and not of the author) but, what is more valuable, it permits us to understand better the apparently anomalous cases.[4] Being a historian, Michelet made all historical time pivot around a point of discourse with which he identified himself—the Revolution. His history is a narrative without the aorist, even if the simple past abounds in it; inversely, the preterit can very well serve to signify not the objective *récit*, but the depersonalization of the discourse—a phenomenon which is the object of the most lively research in today's literature.

What I would like to add to this linguistic analysis, which comes from Benveniste, is that the distinction between the temporal system of discourse and the temporal system of history is not at all the same distinction as is traditionally made between objective discourse and

[4] Cf. Jean-Paul Sartre, "Explication de *L'Etranger*," *Situations* I (Paris, 1947), pp. 99–121.

subjective discourse. For the relationship between the speaker [*énon-ciateur*] and the referent on the one hand and that between the speaker and his utterance [*énonciation*] on the other hand are not to be confused, and it is only the second relationship which determines the temporal system of discourse.

It seems to me that these facts of language were not readily perceptible so long as literature pretended to be a transparent expression of either objective calendar time or of psychological subjectivity, that is to say, as long as literature maintained a totalitarian ideology of the referent, or more commonly speaking, as long as literature was realistic. Today, however, the literature of which I speak is discovering fundamental subtleties relative to temporality. In reading certain writers who are engaged in this type of exploration we sense that what is recounted in the aorist doesn't seem at all immersed in the past, in what has taken place, but simply in the impersonal [*la non-personne*], which is neither history, nor discursive information [*la science*], and even less the *one* of anonymous writing. (The *one* is dominated by the indefinite and not by the absence of person. I would even say that the pronoun *one* is marked in relation to person, while, paradoxically, *he* is not.) At the other extreme of the experience of discourse, the present-day writer can no longer content himself with expressing his own present, according to a lyrical plan, for example. He must learn to distinguish between the present of the speaker, which is grounded on a psychological fullness, and the present of what is spoken [*la locution*] which is mobile and in which the event and the writing become absolutely coincidental. Thus literature, at least in some of its pursuits, seems to me to be following the same path as linguistics when, along with Gustave Guillaume (a linguist not presently in fashion but who may become so again), it concerns itself with operative time and the time proper to the utterance [*énonciation*] itself.[5]

A second grammatical category which is equally important in linguistics and in literature is that of *person*. Taking linguists and especially Benveniste as my basis once more, I would like to recall that person (in the grammatical sense of the term) certainly seems to be a

[5] Gustave Guillaume, *L'Architectonique du temps dans les langues classiques* (Copenhagen, 1945). The work of Guillaume (who died in 1960) toward a "psycho-systématique" has been continued in the contributions of Roch Valin (*Petite introduction à la psychomécanique du langage* [Québec, 1954]). For a statement by Guillaume about his relation to the tradition of Saussure, see *La langue est-elle ou n'est-elle pas un système? Cahiers de linguistique structurale de l'Université de Québec*, I (1952), p. 4.

universal of language, linked to the anthropology of language. Every language, as Benveniste has shown, organizes person into two broad pairs of opposites: a correlation of personality which opposes person (*I* or *thou*) to non-person, which is *il* (*he* or *it*), the sign of absence; and, within this first opposing pair, a correlation of subjectivity (once again in the grammatical sense) which opposes two persons, the *I* and the *non-I* (the *thou*). For our purposes we must, along with Benveniste, make three observations. First, the polarity of persons, a fundamental condition of language, is nevertheless peculiar and enigmatic, for this polarity involves neither equality nor symmetry: *I* always has a position of transcendence with respect to *thou*, *I* being interior to the *énoncé* and *thou* remaining exterior to it; however, *I* and *thou* are reversible—*I* can always become *thou* and vice versa. This is not true of the non-person (*he* or *it*) which can never reverse itself into person or vice versa. The second observation is that the linguistic *I* can and must be defined in a strictly a-psychological way: *I* is nothing other than "la personne qui énonce la présente instance de discours contenant l'instance linguistique *je*" (Benveniste ["the person who utters the present instance of discourse containing the linguistic instance *I*"]).[6] The last remark is that the *he* or the non-person never reflects the instance of discourse; *he* is situated outside of it. We must give its full weight to Benveniste's recommendation not to represent the *he* as a more or less diminished or removed person: *he* is absolutely non-person, marked by the absence of what specifically constitutes, linguistically, the *I* and the *thou*.

The linguistic explanation provides several suggestions for an analysis of literary discourse. First, whatever varied and clever forms person may take in passing from the level of the sentence to that of discourse, the discourse of the literary work is rigorously submitted to a double system of person and non-person. This fact may be obscured because classical discourse (in a broad sense) to which we are habituated is a mixed discourse which alternates—very quickly, sometimes within the same sentence—personal and a-personal *énonciation*, through a complex play of pronouns and descriptive verbs. In this type of classical or bourgeois story the mixture of person and non-person produces a sort of ambiguous consciousness which succeeds in keeping the personal quality of what is stated while, however, continuously breaking the participation of the *énonciateur* in the *énoncé*.

[6] Benveniste, *Problèmes*, p. 252.

Roland Barthes

Many novelistic utterances, written with *he* (in the third person), are nevertheless discourses of the *person* each time that the contents of the statement depend on its subject. If in a novel we read "*the tinkling of the ice against the glass seemed to give Bond a sudden inspiration,*" it is certain that the subject of the statement cannot be Bond himself —not because the sentence is written in the third person, since Bond could very well express himself through a *he*, but because of the verb *seem*, which becomes a mark of the absence of person. Nevertheless, in spite of the diversity and often even the ruse of the narrative signs of the person, there is never but one sole and great opposition in the discourse, that of the person and the non-person; every narrative or fragment of a narrative is obliged to join one or the other of these extremes. How can we determine this division? In "re-writing" the discourse. If we can translate the *he* into *I* without changing anything else in the utterance, the discourse is in fact personal. In the sentence which we have cited, this transformation is impossible; we cannot say "*the tinkling of the ice seemed to give me a sudden inspiration.*" The sentence is impersonal. Starting from there, we catch a glimpse of how the discourse of the traditional novel is made; on the one hand it alternates the personal and the impersonal very rapidly, often even in the course of the same sentence, so as to produce, if we can speak thus, a proprietary consciousness which retains the mastery of what it states without participating in it; and on the other hand, in this type of novel, or rather, according to our perspective, in this type of discourse, when the narrator is explicitly an *I* (which has happened many times), there is confusion between the subject of the discourse and the subject of the reported action, as if—and this is a common belief—he who is speaking today were the same as he who acted yesterday. It is as if there were a continuity of the referent and the utterance through the person, as if the declaring were only a docile servant of the referent.

Now if we return to the linguistic definition of the first person (the one who says "I" in the present instance of discourse), we may better understand the effort of certain contemporary writers (in France I think of Philippe Sollers's latest novel *Drame*) when they try to distinguish, at the level of the story, psychological person and the author of the writing. When a narrator recounts what has happened to him, the *I* who recounts is no longer the same *I* as the one that is recounted. In other words—and it seems to me that this is seen more and more clearly—the *I* of discourse can no longer be a place where a previously stored-up person is innocently restored. Absolute recourse to the instance of discourse to determine person is termed *nyn-egocentrism* by Damourette and Pichon (*nyn* from the greek *nun*, "now").[7] Robbe-Grillet's novel *Dans le labyrinthe* begins with an admirable declaration of nyn-egocentrism: "Je suis seul ici maintenant." [I am alone here now.][8] This recourse, imperfectly as it may still be practiced, seems to be a weapon against the general "bad faith" of discourse which would make literary form simply the expression of an interiority constituted previous to and outside of language.

To end this discussion of person, I would like to recall that in the process of communication the course of the *I* is not homogenous. For example, when I use [*libère*] the sign *I*, I refer to myself inasmuch as I am talking: here there is an act which is always new, even if it is repeated, an act whose sense is always new. However, arriving at its destination, this sign is received by my interlocutor as a stable sign, product of a complete code whose contents are recurrent. In other words, the *I* of the one who writes *I* is not the same as the *I* which is read by *thou*. This fundamental dissymmetry of language, linguistically explained by Jespersen and then by Jakobson under the name of "shifter" [*embrayeur*] or an overlapping of message and code, seems to be finally beginning to trouble literature in showing it that intersubjectivity, or rather interlocution, cannot be accomplished simply by wishing, but only by a deep, patient, and often circuitous descent into the labyrinths of meaning.[9]

There remains one last grammatical notion which can, in my opinion, further elucidate the activity of writing at its center, since it concerns the verb *to write* itself. It would be interesting to know at what point the verb *to write* began to be used in an apparently intransitive manner, the writer being no longer one who writes *something*, but one who writes, absolutely. (How often now we hear in conversations, at least in more or less intellectual circles: "What is he doing?"—"He's writing.") This passage from the verb *to write*, transi-

[7] J. Damourette and E. Pichon, *Des mots à la pensée: Essai de grammaire de la langue française* (Paris, 1911–36), V, #1604 and VII, #2958. "Le langage est naturellement centré sur le moi-ici-maintenant, c'est-à-dire sur la personne qui parle s'envisageant au moment même où elle parle; c'est ce qu'on peut appeler le *nynégocentrisme* naturel du langage" [#1604].

[8] *Dans le labyrinthe* (Paris: Editions de Minuit, 1959). For essays by Roland Barthes bearing on the fictional method and theory of Robbe-Grillet, see *Essais critiques* (Paris, 1964), pp. 29–40, 63–70, 198–205.

[9] Cf. Jakobson, *Shifters, Verbal Categories, and the Russian Verb* (Cambridge [Mass.], 1957). [Translated into French by Nicolas Ruwet in *Essais de linguistique générale* (Paris, 1963), pp. 176–96.] For the origin of the term "shifter," see Otto Jespersen, *Language, its Nature, Development and Origin* (London, 1922), p. 123, and *ibid.*, *The Philosophy of Grammar* (London, 1923), pp. 83–84.

tive, to the verb *to write*, apparently intransitive, is certainly the sign of an important change in mentality. But is it really a question of intransitivity? No writer, whatever age he belongs to, can fail to realize that he always writes *something:* one might even say that it was paradoxically at the moment when the verb *to write* appeared to become intransitive that its object, the book or the text, took on a particular importance. It is not, therefore, in spite of the appearances, on the side of intransitivity that we must look for the definition of the modern verb *to write.* Another linguistic notion will perhaps give us the key: that of *diathesis*, or, as it is called in classical grammars, *voice* (active, passive, middle). Diathesis designates the way in which the subject of the verb is affected by the action [*procès*]; this is obvious for the passive (if I say "I am beaten," it is quite obvious that I am profoundly affected by the action of the verb *to beat*). And yet linguists tell us that, at least in Indo-European, the diathetical opposition is actually not between the active and the passive, but between the active and the middle. According to the classic example, given by Meillet and Benveniste, the verb *to sacrifice* (ritually) is active if the priest sacrifices the victim in my place for me, and it is middle voice if, taking the knife from the priest's hands, I make the sacrifice for myself.[10] In the case of the active, the action is accomplished outside the subject, because, although the priest makes the sacrifice, he is not affected by it. In the case of the middle voice, on the contrary, the subject affects himself in acting; he always remains inside the action, even if an object is involved. The middle voice does not, therefore, exclude transitivity. Thus defined, the middle voice corresponds exactly to the state of the verb *to write:* today to write is to make oneself the center of the action of speech [*parole*]; it is to effect writing in being affected oneself; it is to leave the writer [*scripteur*] inside the writing, not as a psychological subject (the Indo-European priest could very well overflow with subjectivity in actively sacrificing for his client), but as the agent of the action.

I think the diathetical analysis of the modern verb *to write*, which I have just tried to show a verb of middle voice, can be carried even further. You know that in French—for I am obliged to refer to strictly French examples—certain verbs have an active meaning in the simple form, for example, *aller, arriver, rentrer, sortir* [to go, to

[10] Benveniste, "Actif et moyen dans le verbe," *Problèmes*, pp. 168–75. Cf. the distinction initiated by Pānini (fl. 350 B.C.): *parasmaipada*, "word for another," i.e., active, and *āmanepada*, "word for self, i.e., middle. Thus *yajati* ("he sacrifices" [for another, *qua* priest]) vs. *yajate* ("he sacrifices" [for himself, *qua* offering]). Cf. Berthold Delbrück, *Vergleichende Syntax der Indogermanischen Sprachen* (Strassburg, 1893).

arrive, to return, to go out], but, curiously, these active verbs take the passive auxiliary, the verb *être* [to be] in the forms of the *passé composé*. Instead of saying *j'ai allé*, we say *je suis allé, je suis sorti, je suis arrivé, je suis rentré*, etc. To explain this bifurcation peculiar to the middle voice, Guillaume distinguishes between two *passés composés*. The first, which he calls *diriment*, "separated," is a *passé composé* with the auxiliary *avoir* [to have]; this tense supposes an interruption of the action due to the initiative of the speaker. Take for example the verb *marcher* [to walk], an entirely commonplace active verb: *"je marche; je m'arrête de marcher; j'ai marché* [I walk; I stop walking (by my own initiative); I have walked]—this is the *passé composé diriment*. The other *passé composé* that he calls *intégrant* is constructed with the verb *être* [to be]; it designates a sort of semantic entity which cannot be delivered by the simple initiative of the subject. *"Je suis sorti"* or *"il est mort"* ["I went out" or "he died"] (for I can't say "I am dead") never refer to an interruption that would be at all like the *diriment* of the going out or the dying. I believe that this is an important opposition, for we see very well that the verb *to write* was traditionally an active verb and that its past tense is still today formally a *diriment* past: *"j'écris un livre; je le termine; je l'ai écrit."* [I write a book; I end it; I have written it.] But in our literature, it seems to me, the verb is changing status, if not form, and the verb *to write* is becoming a middle verb with an *intégrant* past. This is true inasmuch as the modern verb *to write* is becoming a sort of indivisible semantic entity. So that if language followed literature—which, for once perhaps, has the lead—I would say that we should no longer say today *"j'ai écrit"* but, rather, *"je suis écrit,"* just as we say *"je suis né, il est mort, elle est éclose."* There is no passive idea in these expressions, in spite of the verb *to be*, for it is impossible to transform *"je suis écrit"* (without forcing things, and supposing that I dare to use this expression at all) into *"on m'a écrit"* ["I have been written" or "somebody wrote me"]. It is my opinion that in the middle verb *to write* the distance between the writer and the language diminishes asymptotically. We could even say that it is subjective writings, like romantic writing, which are active, because in them the agent is not interior but *anterior* to the process of writing. The one who writes here does not write for himself, but, as if by proxy, for a person who is exterior and antecedent (even if they both have the same name). In the modern verb of middle voice *to write*, however, the subject is immediately contemporary with the writing, being effected and affected by it. The case of the Proustian narrator is exemplary: he exists only in writing.

These remarks suggest that the central problem of modern writing exactly coincides with what we could call the problematic of the verb in linguistics; just as temporality, person, and diathesis define the positional field of the subject, so modern literature is trying, through various experiments, to establish a new status in writing for the agent of writing. The meaning or the goal of this effort is to substitute the instance of discourse for the instance of reality (or of the referent), which has been, and still is, a mythical "alibi" dominating the idea of literature. The field of the writer is nothing but writing itself, not as the pure "form" conceived by an aesthetic of art for art's sake, but, much more radically, as the only area [*espace*] for the one who writes.

It seems to me to be necessary to remind those who might be tempted to accuse this kind of inquiry of solipsism, formalism, or, inversely, of scientism, that in returning to the fundamental categories of language, such as person, tense, and voice, we place ourselves at the very heart of a problematic of *inter*locution. For these categories are precisely those in which we may examine the relationships between the *je* and that which is deprived of the mark of *je*. Inasmuch as person, tense, and voice imply these remarkable linguistic beings—the "shifters"— they oblige us to conceive language and discourse no longer in terms of an instrumental and reified nomenclature but in the very exercise of language [*parole*]. The pronoun, for example, which is without doubt the most staggering of the "shifters," belongs structurally to speech [*parole*]. That is its scandal, if you like, and it is on this scandal that we must work today, in linguistics and literature. We are all trying, with different methods, styles, perhaps even prejudices, to get to the core of this linguistic pact [*pacte de parole*] which unites the writer and the other, so that—and this is a contradiction which will never be sufficiently pondered—each moment of discourse is both absolutely new and absolutely understood. I think that, with a certain amount of temerity, we could even give a historical dimension to this research. We know that the medieval *septenium*, in its grandiose classification of the universe, prescribed two great areas of exploration: on the one hand, the secrets of nature (the *quadrivium*) and, on the other, the secrets of language [*parole*] (the *trivium: grammatica, rhetorica, dialectica*). From the end of the Middle Ages to the present day, this opposition was lost, language being considered only as an instrument in the service of either reason or the heart. Today, however, something of this ancient opposition lives again: once again the exploration of language, conducted by linguistics, psychoanalysis, and literature, corresponds to the exploration of the cosmos. For literature is itself a science, or at least knowledge, no longer of the "human heart" but of human language [*parole*]. Its investigation is not, however, addressed to the secondary forms and figures that were the object of rhetoric, but to the fundamental categories of language. Just as in Western culture grammar was not born until long after rhetoric, so it is only after having made its way for centuries through *le beau littéraire* that literature can begin to ponder the fundamental problems of language, without which it would not exist.

Barthes–Todorov Discussion

GEORGES POULET: I would like to express the very great pleasure that I felt in listening to Roland Barthes and also a certain feeling of melancholy, for there seems to exist between us a sort of misunderstanding. We are a little like people who live in the same building but on different floors. This difference can be seen in our use of the word *language*, a word that I, myself, never like to pronounce—and this was perhaps the tendency of thinkers of an earlier period—but one which has recently become an extremely important word. The current popular regard for this word is accompanied by a certain number of corresponding negative phenomena. For example, you seem to avoid the word *thought* as if it were becoming rapidly obscene. Nearly every time you use the word *language*, I could replace it by the word *thought* almost without incongruity. I think that if you tried the same exercise, inversely, you would make the same discovery. For example, you said that in a certain perspective of science, which is not your own, there is an objectivity of the given. I think your idea was that there are much more interesting things than objectivity of the given, namely, objectivity of the giving (*donnant*), that is, objectivity of language. Now that seems to be exactly the position that I hold in relation to thought. When you speak, along with Saussure, of the signifier (*signifiant*) in relation to the signified, and of a signifier that could be spoken of even without speaking of the signified, you could speak, in the same way, of a container (*contenant*) without content or with all contents. I would say—but would you—that there could also be a thinker (*pensant*) who might have all thoughts. Therefore it seems to me that we are at the same time very close and yet separated by an abyss—an abyss that we could leap if we wanted to.

ROLAND BARTHES: I am very touched by what you have said, but I can't really reply because, as you said, there is a separation and, if I may say so, what separates us is precisely language. But having said that, I see that there are a number of digressions suggested by your remarks, notably, the fact that we all perhaps reveal more by the words that we *avoid* than by the words that we use. In literature it would be extremely interesting to have a statistical analysis of words avoided by an author. But if I don't use the word *thought*, it is not at all because I find it obscene; on the contrary, it is because it is not obscene enough. For me, language is obscene, and that is why I continually return to it.

JAN KOTT: During dinner Mr. Donato said, "Les avocats sont durs." (The lawyers [avocados] are hard.) This was an *énoncé* oriented toward me, a message oriented toward the recipient. This sentence has something poetic about it. I think it was an *énoncé* which has become *énonciation* and a message which, in the terms of Jakobson, is "oriented toward the structuralization of the message." It is an example of the "duplicity" spoken of by Barthes. Another example of this duplicity in language would be this phrase of the Surrealists that I remember from my youth: "Elephants are contagious" (*Les éléphants sont contagieux*) [*Les oreillons sont contagieux?*]. But what is characteristic of our own time is that literature has become deliberately, consciously, the criticism of language. This is obvious in poetry, but perhaps also in the case of drama. I was especially interested in the problem of dissymmetry in language: the *je* (I) which is always new, but always the same for the recipient. We might say that the great break between the theater of Chekhov and the theater before him is based on this phenomenon. In Chekhov there is a new *je* (I) which is the *tu* (thou) of the other characters. For another example, I recall a telephone conversation with Ionesco, one afternoon in Spoleto. He said, "Come to my house." I said, "No, come here to my house." He said, "No, here is here and not there. I'm here; you're there." "No," I said, "I'm here; you're there." This conversation is very typical of Ionesco's plays. Although it is impossible to say *"Je suis mort"* (I am dead), I can very well imagine a play by Ionesco ending with the *passé composé:* "J'ai mort" (I have deaded).

JEAN HYPPOLITE: I agree with you almost too much to take the floor, and, yet, in view of the title of your paper, I wonder if the *pacte de la parole*, a "complicity of speech," that you mention at the end of your talk, is wholly maintained in writing. Or, when one writes, doesn't interlocution undergo a sort of transformation, so that writing often becomes a phantasm of interlocution? To cite again the example of Proust in *Contre Sainte Beuve*, how does Proust succeed in writing? By addressing the phantasm of his mother in an interlocution which profoundly changes the *pacte de la parole*, transforming it into a sort of mimicry of the *pacte de la parole* in writing. What transformation does the *pacte de la parole* undergo in a creation like writing which, paradoxically, is capable of uniting with a sort of monologue, curiously cut off from real interlocution? This is my question—the aspect that you simply mentioned in bringing us back to the *pacte de la parole*.

In *La Jalousie* is there interlocution or is there phantasm, with changing of the past and of beings in relation to interlocution? Is the *pacte de la parole* maintained or do we have an imitation of this *pacte de la parole*? I am purposely taking *La Jalousie* for my example, as a type of work which questions the poetics of the novel.

BARTHES: So, an homological analysis of person at the level of the signs of discourse in *La Jalousie*—I can't really prejudge the answer. I remember that you have a very high opinion of *La Jalousie* and I share this judgment. It would be a magnificent subject for a "troisième-cycle" doctorate to ask someone to find out what becomes of the proper signs, the indications of person at the level of discourse. We are beginning to concern ourselves with these problems at the level of the story and of the analysis of the story, and to look for the discursive signs of the one for whom the story is intended; for even in a story of the monologue type there are always specific signs of the *thou*, of this recipient (*destinataire*). I think you have pointed to the area of a very important problem: the relation between the story, or phantasm, and interlocution.

LUCIEN GOLDMANN: I speak as a sociologist, and I believe that it is important to look at the situation and the movement of an idea from the outside. For the past six days, during the seminars which preceded this colloquium, many important thinkers here have spoken of a radical breaking-point within French culture. For me this was made most clear in Charles Morazé's talk which compared two plays, Sagan's *Château en Suède* and Sartre's *Séquestrés d'Altona*. Both plays have the same factors, the same problematic: the fact that history has disappeared. However, while this fact constitutes a tragedy in Sartre's play, Sagan's play affirms that it doesn't matter and that one can very easily live without history. M. Hyppolite mentioned that it is very difficult to find an unbroken line of continuity between thought in France from 1945–50 and intellectual life today: there is a breaking point between existentialism and structuralism. For Sartre the essential point was to accede to history, and, starting from the *cogito* of the individual ego, it was very difficult to put history back into the center of things. However, for the present intellectual posture history doesn't matter, the essential is to avoid history or historicity. The perspectives are very different. Barthes also spoke very clearly of a breaking point. He differs from Todorov in that he emphasizes the *modernity* of the present situation rather than the scientific perspective. I might also mention Althusser who has managed in his two books, *Pour Marx* and *Lire le Capital* to eliminate history from Marxist thinking. Here there is obviously a mutation, and I would say that that accounts for M. Poulet's intervention and Barthes' reply. Poulet feels sympathetic toward Barthes rather than Todorov because both Barthes and Poulet are aware of the non-scientific character of their positions. All this is to say that we are faced by a very important ideological phenomenon.

To approach it from the inside, we might ask the question— What is the subject that has changed? Why is language the common element of this new an-historical current of thought? Why has priority been given to the study of language? My hypothesis is that it is because language changes more slowly than content and literary structures. The problem was to eliminate thought and content, so there is only language left, and the speaking subject. Todorov sees language as the active element of the story. I would like to go even further. I agree that the *I* who speaks is not homologous with the *I* who writes. And as Barthes observed, we can distinguish the two types of structuralism on the basis of who uses diachronic methods and who uses genetic methods. We sociologists and historians have been saying that for a long time, but we also say that there is still an *I* who *becomes*, who is transformed, while there was no question of this in Barthes's talk. I also agree that man does not pre-exist language. But your conclusion that man must be defined in terms of language appears to me questionable. Man, as a whole, does not identify with language. To be sure, man speaks, but he also does other things that cannot be reduced to language, although language is, of course, involved—eating for instance. For me, what is interesting about this scientific perspective is to see what is ideological about it. The sociologist must analyze this current of thought which tries to eliminate the psychological and sociological subject, to see if it isn't a way for a collective subject to view the status of man in terms of a certain ideology.

Tzvetan Todorov: I would like to reply to only two of M. Goldmann's numerous remarks. The first was on the definition of man according to language, or of language according to man. Of course, man does not *only* speak, but he is the only creature who speaks, while there are many others who eat. Secondly, in regard to language changing more slowly than literature, if you say that, it is because you are reducing language to vocabulary and syntax, but beyond that, there is discourse. There is a typology of discourse, which remains to be elaborated, but which exists and which would account for the change in discourse, which is just as great as in literature, for literature itself is only a discourse.

RICHARD MACKSEY: This may only interest our French friends, but I think you have distorted Althusser's thought on history. Althusser never eliminated history; on the contrary, he is trying to rethink it within a coherent epistemology. But it would seem that he is trying to rescue Marx from Hegel's dialectical monism of the absolute subject as the single genetic principle. Now if you replace the absolute subject, indivisible genetic totality, with pre-existing, concrete structures, you escape some of the problems of Hegel's essentialism, but you undoubtedly open a different kind of development between ensembles. This has admittedly opened some *ruptures* in the historical process.

GOLDMANN: To be precise in regard to Althusser, he, himself, indicates in his books that the problem of change is the most difficult. The problem of history is the problem of becoming and of change. He says that it is treated by Balibar in the collaborative work. Balibar has three pages in these three big volumes which tell how the machine replaces "making by hand," but never how the machine, the new element, appeared. When I asked him about this problem, Althusser said it is a problem which will perhaps eventually be solved by research. He absolutely resisted saying that man defines himself from the relationships of production, which is the fundamental historical element of dialectical thought. Here there is obviously analysis of fact and elimination of becoming; there are no more classes—in these three volumes no element of becoming is clear except that it is a difficult problem.

BARTHES: I would simply like to recall that among the recent books of importance, the problem of history is often posed in new terms. Foucault's book on insanity is not lacking in historical dimensions, although it may be a new historical dimension. I don't believe we can dismiss what is being elaborated at the present moment, and in very different ways. We can't say that history is henceforth dismissed. I think

Discussion

it is something that is in the process of evolving new definitions of the historical process.

PAUL DE MAN: I would like to speak a moment of Roland Barthes's treatment of history. I find that you have an optimistic historical myth (the same one I saw in Donato) which is linked to the abandonment of the last active form of traditional philosophy that we know, phenomenology, and the replacement of phenomenology with psychoanalysis, etc. That represents historical progress and extremely optimistic possibilities for the history of thought. However, you must show us that the results you have obtained in the stylistic analyses that you make are superior to those of your predecessors, thanks to this optimistic change which is linked to a certain historic renewal. I must admit, I have been somewhat disappointed by the specific analyses that you give us. I don't believe they show any progress over those of the Formalists, Russian or American, who used empirical methods, though neither the vocabulary nor the conceptual frame that you use. But more seriously, when I hear you refer to facts of literary history, you say things that are false within a typically French myth. I find in your work a false conception of classicism and romanticism. When, for example, concerning the question of the narrator or the "double ego," you speak of writing since Mallarmé and of the new novel, etc., and you oppose them to what happens in the romantic novel or story or autobiography—you are simply wrong. In the romantic autobiography, or, well before that, in the seventeenth-century story, this same complication of the ego (*moi*) is found, not only unconsciously, but explicitly and thematically treated, in a much more complex way than in the contemporary novel. I don't want to continue this development; it is simply to indicate that you distort history *because* you need a historical myth of progress to justify a method which is not yet able to justify itself by its results. It is in the notion of temporality rather than in that of history that I see you making consciousness undergo a reification, which is linked to this same optimism which troubles me.

BARTHES: It is difficult to reply because you question my own relationship to what I say. But I will say, very recklessly and risking redoubled blows on your part, that I never succeed in defining literary history independently of what time has added to it. In other words, I always give it a mythical dimension. For me, Romanticism includes everything that has been said about Romanticism. Consequently, the historical past acts as a sort of psychoanalysis. For me the historical past is a sort of gluey matter for which I feel an inauthentic shame and from which I try to detach myself by living my present as a sort of combat or violence against this mythical time immediately behind me. When I see something that might have happened fifty years ago, for me it already has a mythical dimension. However, in telling you this, I am not excusing anything; I am simply explaining and that does not suffice.

PIERO PUCCI: As a classical philologist, I am very happy to see that rhetoric has returned to a place of importance in modern literature and to hear this return of rhetoric spoken of and justified by a sort of discourse on rhetoric in the classical world. Finally, I hope it can be seen that while rhetoric in the classical world was essentially taught in secondary school, the classical world produced not only schoolmasters in rhetoric but also Plato, Longinus, and St. Augustine—and that Aristotle wrote a *Poetics* as well as a *Rhetoric*. What we have heard this evening has been interesting and these studies seem important to me. I also see that this modern rhetoric is much more sophisticated than the ancient rhetoric. I only want to recall again that the Ancients not only saw rhetoric in images, in figures, but also saw that poetry could be insanity and madness—that is also a form of creation. When Aristotle considered poetry and art, tragedy for example, he didn't limit himself to rhetorical categories. This is what I think must be added.

BARTHES: I thank you very much for the enlargement of the problem. I have always conceived rhetoric very broadly, including all reflections on all forms of work, on general technique of forms of work, and not only in the restricted sense of rhetorical figures. We know very well that Aristotle's *Poetics* is also a formal study, in the deepest sense, of all "mimetic" works. And it is obviously in that perspective that we must think of literary works today.

VERNANT: I would like to question Barthes on the problem of the middle voice. If I understood correctly, he was referring to an article that Benveniste published in a psychological journal and in which he showed that the original fundamental opposition is between the active and the middle voice and not between the active and the passive, the middle designating the type of action where the agent remains enveloped in the released action. Barthes considers that this furnishes a metaphorical model for the present status of writing. Then I would ask, is it by accident that the middle voice disappeared in the evolution of Indo-European? Already in ancient Greek the opposition was no longer situated between the active and the middle voice but between the active and the passive voice, so that the middle voice became a sort of vestige with which linguists wondered what to do. If we look at a more fully developed version of Benveniste's study, called "Nom d'action et nom d'agent dans les langues indo-européennes" ["The Name of Action and of Agent in Indo-European Languages"], we see two cases, one in which the action is ascribed to the agent like an attribute to a subject, and another in which the action envelopes the agent and the agent remains immersed in the action—that is the case of the middle voice. The psychological conclusion that Benveniste doesn't draw, because he is not a psychologist, is that in thought as expressed in Greek or ancient Indo-European there is no idea of the agent being the *source* of his action. Or, if I may translate that, as a historian of Greek civilization, there is no category of the *will* in Greece. But what we see in the Western world, through language, the evolution of law, the creation of a vocabulary of the will, is precisely the idea of the human subject as agent, the source of actions, creating them, assuming them, carrying responsibility for them. Therefore, the question I ask you, Barthes, is this: Are we seeing, in the literary domain, a complete reversal of this evolution and do you believe that we are going to see, on the literary level, the reappearance of the middle voice in the linguistic domain? For, if not, we are at the level of pure metaphor and not at the level of reality in regard to the fact that the literary work is already a sign which announces a change of psychological status of the writer in his relationship to his work.

Barthes: I believe that one of the tasks of militant literature is to try, often by extremely violent and difficult methods, to compensate for the falling away of linguistic categories, that is, those which have disappeared from the language in the course of history. One tries to rethink the lost category and to take it as a metaphorical model—I understand the ambiguity of my position but I maintain it—to reclaim it by raising it to the level of discourse. For the writer cannot act directly on the forms of language. He cannot invent new tenses. He has enough trouble inventing new words; he is reproached for every one that he invents. Yet when he passes beyond the sentence or discourse, he finds again a certain freedom for resistance and for violence. That is all I can say for the moment, but I think the question is a timely one and very well put.

Richard Schechner: The theater was taken in by the Church in the Middle Ages and then some time around the Renaissance it was emancipated, or thrown out from the Church, whence it was taken in by literature; and I think in these last few days it's being thrown out by literature. This may be advantageous both to literature and to the theater, but I come here because I truly believe that what the structuralists have to offer to literature they perhaps also, in a different mode, have to offer to the criticism of theater. I want to raise some general problems, because it seems to me that you describe language and literature as implosive, in other words, turned in on its own laws and explicated by its own laws, while in theater at least language is explosive—language is a matrix of action. It doesn't make any sense in the theater unless language gives rise to action, which is the performance. One reads a theater text and situates it in two matrices of action: first the matrix of action out of which the words come, and then the matrix of action which the words give birth to. One doesn't read a theater text purely as literature, but in relationship to the action out of which it was born and in relationship to the action into which it must be cast if people are to see it. I think this can be historically borne out because no closet drama that has not seen continuous performance remains in the consciousness even of literary critics. They constantly refer to these dramas being performed. In the United States for example, we do not write about Racine very much; in France you do, simply because Racine is performed in France and not in the United States. In the theater, therefore, there is a separation between text and gesture and a relationship between text and gesture and no way to consider one without the other. I don't think that what you've done here really helps me, at least, make this relationship clear because you're trying to tell me there is no gesture; and you tend to forget entirely about the spoken word. I watch MM. Goldmann, Barthes, Todorov, Poulet, and so on, arguing here, and there is something present which I could never find on a printed page.

What I want to ask you is whether you consider the realization of the text, the performance of the text, just an incidental adjunct to the literary product or an integral part of the literary project? If you consider it incidental, then we part ways; but if you consider it integral then you have to explain to me what insight you give to both the gesture and the language; you have to explain to me what relationship there is between these linguistic laws and this gestural world.

BARTHES: I can give you a preliminary, banal reply of "semiological common sense" which is, that human gestures constitute a semiotic system and that, consequently, we will find—when we concern ourselves

Discussion

with this problem—on the level of gestures, approximately the same problems posed by any system of signs. But if I, myself, am not tempted by this problem at present, it is because the system of gestures (*la gestuelle*) in our bourgeois theater remains still entirely *naturalistic*. If we had to deal with a theater (as Brecht saw) such as the Chinese or Japanese, in which the gestures are denaturalized to the profit of a very strong code, then we might find an interesting problem. But, frankly, I find it difficult to be intellectually interested in the cinema, for example. Precisely because the cinema is an art that was born during a period dominated by an aesthetic and a general ideology of the naturalistic type. The cinema has still not made the experiment of a coded art. It is simply the problem of an entire code, of an entirely "constituted" code.

SCHECHNER: What would you say about Molière?

BARTHES: We don't know exactly how Molière was played. I don't respond to Molière very much myself, because I sense in Molière all the myths of modern, bourgeois dramaturgy.

SCHECHNER: My question was really methodological. Assuming that the theater is not naturalistic, how could your methodology, your approach to linguistics, to language, and to literature, be applied fruitfully to drama, without considering drama entirely a literary and therefore a nonproduced medium? Granting that drama must be produced to be an aesthetic object, how does your methodology apply to it, or are you, as I suspect you may be, separating drama and literature, as it was separated before the Renaissance?

BARTHES: I repeat, since it is a semiotic system like any other, the instruments and concepts of approach and analysis that are those of semiology in general should apply to it.

SCHECHNER: But in semiology you have a language in which the work of Saussure and the other linguists have given you an insight. Where is the similar insight into the "language of gesture"?

BARTHES: If you are to be the Saussure of theater, that will be wonderful.

MACKSEY: Pending Mr. Schechner's undertaking, I might add that you, M. Barthes, have already made an initial contribution, along with Christian Metz, toward a semiotics of that scapegrace art which you suspect, the film. When you talked in *Communications* of the "Rhétorique de l'image," I was reminded of our own Peirce on indexical signs and the way in which he speaks of the photograph as a "quasi-predicate" composed by the "quasi-subject," light.

DERRIDA: I also think, as Barthes said, that present-day literature is an attempt, not really to return to a buried experience under the name of the middle voice, but to *think* the adventure (voluntarist, if you will) that was Western history, the history of metaphysics. It cannot be a factual re-creation, but an effort to think history, and I think that history is less than ever neglected in that experiment. I was very much in agreement with what we have heard this evening, and I wouldn't have spoken except that what was said about "je suis mort" reminded me of that extraordinary story of Poe about M. Valdemar, who awakens at a certain moment and says, "I am dead." Then I wondered if underneath my agreement with you there wasn't something that I would like to formulate, which would be perhaps a question or a disagreement. I still start from the difference which you drew from Benveniste between discursive time and historical time. This distinction appears unquestionable in the system where Benveniste states it. But when I look for the *present* of discursive time, I don't find it. I find that this present is taken not from the time of the *énonciation* but from a movement of temporalization which poses the difference and consequently makes the present something complicated, the product of an original synthesis which also means that the present cannot be produced except in the movement which retains and effaces it. Consequently, if there is no pure present, as tense of the pure *énonciation*, then the distinction between discursive time and historical time becomes fragile, perhaps. Historical time is already implied in the discursive time of the *énonciation*.

How does that lead us to "I am dead"? Regarding person, you said that when I use *je* in discourse, it is always new (*inédit*) for me but not for the reader or the hearer, whence the irreducible dissymmetry of language. However, I wonder if for me the *je* is not always already repeated, in order to be language, and if, consequently, when I pronounce the word *je*, I am not dealing with absolutely original singularity. I am always already absent from my language, or absent from this supposed experience of the new, of singularity, etc. That would mean that in order for my pronounciation of the word *je* to be an act of language, it must be a signal word, that is, it must be originally repeated. If it were not already constituted by the possibility of repetition, it would not function as an act of language. If the repetition is original, that means that I am not dealing with the new (*l'inédit*) in language. You were reticent about saying "I am dead." I believe that the condition for a true act of language is my being able to say "I am dead." Husserl distinguished two kinds of lack of meaning in language. When I say, "the worm is off," it is obvious that this sentence does not make sense, because it is not in accordance with what Husserl called the rules of pure logical grammar. Husserl would say that it is not language. But when I say "the circle is square," my sentence respects the rules of grammaticality, and if it is a *contre-sens*, at least it is not nonsense. The proof is that I can say that the sentence is false, that there is no such object. The rules of pure grammaticality are observed and therefore my language signifies, in spite of the lack of object. That means that the power of meaning of language is, to a point, independent of the possibility of its object. "I am dead" has a meaning if it is obviously false. "I am dead" is an intelligible sentence. Therefore, "I am dead" is not only a possible proposition for one who is known to be living, but the very condition for the living person to speak is for him to be able to say, significantly, "I am dead." Consequently, the security in which you have placed the "dissymmetry of language" which is linked to the *pacte de la parole* in which writing, which can only function in the opening of "I am dead," would be somewhat effaced or held at a distance. I wonder if everything you have said about writing, with which I entirely agree, doesn't imply that the *pacte de la parole* is not a living *pacte de la parole* as M. Hyppolite said, in opposing it to the phantasm. Because I wonder if one can distinguish the *pacte de la parole* from the phantasm, and if things are really as clear as they seemed a little while ago after M. Hyppolite's intervention.

The Structure of Philosophic Language According to the "Preface" to Hegel's Phenomenology of the Mind [1]

Jean Hyppolite
Collège de France

Isn't it too late to speak of Hegel in our age, when the sciences have gradually replaced metaphysical thought? Even the humane sciences—and especially the first among them, linguistics—have been successful in liberating themselves from philosophic hypotheses, or so they believe. Is there still a place for what many generations have called philosophic thought? The theme of this talk (supposing that philosophers will always exist, although perhaps not in the same way) is to ask whether there is a style or character proper to philosophic thought and language, to the presentation of philosophic ideas, just as there is a style and a character proper to great literary works.

It has often been said that Hegel was the last of the classical philosophers. With him perhaps, or certainly after him, begins the decline of metaphysics. (Who would dare call himself a metaphysician today?) There have been great seekers since Hegel who have opened new paths—Nietzsche, Marx, Freud. But the question is whether they have continued philosophical or metaphysical thought or whether they have written its criticism. What can that thought mean which belongs neither to positive science nor to classical ontology? What is the place of this thought and of its language? It is

[1] "Structure du langage philosophique d'après la 'Préface de la Phénoménologie de l'esprit' de Hegel." The text which follows is a translation from the transcription of M. Hyppolite's address. The French text of the preliminary communication which was distributed in advance to the Symposium participants differs in a number of details and emphases. It is printed as an appendix to this volume. The footnotes to the English text have been supplied by the translator, who is indebted to Professor George Boas for reviewing this version.

precisely because Hegel is the last of the great metaphysicians—not only for us; he, himself was clearly conscious that philosophical thought as such was coming to an end with him—that his thought interests us. We are to Hegel what the late Middle Ages were to Aristotle. His great shadow falls over all the philosophical essays which have been written either for or against him. Only yesterday Hegel was considered as the inspiration for historical and genetic thought—the history of philosophy taking the place of philosophy. Now, since the new recovery of the *Phenomenology of the Mind,* Hegel is considered one of the sources of contemporary thought and of existentialism. The most modern thought, however, is detaching itself from this historical and existential preoccupation while growing more sensitive to formal systems, relationships within formal systems, and systematic properties of systems. Here it is another great philosopher who might be considered the precursor of modern thought—Leibniz rather than Hegel. But I would like to think that there is a certain resemblance between these two universal minds. The formalism of Leibniz is so inventive and fertile that it approaches a philosophy of content. And while Hegel said, "In art as in everything, it is the content that counts," in his philosophy of content he sought systematicity and totalization, to such a degree that his ultimate goal seems to parallel that of Leibniz. Perhaps the day will come when history will reconcile Leibniz and Hegel, for after all Hegel was profoundly influenced by Leibniz.

But to return to our original question, isn't it too late to focus our attention on Hegel? What can we learn from him? What have we to ask him? I hasten to say that I have no intention of reviving a system of the past nor of taking a position among the Hegelians—right, left, or center. That is not the question. But Hegel's work, particularly the *Phenomenology of the Mind* and the *Science of Logic,* can be taken as models of a presentation or of a philosophic discourse. Just as the *Divine Comedy* of Dante, the *Don Quixote* of Cervantes, or the *Human Comedy* of Balzac are works whose structure and organization of discourse we can study, thus in these philosophic works of Hegel we may also consider philosophic discourse as such. The comparison with literary works is all the more indispensable since Hegel drew it himself; however, the difference between a literary discourse and a philosophical discourse is very important. While literary discourse is an imaginative speculation, philosophical discourse involves a norm of truth. Finally, and most important, philosophical discourse contains its own criticism within itself. (I realize that Robbe-Grillet, for example, writes criticism on his own novels, in my opinion inferior to the fiction, but this criticism does not constitute an essential part of the novel itself.) In philosophic discourse, someone speaks (in a moment we shall ask *who*), but he also speaks *about* his own speech (*parole*). And the speech about the speech is an integral part of philosophic language.

It is for this reason that it is interesting to study the "Preface" to the *Phenomenology*. Hegel wrote this preface in 1807, after he had finished the main work, that astonishing novel of culture. He had written under extraordinary conditions, hurried by the editor, and without knowing, when he started, what the end would be. Of course he had been meditating and outlining his system for many years. And finally he presented nearly all his thought in one work, the *Phenomenology*, in 1807. Hegel thought (wrongly in my opinion) that this work was immediately accessible, for after all it dealt with ordinary or common consciousness or, as we would say today, ordinary language. It was, nevertheless, one of Hegel's most difficult works. (Perhaps it is most difficult of all to deal with ordinary language.) When Hegel had finished the *Phenomenology*, therefore, he reflected retrospectively on his philosophic enterprise and wrote the "Preface," different from the original introduction. It is here that he tells what he conceives a philosophic discourse to be. However, it is a strange demonstration, for he says above all, "Don't take me seriously in a preface. The real philosophical work is what I have just written, the *Phenomenology of the Mind*. And if I speak to you outside of what I have written, these marginal comments cannot have the value of what I have written, these marginal comments cannot have the value of the work itself. Furthermore, I am going to write another, very different work, which will be speculative logic." The "Preface" is thus situated between Hegel's two main works (in my opinion, the rest of the system doesn't have the same importance) both of which are very close to our problem of language, the one which he has just written, the *Phenomenology of the Mind*, and the one that he is contemplating, the *Science of Logic*. On one hand, let us say, is speech [*parole*] and on the other language [*langue*], or something even deeper than language. On one hand we have ordinary consciousness, which speaks and about which the philosopher speaks, and on the other is that entity which speaks within a structure of unfathomable depth, which is philosophic thought *par excellence*. The *Phenomenology* and the *Logic*, these are the two works that Hegel presents in this preface, while adding, "Don't take a preface seriously. The preface announces a project and a project is nothing until it is realized. This is true for philosophy as well as for mathematics, the sciences, and literature." And here I am being very

Jean Hyppolite

unfaithful to Hegel, presenting his "Preface" alone, as if I were insensitive to what he says: "A preface is for people who want to speak *about* rather than for those who want to speak from *within*." What can I give as an excuse? It is because I am not a Hegelian or, more precisely, because however great our admiration may be for the *Phenomenology of the Mind* or the *Science of Logic*, we know that we cannot consider them as the expression of totality. We are more interested in Hegel's *projects* of totalization and in what he tells us of what philosophic discourse, or the style of philosophic discourse (what Hegel calls the dialectic), *can* be. Just as in the "Preface" Hegel considers the *Parmenides* to be the greatest philosophical work of antiquity, we shall continue to consider the *Phenomenology of the Mind* and the *Science of Logic* as great philosophical works, but what interests us more today is to know what Hegel considered the style and structure of a philosophic work to be. For my part, I believe not only that Hegel's philosophic project interests us, but that we are obliged to take it up again, to redo what he attempted on the two levels of phenomenology and logic. For, whether we want to or not, and however remarkable the successes of the positive sciences are, we cannot do otherwise than to attempt to translate for mankind the meaning that they hold for us. Naturally we will follow Hegel with the necessary reservations, but we will follow the project that was his in the "Preface" when he described his understanding of the philosophic work.

Before trying to define this style of philosophic work, I would like to explain why I have selected as my title *Philosophic Language in the "Preface" to the* Phenomenology, rather than *The Philosophic Thought of Hegel in the "Preface" to the* Phenomenology. That is, why have I said philosophic language? Don't believe that it is merely a desire to be fashionable. It is because for Hegel himself there is no thought outside of the unity of signifier and signified. Moreover, for Hegel this unity is not the world but rather the meaningful "mapping" [*découpage significatif*] of the world and the structure which this mapping describes. There is no thought outside of language. Therefore I do not believe it is in vain that I insist on the terms *language, discourse,* or even *style*. I have not contented myself to speak of philosophic thought as opposed to other forms of thought such as mathematical or dogmatic thought. Instead of common thought I shall say ordinary language, and instead of philosophic thought, philosophic language. Why? It is because Hegel's philosophy is dominated by the problem of language, which he called "the child and the instrument of intelligence"; the *child*, because language is consubstantial with thought, because language is our original milieu, and because language cannot be separated from thought nor thought from language; and the *instrument* because it is the means by which meaning is transmitted and therefore the means of communication, but a means which never has the total objectivity of a tool. Language is the subject-object or the object-subject. However perfected this tool may become, it must be translated into a language that is closer to us, that is inseparable from us, that is, ordinary language. And without this ordinary language there is no thought, for the *découpage*, the organization, of the world is achieved through this ordinary language. But as Hjelmslev has said, "All technical languages can be translated into ordinary language, but ordinary language can never be translated into a technical language—it cannot be translated *without remainder* [*sans reste*], evenly, into a technical language." [2] That is what Hegel means when he calls language "the child and the instrument of intelligence." To cite another linguist, when Benveniste examines the differences which can exist between determinations of thought and categories of language, he looks for the determinations of thought in Aristotle and discovers that his categories are those of the Greek language and that his very forms are mediated by this language.[3] Doubtless, languages are mutually translatable. Doubtless, we must speak of a dialectically universal language. There is, then, a dialectical element, but there is also an absolute inseparability from the *découpage* of the world. For to delineate a concept is to delineate it with *language,* and to organize things is to organize them *with language.* Which is not to say that it is not necessary—and this is what we owe to Saussure and to Husserl—to distinguish between the meanings which are tied to the signs and what is called the referent, that is, the world. The world is affected by meanings, and meanings and signs (or the divisions of signs) are interdependent. There is here a community which constitutes what Hegel called the concrete universal. The whole problem of language is posed here, and its subject too, for *who* speaks?

So that is why I speak of "language" and not of "thought." In language, Hegel tells us, the *I* (this universal unlike other universals) is both subjective and understood by others. It is existential since it designates the speaker at the very moment when he is speaking. It is only in language that the *I* exists for others, that, as Hegel says, it is universal and singular at the same time. Language, according to Hegel, is that object which is reflected in itself. It is in language that the

---

[2] Louis Hjelmslev, *Le Langage* (Paris: Editions de Minuit, 1966), p. 139.
[3] Emile Benveniste, *Problèmes de linguistique générale* (Paris: Gallimard, 1966), pp. 63–74.

world takes on meaning and that thought is for itself both subject and object. The linguistic environment is the universal consciousness-of-self, of Being; it is the *Logos*. (This is Hegelian metaphysics.) The whole *Phenomenology* develops this thesis on language and repeats it at different levels. Knowledge is possible because from the first certainty of the senses, from the first stammering of the ordinary consciousness, these "shifters," the personal pronouns *I* and *thou*, are in play as well as these original determinations of the "this," the "here," and the "now," which express the universal within the individual field of vision. Hegel said that the very conditions of inter-subjectivity were already contained in language itself. It is starting from them that dialogue and determination can become effective. Ordinary consciousness, which Hegel investigates in the *Phenomenology*, doesn't always know what it is saying nor who is speaking through it; another consciousness sometimes understands it better than it understands itself as the psychiatric dialogue confirms. Nevertheless, it is in language and in its exercise that the mind exists. If there is a diversity of languages, as there is an inter-subjectivity, this diversity is dialectically contained in the universality of human language. We regret that Hegel is not alive today and that he didn't push his reflection on language further. We can only attempt to extend his thought.

Language, then, is not only the fundamental element of thought, the condition of dialogue and of knowledge. We have already remarked that from the first sense-determinations and earliest "babblings of common consciousness" it is through specific yet universal significations such as *I, thou, here, now* that we reach differentiated objects in the world. But Hegel went further—and in this case he was doing some Barthes before the fact—for language is the style or the fundamental expression of a culture, and the rhetoric of a culture. We have only to look at the table of contents to see on how many levels language functions. There is, first of all, the language of commandment in the ethical life; then there is the language which, instead of having content, *acts*, solely by its form as language, as in an oath: *I swear, I promise*. And finally there is the language which expresses the style of a particular culture: honor, flattery, *déchirement* (as in Diderot's *Neveu de Rameau*, analyzed in the *Phenomenology*). At the end of the *Phenomenology* when Hegel deals with religion, he speaks of the spiritual work of art and explains how the world is expressed in the epic (later in the *Aesthetics* he will say that the novel is the epic of the modern age and he will discover in *Don Quixote* the turning point where the novel of chivalry is succeeded by the "prose of the world"), how subjectivity expresses itself in the fluidity of the lyric work, and finally how the theater, comedy and tragedy, reconciles the subjectivity of the self with the objectivity of the world—liberty with destiny. With religion, with these aesthetic expressions (which Hegel later shows finally culminating in poetry, in a very general sense) we are close to philosophic discourse, but for Hegel this new "novel" is no longer the novel of representation but of the concept. It is the very essence of language, of meanings as such and of their mediations. In the "Preface" to the *Phenomenology* Hegel examines philosophic language as the successor to religion. The world must still be expressed in some way, different from the way of the novel or the myth, but expressed nevertheless. And the philosophic work will be precisely the novel that follows a norm of truth, and it will be (we can say this today without being Hegelian) a project of totalization—much more than a totality reinstating finitude, which, as I shall try to show in a minute, is never absent in Hegelianism itself.

We will understand Hegel better if we keep in mind his early studies and the first manifestations of his thought. He didn't begin by being a philosopher in the technical sense of the term. It was only afterward that he said to himself, in effect, "this must be philosophy." He was doing something that he had conceived in relation to the French *philosophes* of the eighteenth century. (I was taught in philosophy class that the *philosophes* were not really philosophers at all, but Hegel thought that they were the true philosophers.) He read Diderot, Voltaire, and especially Rousseau, just as Kant had read Rousseau. He tried to understand what he saw as the substitution of philosophy for religion which had, at one time, been the means by which people became conscious of the world and talked about it. But this philosophy takes account of the entire history of philosophy, and so Hegel became a technician of philosophy. It is wrong to believe that Hegel began by reading the *Critique of Pure Reason*. He read religion as pure religion, and he read Fichte's critique of all revelation and discussed it. For his time, he had an admirable knowledge of Greek thought, and he asked himself what it had or had not contributed. Hegel was also a very positive thinker. From Lukács as well as from Hegel's theological writings, commented on by Nohl, we know how interested Hegel was in the economic problems of his times, surprisingly, considering the situation of Germany. He read Adam Smith and later Ricardo. Hegel tried to take up again, in a strictly philosophical work, a problem to which in former ages religion had spontaneously replied. If we can grasp that, we will understand better what Hegel wanted to do. By a

Jean Hyppolite

sort of paradox, the *Phenomenology of the Mind,* which seems so difficult to us, is a reflection on ordinary consciousness and, as we would say today, on ordinary language. To scrutinize, to sound the depths of ordinary language, ordinary consciousness, and ordinary experience is what Hegel wanted to do in the *Phenomenology of the Mind.* At the end of his preface Hegel, who must have been naïve, like all speculative philosophers, said that he would soon be understood and that a work never appears unless there is a public prepared to receive it. I think it has taken a long time for Hegel's *Phenomenology* to be understood. The Hegelian system, the *Encyclopedia,* and the *Philosophy of Right* have been widely commented upon. An Hegelian influence has been felt in all of Europe. However, one might say that the *Phenomenology of the Mind* has been discovered by the present generation (and I am thinking not of myself but of Kojève), that we have discovered the extraordinary richness of this work and the originality of its intent.

To speak in my own name and about my own past, I must admit that literature used to interest me more than philosophy and that I turned to the latter because I was so troubled by the idea of being subjected to the tyranny of literary criticism. But how could I find a work in which I could reread—or read for the first time—all the great works of literature? When I was a student at the Ecole Normale Supérieure I went to see Lanson and asked his permission to take a little trip to Spain. "To do what?" he asked me. "To study *Don Quixote,*" I told him. He asked me if I knew Spanish. I told him that I would learn it. Some time later I found a note from Lanson in my box: "My dear friend, you must be a little tired. Here is a scholarship and my recommendation to go spend a little time in Brittany. I advise you not to go to Spain."

Well, if Hegel had not existed in addition to Lanson, I would never have read *Don Quixote.* But thanks to Hegel, I discovered *Don Quixote,* and Greek tragedy (before reading Nietzsche), and so many other things. This work, then, gave me the unhoped for opportunity of working scrupulously on a text while, at the same time, entering the immense field of the vast literature which Hegel had not feared to take on, and where I, timid philosopher that I was, could follow him in his discoveries. This Hegelian voyage of discovery, *The Phenomenology of the Mind,* is a great novel of culture. When I wrote my thesis on it, I said that it was *Wilhelm Meister*; today I know that it is also *La Vie de Marianne.* Hegel knew all the novels of the eighteenth century and he, himself, wrote a philosophic novel. But instead of disputing whether this great novel, this "terrestrial comedy," is literature or philosophy, let us observe that in writing it Hegel opened an extraordinarily original avenue of inquiry, and one which is still a very real problem today. In fact, what the *Phenomenology* represents is the science of ordinary experience and of ordinary language. Hegel's *Phenomenology of the Mind* of 1807 may not be *our* solution to the problem, but in any case it opened a very important path. In his "Preface" Hegel tells us that if science (meaning philosophy rather than the natural sciences) remained outside of ordinary self-consciousness, ordinary language, and everyday life it would be ineffectual and without reality. Science must start from ordinary experience and it must return to it. If all the positive sciences today develop absolutely rigorous technical languages permitting them to attain successive triumphs, is it not to be required that these technical languages find their meaning once again in ordinary consciousness? How will this be possible? But if it were not possible, that is, if the path between technically organized consciousness and ordinary consciousness could not be crossed in both directions, then we would have to despair of humanity to a great extent. We *must* be able to do this—of course it will always be a project and never a completed totality. (In this I am not Hegelian.) Ordinary consciousness must, then, discover in itself the awakening of science; thus will it overcome its profound lack of consciousness, for it does not understand itself, it doesn't know what it is doing or saying. However, the philosopher must not substitute himself for the ordinary consciousness, says Hegel, but rather *follow* it in its theoretical and practical experiences, gathering these experiences in the "element" of knowledge (and Hegel uses *element* as we do for example in "marine element") until the point where, in what Hegel calls absolute knowledge, the ordinary consciousness will finally say, "But what you have just discovered—I knew it all along." (A little bit as Oedipus says it at the end of that immense quest which leads him to such tragic results.) It is only when ordinary consciousness recognizes itself in philosophic consciousness, and the latter in the former, that psychoanalysis will be achieved, that science will be alive, and ordinary consciousness will be scientific. For the remarkable thing in this history of ordinary consciousness and of its language is that it is always, from the beginning, a human dialogue. Whatever is the communicating element must pass through the element of dialogue, the "I" and other "I" being in permanent confrontation. Knowledge passes through communication and first of all, as you know, through the inequality of the consciousnesses which meet. (This master-slave inequality is an all too familiar problem.)

This attempt to present ordinary consciousness, to follow its history, to see in it the growth of a deeper knowledge of self, is a definite acquisition of our thought. We may find that Hegel has not resolved the question that he asked, that he did not take into account (how could he have, at that date?) the development of all the positive sciences and their relation to ordinary consciousness, a problem which is so important for us and which Husserl took up in his last works, when he considered the relationship between the technical sciences and their common origin. But we cannot fail to recognize the problem, which Hegel stated, of the relationship between scientific knowledge and ordinary knowledge and between scientific language and ordinary language. If the literary work, the novels of culture, to which Hegel explicitly referred, is an imaginary presentation of an exemplary life, what then will the philosophic work be—inasmuch as it is a presentation of ordinary consciousness? What will be the character of this presentation? Under what conditions will ordinary discourse become philosophic discourse? You will excuse me if, in order to enliven the discussion, I try to characterize philosophic discourse in the form of a paradox: It was once said of a philosopher, "You know he is a philosopher because when you ask him a question, and when he consents to reply—which is not always the case—you no longer recognize the question you asked." In the discourse of a philosopher we don't know *who* is talking, nor *what* is being talked about. This is not meant ironically, for Hegel's whole effort in the "Preface" is to show that if there is a philosophic discourse it is one which does not make a distinction between the self of knowledge and the self of the object. The self of the object is the thing in-itself, the nucleus, the irreducible *thing* which is the basis of objectivity, for generally one falls back on a subject which, failing to discover the object, itself joins the predicates together and achieves coherence. So that Hegel criticizes both representative thought, in which there is always recourse to an explanation by exterior content, and formal thought, which creates a framework for what is received from the outside. For Hegel, true philosophic thought is thought in which knowledge is not an instrument exterior to the thing that is known; it is the thing known which speaks and which expresses itself. The style of such a process of thought is called dialectic. It is the rhythm of the *I* which has forgotten itself and of the things which think themselves within the *I*. (One might almost say that it is God speaking, which seems a bit strong, but there really is something of that nature in a true discourse which intends to be philosophical.) The critique that Hegel makes of formalism is a critique of frameworks and of means of understanding distinct from the thing known. In the philosophic style the thing presents itself and discourse is the very presentation of the object. How is that possible? How can the one who speaks and who knows and the thing that is known form a single movement—which Hegel often presented as a story or a historical genesis. How can such a narrative be conceived, and what is its style? That is what Hegel has tried to present to us. Of course there is the difficulty—for which I refer you to the "Preface"—of showing how there are two types of thought which Hegel rejected. The first is material thought, buried in content, actually egocentric, but unaware of its own involvement in the affair. The other is formal thought which builds up frameworks of relationship, for which the object reference becomes an unknowable nucleus and which must always seek its content outside. Between formal thought and material thought is there the possibility of a style of narrative in which the one who knows is himself involved in the thing that is known?

I think of Diderot who said, "I know how to 'alienate' myself sometimes, and that is indispensable in a great literary work." That is what Hegel is proposing to us—that the philosopher create a discourse which is the discourse and the rhythm of things, themselves. His proposition takes on two different forms, which I am taking up again because I think they constitute what we still owe to Hegel and what we can still borrow from him. There are, shall we say, speech and language, and there are also phenomenology and logic. Hegel undertook the philosophic work along two different lines. On one hand there is ordinary language and common consciousness, the philosopher who speaks through common consciousness and discovers at its heart (even when he doesn't realize it) the fundamental determinations and articulations which give structure to all discourse that, in turn, gives life to common consciousness. There is also the language which contains the determinations and articulations of thought and which is what Hegel calls Logos, a logic which is not the formal logic of the past, but which is the architecture of universal language and of the structures of language, in which all the determinations of thought are linked together. One might say that Hegel was obsessed, from the point of view of this logic, by a sense of the artificial nature of the culture in which we live. He was obsessed by writing certainly, and what he wanted to do in his Logic was to give back to writing the vitality of living speech. Writing is an accumulation of determinations and articulations in which thought has fixed itself in order to express itself in written works. Hegel was obsessed by the danger that we may someday be completely buried by libraries (I am exaggerating somewhat), and he wanted to show that all articulations are themselves a dialectic. The two projects that Hegel leaves us (naturally with the requirement that we conceive them a little differently from the way in which he did) are the projects of the phenomenology and of the logic. On the one hand, the analysis of ordinary language by the philosopher, implying everything that is called phenomenology of perception—this is the *Phenomenology of the Mind.*

On the other hand, the search for all the articulations which make up the structure and the architecture of languages—this is the *Logic.* Is such an enterprise possible? In one case the philosopher loses himself in the system and in the architectonics of the determinations of thought, while in the other he finds himself immersed in the common consciousness. In my opinion Hegel's greatest moment is the point of oscillation between the architecture of the *Logic* and the common consciousness of the *Phenomenology.* Afterward he tried to build a system, the *Encyclopedia,* but it is the movement between these two works which is fundamental for us. For the common consciousness, as it appears in the *Phenomenology,* is not without the consciousness of the philosopher which follows it, narrates it, and records it. But inversely the consciousness of the philosopher is not the consciousness of God, speaking through the philosopher. Nobody could push pride that far. Thus Hegel's two great works are relative, each to the other. Ordinary consciousness accompanies the search for the articulations of thought, and inversely these articulations underlie, in their discovery, the history of ordinary consciousness. So that the rhythm of philosophical discourse (where the search for the "speaker" is simultaneous with the treatment of the object spoken of) is attenuated by the sense of finitude which accompanies it. Hegel has been reproached for not recognizing this finitude, for "putting himself in the place of God," but he knew finitude very well. He knew that there is meaninglessness [*nonsens*] and that it is sometimes irredeemable. As there are lost letters and lost causes, so too there is lost meaning. But whereas a negative theology admits a meaning beyond meaning, for Hegel what is redeemable has meaning, but what is irredeemable is the measure of meaninglessness that invests all meaning. And this difference he calls the Absolute Difference. Hegel therefore recognized finitude in terms of this meaninglessness investing meaning. It cannot be said that he put himself in the place of God, for he well knew that when he was searching for the universal articulations of thought it was still as one concrete philosopher that he was carrying on the quest. He well knew, in the words of my friend Merleau-Ponty, that there is no philosopher without a shadow.

Discussion

J. LOEWENBERG: I certainly welcome the opportunity to make a few brief comments on a paper which is so full of ideas and has behind it erudition as exemplified in M. Hyppolite's translation of the *Phenomenology* and his commentary. His certainly remarkable feat of condensation included practically his whole interpretation of Hegel into such a brief compass. I know he excluded a great deal, but what he included is all in his great books. I am to a large extent in agreement with the general view expressed in M. Hyppolite's paper, especially his appreciation of the *Phenomenology* as a work of literary art comparable to the great masterpieces which he mentions, such as *The Divine Comedy*. Obviously he does not try to compare in structure or in development Hegel's *Phenomenology* to, say, Spinoza's *Ethics*.

The crucial problem—of course, any comparison between a literary work of art and a philosophical work of art, which also has the imagination and the vision and the perspective of a literary work of art—is its truth. And that is the crucial problem—the truth of Hegel's *Phenomenology*, whether judged by any standard other than Hegel's (admitting there are standards other than Hegel's) and even by Hegel's standard itself, the question is whether it's true. But M. Hyppolite limited himself largely to a discussion about the "Preface," and as he knows, as he has expressed it in his books, though written ostensibly to the *Phenomenology*, it certainly was written after the work had been completed. Then not only did he limit himself to the "Preface" but his main center of attack was the language in the "Preface." Now the "Preface" is a philosophical manifesto, couched in a form and diction which presupposes the subsequent system. And Hegel himself disavowed the intention of telling in the "Preface" what he was going to develop in the system. The trouble is, you see, that there is a certain circular relation between the "Preface" and the system for which the vocabulary, the language that Hegel uses, was needed. As a matter of fact you can't understand Hegel's language, if you read the "Preface" alone, until you know the system, and you can't know the system until you know the language; that is one of the difficulties of Hegel's work. Unless you learn the vocabulary, you don't understand it; but on the other hand, the vocabulary is already presupposed . . . I mean you have here a very, very serious circle.

Now the language: there is a relation in Hegel's language, which he needs for the articulation of his system of philosophy, and the languages used in other philosophies: and M. Hyppolite shows in his paper that Hegel seems to condemn as nonphilosophical any language other than his own. Which is another difficulty. After all, there are other languages and we didn't reject them as nonphilosophical until Hegel established in his system that the *only* philosophical language is a dialectical method as he propounded and developed it. So there is another difficulty about the "Preface": it is a manifesto which is couched in a language which, to the ordinary user of language, is simply unintelligible. Hegel himself says it requires of a person that kind of effort comparable to one walking on his head. So Hegel himself is quite aware of the difficulty of the problem.

Now there is another problem about language: the relation of Hegel's own language which he employs to characterize his philosophy and especially the ways of thinking, or forms of consciousness, as developed in *Phenomenology*. The dialectic in the *Phenomenology* is based on the linguistic expressions of various ways of thinking, beginning with uncertainty, through perception, understanding, self-consciousness, various forms of rationalism, and then going on to ethics, religion, etc. But, after all, the *Phenomenology* is based upon the law of contradiction: that which is contradictory cannot be sustained. But, after all, what but diction can be contradicted? Only diction can be contradicted. And it is that, I think, that is the key to what M. Hyppolite has so eloquently and persuasively shown—that thought and language are interdependent (what he calls consubstantial); one cannot exist without the other. Language expresses thought and thought can only express itself in language: hence, only diction can be contradicted. Without diction there can be no contradiction. And that is really a key to what Hegel is doing with the various languages that are employed in the *Phenomenology*. Each way of thinking has its language peculiar to it. Every way of thinking has a language which is idiomatic. There is an idiom for every way of thinking, and it's that *idiom* which Hegel pushes to an extreme to show that the idiom, obviously necessary for the expression of a certain way of thinking, becomes self-inconsistent; it doesn't say what it means, and it can't mean what it says. The language that it *has* to use is self-contradictory and then, of course, has to be transcended, has to be outgrown. Now, I should say that all philosophical languages are idiomatic in the sense of their being peculiar to different systems of thought. They are embodied in them. To demand one philosophy to speak another language or to demand one philosophy to give up its method of using a certain language is to demand that it give up its philosophy; because, for example, we can't expect vitalism to speak the language of mechanism. Nor can we expect mechanism to speak the language of vitalism. To ask mechanism to give up its language, is to ask it to give up mechanism. But whether mechanism is sound philosophy or not or whether vitalism is truer than mechanism, that's another matter. As far as language is concerned, it can't use any other language: hence, we heard last night theories about language having to do with different languages; so whatever theory you propose, whatever subject matter the theory is about, calls for a certain language and for a certain method.

There is a difference between genus and species when applied to philosophical languages. Is there a generic language of which other languages are species, or is every language *sui generis?* To apply this to Hegel. Is Hegel's language, in the "Preface" of the *Phenomenology, sui generis,* or is it but a specific mode of thinking, which we are not obliged to adopt? In other words is it *the* philosophical language, or is it *a* philosophical language? Now I have tried to follow the résumé of M. Hyppolite's paper where he seems to argue that it is the structure of philosophical language, as if it were *the* philosophical language, and he seems to agree that languages which Hegel himself in the "Preface" rejects as nonphilosophical are *not* truly philosophical. That is a very crucial point.

Now a plea for the philosophical language as generic, which Hegel seems to make in the "Preface" of the *Phenomenology*, must wait until proved in its *application* through the *Phenomenology*; this Hegel himself maintains. He claims that philosophy can only be judged by its results. You can't announce at the beginning a program of philosophy. A program of philosophy is not a philosophy; only the development of the program can be called philosophical. And yet the language seems to be presented in the "Preface" as if it *were* the only language in which to develop the program of philosophy which he announces. That seems to me a great difficulty, and in the last analysis the stumbling block to Hegel has always been, and will always remain, his absolutism.

There seem to be two *Phenomenologies*, and not just one. M. Hyppolite himself recognizes the twofold nature of the *Phenomenology*. In his translation, he groups in one volume the first three main divisions of the *Phenomenology*, namely consciousness, self-consciousness, and reason; and he justifies it by indicating the difference between the three first parts of the *Phenomenology* and the last part, called Spirit, to which he devotes a separate volume. He himself seems to feel that there is a great difference between the two *Phenomenologies*, namely the *Phenomenology* comprising what Hegel calls consciousness, self-consciousness, and reason, and another which is equal in bulk to the first three—Spirit—which is a separate *Phenomenology*. What is the difference?

Now, I know M. Hyppolite will disagree, and I propose it merely for discussion. I will ask a question so that M. Hyppolite can answer it. I myself would feel that the first *Phenomenology* consisting of consciousness, self-consciousness, and reason is a humanistic *Phenomenology*. The other, dealing with Spirit, seems to me a superhumanistic *Phenomenology*. For there Hegel introduces his absolute Spirit, his absolute Being, self-revealing, self-sustaining, as if, for example, the absolute Spirit were present in the dialectic of culture, in the dialectic of the social evolution, the French Revolution, in the manifestation of the Enlightenment, in the manifestation of the various religions; so that if God is light, it is the absolute Spirit that appears as light and knows itself as light. Now that is a very difficult conception to adopt. Hence, the "Preface," as M. Hyppolite interprets it, seems to me more germane to the second *Phenomenology*, dealing with Spirit, dealing with spiritual phenomena, rather than dealing with the first part, that is with the first *Phenomenology*, which I call the humanistic part. After all, what is important here is to find out what the subject is that experiences all these things. M. Hyppolite speaks of common sense—you meant probably a generic mind, mind viewed generically, and there are many, many examples of the various forms of consciousness or ways of thought of which Hegel traces the dialectical as well as the historical development. Now, the generic mind is one thing; a superhuman being, an absolute Spirit, or the Christian God transmogrified into an absolute is quite another thing. It's the subject whose experiences are recorded and that's a great stumbling block.

I always feel that the search for a universal language is comparable to the search for a universal method. Philosophers have been engaged for a good many centuries in attempting to arrive at a universal method of philosophizing. Now, if we admit different kinds of philosophy, if we admit of a philosophical pluralism (I don't mean metaphysical Pluralism, I mean the possibility of plural philosophies, many philosophies), obviously each philosophy will have its own method. And it's absurd to ask one philosophy to give up its method, for then it gives up its philosophy, unless we assume, as Hegel insists the philosopher seems to assume, that all philosophies, each with its own method, are steppingstones to an all-comprehensive philosophy, with its own method and the final and the absolute philosophy. And Hegel remains, as the Germans called him soon after his death, *der unwiderleglich Weltphilosoph*. Now, if one doesn't accept that dictum, one is naturally critical of Hegel's method as the only method. To demand that one method and one method alone be suitable to all subject matter (I'm speaking of philosophical subject matter) is a case where methodology becomes methodolatry, the worship of one method. I am in the habit of speaking of methodology in the plural. There's the generic methodology, of which there are many species. I don't know why the mathematical language, that Hegel so dismisses as nonphilosophical, should not be used in a certain philosophical system. Hence, the philosophical search for a universal language presents the same predicament, namely, one language alone is to be called philosophical, others being pseudophilosophical, partially philosophical, erroneously philosophical, and so on. Well, if I may engage again in a word-play, if we speak of lingology as the science of languages, lingology may easily turn into lingolatry, worship of *a* language as *the* language, and I think that is a very important consideration in commenting on M. Hyppolite's paper.

The ultimate choice in dealing with Hegel is between a Hegel *with* and a Hegel *without* the language announced in the "Preface" as exclusively philosophical. *Tout est là*. Whether we ought to take Hegel, one Hegel, namely with the language as announced in the "Preface" as exclusively philosophical, or Hegel without that language, in another language. Hegel's message couched in a language other than his is still pertinent, and M. Hyppolite shows how pertinent it is. It's strange he didn't choose Hegel's language—he used his own wonderful French in conveying Hegel's message. He didn't need Hegel's language, which shows the potency of Hegel's thought, because it isn't dependent on his language. Hence what we have after all, the distinction in Hegel's whole *Phenomenology*, is a difference between a truth-claim and truth-value. Hegel shows that any philosophical thought, any philosophical way of thinking, any human persuasion can make a truth-claim. It claims to be true, and it claims to be absolutely true, and its claim is not identifiable with its value. It may have a truth-claim, but no truth-value. Hegel shows that its truth-value is relative to a higher value. We can admit that any philosophical way of thinking can make a claim to being considered true, as long as it doesn't ask to be considered absolutely and exclusively true, and that holds for Hegel's system too. If I were to express what I learned from Hegel's *Phenomenology*, although I can't claim to have been such a profound student as M. Hyppolite, I would speak of it as dialectical pluralism. Hegel's dialectic justifies the assumption of a pluralism in philosophical ways of thinking, and Hegel's own method might well be regarded as inconsistent with his conclusion. If we accept the dialectical method as a valid method, we can't terminate the method by arriving at an absolute. On the other hand, if you want an absolute, you can't get it by a dialectical method. I'm suggesting this as a subject for discussion; perhaps M. Hyppolite will throw some light on it.

JEAN HYPPOLITE: First of all, Mr. Loewenberg is a great connoisseur of Hegel. He has given lectures on the *Phenomenology* which constitute a truly important work and in which one may find the few remarks—for they are not objections—that he has just presented. I am obliged to say that I am in agreement with Mr. Loewenberg on nearly all the points presented. It is certain that the plurality of philosophies is grouped by Hegel into every possible philosophic system. It is also certain that the idea of an absolute knowledge is inconceivable unless it is given a certain problematic sense, which I am quite willing to give it. There is one point on which I might make an explanation. That is in regard to language. I believe Mr. Loewenberg asked, "Is there then a philosophic language which would be distinct from all other languages?" I think that I must reply for Hegel that there is no philosophic language peculiar to philosophy, as there is, for instance, a mathematical language. Hegel is an adversary of all formalism. It is interesting to see in the *Logic* or in the "Preface" to the *Phenomenology* how Hegel finds fault with everything which is a formal system. When it is said that Hegel reduced philosophy to logic, it must be understood that it is not a question of formal logic. Absolutely not. For Hegel there is no one technical language which would permit the solution of philosophical problems. The language that Hegel speaks is the German language, and the play on words is difficult in translation, of course, but it is nothing more than that. It gives the appearance of a jargon, I realize. For instance, *extranéation* gives me a feeling of uneasiness, but I don't know how else to render it. It is to distinguish *entfremden* and *entäussern*. These words exist commonly in German, but in French *extranéation* is obviously a Latin word. The translation of Hegel is a perpetual betrayal. Just a small anecdote to enliven things —I corrected one error of translation which is very special and which shows Hegel's thought very well. It was simply a question of reading *der* or *den*, and I was told, "You know, Hegel wrote so badly that it might be either an *r* or an *n, der* or *den.*" Actually I was the one who was making the mistake, because I was being carried along by the meaning. Hegel said, "and the result is the corpse," and I translated, "one leaves a corpse behind and one waits." But no, Hegel says precisely "and the result is the corpse which has left enthusiasm behind." That is much more profound; it is as much as to say that youthful enthusiasm is missing in the end result. Hegel was extraordinarily sensitive, for what one expects is an enthusiasm which leaves something behind, and not the loss of enthusiasm. And that says a lot about Hegelian thought. Now, I haven't told this anecdote simply for the pleasure of telling it, but to show that Hegel's philosophic style is fundamental, and that one cannot deny the *way* in which Hegel tells his history of the world. It is not a novel; it is something other than a novel, but still something in which language is fundamental. And it is quite different from a technical language. But Mr. Loewenberg has said all that in a book on the *Phenomenology of the Mind* in which he follows its developments very closely.

As to saying that in effect one cannot understand the "Preface" without the works—very well. However, the "Preface" that I misunderstood and scorned a little the first time I read the *Phenomenology* appears to me today to be a capital piece of work. I wasn't able to show here the sort of technique, a living technique, by which Hegel shows how the nonphilosophical public complains and laments because it is obliged to reread philosophical works two or three times. And why doesn't the public understand? It is because a philosophical statement isn't like an ordinary statement. In a philosophical statement, the subject has started to disappear. In an ordinary proposition, there is a subject. What are you talking about? I am talking about a worm. What is this worm? It is round; it is white; it is black. There is a basis, a support, and then there are the properties of the support, which is called the predicate. Whereas in a philosophical subject, the support disappears. There is nothing to hang on to. There is no nucleus. It has passed into the predicate. Russell didn't understand. He is a great mathematician, who started out as a Hegelian. And he said to himself, "But what is Hegel doing? He is making identical propositions and he is confusing the copula with the identity." No, Hegel's identical proposition is not an identity in the sense of the mathematician: $A = B$, where A remains fixed and B remains fixed. A *passes into* B. And the only subject is the becoming. It is because of the disappearance of the subject and this continual mediation that people don't understand. They don't understand because they *want* a support. But leaving aside the question of the support, ordinary thought also admits critical thought. That is, thought oscillates between the support and what I have called argument. (I translate *raisonnieren* as *argument* rather than *ratiocination*, because Hegel applies it to mathematics, to literature, and to conversation. The only thing to which he doesn't apply it is philosophy. Therefore to translate it as *ratiocinate* doesn't work, but to translate it as *argue* works very well.) That is to say, ordinary thought *argues*. Once it has the support it attaches the predicates like cars to a train. Philosophic thought crushes ordinary thought because the support collapses. Hegel describes this in dynamic terms. He says that ordinary thought experiences a sort of shock—it is in the process of passing into the predicate and suddenly it is sent back, repulsed, to the subject that it has lost. It tries to find itself outside of the thing and there it is in the thing just at the moment when it would like to lose itself. There is something which has never existed before—technical philosophers who try to refine or reflect on their instrument. Hegel put criticism inside the instrument; more exactly, he put criticism in the movement of things. Excuse me for this digression, but everything that Mr. Loewenberg has just said allows me to say a few words, for we are in agreement on the impossibility of being absolutely Hegelian and in admiration for Hegel's achievement.

GEORGES POULET: Just a moment ago M. Hyppolite said of Hegel that his style was fundamental. Let us return to something that he said at the beginning of his talk, when he asked what the style of a philosophic work is and when he proposed Hegel's style as the perfect example of the philosophic style. At that point I said to myself, isn't M. Hyppolite putting himself at an advantage? Isn't Hegel's case a special case, an entirely exceptional case, the case of a success of philosophic language such as we find nowhere else? For example, when we consider the Hegelian language we find ourselves before something which is fundamental and which is maintained throughout the development, so that the language is the very act by which the fundamental is preserved and develops. This seems to me to be true only in the case of Hegel, and it seems particularly inexact, and I think you will agree with me, in the case of the one whom you have both joined and opposed to Hegel, that is Leibniz. In the case of Leibniz, it is not the development that is important, it is the *envelopment* (if I may express it this way). And then we find ourselves in the presence of a problem which I don't believe has been raised yet but which merits consideration in the line of your discussion—the problem of what we might call the *implicitation* and *explicitation* in and through language. Leibniz's thought, as expressed by Leibniz, is a form of language which always remains as condensed as possible. This is the category of maximum density. On the contrary, a thought like Hegel's can satisfy itself only to the degree that it develops itself through language. There seems to be an extremely curious paradox here, in that Hegel's philosophy begins as the story of unhappy *consciousness* and ends as the story of happy *speech*. Don't we find the opposite in philosophies such as that of Leibniz? Isn't that also what we would find if we considered poetry briefly? Poetry is generally speech [*parole*] which seeks to remain as far as possible in its *implicitation*, so much so that if it develops itself, it is lost. It deteriorates to the degree that it develops, to the degree that it abandons itself to its "gift of speech." This is especially true for, let us say, the poetry of Victor Hugo. Let us oppose to this sort of poetry a poetry like that of Char. This is a poetry in which density of language corresponds to a sort of immediate grasp of poetic truth in a sort of *prélocution* or *pro-locution* which is the opposite of elocution—of a certain philosophical elocution which might be the Hegelian type. Therefore, alongside the success of philosophical speech which you have proposed, with Hegel as example, there is a failure of *explicit* speech. We can see an example of this in a work which is somewhat earlier than Hegel's, namely Sterne's *Tristram Shandy*. What is *Tristram Shandy?* It is the story of somebody who, just as in the *Phenomenology of the Mind*, wants to present the story of the very fluctuation of his thought. He finds himself, however, in conditions that make it more and more impossible for him to tell this story. This is because speech is too slow while, on the contrary, thought is too fast; and the initial lag between thought and speech grows steadily worse while speech is progressing, so much so that the progression becomes a digression. Here we see the passage from the triumph of language to the failure of language.

Hyppolite: This is a fine development, an excellent and necessary detour that you have made rescue the thought. You score against me here, because you are aiming at my weak point. You are aiming at me, in fact, by accusing Victor Hugo (which isn't bad). You accuse him of this language which generates itself, of bad rhetoric, actually. You accuse him of too much eloquence, with which you contrast that condensation which overlays an interior silence and which is deeper than speech. That is how you save the thought. Fortunately, one of your examples, may I say, doesn't hold. It is that of Leibniz. Your position is correct; but for Leibniz, it suffices to climb to the summit of his theodicy (in that building of I don't know how many stories), where all the possible worlds are unfolding, to see his prodigious imagination.

There are cases where Hegel tries to condense and there are unfortunate cases where he develops, which is very understandable, and where he seems to try to be witty. Yes, that is rather unfortunate for the *Phenomenology*. There are also some very profound things, in particular the *Hic et Nunc*, that he expresses in a very condensed way. For Leibniz, as for Aristotle, I think that we must say that his envelopment is also a development. He tries to condense his thought, but he doesn't always succeed. You are right in regard to the poet, the profound poet who only pronounces monosyllables, or little more, because he seeks such a great density. Hegel gives him a place, he calls him the beautiful soul. The beautiful soul excludes itself from dialogue. In its purity it faints before the problem. It disappears because it refuses communication. This is his formula, and if you apply it to Leibniz, I think that I could show that the density of Leibniz doesn't exclude developments and myths.

Naturally, there are two rather different philosophic structures here, but when you take up poetry itself, there I have difficulty in answering you. You bring up a very difficult point. For instance, what is the meaning of Hölderlin's last poems? What did Hegel think of Hölderlin? There is a deep question. At a certain point, Hölderlin wrote to Hegel, who was going through a crisis of melancholy in Frankfort, "You will recover, but I won't." The question is, which one touched the depth of the absolute: the one who didn't recover, Hölderlin, or the one who recovered and maintained communication, Hegel? And here you have me, because I can't reply to the heart of the question. What is the meaning of Hölderlin's last poems, the poems of insanity, in relation to the Hegelian discourse? You have a very good point, because there is something which is quite superior to all eloquence, in the best sense of the term. I cannot exclude that speech which is so condensed as to evoke silence—Hegel follows its trail wherever he meets it. In regard to the final speech which triumphs over the unhappy consciousness, yes, of course, you are right. Hegel admitted it also. You know for Leibniz this is the least bad of all possible worlds. The least bad, that is something prodigious. Hegel and Leibniz are very much alike; they both have a sort of prodigious speculative power, and they are both realists. You have a very good question in regard to poetry. Once again, is there something in poetic thought which escapes speech and language? You could not have taken a detour that would have made it more impossible for me to answer you simply by *speaking*. Is poetry superior to philosophy?

POULET: But poetry is still language.

HYPPOLITE: To be sure, you are providing me with an argument. It is *another* language and this other language—there, I concede.

RICHARD MACKSEY: I am reminded of a poet who is sometimes reproached for trying to be philosophical, Wallace Stevens. In his essay "A Collect of Philosophy," which was, by the way, refused by a professional journal and remained unpublished at the poet's death, he plays with parallels and oppositions between the philosophic and the poetic activities. He quotes from his correspondence with Jean Wahl on this topic, where the latter speaks of the relationship of Novalis to Fichte, Hölderlin to Hegel, Hegel to Mallarmé, and so on. But Stevens insists that the poet and the philosopher occupy adjacent and not identical linguistic worlds: they share the habit of forming concepts and they both seek a kind of integration of these concepts in their works, but Stevens quickly and gnomically adds that the poet's "integration" is intended to be "effective." He says that the philosopher, once he has been given his initial donnée, "walks" carefully, deliberately, in language while the poet is "light-footed" and is concerned with the immediate rather than the mediated. To be sure, in his own poetry Stevens seems to be concerned with the criticism of his own fictions, with his own predication, in a way which is almost reminiscent of your description of Hegel's enterprise, but this is all intended to be in his phrase "effective" rather than "fateful" (mimetic rather than discursive someone else might say). Yet he concludes this rather unsatisfying essay on differences with a phrase he borrows from his correspondence with Jean Paulhan, a phrase which hardly resolves the ancient antagonism of which Plato speaks, but a formula which Stevens feels unites the poet and the philosopher in their separate vocations: the need to create "confidence in the world," however differently those worlds may then be explored. Against the negation of death which fascinated Hegel too, in the impending silence of his last poems, Stevens, his own "credible hero," keeps reaffirming through the very obliqueness and partiality of his language this confidence at the center of his poetic utterance:

> It was not important that they survive.
> What mattered was that they should bear

> Some lineament or character,
> Some affluence, if only half-perceived,
> In the poverty of their words,
> Of the planet of which they were part.

RENÉ GIRARD: You have spoken of Hegel's interpretation of *Don Quixote*, which seems to me to reveal the whole historical myth of the *Phenomenology*. Don Quixote is essentially the hero who refuses the *prose du monde*. That is, he is the hero of the past, the hero who belongs to a finished world. This interpretation, as we know, has dominated all the reading of Cervantes ever since, Marxist reading in particular. But we know that this interpretation is false, and there are many ways of showing it, though I shall cite only one point. That is the chapter where Don Quixote is in a printer's shop and where he sees his own novel printed, and says "my character will be multiplied to infinity." One can easily see there a kind of prophecy of what happens in our world, not only with reading, but with the other means of reproduction of word and image. It seems to me that your talk and Hegel himself unite the idea of the novel, the *Bildungsroman*, to that of the *Phenomenology*. It seems to me that the structure of the novel is quite different from the passage from a *tabula rasa* to the sort of accumulation of knowledge which is made, with a lot of contradiction perhaps, in Hegel. It seems to me that the word *Bildungsroman* in German can be translated by the word *desengaño*, or the French word, *éducation*, that is, the novel in the sense of Cervantes. Myth is always present in the individual, and if one looks at the structure of the novel, far from diminishing more and more to be replaced by "true knowledge," on the contrary, the myth extends further and further. In the second part of *Don Quixote*, all the characters become insane, and especially those who, wanting to ridicule Don Quixote, imagine that they know the truth, and, in reality, fall into the trap which he, unknowingly, sets for them. Also I think of your article in which you compare the *Phenomenology* to myth, an article which I admire very much, but where it seems to me that there is, after all, an essential difference between the movement of myth and the movement of the *Phenomenology*, one which is not recognized. The difference is that in myth, Oedipus's illusion becomes better and better formulated in the course of the myth; it becomes deeper and more intensified. Consequently, I would personally interpret the *Phenomenology* as a myth *manqué* or as the outline of a myth, rather than as a myth. It seems to me that today myth expresses language and temporality, as well as the relationship between myself and another, much better than does the *Phenomenology*. But this brings in the question of the conclusion. You say that it is impossible to be Hegelian because of the reconciliation, and I agree with you, to the degree that the reconciliation is *catharsis*. But I say that the *Phenomenology* is a myth, a myth *manqué*, to the degree to which it reproduces structure, and to be a myth *manqué* is something extraordinary after all, something that very few works are. But precisely what we must succeed in conceiving is the distance between the conclusion of the *Phenomenology*, interpreted as reconciliation, that is as *catharsis*, and the experience of the conclusion of myth, which is a fleeting revelation of truth, but a unique revelation, and in *death*, not in general reconciliation.

HYPPOLITE: I am very sorry that Lanson didn't let me go to Spain to become acquainted with so many interpretations of *Don Quixote* —a work which will never cease to be interpreted. Nevertheless, perhaps you have read the book of Marthe Robert on *Don Quixote* and *The Castle*. And I am tempted to answer you that when Don Quixote notices that books are being made on Don Quixote, yes, he becomes a part of literature—that is what Hegel means. The problem of Don Quixote meeting the *prose du monde* becomes the problem of going to see if literature is, in fact, *in* the world. But if, by chance, literature were *not* in the world, were something totally other, then Don Quixote would to a large extent be stranded, left high and dry. The problem of Don Quixote becoming a hero of literature is the failure of Don Quixote as himself, as an individual.

GIRARD: Is Don Quixote really a work of the past? Is there a *prose du monde?* Or, on the contrary, are we entering into an era which is more mythical than any previous era, precisely because it believes itself deprived of myth?

HYPPOLITE: Yes, Hegel's interpretation of *Don Quixote*, especially in the *Aesthetic*, is in fact the passage to the *prose du monde* in which there are still novels but no more epics. The *prose du monde* is the universal separation of law, economy, and men, who are obliged to pass through abstraction. And I see there is nevertheless something very profound which you have failed to rescue. That is the problem of Don Quixote generating a literature, in saying that Don Quixote recognizes that he is now in books. Because the question is precisely to know whether books are in the world. The question is to know, if we remain within literature, can we—you seem to have a confidence that I don't have—can we construct new myths today, myths of the future?

GIRARD: I say, on the contrary, that perhaps we *are* in a myth which we don't recognize. It is not a question of constructing myths, but of recognizing the ones that we are now living and from which we believe ourselves to be free.

HYPPOLITE: In regard to what you have said of the myth *manqué* in Hegel—I think that it is *demythification* which is *manqué* in Hegel. Here we come back to my study of the "Preface" to the *Phenomenology*: to what degree does philosophy conserve the creative power of the novel and yet remain critical? It is the unity of these two things which comprises philosophical discourse. It is to be at the same time itself and the criticism of itself, and for there to be no separation between itself and the criticism. That doesn't answer your problem, which is one of the many interpretations of the *Don Quixote* (which have no end), but it does respond to Don Quixote's problem, for if he sees that he is in a book, then that's the end of it; he has become himself a chivalric novel in fact.

NORMAN HOLLAND: I wanted not so much to ask a question as to make a comment, and perhaps a naïve comment, on Professor Hyppolite's paper. You introduced a word which I thought was tabu at this conference, namely *style*. And to me as an English critic, this has a very wide usage. To take a crude example, I learned recently that the first thing General DeGaulle wrote was a tragedy in the manner of Corneille. And one could say, in fact I'm sure the American State Department might say, that he is still writing a tragedy in the manner of Corneille. But the point is that one would use style both for his language and his writing, and also for his political behavior. So I would ask M. Hyppolite why he didn't use the word *structure* in speaking in a combined way of Hegel's language as well as his method of thought or does he feel this would be an inappropriate use of the word? Alternately, I would ask M. Poulet and M. Barthes if they would feel that the word structure would be more appropriate?

HYPPOLITE: If I didn't use the word *structure* it was no doubt to avoid a word that is, shall I say, too fashionable: but I certainly don't refuse to use it: it is in the title of my paper. If you think that the word *structure* points toward both method and style, I agree with you. However, the question is what is a structure and what do we mean when we use the word *structure*. A structure is a whole in which the terms are determined by the whole and mutually determine each other within the whole. I think that in Hegel there is no method separable from the development, taken in itself. That is, there is no structure of method anterior to the structure of the discourse itself. That is very difficult for the structuralists to conceive of. That is why they have more recourse to Leibniz, who is the real father of their thought. For Leibniz first has structural models which function in very different cases. Do we find something of this order in Hegel, inasmuch as there is an eidetic reduction? Hegel doesn't speak of X or Y, but he has carried out a reduction of meanings to a structure of meanings, certainly. In every chapter of the *Phenomenology* there are reductions of this order. He says himself in the "Preface," in that astonishing sentence, that it is *things* which essentialize themselves. It is here that we must reverse the question: Where does the fact of an eidetic reduction serve? It is the philosopher who, by variations, determines the meanings. But for Hegel, it is *things* which show themselves in their essence. They carry out their own eidetic reduction. Hegelian thought is in one sense a very reified, realistic thought. You will excuse me for not developing too much. If you want to say that structure, style, and method are connected, I grant it to you. If you want to ask me more about structure, that is very difficult. I am not refusing, it is simply that we would have to discuss the usage of the word *structure*. I think it is correct to use the word for Hegel, but . . .

REINHARDT KUHN: After what M. Poulet said about poetic language and what M. Girard said about the language of the novel, I have gained the courage to ask a question which may seem to you like "the stammering of an ordinary consciousness." At the beginning of your talk you spoke of the difference between philosophic language and literary language. And if I followed you correctly, the two essential differences were that philosophic language is based on what you called a norm of truth, and the second difference was that philosophic language carries its own criticism in itself. Then you spoke of Robbe-Grillet and of the failure of the attempt to combine critical and literary thinking. I am completely in agreement with you. There is, in my opinion, especially in Robbe-Grillet's weakest novels, a distance between literary language and critical language. However, it seems to me that in most great novelists and even poets there is a combination of poetic and critical language. I am thinking of Stendhal and of Mallarmé. This especially troubled me when you defined the philosophical statement, which seemed to me to be the poetic statement, or, more precisely, the poetic statement of Mallarmé.

HYPPOLITE: What you say doesn't appear at all like "the stammerings of ordinary consciousness." Everything you say interests me and appears to be within the scope of my own problematic. You said that there are novelists or poets who are at the same time critics of themselves, in whom critical language accompanies poetic language. I don't dispute that, but while it is characteristic of philosophical language, it is not absolutely characteristic of poetic language. In philosophic language criticism is not isolated, on the contrary, it is creative. And you take as an example one who is said to have been a Hegelian. I don't know whether he was, but there are resemblances; for his thought is a message and a message about the message. That is the throw of dice that will never abolish chance. Even when it came from extraordinary circumstances, when it is like a constellation, this strange success is an emergence of meaning—and it is also something of this order that Hegel is seeking. As an example, Mallarmé couldn't please me more. I don't dispute that there are literary works which are *also* philosophical works. Are philosophical works also literary works? We are touching on what I wanted to do in speaking of the status of the philosophical work. And M. Poulet was, in speaking of the density of Leibniz, making a literary criticism of a philosophical work, just as I tried to show that Hegel studied the style and the rhythm of the philosopher. This aspect particularly interests me, and I don't think that in philosophy today we can do anything else but attempt with the critic to do for philosophy what the technical sciences are developing. I am trying to situate the work of philosophy and you render me a service in confronting it with literary works, which I am also trying to situate.

PAUL DE MAN: For me, what was missing in your talk, when you spoke about what remains present and real for us in Hegel, was the passage, the point of departure from everyday facticity, then the return to everyday facticity through the mediation of a coherent language. You didn't speak of the moment of negation, nor of what seems to me to remain central in Hegel, namely, the problem of death, that you have commented upon with a great deal of eloquence in your own works on Hegel. The problem of death, the problem of negation, which seems to be the most difficult problem on the level of language, is connected with the opposition which you proposed (in response to

M. Derrida) between the *belle âme* which would be the poetic soul and philosophical language. You make use of something which has not been established, that is, that in the passage of the *Phenomenology* where Hegel speaks of the *belle âme*, it is Hölderlin of whom he is thinking. In any case it would not be the Hölderlin of the end. And this Hölderlin does not differ from Hegel as the poetic *belle âme* differs from philosophical discourse, but rather as one who has become totally de-mystified through a real experience of death in contrast to one who knows this experience only through the others, as was, after all, the case for Hegel.

My last remark is addressed to M. Girard. I don't understand how he accuses the *Phenomenology* of not having faced the problem of death or of having replaced this problematic with a mythological vision, in which I don't recognize, in any case, the work of a phenomenologist, Heidegger, who, on the problem of death, seems to me to have taken up again certain essential themes of the Hegelian tradition.

HYPPOLITE: To be sure, I didn't speak about death. But I will ask you a question: the *belle âme* in Hegel's *Phenomenology* disappears like a vapor in the air. It is what I have called a lost meaning. And so, Hegel's whole effort is to redeem [*récupérer*] death: does he succeed? I don't believe he does. Furthermore, I don't believe there is any way of redeeming death. Hegel has only transformed death into negation. We can discover, on the contrary, that negation is death: we can go in this circle. In my talk, I have given a certain place to death, that of lost meaning, although this is not exactly the place that Hegel gives it. For, in fact, everything that Hegel recovers from death is everything that is not a lost meaning. Hegel spoke of passage, but also of determination and of fixation. What is called death in the "Preface" is fixation. What is understanding? It is to divide and to fix to such a degree that movement is introduced at the center of things. In that way, he thinks that negation appears in a determination (that limitations at their extreme become negation?). What relationship is there between death and negation and how can death pass into language? I am quite willing to say that it does this, but the question is to know whether it is completely overcome in the passage. I would agree with M. Poulet here: there is a part which is not redeemed. That is not to say that thought is not redeemed, but in any case there is something which is not redeemable, and I would not follow Hegel to the end; I can't.

Of Structure as an Inmixing of an Otherness Prerequisite to Any Subject Whatever[1]

Jacques Lacan
Ecole Freudienne de Paris

Somebody spent some time this afternoon trying to convince me that it would surely not be a pleasure for an English-speaking audience to listen to my bad accent and that for me to speak in English would constitute a risk for what one might call the transmission of my message. Truly, for me it is a great case of conscience, because to do otherwise would be absolutely contrary to my own conception of the message: of the message as I will explain it to you, of the linguistic message. Many people talk nowadays about messages everywhere, inside the organism a hormone is a message, a beam of light to obtain teleguidance to a plane or from a satellite is a message, and so on; but the message in language is absolutely different. The message, our message, in all cases comes from the Other by which I understand "from the place of the Other." It certainly is not the common other, the other with a lower-case *o*, and this is why I have given a capital *O* as the initial letter to the Other of whom I am now speaking. Since in this case, here in Baltimore, it would seem that the Other is naturally English-speaking, it would really be doing myself violence to speak French. But the question that this person raised, that it would perhaps be difficult and even a little ridiculous for me to speak English, is an important argument and I also know that there are many French-speaking people present who do not understand English at all; for these my choice

[1] Since Dr. Lacan, as he remarks in his introduction, chose to deliver his communication alternately in English and French (and at points in a composite of the two languages), this text represents an edited transcription and paraphrase of his address.

of English would be a security, but perhaps I would not wish them to be so secure and in this case I shall speak a little French as well.

First, let me put forth some advice about structure, which is the subject matter of our meeting. It may happen that there will be mistakes, confusion, more and more approximative uses of this notion, and I think that soon there will be some sort of fad about this word. For me it is different because I have used this term for a very long time—since the beginning of my teaching. The reason why something about my position is not better known is that I addressed myself only to a very special audience, namely one of psychoanalysts. Here there are some very peculiar difficulties, because psychoanalysts really know something of what I was talking to them about and that this thing is a particularly difficult thing to cope with for anybody who practises psychoanalysis. The subject is not a simple thing for the psychoanalysts who have something to do with the subject proper. In this case I wish to avoid misunderstandings, *méconnaissances*, of my position. *Méconnaissance* is a French word which I am obliged to use because there is no equivalent in English. *Méconnaissance* precisely implies the subject in its meaning—and I was also advised that it is not so easy to talk about the "subject" before an English-speaking audience. *Méconnaissance* is not to *méconnaitre* my subjectivity. What exactly is in question is the status of the problem of the structure.

When I began to teach something about psychoanalysis I lost some of my audience, because I had perceived long before then the simple fact that if you open a book of Freud, and particularly those books which are properly about the unconscious, you can be absolutely sure —it is not a probability but a certitude—to fall on a page where it is not only a question of words—naturally in a book there are always words, many printed words—but words which are the object through which one seeks for a way to handle the unconscious. Not even the meaning of the words, but words in their flesh, in their material aspect. A great part of the speculations of Freud is about punning in a dream, or *lapsus*, or what in French we call *calembour, homonymie*, or still the division of a word into many parts with each part taking on a new meaning after it is broken down. It is curious to note, even if in this case it is not absolutely proven, that words are the only material of the unconscious. It is not proven but it is probable (and in any case I have never said that the unconscious was an assemblage of words, but that the unconscious is precisely structured). I don't think there is such an English word but it is necessary to have this

Jacques Lacan

term, as we are talking about structure and the unconscious is structured as a language. What does that mean?

Properly speaking this is a redundancy because "structured" and "as a language" for me mean exactly the same thing. Structured means my speech, my lexicon, etc., which is exactly the same as a language. And that is not all. Which language? Rather than myself it was my pupils that took a great deal of trouble to give that question a different meaning, and to search for the formula of a reduced language. What are the minimum conditions, they ask themselves, necessary to constitute a language? Perhaps only four *signantes*, four signifying elements are enough. It is a curious exercise which is based on a complete error, as I hope to show you on the board in a moment. There were also some philosophers, not many really but some, of those present at my seminar in Paris who have found since then that it was not a question of an "under" language or of "another" language, not myth for instance or phonemes, but language. It is extraordinary the pains that all took to change the place of the question. Myths, for instance, do not take place in our consideration precisely because they are also structured as a language, and when I say "as a language" it is not as some special sort of language, for example, mathematical language, semiotical language, or cinematographical language. Language is language and there is only one sort of language: concrete language— English or French for instance—that people talk. The first thing to state in this context is that there is no meta-language. For it is necessary that all so called meta-languages be presented to you with language. You cannot teach a course in mathematics using only letters on the board. It is always necessary to speak an ordinary language that is understood.

It is not only because the material of the unconscious is a linguistic material, or as we say in French *langagier*, that the unconscious is structured as a language. The question that the unconscious raises for you is a problem that touches the most sensitive point of the nature of language, that is the question of the subject. The subject cannot simply be identified with the speaker or the personal pronoun in a sentence. In French the *ennoncé* is exactly the sentence, but there are many *ennoncés* where there is no index of him who utters the *ennoncé*. When I say "it rains," the subject of the enunciation is not part of the sentence. In any case here there is some sort of difficulty. The subject cannot always be identified with what the linguists call "the shifter."

The question that the nature of the unconscious puts before us is, in a few words, that something always *thinks*. Freud told us that the unconscious is above all thoughts, and that which thinks is barred from consciousness. This bar has many applications, many possibilities with regard to meaning. The main one is that it is really a barrier, a barrier which it is necessary to jump over or to pass through. This is important because if I don't emphasize this barrier all is well for you. As we say in French, *ça vous arrange*, because if something thinks in the floor below or underground things are simple; thought is always there and all one needs is a little consciousness on the thought that the living being is naturally thinking and all is well. If such were the case, thought would be prepared by life, naturally, such as instinct for instance. If thought is a natural process, then the unconscious is without difficulty. But the unconscious has nothing to do with instinct or primitive knowledge or preparation of thought in some underground. It is a thinking with words, with thoughts that escape your vigilance, your state of watchfulness. The question of vigilance is important. It is as if a demon plays a game with your watchfulness. The question is to find a precise status for this other subject which is exactly the sort of subject that we can determine taking our point of departure in language.

When I prepared this little talk for you, it was early in the morning. I could see Baltimore through the window and it was a very interesting moment because it was not quite daylight and a neon sign indicated to me every minute the change of time, and naturally there was heavy traffic, and I remarked to myself that exactly all that I could see, except for some trees in the distance, was the result of thoughts, actively thinking thoughts, where the function played by the subjects was not completely obvious. In any case the so-called *Dasein*, as a definition of the subject, was there in this rather intermittent or fading spectator. The best image to sum up the unconscious is Baltimore in the early morning.

Where is the subject? It is necessary to find the subject as a lost object. More precisely this lost object is the support of the subject and in many cases is a more abject thing than you may care to consider—in some cases it is something done, as all psychoanalysts and many people who have been psychoanalyzed know perfectly well. That is why many psychoanalysts prefer to return to a general psychology, as the President of the New York Psychoanalytical Society tells us we ought to do. But I cannot change things, I am a psychoanalyst and if someone prefers to address himself to a professor of psychology that is his affair. The question of the structure, since we

Jacques Lacan

are talking of psychology, is not a term that only I use. For a long time thinkers, searchers, and even inventors who were concerned with the question of the mind, have over the years put forward the idea of unity as the most important and characteristic trait of structure. Conceived as something which is already in the reality of the organism it is obvious. The organism when it is mature is a unit and functions as a unit. The question becomes more difficult when this idea of unity is applied to the function of the mind, because the mind is not a totality in itself, but these ideas in the form of the intentional unity were the basis, as you know, of all of the so-called phenomenological movement.

The same was also true in physics and psychology with the so-called Gestalt school and the notion of *bonne forme* whose function was to join, for instance, a drop of water and more complicated ideas, and great psychologists, and even the psychoanalysts, are full of the idea of "total personality." At any rate, it is always the unifying unity which is in the foreground. I have never understood this, for if I am a psychoanalyst I am also a man, and as a man my experience has shown me that the principal characteristic of my own human life and, I am sure, that of the people who are here—and if anybody is not of this opinion I hope that he will raise his hand—is that life is something which goes, as we say in French, *à la dérive*. Life goes down the river, from time to time touching a bank, staying for a while here and there, without understanding anything—and it is the principle of analysis that nobody understands anything of what happens. The idea of the unifying unity of the human condition has always had on me the effect of a scandalous lie.

We may try to introduce another principle to understand these things. If we rarely try to understand things from the point of view of the unconscious, it is because the unconscious tells us something articulated in words and perhaps we could try to search for their principle.

I suggest you consider the unity in another light. Not a unifying unity but the countable unity one, two, three. After fifteen years I have taught my pupils to count at most up to five which is difficult (four is easier) and they have understood that much. But for tonight permit me to stay at two. Of course, what we are dealing with here is the question of the integer, and the question of integers is not a simple one as I think many people here know. To count, of course, is not difficult. It is only necessary to have, for instance, a certain number of sets and a one-to-one correspondence. It is true for example that there are exactly as many people sitting in this room as there are seats. But it is necessary to have a collection composed of integers to constitute an integer, or what is called a natural number. It is, of course, in part natural but only in the sense that we do not understand why it exists. Counting is not an empirical fact and it is impossible to deduce the act of counting from empirical data alone. Hume tried but Frege demonstrated perfectly the ineptitude of the attempt. The real difficulty lies in the fact that every integer is in itself a unit. If I take two as a unit, things are very enjoyable, men and women for instance —love plus unity! But after a while it is finished, after these two there is nobody, perhaps a child, but that is another level and to generate three is another affair. When you try to read the theories of mathematicians regarding numbers you find the formula "*n* plus 1" ($n + 1$) as the basis of all the theories. It is this question of the "one more" that is the key to the genesis of numbers and instead of this unifying unity that constitutes two in the first case I propose that you consider the real numerical genesis of two.

It is necessary that this two constitute the first integer which is not yet born as a number before the two appears. You have made this possible because the *two* is here to grant existence to the first *one*: put *two* in the place of *one* and consequently in the place of the *two* you see *three* appear. What we have here is something which I can call the *mark*. You already have something which is marked or something which is not marked. It is with the first mark that we have the status of the thing. It is exactly in this fashion that Frege explains the genesis of the number; the class which is characterized by no elements is the first class; you have one at the place of zero and afterward it is easy to understand how the place of one becomes the second place which makes place for two, three, and so on. The question of the two is for us the question of the subject, and here we reach a fact of psychoanalytical experience in as much as the two does not complete the one to make two, but must repeat the one to permit the one to exist. This first repetition is the only one necessary to explain the genesis of the number, and only one repetition is necessary to constitute the status of the subject. The unconscious subject is something that tends to repeat itself, but only one such repetition is necessary to constitute it. However, let us look more precisely at what is necessary for the second to repeat the first in order that we may have a repetition. This question cannot be answered too quickly. If you answer too quickly, you will answer that it is necessary that they are the same. In this case the principle of the two would be that of twins—and why not triplets or quintuplets? In my day we used to teach children that they must not add, for instance, microphones with dictionaries; but this is absolutely absurd, because we would not have addition if we were not able to add microphones with dictionaries or as Lewis Carroll says, cabbages with kings. The sameness is not in *things* but in the *mark* which makes it possible to add things with no consideration as to their differences. The mark has the effect of rubbing out the difference, and this is the key to what happens to the subject, the unconscious subject in the repetition; because you know that this subject repeats something peculiarly significant, the subject is here, for instance, in this obscure thing that we call in some cases trauma, or exquisite pleasure. What happens? If the "thing" exists in this symbolic structure, if this unitary trait is decisive, the trait of the sameness is here. In order that the "thing" which is sought be here in you, it is necessary that the first trait be rubbed out because the trait itself is a modification. It is the taking away of all difference, and in this case, without the trait, the first "thing" is simply lost. The key to this insistence in repetition is that in its essence repetition as repetition of the symbolical sameness is impossible. In any case, the subject is the effect of this repetition in as much as it necessitates the "fading," the obliteration, of the first foundation of the subject, which is why the subject, by status, is always presented as a divided essence. The trait, I insist, is identical, but it assures the difference only of identity—not by effect of sameness or difference but by the difference of identity. This is easy to understand: as we say in French, *je vous numérotte*, I give you each a number; and this assures the fact that you are numerically different but nothing more than that.

What can we propose to intuition in order to show that the trait be found in something which is at the same time one or two? Consider the following diagram which I call an inverted eight, after a well-known figure:

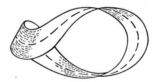

You can see that the line in this instance may be considered either as one or as two lines. This diagram can be considered the basis of a sort of essential inscription at the origin, in the knot which constitutes the subject. This goes much further than you may think at first, because you can search for the sort of surface able to receive such inscriptions. You can perhaps see that the sphere, that old symbol for totality, is unsuitable. A torus, a Klein bottle, a cross-cut surface, are able to receive such a cut. And this diversity is very important as it explains many things about the structure of mental disease. If one can symbolize the subject by this fundamental cut, in the same way one can show that a cut on a torus corresponds to the neurotic subject, and on a cross-cut surface to another sort of mental disease. I will not explain this to you tonight, but to end this difficult talk I must make the following precision.

I have only considered the beginning of the series of the integers, because it is an intermediary point between language and reality. Language is constituted by the same sort of unitary traits that I have used to explain the one and the one more. But this trait in language is not identical with the unitary trait, since in language we have a collection of differential traits. In other words, we can say that language is constituted by a set of signifiers—for example, *ba, ta, pa,* etc., etc.—a set which is finite. Each signifier is able to support the same process with regard to the subject, and it is very probable that the process of the integers is only a special case of this relation between signifiers. The definition of this collection of signifiers is that they constitute what I call the Other. The difference afforded by the existence of language is that each signifier (contrary to the unitary trait of the integer number) is, in most cases, not identical with itself—precisely because we have a collection of signifiers, and in this collection one signifier may or may not designate itself. This is well known and is the principle of Russell's paradox. If you take the set of all elements which are not members of themselves,

$$x \notin x$$

the set that you constitute with such elements leads you to a paradox which, as you know, leads to a contradiction. In simple terms, this only means that in a universe of discourse nothing contains everything, and here you find again the gap that constitutes the subject. The subject is the introduction of a loss in reality, yet nothing can introduce that, since by status reality is as full as possible. The notion of a loss is the effect afforded by the instance of the trait which is what, with the intervention of the letter you determine, places—say a_1 a_2 a_3—and the places are spaces, for a lack. When the subject takes the place of the lack, a loss is introduced in the word, and this is the definition of the subject. But to inscribe it, it is necessary to define it in a circle,

Jacques Lacan

what I call the otherness, of the sphere of language. All that is language is lent from this otherness and this is why the subject is always a fading thing that runs under the chain of signifiers. For the definition of a signifier is that it represents a subject not for another subject but for another signifier. This is the only definition possible of the signifier as different from the sign. The sign is something that represents something for somebody, but the signifier is something that represents a subject for another signifier. The consequence is that the subject disappears exactly as in the case of the two unitary traits, while under the second signifier appears what is called meaning or signification; and then in sequence the other signifiers appear and other significations.

The question of desire is that the fading subject yearns to find itself again by means of some sort of encounter with this miraculous thing defined by the phantasm. In its endeavor it is sustained by that which I call the lost object that I evoked in the beginning—which is such a terrible thing for the imagination. That which is produced and maintained here, and which in my vocabulary I call the object, lower-case, *a*, is well known by all psychoanalysts as all psychoanalysis is founded on the existence of this peculiar object. But the relation between this barred subject with this object (*a*) is the structure which is always found in the phantasm which supports desire, in as much as desire is only that which I have called the metonomy of all signification.

In this brief presentation I have tried to show you what the question of the structure is inside the psychoanalytical reality. I have not, however, said anything about such dimensions as the imaginary and the symbolical. It is, of course, absolutely essential to understand how the symbolic order can enter inside the *vécu*, lived experienced, of mental life, but I cannot tonight put forth such an explanation. Consider, however, that which is at the same time the least known and the most certain fact about this mythical subject which is the sensible phase of the living being: this fathomless thing capable of experiencing something between birth and death, capable of covering the whole spectrum of pain and pleasure in a word, what in French we call the *sujet de la jouissance*. When I came here this evening I saw on the little neon sign the motto "Enjoy Coca-Cola." It reminded me that in English, I think, there is no term to designate precisely this enormous weight of meaning which is in the French word *jouissance*—or in the Latin *fruor*. In the dictionary I looked up *jouir* and found "to possess, to use," but it is not that at all. If the living being is something at all thinkable, it will be above all as subject of the *jouissance*; but this psychological law that we call the pleasure principle (and which is only the principle of displeasure) is very soon to create a barrier to all *jouissance*. If I am enjoying myself a little too much, I begin to feel pain and I moderate my pleasures. The organism seems made to avoid too much *jouissance*. Probably we would all be as quiet as oysters if it were not for this curious organization which forces us to disrupt the barrier of pleasure or perhaps only makes us dream of forcing and disrupting this barrier. All that is elaborated by the subjective construction on the scale of the signifier in its relation to the Other and which has its root in language is only there to permit the full spectrum of desire to allow us to approach, to test, this sort of forbidden *jouissance* which is the only valuable meaning that is offered to our life.

Discussion

ANGUS FLETCHER: Freud was really a very simple man. But he found very diverse solutions to human problems. He sometimes used myths to explain human difficulties and problems; for example, the myth of Narcissus: he saw that there are men who look in the mirror and love themselves. It was as simple as that. He didn't try to float on the surface of words. What you're doing is like a spider: you're making a very delicate web without any human reality in it. For example, you were speaking of joy [*joie, jouissance*]. In French one of the meanings of *jouir* is the orgasm—I think that is most important here—why not say so? All the talk I have heard here has been so abstract! . . . It's not a question of psychoanalysis. The value of psychoanalysis is that it is a theory of psychological dynamism. The most important is what has come after Freud, with Wilhelm Reich especially. All this metaphysics is not necessary. The diagram was very interesting, but it doesn't seem to have any connection with the reality of our actions, with eating, sexual intercourse, and so on.

HARRY WOOLF: May I ask if this fundamental arithmetic and this topology are not in themselves a myth or merely at best an analogy for an explanation of the life of the mind?

JACQUES LACAN: Analogy to what? "S" designates something which can be written exactly as this S. And I have said that the "S" which designates the subject is instrument, matter, to symbolize a loss. A loss that you experience as a subject (and myself also). In other words, this gap between one thing which has marked meanings and this other thing which is my actual discourse that I try to put in the place where you are, you as not another subject but as people that are able to understand me. Where is the analogon? Either this loss exists or it doesn't exist. If it exists it is only possible to designate the loss by a system of symbols. In any case, the loss does not exist before this symbolization indicates its place. It is not an analogy. It is really in some part of the realities, this sort of torus. This torus really exists and it is exactly the structure of the neurotic. It is not an analogon; it is not even an abstraction, because an abstraction is some sort of diminution of reality, and I think it is reality itself.

NORMAN HOLLAND: I would like to come to Mr. Lacan's defense; it seems to me that he is doing something very interesting. Reading his paper before the colloquium was the first time I had encountered his work and it seems to me that he has returned to the *Project for a Scientific Psychology*, which was the earliest of Freud's psychological writings. It was very abstract and very like what you have written here, although you are doing it with algebra and he is doing it with neurons. The influence of this document is all through *The Interpretation of Dreams*, his letters to Fliess, and all the early writings, although often merely implicit.

ANTHONY WILDEN: If I may add something, you spoke at the beginning of your talk of repudiation or nonrecognition [*méconnaissance*], and we have begun with such an extreme case of this that I don't know how we're going to work our way out of it. But you have started at the top (at the most difficult point of your work), and it is very difficult for us to recognize the beginnings of this thought, which is very rich and very deep. In my opinion, as your unhappy translator, you are absolutely faithful to Freud and it is absolutely necessary for us to read your works before talking a lot of nonsense—which we may very well do here tonight. And after they have read your work, I would urge these gentlemen to *read Freud*.

RICHARD SCHECHNER: What is the relationship between your thought about nothingness and the work that Husserl and Sartre have done?

LACAN: "Nothingness," the word that you have used, I think that I can say almost nothing about it, nor about Husserl, nor about Sartre. Really, I don't believe that I have talked about nothingness. The sliding and the difficulty of seizing, the never-here (it is here when I search there; it is there when I am here) is not nothing. This year I shall announce, as a program of my seminar, this thing that I have entitled *La Logique du phantasme*. Most of my effort, I believe, will be to define the different sorts of lack, of loss, of void which are of absolutely different natures. An absence, for instance. The absence of the queen, it is necessary to make an addition with this sort of element, but to find the absence of the queen. . . . I think that the vagueness of the mere term *nothing* is not manageable in this context. I am late in everything I must develop, before I myself disappear. But it is also difficult enough to make the thing practicable to advance. It is necessary to proceed stage by stage. Now I will try this different sort of lack.

[M. Kott and Dr. Lacan discuss the properties of Möbius strips at the blackboard.]

JAN KOTT: There is a curious thing which is probably accidental. We find all these motifs in Surrealist painting. Is there any relationship here?

LACAN: At least I feel a great personal connection with Surrealist painting.

POULET: This loss of object which introduces the subject, would you say that it has any connection with the void [*le néant*] in Sartre's thinking? Would there be an analogy with the situation of the sleeper awakened that we find at the beginning of Proust's work? You remember, the dreamer awakens and discovers a feeling of loss, of an absence, which is moreover, an absence of himself. Is there any analogy?

LACAN: I think that Proust many times approached certain experiences of the unconscious. One often finds such a passage of a page or so in Proust which one can *découper* very clearly. I think you are right; Proust pushes it very close, but instead of developing theories he always comes back to his business, which is literature. To take the example of Mlle. Vinteuil, as seen by the narrator with her friend and her father's picture, I don't think that any other literary artist has ever brought out a thing like this. It may be because of the very project of his work, this fabulous enterprise of "time recovered"—this is what guided him, even beyond the limits of what is accessible to consciousness.

SIGMUND KOCH: I find a pattern constantly eluding me in your presentation, which I can only attribute to the fact that you spoke in English. You placed a great deal of emphasis on the integer 2 and on the generation of the integer 2. Your analysis is, as I recall, that if one starts with a unitary mark, then there is the universe of the nonmarked, which brings you, presumably, to the integer 2. What is the analogical correspondence between the marked and the unmarked? Is the marked the system of consciousness and the nonmarked the unconscious system? Is the marked the conscious subject and the nonmarked the unconscious subject?

LACAN: From Frege I only recalled that it is the class with characteristic numbers *o*, which is the foundation of the *1*. If I have chosen *2* for psychoanalytical reference, it is because the *2* is an important scheme of the Eros in Freud. The Eros is that power which in life is unifying, and it is the basis on which too many psychoanalysts found the conception of the genital maturity as a possibility of the so-called perfect marriage, for instance, which is a sort of mystical ideal end, which is promoted so imprudently. This *2* that I have chosen is only for an audience which is, at first, not initiated to this question of Frege. The *1* in relation with the *2* can, in this first approach, play the same role as the *o* in relation to the *1*.

For your second question, naturally, I was obliged to omit many technical things known by those who possess Freud perfectly. In the question of repression it is absolutely necessary to know that Freud put as the foundation of the possibility of repression something that in German is called the *Urverdrängung*. Naturally, I could not afford here the whole set of my formalization, but it is essential to know that a formalism of the metaphor is primary for me, to make understood what is, in Freudian terms, *condensation*. [Dr. Lacan concluded his comment with a reprise of "L'Instance de la lettre" at the blackboard.]

GOLDMANN: Working in my method on literature and culture, what strikes me is that in dealing with important, historical, collective phenomena and with important works, I never need the *unconscious* for my analysis. I do need the *nonconscious;* I made the distinction yesterday. Of course there are unconscious elements; of course I can't understand the means by which the individual is explaining himself— and that, I have said, is the domain of psychoanalysis, in which I don't want to mix. But there are two kinds of phenomena which, according to all the evidence, seem to be social and in which I must intervene with the nonconscious, but not the unconscious. I think you said that the unconscious is the ordinary language, English, French, that we all speak.

LACAN: I said *like* language, French or English, etc.

GOLDMANN: But it's independent from this language? Then I'll stop; I no longer have a question. It's linked to the language that one speaks in conscious life?

LACAN: Yes.

GOLDMANN: All right. The second thing that struck me, if I understood you. There were a certain number of analogies with processes that I find in consciousness, on the level where I get along without the unconscious. There is something that since Pascal, Hegel, Marx, and Sartre we know without recourse to the unconscious: man is defined by linking these invariants to difference. One doesn't act immediately dépasse l'homme" Pascal said. History and dynamism, even without reference to the unconscious, cannot be defined except by this lack. The second phenomenon I find on the level of consciousness: it seems obvious that consciousness, inasmuch as it is linked to action, cannot be formulated except by constituting invariants, that is objects, and by linking these invariants to difference. One doesn't act immediately on a multiplicity of givens. Action is closely linked to the constitution of invariants, which permit a certain order to be established in the difference. Language exists before this particular man exists—is this language (French, English, etc.) linked simply to the problem of the phantasm? There is no subject without symbol, language, and an object. My question is this: Is the formation of this symbolism and its modifications linked solely to the domain of the phantasm, the unconscious, and desire, or is it also linked to something called work, the transformation of the outside world, and social life? And if you admit that it is linked to these also the problem comes up: Where is the logic, where is the comprehensibility? I don't think that man is simply aspiration to totality. We are still facing a mixture, as I said the other day, but it is very important to separate the mixture in order to understand it.

LACAN: And do you think that work is one of the "mooring-points" that we can fasten to in this drift?

GOLDMANN: I think that, after all, mankind has done some very positive things.

LACAN: I don't have the impression that a history book is a very structured thing. This famous history, in which one sees things so well when they are past, doesn't seem to be a muse in which I can put all my trust. There was a time when Clio was very important—when Bossuet was writing. Perhaps again with Marx. But what I always expect from history is *surprises,* and surprises which I still haven't succeeded in explaining, although I have made great efforts to understand. I explain myself by different co-ordinates from yours. In particular, I wouldn't put the question of work in the front rank here.

Discussion

CHARLES MORAZÉ: I am happy to see in this discussion the use of the genesis of numbers. To reply to Mr. Goldmann, when I study history, I depend on this same genesis of numbers as the most solid reality. Apropos of this, I would like to ask this question to see if our postulates are really the same or different. It seems to me that you said at the beginning of your talk that for you the structure of consciousness is language, and then at the end you said the unconscious is structured like language. If your second formulation is the correct one, that is also mine.

LACAN: It is the unconscious that is structured like language—I never varied from that.

RICHARD MACKSEY: We have perhaps exhausted our quota of *méconnaissances* for this session, but I'm still a bit confused about the consequences which your invocation of Frege and Russell imply for your ontology (or at least your ontics). Thus, I'm concerned about the extreme realist position which your mathematical example would seem to imply. I'm not troubled by the argument that the incompletability theorem undermines realism, since Gödel himself has maintained his realist position, simply seeing the theorem as a basic limitation on the expressive power of symbolism. Rather, I think that the logistic thesis itself has been subjected to serious criticism. If the authors of the *Principia* attempt to define the natural numbers as certain particular sets of sets, apart from other metalinguistic difficulties in the theory of types one could counter that their derivation is arbitrary, since in a set theory, not based on a theory of types, "one" could be defined as, say, the set whose sole number is the empty set, and so on, so that the natural numbers could retain their conventional properties. Ergo, one might ask *which* set is the number one? A few months ago Paul Benacerraf carried this line of argument further, asserting that the irreducible characteristic of the natural numbers is simply that they form a recursive progression. Thus, any system that forms such a progression will do as well as the next; it's not the mark which particular numbers possess, but the interrelated, abstract *structure* (rather than the constituent objects) which gives the properties of the system. This attacks any realist position that equates numbers with entities or objects (and proposes a kind of conceptualist or nominalist structuralism).

LACAN: Without enlarging on this comment, I should say that concepts and even sets are not objects. I have never denied the structural aspect of the number system.

The Voice and the Literary Myth[1]

Guy Rosolato
Clinique Delay, Paris

In dealing first of all with the Voice and with what it tells us, I propose to take it as a starting point in order to retrace my way back to the literary myth itself, and this to the extent that the Voice serves to fix and locate the myth.

Among all the voices to be heard in the literary work, there is one which sets itself apart by its singularity: it seems to be independent of both the representations and

[1] "La Voix et le mythe littéraire." The text which follows is a translation of Dr. Rosolato's communication with some minor emendations and additions from the tape-recording. Certain capitalized terms have a privileged status in Lacanian psychoanalytic theory. For a concise discussion of the Symbolic [*le symbolique* or *l'ordre symbolique*, which is to be distinguished from *la symbolique* or *die Symbolik*, a descriptive, comparative inventory of signs], see Rosolato, "Le Symbolique," *La Psychanalyse*, V (1959): 225-33. For the Name of the Father [*le nom du père*] as "the signifier of the function of the father," see Lacan, "D'une question préliminaire à tout traitement possible de la psychose," *Ecrits* (Paris, 1966), pp. 531-83, a theoretical article to which Dr. Rosolato refers in the course of his communication, as well as a shorter discussion in Lacan, 'La Psychanalyse et son enseignement," *op. cit.*, pp. 437-58. For the notion of the Dead Father [*le père mort*, which plays on *le mort* or 'dummy," as in bridge], see Lacan, "Le Mythe individuel du névrosé ou 'Poésie et vérité' dans la névrosé," Paris, 1953 [mimeographed]. For a discussion of the spoken Word [*la parole*] which has influenced Lévi-Strauss as well as Lacan, see Maurice Leenhardt, *Do Kamo: La personne et le mythe dans le monde mélanésien* (Paris, 1947), Ch. IX and X. Finally, an English translation of Lacan's crucial essay "Fonction et champ de la parole et du langage en psychanalyse," with extensive commentary and notes by Anthony Wilden, is available in *The Language of the Self* (Baltimore, 1968). All notes and citations to the present essay have been supplied by the translator.

Guy Rosolato

the masks of the work, so that even if it reaches us as if through a veil, even if it is only a refracted voice, it is not necessarily indefinable. This voice is not that of the protagonists of the narrative, nor that of the author, nor is it the voice of the "narrator."

Can we define it more precisely and go beyond these purely negative characteristics?

The term "double" is often used in relation to the work of art. It is with the *subject*, therefore, that our explorations should begin.

The aesthetic movement is played in two registers. Generally speaking, it can be said that its celebration depends upon a fundamental oscillation between *metonymic organization* and *metaphorical substitution*, in other words, between the two constitutive modes of language. The most deliberately metonymic work, the most descriptive or most realistic work culminates in a metaphor which it secretly sustains by the continuity of its narrative, and which is revealed at certain points, notably at its end: metaphor of a "life," a "reality," an "object" thus put into the flow of the work, defined by the limits of the book and by the break of its ending. Whatever fascination is exerted by the work is a result of this metaphoro-metonymic movement. Inversely, a poetic text, the most dense with metaphors, must rely on a metonymic articulation, on a flexibility of interpretation which gives it a completely subjective coherence, momentary, variable, but certainly discernible.

Consequently this oscillation assures—by means of the possibility of doubling of meanings—a correlative duplication as both sender [*destinateur*] and addressee [*destinataire*] of the message: when I use the term *double* it is relating to this effect of correspondence between these two duplications. It already appears that representation cannot be understood in its most conventional meaning, as a sort of copy of the outside world: it is a question of an auto-representation, in which the work finds itself within itself by a symmetry which is successively destroyed and reborn, parallel to the metaphoro-metonymic oscillation. This doubling can even be represented in the work as a sort of baring of its inner workings [*ressort*]: doubling of characters (as in the *Tales of Hoffmann*) or doubling of the *récit* (precisely as shown by J. Ricardou).[2] This auto-representation, which concerns the very construction and progress of the work, also contains—let me emphasize this—a reminder, *a correspondence with the splitting of the subject.*

Can it therefore be said that this voice I spoke of—which for greater

[2] Jean Ricardou, "L'Histoire dans l'histoire," *Critique* no. 231–32 (1966): 711–29, a discussion of the fiction of Novalis and Poe.

202

clarity I shall call the *relative voice*—depends only upon this doubling effect? It is no doubt related to it as its basis, but it also serves as a link between this organization and another, ternary, organization, which I shall consider in a moment.

Let it be noted for the moment that this voice is first and foremost an anonymous voice. It is present like a thread woven through the narrative, and yet it is outside it, "off-stage." What must be demonstrated, therefore, is how it detaches itself from the particular voices in the text, and by what means—means which will naturally be those proper to fascination—it imposes this difference and this distance. What is more, the very fact of its being anonymous implies something about it: that its task is to focus our attention upon a secret, upon a vanishing point, near which is to be found the question of the Name.

Let me begin, then, by examining this first relationship, this fact of the relative voice being out of phase in relation to the protagonists, by distinguishing a series of three oppositions.

1) In the first place, let us consider what is related to the third person (*il*) (the non-person) in the form of the narrated event [*l'énoncé*] in relation to what depends on the first two persons, mainly on the first (*je*), which, as the subject, puts the speech event [*l'énonciation*] in question. (And this relationship which links the process of the narrated event [*énoncé*] to its protagonists, without reference to the speech even [*l'énonciation*], has very properly been defined as a *voice* by Roman Jakobson.)[3] The literary enterprise in fact consists in a continual reverberation between these two orders: it could even be said that here again the metaphoro-metonymic interplay continues to function, the metonymy on the side of the "*il*," as a substitute, as displacement-effect, and as a perpetuated description; whereas the metaphor remains attached to the side of the "shifters" [*embrayeurs*] (*je–tu*) which determine the subject in himself through the discourse.

This situation becomes clearer when one makes the point of distinguishing in a literary text (as does Emile Benveniste),[4] between the "historical" speech event [*l'énonciation*] as opposed to the speech event of "discourse." A correlation is in fact established between the use of person and the tense of the verb; let it be remembered that the "present" is obviously the time in which one speaks and that there is no way to avoid referring it to the "*je*" which is speaking. From this point the narration of past, historical, events employs the *passé simple* [the historic past tense in French], the imperfect, the pluperfect, all in the

---

[3] Roman Jakobson, *Essais de linguistique générale* (Paris, 1963).
[4] Emile Benveniste, *Problèmes de linguistique générale* (Paris, 1966), pp. 237–50.

Guy Rosolato

third person. For "discourse," on the other hand, all three persons can be used (*je–tu–il*) and all tenses, except the *passé simple* [which is replaced by the *passé composé* or perfect tense in "spoken" French].

It goes without saying that matters can easily become more complex, depending upon whether the relationship between the *je* of the narrator and the *il* of the hero is in equilibrium or is reversed. Todorov[5] feels that this consideration would account for what Jean Pouillon has called the *visions du récit* [the perspectives of the narrative]: the *vision du dehors* [view from outside] where the *il* dominates; the *vision par derrière* [view from behind] (with the *je*); or the *vision "avec"* [the view "with"] (i.e., where the two points of view are in equilibrium, therefore also in the first person).

Here we can see a system functioning in such a way that even in a "historical" narrative, both the *je* of the one who *speaks* the narrative and the inclusive "*nous*" and "*vous*" are implicated. The relative voice is consequently perceived by us only in so far as we recognize not only this or that particular voice which is *in danger of failing because it is only a partial voice*, but also the whole which comprehends the various opposed elements: the relative voice accounts for this relationship. Here then we have a first means of approaching the question.

In the same spirit, it would also be possible to try to attribute another type of conjunction to "scientific" language; the third person commands the present, but a present which is that of Law and which has value in so far as it endures (e.g., the earth revolves); something which does not nevertheless allow us to forget the personal *je* of a Galileo and his first enunciation of that Law, from which point the Law prevails, for us, in his formulation of it. And the traveler's account of his voyages can consequently be seen as involving three tableaux: discursive, historic, and scientific.

2) The second opposition I mentioned is one which still concerns the status of the subject (*je*) in a comparison between the performative and the constative (Benveniste). The first category is par excellence that of the subject: for through him the speech-event [*l'énonciation*] in itself dominates the act performed, the subject is the origin, in speech, of the *pact*, of the Law, of the symbolic relationship which unites the subject to others ("I swear, I name, I declare"). If the literary text pursues its course in the "constative" mode ("the Marquise comes down at five o'clock"), the text does not as a result remain any the less metonymic, it can be put into parentheses in relation to a speech-event

[5] See Todorov in *L'Analyse structurale du récit* [*Communications* No. 8] (Paris, 1966), and Jean Pouillon, *Temps et roman* (Paris, 1946).

[*énonciation*] of the author: "I say that . . . ." But this expression remains ambiguous. In order to pass into the performative mode, in order
not to be a simple affirmation which "constates" that certain remarks
are made, the *saying* of it must inaugurate a new situation (Benveniste),[6] which itself must be accepted as a recognition by a social group
which would also accept the "I say that . . ."; in other words, a pact is
implied: the metonymy of the text (the constative mode) introduces,
by the formed totality, the metaphor of the Name, as a result of
which we see the "I say that . . ." take on its meaning as a full (performative) declaration. In this way the metaphoro-metonymic oscillation reappears in the subject's assumption [of a function]. Here again
the relative voice includes this opposition.

3) There is a third confrontation worth mentioning, a confrontation
which, if it is applied to the verb, also makes more precise the articulation of the subject to the process: it is a question of *voices*, in the usual
grammatical sense. The classic distinction is of three voices: the active,
where the action is exerted by the subject; the passive, where it is
undergone by him; and the middle (or pronominal voice in French,
that is to say the voice of the reflexive verb), where the action turns
back on itself or upon the subject (A. Dauzat).[7] It has been remarked
that the category of voice in Indo-European is nevertheless independent of the state and of the action which allowed me to make the preceding definitions: voice could be better defined in the opposition
between the active and the middle, according to whether the process
of the action is brought about starting from the subject and acting
externally to him (the active voice) (Benveniste).[8] Above all it is the
transformations, the transpositions between these voices which concern us here, especially if we wish to uncover the conditions which
make them possible.

Starting from "je parle" [I speak, I am speaking], a series of modifications can be envisaged: "je te parle" [I speak you or to you]; "je
parle ce texte" [I speak this text]; "je suis parlant" [I am (constituted
as) speaking]; "je suis parlé"[I am spoken]; "on parle" [one (someone)
speaks]; "ça parle" [it or *id* speaks]; "on me parle" [someone speaks
me or to me]; "il me parle" [he speaks me or to me]; and so forth.

[6] Benveniste, *Problèmes*, pp. 267–76; for a more extended discussion of "perform-
atives" and "constatives," the distinction made in the Royaumont colloquium on
"la philosophie analytique" by John Austin, see his Harvard lectures *How to Do
Things with Words* (Cambridge, Mass., 1962).

[7] A. Dauzat, *Grammaire raisonnée de la langue française* (Paris, 1947).

[8] Benveniste, *Problèmes*, pp. 168–75.

These are formulations which, while not exactly current usage, may very well serve in pathological situations, ranging themselves in a series of levels according to the three voices of the verb.

But if we remain at the level of the "je parle" and its derivatives, we simply perpetuate a suspension and a rupture, through a fixation on the middle voice and on the constative mode. There may be a pathological alteration in this blocking which obstructs the symbolic (and performative) liaison of *une parole-qui-dit* [a Word-which-speaks], because neither the articulations of language, nor even those which are particular to neurotic symptoms can be assumed. The theory of hallucination would thus be enriched if it took into account this irreducible interruption of what cannot be said, by an impossible reference to what I shall call the "anterior voice" in order to show how an *active* "voice" comes to *double* the passive form ("je suis parlé; on me parle") and to complete the rupture of the "je parle" if it is sustained. It will be noted that "I speak" occupies a privileged position in relation to "I hear," "I see," or "I feel."

Jacques Lacan has already demonstrated the particular aspects of the hallucinations of President Schreber, whose *Memoirs of my nervous illness* was analyzed by Freud, considered as interrupted messages centered around "shifters" [*embrayeurs*].[9]

This relative voice, then, can be considered as the index of a series of oppositions through which the subject, in relation to discourse, accomplishes his movement of fading and return, his movement of pulsation. In this way, the relative voice, because the literary work exists and we read it, maintains this distance, this divergence, this hiatus, which is integral to the subject, and which the metaphoro-metonymic oscillation supports.

But in taking into account only this relationship to the division or doubling [of the subject], we neglect the triadic organization of the voices which are anterior, relative, or actually present, and consequent —but this time in a succession or a subordination which tends to cut into the triangle of the voices in the grammatical sense.

The relative voice which serves as the breath of the literary work

[9] Jacques Lacan, "D'une question préliminaire à toute traitement possible de la psychose," *Ecrits* (Paris, 1966), pp. 531–83, especially pp. 535–41. For the Schreber case, see *Memoirs of my nervous illness,* translated by Ida Macalpin (London, 1925); Strachey retranslates the quotations from the *Denkwürdigkeiten* in Freud's commentary on the Schreber hallucinations, *Standard Edition*, XII (London, 1958), pp. 1–82. For Jakobson's discussion of "shifters," a concept derived from C. S. Peirce's pioneer work in semiology, see Jakobson, *Shifters, Verbal Categories, and the Russian Verb* [Russian Language Project] (Cambridge, Mass., 1957).

seems to perpetuate *another* voice, one we are already acquainted with, an *anterior voice*, from which the relative voice is distinguished so as not to be simply an echo.

The sonorousness of the voice must also be understood, and the way it was *heard* in childhood; in its anteriority and its organization, that is to say, in its selection of sounds and its particular timbre, which the child attempts to reproduce. This far-off voice, the voice of the Father, contains distinctions, a meaning which is progressively unfettered, and a law to which the mother defers; this is the best, if not the only *means of access* to language. This precession can be found with the work of art as well; like a ready-made and particular language, a language established in a far-off time, but also privileged to the detriment of others—therefore a language established according to a *chosen code*. Note the ternary distribution: the relative voice is caught between the anterior and the consequent voices. Thus it serves as a means of transmission between the two.

As for the last voice, whether it is only a virtual voice, like a mute commentary, the commentary of the reader, or whether it is limited to simple reproduction, this last voice can become the support of an act of literary criticism, or accentuate the particularities of the original literary work, in a diacritical sense, but in this event it becomes itself engaged in its own enterprise, which is to be heard, and therefore in its turn this voice becomes a relative voice: a retransmission or relaying is involved.

Nevertheless, the relative voice, whether it is actually present or simply a median, only compels recognition in so far as it surpasses and abolishes the two other voices: but, in return, they are also regenerated and recovered, brought into perspective, as the upshot of this "sacrifice."

It is now possible to formulate our central question: how does the relative voice maintain and support the literary myth?

In the first place we must be prepared to visualize a separation between fiction and myth. This does not mean that such a division is invariably possible in any historical epoch whatever. It even seems to be true that when the myth is patent and active (like a religious myth), fiction is subordinated to the myth to such an extent that the myth itself may be indiscernible for those who are subjected to it.

This relative voice, covered as it is by the voice of God, cannot in this case possess any sort of autonomy. But the fact that with Leonardo da Vinci there is an increasing uneasiness before each picture to be painted, something lying in wait for the first man to call it up, shows clearly to what extent the Renaissance is involved in this process of disengagement.

Aesthetic fiction will present itself from that time on under the index of the greatest and most slippery fluidity: its figuration, for its author or for any man, will remain infinitely fragile, oscillating between the extreme fragility of belief, as for a myth, and an illusion always on the point of being exposed, like the nothing itself; and this in an alternating movement of capture and liberation. Fiction thus participates in myth and in the firmly established belief in it, and yet it is at every instant capable of escaping it. It is for this reason that we are justified in calling fiction an intermediary myth.

The voice will therefore be the wedge which inserts itself between fiction and myth, revealing as it does so the close relationships between religion and art, relationships which are matters for the Symbolic.

But fiction only takes full flight—and not at any time whatever, but probably only in the course of certain historical upheavals—from the moment when, thanks to it, *all and anything can be said.* Speech [*parole*] then begins an interminable process of uttering what still remains to be said, cutting through what cannot be said. It must be emphasized that here it is a question of laying open the very meaning of fiction, that is to say, the most radical means of bringing out the voice, in such a way that, without it, without its being perceived, the literary work becomes no more than an object of refusal and repulsion: formerly Sade, recently Bataille, and now Genêt have brought us to that extremity where, in spite of and because of all that is an obstacle to the voice and which is readily mobilized at this juncture, only the voice must find its tenor—its tonality.

To tell all is still to take over, or to surmount, all the voices which may have something to say: the totalitarian enterprise of the work is immediately obvious. Under the cover of moral voices, of improper or antiquated voices, it is the anterior voice which finds itself pushed aside, whereas the consequent voice, that of commentary and reaction, is not considered at all: and, since the literary work has been completed, one can only surmise that the three voices have not for all that been abolished, but, on the contrary, that their arrangement in levels assumes a maximum amount of relief and that exasperated protestation, like indifferent acceptance, is at one and the same time an incomprehension and a deafness in relation to the voice borne by the work. On this string, therefore, the theme of transgression is played, as a limit around which the telling-all [*le tout-dire*] is developed. But is the least restriction on this project actually conceivable? Telling all—isn't this to accept the commonplace, the anecdote, and the everyday? The voice takes into its flux all that is not said, as a sort of collection of all that has been sacrificed.

Why not consider this division of the various voices as a symbolic renewal, according to a model which is not in the least arbitrary, from the level of the physical constitution of sound and voice? To the tension and stiffness which the breath encounters in the vocal cords where it takes on life, succeeds the expansion of a resonant chamber where the obstacle of a wall coincides with the bursting forth and the modulation of the sound. We could even follow a similar schema in the ways in which the voice is picked up by radio: from the crystal and the transistor, both resistant matter, to the vibrations issuing from the *loud*-speaker. Like a variation, we encounter this conflict between the inert and the animated at the level of the voices which split themselves up in the eradication of the distal voices, on behalf of the central voice.

The musical instrument, in its first patriarchal simplicity—the horn— fills itself with an ancient murmur, and by its rigid body participates in the formation of the sound which traverses it. Do we need to recall the sense that Theodor Reik reveals as the paternal voice invoked in the ritual usage of the *Shofar*, and more generally in the order of music? [10]

This tension and subordination is probably also to be discovered in the attitude of submission which characterizes the act of listening— what is called inspiration. By this soliciting of the "unconscious," surrealist automatic writing pursues this same division, where certain echoes are supposed to fall silent, where the "control exercised by reason" or some "moral or aesthetic preoccupation" (André Breton)[11] supposedly fall away. But syntax is nevertheless respected. The body itself, with its weight, its somnolences, joins itself to the mortified or supplanted voices in order that the voice may escape from the depth of their inertia. One could even imagine a "narrative" which might try to maintain itself as near as possible to its own advent and which would suppress the intermediaries, the accents, the objects, the plenitude of a plot—as in the fiction of Blanchot—,[12] and which would let only its own first moment well forth; or in order that the body and

[10] Theodor Reik, "The Shofar," in *The Psychological Problems of Religion: I: Ritual: Psychoanalytic Studies* (New York, 1946), pp. 221–361.

[11] André Breton, *Manifestes du surréalisme* (Paris, 1965).

[12] For a discussion of Blanchot's fictional method and its relation to his hyperbolic reduction of the creative act, see Jean Starobinski, "*Thomas l'obscure,* chapitre premier," *Critique,* 229 (1966): 498–513.

Guy Rosolato

the mouth which speaks might remain in the tension called forth by the cry—with drugs. The miserable miracle would be this sacred putting-to-death, the body separated by its biology which is manipulated by a vacillating breath, to the voices picked out, this body returned to that "grasped metaphysics," as Henri Michaux has said, "by means of mechanics"—"when one is no more than a line." [13] It is to be understood that the three voices in question here presuppose two orders: an *anteriority* of an "already there" of the Law, an anteriority of the voice of the Father in language, and a *succession*, as a consequent voice, an anticipated recourse to a possible alteration or degeneration of what is borne by the voice actually present. A ternary organization might equally well be superimposed on this order, which could also be considered as temporal—a ternary order independent of any particular time, where to the anterior voice there corresponds a *primordial affirmation*, and to the consequent voice, a *second contention*, considered as an always possible denial of the relative voice which therefore appears between them as the exercise of a negation applied over these distal voices and so accomplishes in this way their reinstatement as distinct voices.

An identical structure to what I am describing can be found in the sacrifice and the myth. By myth I mean what it is possible to say about man concerning his birth, his destiny, his death, the question of sex, and, in a general way, by regrouping these themes in relation to filiation and succession, genealogy depending on a revelation or an ancient dictum of tradition, rejecting in every case the control of reason. But it must immediately be added that the myth takes on its contours in terms of a reigning *science* or *body of knowledge* which ends by fixing a limit, a "this is how it is," beyond which that science will not go. But this formula, as the Law of science, sets us reflecting on the order of the symbolic Law as a promise and a pact which binds the subject: "I declare that this is how it will be."

I propose therefore that we should see in myth the representation of this Law serving as a common focus for the greatest psychological and pathological variety of individuals in any social group; it is in this that the representation gives rise to interpretations whose collective articulation is assured by the Law common to all, which is to be found, in any particular instance and according to particular requirements, serving as a point of reference. In this sense the myth would have a therapeutic value through the collective whole, by making each one adhere to the Law in spite of particular diversities, bending to its will

[13] Henri Michaux, *Misérable miracle* [*Livres sur mescaline*] (Paris, 1956), p. 87.

in this way whoever might have been capable of deviating from it, even by means of a radical breach making him unfit for accession to the Law.

I would say, perhaps rather abruptly, that myth must be envisaged in terms of what appears as universal for human beings, that is to say, in terms of the incest-prohibition: the confrontation of myth with the wishes integral to the Oedipus complex will be all the more fruitful as we will be able to isolate at the same time the characteristics of the Law which asserts itself in terms of the Father, of the genealogy which he controls and directs, in terms of lineage, and conjointly, in terms of the accession to the Symbolic order.

Let me use as an example the religious myths which dominate or have dominated our culture: in the Judeo-Christian tradition the analysis of two central myths, the Covenant with the sacrifice of Abraham and the Catholic dogma of the Trinity, reveals an organization of which I can only summarize the elements here:

1) The patrilineal order of these societies provides us with the Law which we find as a representation in these myths, that is:

a) The feminine element is excluded: we must consider this negative aspect as a precise indication of the fact that one must orient oneself in the lineage of the fathers, the Law proclaiming for each subject, of whatever sex, that he must leave his mother and that the lineage of the name will be that of the male.

b) Three masculine elements serve to establish the principle of the genealogy (God, Abraham, Isaac, or the three persons of the Trinity). Here again we find the primary affirmation and the terminal content, that of descent and of the Son.

Each one of these elements is to participate in a movement whose agent is that of the center: Abraham, Christ.

2) This symbolic mutation takes place through the sacrifice. It is also clear that the Law is instituted at the same time, since the Name invoked is the murder of the Thing. As for the personal sacrifice, it must be considered that with the Son as victim it is also a question of the *Father*, as Freud and Reik[14] have shown: the putting to death will

---

[14] For Freud's version of the mythical Symbolic Father, see *Totem and Taboo*, Standard Edition, XIII (London, 1955), pp. 1–162; and the late essays in biblical exegesis *Moses and Monotheism*, Standard Edition, XXIII (London, 1964), pp. 1–137; see also Reik, "The Shofar," pp. 282–91, for a discussion of the patriarchal sacrifice of the son as an expression of the father's own hostility toward *his* father. Dr. Rosolato has elaborated his model of the sacrificial myth in the three

therefore also concern the Father, but in an indirect manner through the intermediary of the Son. This is important because in the myths parricide is never directly represented. The mutation takes place with the substitution of the ram for Isaac and the historically dated death of Jesus, once and for all in its soteriological power: thus the substitution is represented, the metaphor itself along with the fall of the sacrificed object.

This negation applied over the distal elements thenceforth permits the symbolic evocation of the Name of the Father, beginning from the Dead Father, and the repetition in perspective of the three persons.

What I want to show is that the religious myth represents that which is recurrent in so far as it is a necessary relation between three masculine persons which delineates a patrilineal succession for three generations and at the same time, through the sacrifice, represents a negation over a primordial affirmation.

Through the mutation and the accession to the Symbolic order, through the substitution of the victim, the Dead Father becomes situated in the unconscious. Thus one passes from a dual confrontation with the Idealized Father, to this Dead Father. Moreover the effect of desire is represented with its phallic implication in the future generations issuing from Isaac, or in the spiritual fecundation by the Holy Spirit. In this way a future contention, by the descendant, along with his Oedipal wishes, is accepted.

Perhaps this digression on the myth may have seemed overfastidious to you, but it is not, because it shows us that at a certain time in history a precise correspondence can be made between the Oedipus complex, the religious myth, and, in particular the Law of the Father and of patrilineal descent. This correspondence is as follows: the Oedipal wishes give order to the unconscious and find their God in it. They only manifest themselves through the detour and the transformations of language (e.g., the manifest content of the dream) or, in the neuroses, through the special language of symptoms. They only appear "directly" in psychosis, although the psychotic delusion seeks to organize them in what Freud considers an attempt to cure itself, a healing scar.

In the monotheistic myth, which is structurally opposite, in a com-

---

great monotheisms as a masculine trinity of three generations in a subsequent paper, "Trois générations d'hommes dans le mythe religieux et la généalogie," *L'Inconscient,* No. 1 (January–March, 1967), pp. 71–108.

plementary way, we note the absence of these forbidden Oedipal desires: neither incest nor parricide is to be found directly. But since the myth also offers a solution, the way left open by what is forbidden, under the Law, it will therefore represent the succession of patrilinearity and its foundation, that is to say, the Symbolic itself, the Dead Father and the Death of the thing which is replaced by perennialized desire.

As for the Law of patrilinearity, it is represented: by symbolic mutation, outside of a metonymic lineage related to the mother and childbearing, the Symbolic whose negation permits a succession, an account due, beginning from the Father: the Law as a pact requires the invocation of his Name, an assurance of acting in his Name.

Let me now return to literary myth. If religious myth does not tell all and if it imposes the recognition that certain things cannot be said, an interdiction which is in any case interpretable by anyone and with a belief which does not allow itself any failing or lapses, and certainly not the approach which we have seen with fiction (the approach of capture and disengagement), then fiction itself, as I have said, detaches itself from the myth precisely through the identification of a voice.

Thus we can perceive in the "telling-all" of fiction a turning away from religious myth and a more exact focusing on the *subject.* But the literary work conceived in this way is nonetheless forced to refer itself this time to its own myth which is not to be confounded with its fiction. One could even say that fiction constitutes for every myth the external danger which ruins it by the enterprise of the "telling-all." The same is true for its having to be apprehended as a representation.

If the nodal point [*le noeud*] of religious myth is sacrifice, one would presumably be justified in seeking its counterpart, which, in the literary enterprise, is paired with fiction.

It could even be said that the unconscious Oedipal wishes are for the religious myth what the content of the work of fiction is for the literary myth.

A tragic destiny which takes on the precise forms of misfortune, such as rupture, after prison, rejection, dereliction, solitude, or more usually malediction, this destiny seems to become what is proper to him who maintains this telling-all, be he poet or writer. Even for the scientist, and by different means, but means which put the same exigency in question, a similar fate could be noted.

Even if there were no other reasons, this would lead us to seek the literary myth in the act of creation itself. This act of creation cannot henceforth take place except in an alternation, a succession, and a choice.

Besides what has been said about them, the voices I have described set up a parallel genealogy, for which one could indicate a correspondence in fetishism with the effects of the object which lay bare the division or splitting of the subject: it is not a question of a genealogy related to sex, since sexual differences have been put aside by the fetishist, or more precisely *disavowed*, but of a genealogy according to the mind.

The alternative then becomes: *either* the author inscribes himself within that genealogy, which has symbolic value, while the distal voices, as I have indicated, suffer this primal sacrifice which introduces us to the relative voice, itself accepted as such by others: in this case, the literary work with the partial voices of its protagonists becomes something that *falls*, as one might say if it were a question of reputation or public image. The author thus protects his split self [*sa refente du sujet*]: in the very break itself, the distance of his recognized technique as a writer, while his authenticity [*vérité*] is already elsewhere, moving toward another work, in the break of a spoken Word [*parole*] in which he can no longer recognize himself, at the best or at the worst.

Or else, the failure of the work means that it comes back to him like a letter that has not reached its addressee; here the fictional genealogy folds back on itself. This may be understood in its mythic sense as a symbolization which has not attained its full realization; in the face of this all-pervasive *telling* which somehow gets stopped up, the sacrifice has not run the necessary symbolic course. Thus, in complete default of another myth, or if the symbolic foundation is limited to this single venture, he will not have the means to find elsewhere this reference to the Dead Father; it will fall his lot to be the victim of the sacrifice as if it were incumbent upon him to find in himself his radical division, in a conjunction of life and death, but one which nevertheless desperately preserves an impossible unity of the subject.

Every writer who undertakes this absolute *telling* is acquainted with this alternative, this choice—to the extent, indeed, that he even chooses to embody it in narrative form.

In its effect of delimiting the literary myth in relationship to the work of fiction, the voice is therefore a link with the Dead Father by which the subject can at once sustain his own internal division and the work its power to charm us.

In this sense Mallarmé proclaimed in his "Tombeau d'Edgar Poe" —and why not recognize its peculiarly relevant ambiguity in this present context—"That death was triumphant in this strange voice" [*Que la mort triomphait dans cette voix étrange*].

Discussion

EUGENIO DONATO: Following what you have said, I seem to see the possibility of a typology of the relationships of the religious myth in society. Let us think of certain societies without writing, where the spoken word [*la parole*] has an absolute value, where the Dead Father is held at the mythical level, but where there is a separation between ritual and myth, where this separation is maintained absolutely. I am thinking of the formula, "I do what I do because my ancestors did as they did," in illiterate societies. From there I see the passage to the oracle of the Oedipus stage, requiring incarnation in the Father, from there to the Absolute Father of the Hebraic world, and from there to the disappearance of the Absolute Father, to be rediscovered in the Dead Father. Thus, there is at least a three-stage evolution.

GUY ROSOLATO: The striking thing, in my opinion, is that in each of the three great monotheistic religions, Judaism, Christianity, and Islam, we find the question of the Dead Father, but always in an *indirect manner*. Parricide is never realized on the mythical level. In Judaism we see it in relation to Isaac and later with the intermediary of the sacrificed ram. In Christianity it is Christ, the Son, who is sacrificed, but here the Son is inseparable from the Father, the two being consubstantial persons of the Trinity. One might ask where parricide is to be found in Islam, for here the problem of sacrifice is not posed in relation to God nor to his prophet. In fact there is here a profound denial of sacrifice which, may I say along with Freud, implicitly assumes the problem of sacrifice. There is a delegation of sacrifice, the ram, and Islam is like a recall to the patriarchal religion of Abraham.

CHARLES MORAZÉ: Perhaps the difference between Islam and the two other religions is that it is a religion of war and, especially in its early movements, the sacrifice takes place on the battlefield.

Have you ever had the occasion to study the phenomenon of certain mental patients whose voice is turned toward the inside, rather than being projected? They seem to speak to themselves without being understood by others. Since you made allusion to the physiological function of the voice, I wondered if you might have studied this strange form of mental illness.

Discussion

ROSOLATO: First in regard to Islam, I think that the question of Holy War is really very important; it seems to be an essential part of the religion.

Then, as to the voice and pathology, I think that the problem of auditory hallucinations in which the patients do articulate silently, is very important. Psychiatrists have long been aware of the curious phenomenon that the subjects of these hallucinations have articulatory movements of the larynx, but that they don't articulate. They don't speak, but they *hear* voices. The voice seems to be made passive, in that, although they speak—this is proved by the articulatory movements—they negate and suppress what they have to say, so that instead of insulting others, they seem to receive insults from others. It seems to me that this could be analyzed in regard to the "shifters" [*embrayeurs*] of hallucination.

MICHAEL BENAMOU: In the historical evolution of Catholicism doesn't the masculine Trinity become a bi-polar quaternity including the Virgin Mary? I believe Jung tries to develop this schema. How would you treat such a development?

ROSOLATO: The Gnostic problem of feminine person existing as part of the Trinity in place of the Holy Spirit was posed during the first centuries of Christianity. Then as the religion continued to evolve, the feminine element was excluded from the Trinity. There are, nevertheless, psychoanalytical interpretations, notably that of Ernest Jones, which consider the Holy Spirit as an androgyne, a masculine-feminine element. Therefore, it becomes an interesting problem to situate the Virgin Mary in relationship to the Trinity. As a virgin, with a very special and fixed cult, she cannot participate in the adoration of the divinity or of the three persons of the Trinity. In this way, Catholic dogma seems to have situated her in such a way as to prevent any possibility of a reappearance of the Gnostic tendency, that is, of the Virgin appearing as the third person of the Trinity. At least this is my interpretation.

JEAN HYPPOLITE: I was struck by your remark about the double. There are many literary themes concerning doubles. I would like to pose the question whether the theme of the double within the literary work doesn't represent the problematic of literature as being itself a double.

ROSOLATO: I think you are asking a very difficult question, but we might try to distinguish various levels of this problem. There is the figuration of the double, such as a double character, in the *Tales of Hoffmann*, for example. There is the story within the story. Finally there is the functional level of, for example, the play of metaphor and metonomy which would account for the split of the subject. That would be the level of representation. But obviously this is all rather tentative.

RICHARD MACKSEY: Since you have suggested such a striking contrast between the basically triangular configuration of the Oedipal myth and the linearity of your monotheistic genealogy, I'd be interested to see if René Girard, who has been so concerned with the mediation of the double in the former, would find a different dynamics in the latter model.

Your model of the religious myth, which you developed so economically, seems remarkably fruitful, not only for demonstrating the similarity of representation in the three great monotheisms but for explicating transformations and deviations within each. Thus, though you associate Islam with the delegated sacrifice and patriarchal moment of Abraham, with the introduction of Ali and his death into Shi'ite belief overt sacrifice once again assumes a central role. In Sunnite belief, though, I should assume that the *Koran* itself completes the primary triad; it is certainly given as primary and unmediated in a way that the Judeo-Christian scriptures are not, separate from Tradition and the Sunna (which are in history), and, of course, untranslatable.

Finally, your analysis of the genesis and three voices of myth suggests the processional and iconic representation of the Trinity in Hellenistic Christianity: Theos/Arche; Logos/Soter; and Pneuma/Ornis. I wonder if you could also trace heretical and additional psychopathological transformations from the model?

ROSOLATO: Although time does not permit me to elaborate here, I have traced some of the suggestions you have mentioned in some detail from the monotheistic triad and the three generations. In a study which will appear shortly [in *L'Inconscient*] I apply the thesis to the three religions, trying to relate the reciprocal currents of Gnosis and Ritual in the theologies; the latter part of the essay is concerned with the therapeutic function of the myth and the way in which certain psychopathological structures are situated in relation to the myth.

Structure and Infrastructure in Primitive Society: Lévi-Strauss and Radcliffe-Brown[1]

Neville Dyson-Hudson

I

The idea of *structure*, as it most interests literary scholars at the present time, derives directly from social anthropology. It will therefore seem ironic—if not downright obstructive—to say that social anthropologists have far greater difficulty than literary scholars in deciding just what a structural explanation (or interpretation) is. This may well be because literary scholars see "structuralism" and the approach of Claude Lévi-Strauss as synonymous, while for social anthropologists this is far from the case. I

[1] This paper was first written in October, 1966; it is being finally checked for the press in January, 1969. A great deal has happened in the interim as far as Lévi-Straussiana is concerned. To take stock of it all would mean an entirely new paper which I do not have the time, and may well not have the talent, to accomplish. I have accordingly left the paper as it was first delivered, except for three matters. First, I have—for the benefit of nonspecialist readers—given footnote indication of some relevant anthropological items that have since appeared. Second, I have made minor textual amendments to avoid what would by now be incorrect statements (regarding an English translation of *Les Structures,* the authorship of *Orpheus with His Myths,* and the like). Third, I have tried to indicate more explicitly than I first did what the notion of praxis implies for me. Only a little more explicitly, however, because I believe now even more firmly that the notion of structure needs supplementing, and in committing myself to the notion of praxis as the appropriate complement I find I have, willy nilly, sketched out several years' work for myself.

But for the great kindness and varied assistance of Eugenio Donato, Robert Gordon, Harriet Greif, Richard Macksey, Bernard and Lilianne Vannier, Walter Weintraub, and Harry and Pat Woolf this paper would never have been presented in the first place. Whether such a slight essay can float the burden of so much indebtedness I do not know, but I would like to record my gratitude to all of them.

too was trained in a tradition different from, and in many respects opposed to, that represented by the views of Lévi-Strauss, but one which nonetheless has consciously considered itself "structuralist." This is to say, that form of analysis associated with the work of A. R. Radcliffe-Brown and for which Lévi-Strauss has been kind enough to provide the distinguishing label of "the naturalist fallacy."

Given that there are different views concerning the notion of structure in social anthropology, it is unfortunate that the varied segments of my profession should be represented here by one small voice. It is an accidental situation—Luc de Heusch and David Schneider also accepted invitations to speak, but were finally unable to attend. But it is an accidental situation we may put to some use since it illustrates the basic paradox of Lévi-Strauss: which is, that anthropology has today a wider audience than ever before because of Lévi-Strauss's writings; yet those writings have drawn greater enthusiasm from outsiders than from anthropologists and have so far had greater impact on other fields than on his own. Let me illustrate that paradoxical situation for you by briefly contrasting two responses to his work, one from within the profession of anthropology, the other from outside it.

Les Structures elémentaires de la parenté was published in 1949, and the main parameters of that book, one might say, were on the one hand "kinship" and on the other "the comparative method." In 1950 Radcliffe-Brown had written what was meant to be an authoritative summary of kinship,[2] and in 1951 had delivered (as the Huxley Memorial Lecture) what was meant to be an authoritative stock-taking of the comparative method.[3] Yet in neither place did he find it necessary to refer to *Les Structures,* or indeed to its author in any way, despite the fact that Lévi-Strauss had, as early as 1945,[4] specifically opposed Radcliffe-Brown's ideas on particular aspects of kinship and on aspects that were reiterated without alteration by Radcliffe-Brown in 1950. Now it is true that Radcliffe-Brown had (except for rare, oblique, and always brief critical comments) also managed to ignore his colleague, countryman, and contemporary Malinowski for a generation. One might therefore be tempted to put this down simply to personal eccen-

[2] "Introduction," in C. Daryl Forde and A. R. Radcliffe-Brown (eds.), *African Systems of Kinship and Marriage* (London, 1950).

[3] Later published in the *Journal of the Royal Anthropological Institute,* 81: 15–22 (1952). Reprinted as ch. 5 in M. N. Srinivas (ed.), *Method in Social Anthropology: Selected Essays by A. R. Radcliffe-Brown* (Chicago, 1958).

[4] See "L'analyse structurale en linguistique et en anthropologie," *Word* 1 (1945): 1–12. Reprinted as ch. 2 of *Structural Anthropology* (New York, 1963).

tricity. Clearly, however, the eccentricity was quite contagious, for year after year went by as the review columns of *Man* remained innocent of any appraisal of *Les Structures*, despite the many British anthropologists who shared an interest in kinship, an interest in the comparative method, and literacy in French.

It was two years after its publication before *Les Structures* received consideration in the English professional journals, and then Leach took up not the whole thesis, but simply one technical aspect of it—the structural implications of matrilateral cross-cousin marriage.[5] Although he praised the stimulating quality of Lévi-Strauss's argument, he had no hesitation in declaring, "his main proposition is back to front," and he is guilty in some of his arguments of "straining the facts to fit a world-embracing theory of social evolution." [6]

Not until 1952 was there any assessment in English of Lévi-Strauss's theory as a whole, and even then it was by a Dutchman writing in a Dutch series.[7] Josselin de Jong called *Les Structures* one of the most important contributions to anthropological theory of the present century, but still felt it necessary to add, "we sincerely hope that the author will not let himself be discouraged by a lack of positive reactions to his work so far." [8]

Six years after it had first appeared, *Les Structures* finally crept into the review pages of *The American Anthropologist*, but it was even then only in the form of a review of Josselin de Jong's book[9] and was cheerfully announced as "a review of a review" of "an important study of the rules of preferential marriage." Nonetheless, the reviewer was quite clear in his opinions about the entire enterprise. "We can often work to advantage with simplified models of society," he declared, "but the models may also get too simple and what Lévi-Strauss discards will live to undo him." And he concluded, "Lévi-Strauss's book is magnificent in almost every respect save its major argument. Criticism of the book should strike at its heart and not just its limbs. De Jong has done a good job of *maiming*." It is perhaps not surprising that those remarks should come from the man (George Homans) who with

[5] E. R. Leach, "The Structural Implications of Matrilateral Cross-Cousin Marriage," *Journal of the Royal Anthropological Institute* 81: 23–55. Reprinted as ch. 3 of *Rethinking Anthropology* (London, 1961).

[6] *Ibid.*, pp. 101 and 103.

[7] J. P. B. de Josselin de Jong, *Lévi-Strauss's Theory on Kinship and Marriage* (*Mededelingen Van Het Rijksmuseum Voor Volkenkunde, No. 10.* Leiden, 1952).

[8] *Ibid.*, p. 59.

[9] *American Anthropologist* 57 (1955): 136–37.

David Schneider published in that same year an intended systematic rebuttal of Lévi-Strauss's arguments.[10] But it is nonetheless sad that they should also come from a man who, on another occasion, had had both the insight and the charity to discern that, "To overcome the inertia of the intellect, a new statement must be an overstatement, and sometimes it is more imporant that the statement be interesting than that it be true." [11]

By the time this paper appears, it will have been twenty years since the first publication of *Les Structures*, and according to present publishers' schedules, an English translation will finally be available. It is even possible that the translated version will finally achieve what the original did not—reviews in the official anthropological journals of the English-speaking world. Though it would be, perhaps, an overly sanguine man who would predict how long those reviews might be, and what they might have to say.[12]

By contrast, let me recall for you a response to Lévi-Strauss from outside the profession, but still in English—the review from *The Times Literary Supplement* titled "Orpheus With His Myths." [13] There the reader finds himself firmly taken in hand, as if he were a student at a tutorial, while his tutor-reviewer inflicts upon him all the paraphernalia of the intellect as (he is given to suppose) the minimum necessary equipment for understanding just what Lévi-Strauss is up to. Some knowledge of moiré patterns is apparently desirable, as well as some understanding of cloud-chamber particles, and in rapid succession the reader is given topology (a term defined for him), etiologies (a term explicated in passing), phonemes, theories of consciousness, poetic metaphor, and post-romantic lyricism in music (with the composers specified, possibly for later homework on the reader's part). The relative

[10] George Homans and David Schneider, *Marriage Authority and Final Causes* (Glencoe, 1955).

[11] George Homans, *The Human Group* (New York, 1950), p. 329.

[12] In the summer of 1964, British anthropologists met to discuss Lévi-Strauss, but even as of that date E. R. Leach was able to say "many of those who attended the A.S.A. [Association of Social Anthropologists] meeting and contributed to the discussion did not appear to have read Lévi-Strauss's work at all. Thus while some of the criticisms raised were genuinely felt and derived from the basically different point of view of the English empiricist and the French intellectual, others seemed to depend either on English arrogance or straight misinformation." (In Edmund Leach [ed.], *The Structural Study of Myth and Totemism* [London, 1967], p. xv.)

[13] April 29, 1965. Reprinted as pp. 239–50 in *Language and Silence* by George Steiner (New York, 1967).

merits of digital and analog computers are touched upon, but only in a coy way, to enable our reviewer to suggest a "well-advised" retreat from this particular complexity.

Against this background of the two-or-more cultures, the reader has Lévi-Strauss presented to him as the perpetual end-product of innumerable intellectual genealogies. Lévi-Strauss is apparently in a line which stretches from Montaigne to Gide, picking up Montesquieu, Diderot, and Rousseau on the way. Lévi-Strauss can apparently be traced backward through Leibniz to Vico. A line passing through Freud will connect with Lévi-Strauss; it happily precludes partisan feelings to know that a line passing through Jung will also connect with Lévi-Strauss. One can go from Marx to Lévi-Strauss. One can also go from Durkheim, Mauss, and Hertz to Lévi-Strauss: and if the reader is an anthropologist, he might well be tempted to rest here in momentary mutual communication. Unfortunately, rest is out of the question as the reviewer calls him to trace Lévi-Strauss's connections with (for example) Bacon and Giordano Bruno, since they all generate lapidary and obscure formulas; or with La Bruyère and Gide because those three share (or their prose does) "austere dry detachment"; or with Pascal, because of a shared "mannered . . . concision and syntax." And somewhere, if the reader will only persist, are connections that will take him from Lévi-Strauss to Broch, Baudelaire, and Mallarmé, to Rilke and to Valéry. Moreover, on the way from Lévi-Strauss to these various termini, one can pick up quick views of other points of interest—of Sartre or of Camus, of Hegel and The Cambridge Platonists, of Wittgenstein.

Faced with this veritable railway map of the intellect, the reader may (if only as the price of escape from an endless tour) be ready to agree with the reviewer's assertions that Lévi-Strauss is indisputably an influence, though what sort of influence is not clear; and that his prose is a very special instrument. But if the reader is also a social anthropologist, he may be forgiven for wondering what on earth this all has to do with his own profession.[14]

[14] When I first wrote these comments, the faceless quality of a *TLS* review facilitated a more savage response than would have been likely had I perceived it as coming from a real individual. In the interim, that anonymity has evaporated with Mr. George Steiner's reprinting of the essay in his *Language and Silence* (New York, 1967). I have failed to moderate my response (despite some effort) because that review still seems to me far more a windy self-advertisement than an honest attempt to delineate a new style of thought, and to be typical of the kind of distraction which has prevented Lévi-Strauss's colleagues from granting him a fair hearing as simply—and above all—a fellow professional.

I do not believe I have caricatured the situation by selecting these two particular examples of response to Lévi-Strauss's work. The near-comic pomposity of *The Times Literary Supplement* is, for instance, paralleled in the faintly hysteric ignorance of *The New York Review of Books*.[15] There Miss Susan Sontag hails Lévi-Strauss as "the man who has created anthropology as a total occupation" (whatever that means); and shows her clear grasp of the subject by revealing that "Anthropology has always struggled with an intense, fascinated repulsion towards its subject"; and what's more, that the anthropologist is a man "who submits himself to the exotic to confirm his own inner alienation as an urban intellectual." Even if one dispenses with the expected inanities of the weekly reviews, there is still the more serious and sustained response to Lévi-Strauss represented (for instance) by entire issues of *Esprit*[16] and *Aut Aut*[17] being devoted to his work. Conversely, Homans's bravura dismissal of *Les Structures* has had its parallel in Sahlins's profoundly sceptical review of *Structural Anthropology* for *The Scientific American*.[18] There the same book that prompted the convoluted eulogies of *The Times Literary Supplement* is characterized as "Delphic writings" and its underlying viewpoint considered "bizarre, not to say incomprehensible, to traditional anthropology." And the same author that drew worshipping acclaim from *The New York Review of Books* as "a hero of our time" is here identified as "a complex and subtle Babar" who "may be more French than anthropologist." The same essentially dismissive tone is to be found, for instance, in Murphy's satiric description of Lévi-Strauss's viewpoint as "Zen Marxism."[19] Even Leach—largely responsible for whatever hearing Lévi-Strauss's views have received on the British anthropological scene—is driven into growling when the Lévi-Strauss that is presented is not a fellow professional, but the Sage of the Sixième Section, darling of the humanists: "I can make judgements about Lévi-Strauss's skill as an analyst of ethnographic materials, but when it comes to his still embryonic but potentially much more grandiose reputation as a philosopher I am not only out of my depth but somewhat unsympathetic to his position."[20] Why should there be this real and persistent contrast between intrigued enthusiasm from the humanities and wary scepticism from

[15] *The New York Review of Books*, vol. i, no. 7 (1963), p. 6.
[16] Nov., 1963.
[17] July, 1965.
[18] June, 1966, pp. 131–36.
[19] *Man* 63 (Feb., 1963).
[20] *New Left Review*, Mar., 1966, p. 12.

Neville Dyson–Hudson

anthropologists about a single body of work? There have already been plenty of attempts to explain the Lévi-Strauss syndrome (plenty of "windy exegesis" to use Sahlins's phrase) inside as well as outside the sciences of man. I have no wish to flog a dead horse, but a few simple points may be worth raising. There is first the confusion engendered for many anthropologists by the mere existence of Lévi-Strauss's outside audience, with its many different interests and its diverse pronouncements. Crowds of visitors can create noise in the corridors of any profession and thereby irritate those trying to work quietly in its cubicles. When such crowds are led by guides of the *Literary Supplement* or *New York Review* sort, who with penetrating voices firmly misidentify the geography as they pass through, then the irritation of residents is likely to erupt into sheer bad temper.

Second, this capacity to arouse outside interest comes itself from Lévi-Strauss's taking the whole field of man's activities as his proper field of investigation. Such a wide sweep is (parochially or merely cautiously) considered by most anthropologists to be dangerously delusory, and, because it was last exhibited on this scale some fifty years ago, unfashionable. It means, among other things, that Lévi-Strauss has a habit of proposing answers for questions that are not even thought to be proper questions any longer, and of invoking shadowy categories like "the human mind" in his attempts at explanation.[21] Consistent with this interest in large questions, no doubt, are Lévi-Strauss's large claims for the profession: for instance, "Anthropology is, with music and mathematics, one of the few true vocations."[22] These, too, often cause discomfiture to some of his less phototropic (crustier?) colleagues.

Again, *social* anthropology—by which particular term Lévi-Strauss wishes his subject to be identified—has for some time concerned itself increasingly with the detailed direct observation of human behavior by means of field studies.[23] By contrast, Lévi-Strauss's work characteristically, increasingly (and given his style of interest, of necessity) draws upon the observation of others by means of library study, and the data he uses may be related to societies and observers alike long-dead

[21] E.g., *Indiana University Publications in Anthropology and Linguistics. Memoir 8*: 4.
[22] Tr. John Russell, *A World on the Wane* (London, 1961), p. 58.
[23] Not all anthropologists find this emphasis on field study beyond criticism, of course. See, for example, E. R. Leach, *Rethinking Anthropology* (London, 1961), p. 1; and I. C. Jarvie (1967), "On Theories of Fieldwork," *Philosophy of Science* 34: 223–42.

and so beyond confirmation. Where he has presented the results of his own field studies they seem—to speak bluntly—slight by contemporary professional standards;[24] or they are couched in the form of the-novel-as-autobiography with the observer looming rather larger than the people observed.[25] All this may readily induce a suspicion that Lévi-Strauss's analyses add up to a Poetics for social anthropology, rather than a theory in any scientific sense. Maybury-Lewis on dual organization[26] and Barnes on the Murngin[27] are examples of this uneasiness. But let me offer—arbitrarily and very possibly unfairly—a nontechnical example to illustrate the point. You may remember that in *Tristes Tropiques* Lévi-Strauss has a brief, elegant, penetrating account of Fire Island, New York.[28] He sums up his topographic description of it by saying, "It's Venice back-to-front, with earth that turns to water and canals that hold firm." Then he continues, "The picture is completed by the fact that Cherry Grove is mainly inhabited by homosexual couples—*doubtless drawn to the area by its wholesale inversion of the normal conditions of life.*" Now the statement I have here italicized is, as realistic description let alone anthropological analysis, quite absurd; even apart from the way it quietly slides over the qualification *"mainly* inhabited" (what drew the implicitly indicated noninverted couples?). Now Lévi-Strauss is not a fool, and he has a right to expect his reader not to be a fool. Clearly this is poetics rather than analysis, and it is the central theme of reversal that holds his entire Fire Island passage together in a most effective way. What disturbs some of his colleagues, it seems to me, is the suspicion that it is poetics of this sort (observations symmetrically recollected in tranquility, so to speak) that also invades his accounts of other human groups, and that it is the

---

[24] "La vie familiale et sociale des Indiens Nambikwara." *Journal de la Société des Americanistes, n.s.,* 37 (1948): 1–132, and "The Social and Psychological Aspects of Chieftainship in a Primitive Tribe," *Transactions of the New York Academy of Sciences* 7 (1944): 16–32, for example. In all fairness it should be pointed out that the same could also be said of (for instance) Radcliffe-Brown: indeed has been said quite forcefully by Elkin in *Oceania 26* (1956): 244, 246–48 particularly.

[25] *Tristes Tropiques* (Paris, 1955), tr. John Russell as *A World on the Wane* (London, 1961).

[26] D. Maybury-Lewis, "The Analysis of Dual Organizations," *Bijdragen tot de Taal-, Land- en Volkenkunde* 116: 17–44. (But see also Lévi-Strauss's extended reply, pp. 45–54 of the same volume.)

[27] J. A. Barnes, "Inquest on the Murngin" (Royal Anthropological Institute Occasional Papers, No. 26, London, 1967), especially pp. 19, 31, 45–46.

[28] Lévi-Strauss, *A World on the Wane,* pp. 143–44.

Lévi-Straussian rather than the savage mind that they are summoned to examine.

Two more examples and then I have done with this quick attempt to account for alarums and dispersals. Each has to do with disconcerting changes in direction, and whether real or merely perceived by his audience they nonetheless result in exasperation. Lévi-Strauss has a habit of publicly invoking intellectual ancestors whom his colleagues see as having a confused relation (if any) to his present endeavors. Is he Hegelian? neo-Hegelian? Freudian? a Marxist? a Marxotrope? a Marx-inverter? a Zen Marxist? a Durkheimian? a Durkheim-ignorer? and so on. His colleagues abide the question: Lévi-Strauss, it seems, is free. But the role of Scarlet Pimpernel—particularly when the Frenchies are doing the hiding rather than the seeking[29]—seems not to be well thought of in anthropology. And the result, in part, is clear to Lévi-Strauss himself: "More than my opponents, perhaps, I am responsible for some of their errors with regard to my thinking." [30] The more disconcerting form of his motility, however, seems reserved for Lévi-Strauss's would-be proponents. The brouhaha over the translation of *La Pensée Sauvage* is a recent example.[31] Even clearer is the unfortunate affair of preferential and prescriptive marriage, when Lévi-Strauss declared—with excruciatingly appropriate staging in (of all places) the Royal Anthropological Institute—that his foremost proponents on the English scene did not understand what he was doing (or vice versa, but the effect is the same).[32]

---

[29] With apologies to Baroness Orczy:

> Is he with Durkheim? Marx? or Mauss?
> That demmned elusive Lévi-Strauss.

The reader is invited to try his own versions.

[30] Lévi-Strauss, *Structural Anthropology* (New York, 1963), p. 81.

[31] *Man* (n.s.) 2: 464; 3: 125–26, 300–1, 488.

[32] "The Future of Kinship Studies," *Proceedings of the Royal Anthropological Institute* (1965): 13–22. *Viz:*

If we are to assume that for the time being the study of kinship systems should remain first and foremost a study of models rather than of empirical realities, what place can be left to the distinction between prescriptive and preferential marriage systems? Since such distinguished scholars as Leach and Needham have fully endorsed it and are obtaining important results from the use of it, I feel somewhat embarrassed to confess that I fail to grasp its significance. . . . I find myself in the puzzling situation of having written an enormous book whose theoretical implications are recognized, though practically it would deal with no more than a dozen or so societies. This being the case it becomes hard to

All these are small points, behavioral rather than intellectual, and certainly incomplete. But it may help you to see why Lévi-Strauss is often regarded by his own colleagues not as a prophet with new truths so much as a will-o'-the-wisp who dances irresponsibly and confusingly—but elegantly—across the reaches of social anthropology. And perhaps who even sings, as he goes, a little jingle from a recent musical play:

> For life is like cricket, we play by the rules
> But the secret which few people know
> Which keeps men of class well apart from the fools
> Is to make up the rules as you go.[33]

What, exactly, is at stake in this scene of some confusion? For an answer we must, I think, go back twenty years or so.

II

In the 1944–45 session of the Royal Anthropological Institute of Great Britain and Ireland, its Council accepted a bequest from a Mr. Henry Myers to establish an annual lecture on the place of religion in human development. To deliver this first lecture, the Council not unnaturally chose A. R. Radcliffe-Brown, who was then generally recognized as the world's greatest living social anthropologist. And for his theme Radcliffe-Brown not unnaturally chose the topic "Religion and Society." As a result it was possible to read in 1945 (in the published version of that lecture) an extended consideration of Durkheim's study of thirty years before on the religion of the Australian aborigines (*Les Formes élémentaires de la vie religieuse*, 1912). While commenting critically on the data then available to Durkheim, on his handling of it in some respects, and on his overemphasis of totemism as promoting group unity and solidarity, Radcliffe-Brown unhesitatingly supported the main direction of his thought. "I think," he said, "that Durkheim's major thesis as to the social function of the totemic rites is valid and only requires revision and correction in the light of the more extensive and more exact knowledge we now have." [34]

---

understand, at least for me, why the study of such a limited number of tribes should have such important bearing upon the theory of kinship. (*Ibid.*, p. 17.)

[33] From *The Roar of the Greasepaint—The Smell of the Crowd*, by Leslie Bricusse and Anthony Newley (copyright RCA, 1965). A recent anthropological response along these lines is Marvin Harris's discussion of French structuralism in his *The Rise of Anthropological Theory* (New York, 1968), pp. 483–513.

[34] *Structure and Function in Primitive Society* (London, 1952), p. 166.

Neville Dyson–Hudson

Two years later, in France, Durkheim's study was again the object of extended comment, this time by M. Merleau-Ponty in his essay "The Metaphysical in Man." [35] Merleau-Ponty's response was altogether different: ". . . it does not yet allow us to penetrate the inner workings of religion," he declared. "The identification of the sacred with the social . . . is either all too obvious and begs the whole question, or else it is taken to be an explanation of the religious by the social, in which case it hides the problem from us. . . . Nothing is gained by basing the religious or the sacred on the social since one comes upon the same paradoxes, the same ambivalence, and the same blend of union and repulsion, desire and fear which already existed in the sacred and made it a problem." [36] From a condemnation Merleau-Ponty proceeds to a prescription: "Sociology should not seek an explanation of the religious in the social (or, indeed, of the social in the religious) but must consider them as two aspects of the real and fantastic human bond as it has been worked out by the civilization under consideration, and try to objectify the solution which that civilization invents, in its religion as in its economy or in its politics to the problem of man's relations with nature and with other men." [37]

I have no means of knowing whether either Radcliffe-Brown or Merleau-Ponty read each other's work, or indeed knew of each other's existence: I would think it unlikely. Yet we have here an important, if unconscious, confrontation. For in this last statement, and elsewhere in Merleau-Ponty's essay, we have what seems amazingly close to a programmatic outline for the work of Lévi-Strauss in the twenty years since 1947. As is by now well-known, that gradual unfolding of twenty years work by Lévi-Strauss has (often enough with specific intent) brought into question Radcliffe-Brown's entire view of the nature of society and of social anthropology. Unavoidably, the social

[35] *Rev. de Metaphysique et de Morale*, nos. 3–4, July, 1947. All my page references are to the translated version in Merleau-Ponty, *Sense and Nonsense*, tr. H. L. and P. A. Dreyfus (Northwestern Univ. Press, 1964).

[36] *Ibid.*, p. 89. It is interesting to note that as early as 1925 Malinowski had offered a view of Durkheim's theory quite opposite to that of Radcliffe-Brown, and much more in keeping with Merleau-Ponty's position. In *Magic, Science and Religion*, Malinowski had referred to Durkheim's "strange and somewhat obscure conclusions" (Anchor edn. 22), and asserted "It is . . . only by a clever play on words and by a double-edged sophistication of the argument that 'society' can be identified with the Divine and the Sacred . . . the metaphysical concept of 'Collective Soul' is barren in anthropology (and) we have to reject the sociological theory of religion." (*Ibid.*, p. 59.)

[37] Merleau-Ponty, *Sense and Nonsense*, p. 90.

anthropologist has been brought to reflect once again (as with Malinowski and Radcliffe-Brown in the past) on what exactly it *is* that he studies when he studies man in society, and accordingly, what methods he should employ.

If the least dubious of Miss Susan Sontag's comments on Lévi-Strauss is that he is "a Hero of our Time," then it is to our time as much as to our hero that we should look for an explanation. And here, I suggest, within a two-year period we see revealed, in the judgments of Radcliffe-Brown and Merleau-Ponty on Durkheim, a watershed between time past and time present as far as the sciences of man are concerned. Because Radcliffe-Brown's assessment was, of course, not merely confined to Durkheim: the approval given to *Elementary Forms of the Religious Life* was part of a general argument that insisted on the primacy of action over belief in properly sociological studies of religion. ". . . it is action or the need of action that controls or determines belief rather than the other way about" [38] asserted Radcliffe-Brown; "To understand a particular religion we must study its effects. The religion must therefore be studied *in action*." [39] And as if the emphasis on that last phrase were not enough, he repeats as a separate point, "In the study of any religion we must first of all examine the specifically religious actions, the ceremonies and the collective or individual rites." [40] The idea of the primacy of belief he dismisses as "a mode of thought that was common in the nineteenth century," [41] and additionally as "the product of false psychology," [42] and he most specifically rejects it.[43]

Nor, of course, was Merleau-Ponty's discussion confined merely to an assessment of Durkheim: *Elementary Forms* is for him a convenient,

[38] Radcliffe-Brown, *Structure and Function*, p. 155. This must surely count as one of Radcliffe-Brown's most persistent views. As early as 1923 he had declared, "my own view is that (the search for explanations) is of comparatively minor importance amongst primitive peoples, and that amongst them the basis of the development of custom is the need of action, and of collective action, in certain definite circumstances affecting the society or group, and that the custom and its associated beliefs are developed to fill this need." "The Methods of Ethnology and Social Anthropology," reprinted in M. N. Srinivas (ed.), *Method in Social Anthropology: Selected Essays by A. R. Radcliffe-Brown* (Chicago, 1958), p. 24.
[39] *Ibid.*, p. 177. He uses exactly the same phrase on p. 169 also.
[40] Radcliffe-Brown, *Structure and Function*, p. 177.
[41] *Ibid.*, p. 162.
[42] *Ibid.*, p. 155.
[43] *Ibid.*, p. 162. Taken together, these various comments implicitly constitute a clear opposition to the views which Lévi-Strauss was eventually to develop—action *vs.* cognition as an interpretive principle of human behavior, in fact.

if important, channel to a gradually widening statement on the sciences of man. After noting that "Durkheim treats the social as a reality external to the individual and entrusts it with explaining everything that is presented to the individual as what he has to become," Merleau-Ponty counters fiercely. "But the social cannot perform this service unless it itself bears no resemblance to a thing, unless it envelops the individual, simultaneously beckoning and threatening him, unless each consciousness both finds and loses itself in its relationship with other consciousnesses, unless, finally, the social is not *collective consciousness* but intersubjectivity, a living relationship and tension among individuals." [44] You will recall that it is by this link that he tries to bring sociology as well as Saussurean linguistics and psychoanalysis to a position of benefiting from the philosophical implications of Gestalt psychology. And this he believes possible "if one could show that in general each of the sciences of man is oriented in its own way toward the revision of the subject-object relation." [45]

Correctly or incorrectly, I see this orientation toward the revision of the subject-object relation which Merleau-Ponty so hoped for as providing the logic for the gathering at this symposium of men from such widely divergent fields. Correctly or incorrectly, I see it as the main issue at stake in the two forms of structuralism that confront each other in my own field, social anthropology. Correctly or incorrectly, I see the failure of Lévi-Strauss to meet all the objectives laid open for us by Merleau-Ponty as the reason why his brand of structuralism is only a partial solution to the nature of primitive societies. (As Radcliffe-Brown's brand of structuralism was in its own way a partial solution rather than the "naturalist fallacy" that Lévi-Strauss dismissively terms it.) Let me enlarge upon two of these cryptic comments to indicate why I believe social anthropology's two forms of structuralism to revolve about this issue, and why I find both only partial solutions that have greater need for each other's company than either has for the other's place. I willingly leave my remaining comment—on the logic of this symposium—to the symposium itself.

Radcliffe-Brown and Lévi-Strauss have much in common, I believe: far more, certainly, than anyone who merely reads Lévi-Strauss's remarks on Radcliffe-Brown would gather. Yet it is the central issue of objectivity and subjectivity, both in regard to the nature of social phenomena themselves and the means by which they are to be per-

[44] Merleau-Ponty, *Sense and Nonsense*, pp. 89–90.
[45] *Ibid.*, p. 86.

ceived, that makes a comparison of the two men of general interest. And on this central issue, their stance is one of complete opposition. The opposition arises because both are alike concerned (as any social anthropologist must be) with the dual problem of distinguishing *order* in the complex mass of evidence relating to human behavior that they inspect, and of distinguishing *persistent* features in the transiency that results from the human condition—from the fact that societies and cultures continue, whereas the humans they contain are born, age, and die. It is in an attempt to isolate order and persistence that they employ the concept *social structure,* however they may vary in their individual application of it.

Lévi-Strauss has noted that Radcliffe-Brown believed social structure "to lie at the level of empirical reality, and to be a part of it," [46] that for him "structure is of the order of empirical observation . . . is of the order of a fact"—and that he had "introduced . . . [it] . . . into social anthropology to designate the durable manner in which individuals and groups are connected within the social body." [47] In speaking so he had the clearest possible warrant, since Radcliffe-Brown had declared in his 1940 address on "Social Structure": "In the study of social structure the concrete reality with which we are concerned is the set of actually existing relations, at a given moment of time, which link together certain human beings." [48] And he added: "Every human being living in a society is two things: he is an individual and also a person. As an individual, he is a biological organism. . . . The human being as a person is a complex of social relationships. . . . We cannot study persons except in terms of social structure, nor can we study social structure except in terms of the persons who are the units of which it is composed." [49] "Social structures," he said, "are just as real as are individual organisms" [50] and "it is on this [social structure] that we can make direct observations." [51] "If we take any convenient locality of a suitable size, we can study the structural system as it appears in and from that region, i.e., the network of relations connecting the

[46] Lévi-Strauss, on p. 52 of "On manipulated Sociological Models," *Bijdragen tot de Taal- Land- en Volkenkunde* 116: 45–54.
[47] "The Scope of Anthropology," *Current Anthropology* 7 (1966): 117. This is a translation of Lévi-Strauss's *Discours inaugural* at the Collège de France, January, 1960.
[48] Radcliffe-Brown, *Structure and Function,* p. 192.
[49] *Ibid.,* pp. 193–94.
[50] *Ibid.,* p. 190.
[51] *Ibid.,* p. 192.

inhabitants amongst themselves and with the people of other regions. We can thus observe, describe and compare the systems of social structure of as many localities as we wish." [52]

The very way indeed, for Radcliffe-Brown, in which one distinguishes "social phenomena" as "a distinct class of natural phenomena" is that "they are all, in one way or another, connected with the existence of social structures, either being implied in or resulting from them." [53]

By contrast, Lévi-Strauss believes (to limit my sources of quotation, with which you will all doubtless be familiar) that: social structures are "entities independent of men's consciousness of them (although they in fact govern men's existence)." [54] That all that can be directly observed of societies is "a series of expressions each partial and incomplete, of the same underlying structure, which they reproduce in several copies without ever completely exhausting its reality." [55] And indeed that "If the structure can be seen, it will not be at the . . . empirical level, but at a deeper one, previously neglected; that of those unconscious categories which we may hope to reach, by bringing together domains which, at first sight, appear disconnected to the observer: on the one hand, the social system as it actually works, and on the other, the manner in which, through their myths, their rituals and their religious representations, men try to hide or to justify the discrepancies between their society and the ideal image of it which they harbour." [56] Accordingly, he accuses Radcliffe-Brown of an "ignorance of hidden realities" in believing "that structure is of the order of empirical observation when in fact it is beyond it"; and concludes that in "seeing it where it is not, he deprives the notion of its full force and significance." [57]

And indeed, seven years before, in a written response to Lévi-Strauss's paper on "Social Structure" (given at the 1952 Wenner-Gren Symposium) Radcliffe-Brown had made the only direct response of which we have published record: "I use the term 'social structure' in a sense so different from yours as to make discussion so difficult as to be unlikely to be profitable," he said; and finally concluded, "You will

[52] *Ibid.*, p. 193.
[53] *Ibid.*, p. 190.
[54] Lévi-Strauss, *Structural Anthropology*, p. 121. (From Lévi-Strauss's discussion of "Social Structures of Central and Eastern Brazil," first published in 1952.)
[55] *Ibid.*, p. 130.
[56] "On manipulated sociological models," p. 53.
[57] "The Scope of Anthropology," p. 117.

see that your paper leaves me extremely puzzled as to your meaning." [58]

Thus while both men are concerned—since as scientists they must be—with objectifying social phenomena, the problem that faces them is vastly different. For Radcliffe-Brown, the phenomena he is trying to handle have already, in and of themselves, an objective existence; for Lévi-Strauss, the phenomena that he is trying to handle have, overwhelmingly, a subjective existence, and it is in their objectification that his real problem lies.

However we juggle these concepts around, it seems to me that we finish up in a blind alley. Lévi-Strauss has, it is true, the additional concept of *social relations* or *social organization*;[59] Radcliffe-Brown has, it is true, the additional concept of *structural form*. But we cannot derive matched pairs from these—for the final characteristic of *structural form* in Radcliffe-Brown's sense is that, if persistent, it is still observable—a direct inference from jural or statistical regularities. And the final characteristic of Lévi-Strauss's *social organization* or *social relations* is that, if observable, it is still irrelevant—since the natives themselves do not understand what they are doing, and merely transpose their conscious model into the anthropologist's unconscious one.[60] Whether we try to say that we have a *social structure* (in Radcliffe-Brown's sense) matched with a meta-structure (as social structure in Lévi-Strauss's sense); or a *social structure* (in Lévi-Strauss's sense) matched with an infra-structure (as social structure in Radcliffe-Brown's sense), we still don't solve the points at issue. Which are: whether a social structure in Lévi-Strauss's sense (whatever we call it) exists at all; and if so what sort of relation does it bear to social structure in Radcliffe-Brown's sense (whatever we call it); and by what means this relationship is to be demonstrated? All this seems precisely what still has to be proved. Those who, like Needham, believe they can demonstrate a total structural analysis for a restricted ethnographic context seem to be answered by Lévi-Strauss that its importance is because it is universal, not restricted. Those who haven't attempted such a restricted ethnographic application of it see it not as demonstrated but as merely asserted.

In short, the confrontation as presented in this bare form is irresolvable. Either the reality that the anthropologist should be con-

---

[58] Quoted by Murdock in S. Tax *et al.* (eds.), *An Appraisal of Anthropology Today* (Chicago, 1953).

[59] See, for example, in Tax, *ibid.*, p. 116.

[60] See Lévi-Strauss, *Structural Anthropology*, pp. 130–31, for example.

Neville Dyson-Hudson

cerned with is action—often purposive, apparent, repetitive, observable and subject to demonstration; or it is idea—often unconscious, immanent, refracted, and its pattern demonstrable only after being stripped down and reassembled.

As an anthropologist raised in the empirical tradition, who believes he is dealing in some fairly immediate sense with the real world, I find the suggestion of choice here intolerable. Moreover, I find it unnecessary. I am more than ready to agree with Leach that Lévi-Strauss has a case. I think it a far from proven case; and certainly insufficient to abandon the empiricism on which I was raised. I would rather turn back to the real world, in whose existence I at least believe, and try to apply in it some of the recommendations made by Merleau-Ponty twenty years ago. My grounds for doing so are that Lévi-Strauss has offered only a partial solution to the problem of man in society. In that, he and Radcliffe-Brown stand on equal terms. What I wish briefly to explore is the area in which another partial solution remains to be offered between them, called for by the deficiencies of both and hopefully offering something to each.

That partial solution consists in the proposal to try and bring the individual within the purview of social anthropology again. My argument will be that if Radcliffe-Brown is guilty of a fallacy it is a juralist fallacy rather than a naturalist fallacy; and that although Lévi-Strauss has introduced subjectivity into social anthropology, he has done so only at the collective level. In either case, man as a sentient being attempting to work out his own solutions has disappeared. We have only his residues—as the externally constrained bundle of socially prescribed rights and obligations, as the unconscious instrument of his culture's heritage of ideas. Objective or subjective, all we have is rigidity. Of the man of the poets, of the man of the novelists, of the man of the psychoanalysts, there is no sign.

If there is a fallacy in Radcliffe-Brown it is a *juralist* fallacy, not a "naturalist fallacy," I have suggested: let me explain what I mean by this. First of all, I don't care very much for the word "fallacy" here, and I use it simply as a device for dialogue with Lévi-Strauss. (It smacks too much of an assumption that there is only one form of truth, whichever one possesses and one's opponent does not. Young as they are, the sciences of man have surely been going on long enough to avoid this kind of delusion.) But in that restricted sense let it stand. Radcliffe-Brown, in abandoning Malinowski's usage of *culture* as context and *institution* as isolate, moved in an important direction. As then conceived (as a totality rather than the stripped-down model

234

of a totality) "culture" was too complex a concept for manipulation in that process of comparison-leading-to-generalization, which Radcliffe-Brown believed the proper concern and method of social anthropology. And "institution" was too gross an isolate for adequately dissecting the inner workings of a society. In choosing, instead, "social structure" as his context and "person" as his isolate, Radcliffe-Brown had greater freedom to manipulate, compare, generalize. But in choosing "person" Radcliffe-Brown stifled himself, by choosing a formalized individual with little if any room for thought and maneuver. "The person" was defined by his place in society: he is quite different from an individual: the failure to distinguish them "is a source of confusion in science." [61] But what is this individual that, Radcliffe-Brown explicitly warns us, the person must be distinguished from? Astonishingly, man as "a biological organism, a collection of a vast number of molecules organised in a complex structure"; and while "Human beings as individuals are objects of study for physiologists and psychologists" [62] it is difficult to see what is being left for the psychologist to study here. Between the anatomical object and the socially constrained object there is nothing. In short, Radcliffe-Brown had saddled himself with a lawyer's view of society, and an English lawyer's view at that. For every position in society there were prescribed rights and duties. A person was definable by his position in society—and since he only existed in that dimension by that position, then naturally he behaved as his prescribed rights and duties indicated. His behavioral existence could be adequately circumscribed by reference to those rights and duties. Such a notion not only makes objectification possible (which allowed considerable advances for social anthropology, after all) it makes it inevitable—which is a good deal less satisfactory. In sociological terms, Radcliffe-Brown was using (without, I think, realizing the

[61] Radcliffe-Brown, *Structure and Function*, p. 194. These remarks occur in a lecture ("On Social Structure") which he begins by unusually explicit criticism of Malinowski; they can perhaps be read as implicit and oblique response to a complaint of Malinowski's some years earlier about "The tendency represented largely by the sociological school of Durkheim, and clearly expressed in Professor Radcliffe-Brown's approach to primitive law and other phenomena, the tendency to ignore completely the individual and to eliminate the biological element from the functional analysis of culture." In Malinowski's opinion it was "really the only point of theoretical dissension between Professor Radcliffe-Brown and myself and the only respect in which the Durkheimian conception of primitive society has to be supplemented in order to be really serviceable." (B. Malinowski, "Introduction," in H. I. Hogbin, *Law and Order in Polynesia* [London, 1934], p. xxxviii.)

[62] Radcliffe-Brown, *Structure and Function*, p. 194.

implications) a single, all-concealing role construct. It crippled him. His "social structure" is, in effect, a normative structure, a jural structure—with enough idealist content to make "naturalist fallacy" an inappropriate criticism.

In so far as he has called that into question, Lévi-Strauss has performed a great service, and Leach in refining the view, perhaps as great a one. But a good deal of dissatisfaction had been expressed earlier, in fact, by Schapera who had said: "If we agree that by social structure we mean the relations between human beings, then the primary object of our study should be the relations that actually exist, and not the relations that are supposed to exist. The latter should be studied, but they are important mainly because they help us to determine how far practice corresponds to precept."[63] The solution he prescribed was a statistical approach; its values are now obvious to us. What I have in mind, however, is something different. It consists not in asking how many people how many times observe or do not observe a normative injunction; but in asking, rather, what alternatives lie concealed in such injunctions and how are they differentially chosen. It involves notions of strategy—which presupposes both a plasticity of role and a sentient individual in it, with interests as well as rights and obligations—and its methodological requirements are perhaps rather those of scaling than of statistics.

There is little new in this, as you will see, but what I suggest is that it can be applied to help answer the question posed by Sartre, "Work and anxiety, tools, government, customs, culture—how can we insert the 'person' into all of this? And inversely, how can he be extracted from that which he never tires of spinning, and which incessantly produces him?"[64] If, as Merleau-Ponty claims (and as Lévi-Strauss perpetually tries to demonstrate), our task is to recognize every society as "a totality where phenomena give mutual expression to each other and reveal the same basic theme"[65] then it must surely not be at the expense of his other claim (in respect of which Lévi-Strauss shows us no advance) that the social is "intersubjectivity, a living relationship and tension among individuals." To demonstrate this second feature, *social structure* whether as conceived by Radcliffe-Brown or as conceived by Lévi-Strauss, is not enough. For if Radcliffe-Brown gives

[63] I. Schapera, "The Tswana Conception of Incest," in M. Fortes (ed.), *Social Structure: Studies Presented to A. R. Radcliffe-Brown* (Oxford, 1949), p. 105.
[64] On p. 234 (in his essay on Merleau-Ponty), in *Situations, IV* (Paris, 1964). My references are to the translation by Benita Eisler (*Situations* [New York, 1965]).
[65] Merleau-Ponty, *Sense and Nonsense*, p. 90.

us a relationship among individuals, it is a relationship objectified from the start, in which individuals meet only as the bearers of already defined rights and obligations which specify in advance the patterns of their relationship. And if Lévi-Strauss gives us subjectivity, it is the subjectivity of a collective unconsciousness, and the individuals either know no reasons for what they do, or only the wrong reasons. We must look elsewhere.

III

"Everything," says Sartre, "comes from structure and event at the same time."[66] And to encompass event, we need another notion—*praxis*. To use Sartre's own phrasing again, "the event which makes us by becoming action, action which unmakes us by becoming through us event, and which since Marx and Hegel, we call praxis."[67] It may well seem foolhardy to choose for my argument a term already employed by thinkers as diverse as Aristotle, Marx, and Sartre. (Indeed the simple task of disentangling *praxis* from *phronesis* in Aristotelian usage alone is itself intimidating in the context of my argument,[68] for both are components of what I would assert to be typical social behavior.) However, I do need a brief label complementary to social structure here, and the most logical choice in English—social action—is irremediably muddled for my purpose by its association with the highly abstract formulations of Parsons and his associates.[69]

There are even some advantages to using a term with several overtones here; for it is the echoes of what we are trying to identify, and not merely the usage itself, which trace back variously to Aristotle, to Marx, and to Sartre. The Aristotelian notion of self-realizing and self-justifying, as well as purposive, behavior—"performance" as we might say—is the very essence of role behavior, and it is no surprise to an anthropologist that *praxis* has its place in the *Poetics*,[70] as well as the *Nichomachean Ethics*.[71] As for Marx, we are arguing an extension into the social world of that imprint on the natural world which he

[66] Sartre, *Situations*, p. 294.

[67] *Ibid.*, p. 255.

[68] See, for example, *Nicomachean Ethics*, 1140a–1141b. For this and the following slim gleaning of Aristotelian references I am grateful to Richard Macksey, who offered them from the dense undergrowth of his unpublished study "*Theoria* and *Praxis* in some Ancient Texts: A Relationship Reargued."

[69] E.g., T. Parsons *et al.*, *Towards a General Theory of Action* (Cambridge, Mass., 1952).

[70] 1450a.

[71] 1140b, notably 2–8.

saw as man's species-characteristic.[72] We are arguing that the behavior he attributed to English and French social critics is attributable
to all men; "The real human activity of individuals who are active
members of society and who suffer, feel, think, and act as human
beings." [73] And by reference to Sartre[74] we are recognizing—as everyone after Freud must surely recognize—the duality of a man's subjective views of his situation and the objectively existing situation; the
dépassement by which subjectively motivated individual action can
transform an objectively existing situation; and the fact that the most
purposive of actions can result not just in finalities, but in counter-
finalities as well.

How, precisely, are we to translate a concern with *praxis* into a
working method for social anthropology? I suggest we need three
things. First, we need a concept of the *individual*, not as Radcliffe-
Brown's bag of molecules, but as a sentient being with definable
interests. (And for this second term I would accept the formulation of
a political philosopher, Plamenatz:[75] "the settled and avowed aspirations of a man which he . . . believes to be more or less realizable.")
Third, and a notion on which the other two are dependent, we need a
greatly elaborated concept of role, instead of the single one implicit in
Radcliffe-Brown. Such an elaboration has already been provided by
Levinson[76] and I will not repeat it here, except to point out that in
distinguishing the many facets—role demands, role conceptions (both
individual and modal) role performances and so on—it allows us to see
roles for the plastic, manipulable things they are. And it is because they
are flexible (means to act in alternative ways) and not simply constraints that demand action, with denial of the injunction as the only
alternative, that roles so conceived give us the instrument for dealing
with *praxis*.

There is nothing recondite about all this. The facts of our experience,

[72] "The practical construction of an *objective* world, the manipulation of in-
organic nature, is the confirmation of man as a conscious species-being . . . he no
longer reproduced himself merely intellectually, as in consciousness, but actively
and in a real sense, and he sees his own reflection in a world which he has constructed." (Marx, *Economic and Philosophical MSS*. 1st. MS, xxiv, tr. T. B.
Bottomore.)

[73] Marx, *The Holy Family*, tr. R. Dixon (Moscow, 1956), p. 205.

[74] *Critique de la raison dialectique (précédé de question de methode)* (Paris,
1960).

[75] J. Plamenatz, "Interests," *Political Studies* 2 (1954): 1–8.

[76] D. J. Levinson, "Role, Personality and Social Structure in the Organisational
Setting," *Journal of Abnormal and Social Psychology* 58 (1959): 170–80.

whatever the titles of our papers may be, are that there are good and bad as well as a whole variety of indifferent mother's brothers in the societies we study, and not just "The Mother's Brother"; just as there is a whole range of stepmothers, no doubt, in the western world, whatever our fairy tales may care to emphasize. And the demand of our science is, however difficult it may be, to try to bring our analytical concepts to the point at which our experience is made sense of: not to lop off stretches of our experience in conformity with our limited analytical perceptions.

Unfortunately, there is nothing settled about this either, since it is the problem that has dogged the sciences of man for so long. Durkheim had wrestled with it in 1914 when he attempted to explicate the problem of *homo duplex*:[77] "sociology . . . cannot, in reality, deal with the human groups that are the immediate object of its investigation without eventually touching on the individual who is the basic element of which these groups are composed," he observed. We need not follow him in all his conclusions—surely the sciences of man have made some headway in fifty years, after all?—to agree with him that "our inner life has something that is like a double center of gravity," that "man feels himself to be double: he actually is double. There are in him two classes of states of consciousness that differ from each other . . . in the ends towards which they aim. . . . Strictly individual, the states of consciousness of [one] class connect us only with ourselves. . . . The states of consciousness of the other class, on the contrary . . . turn us towards ends that we hold in common with other men."

If we make such a commitment, what sort of means have we at hand to implement it? I cite a handful of varied possibilities. We have two papers by Raymond Firth[78] in which "the place of individuals in social organization" [79] was first openly confronted in recent anthropology. We have Fredrik Barth's later detailed discussion, essentially in the same tradition, of how "social forms" are generated by individual interaction.[80] We have, as I have already mentioned, Levinson's

---

[77] Emile Durkheim "Le dualisme de la nature humaine et ses conditions sociales" (*Scientia* XV [1914]: 206–21). Reprinted and translated in K. Wolff (ed.), *Essays on Sociology and Philosophy by Emile Durkheim et al.* (New York, 1964). The phrases quoted are to be found on pp. 325, 337 of the translation.

[78] "Social Organisation and Social Change" (1954), and "Some Principles of Social Organisation" (1955). Reprinted as chs. II and III, in R. Firth, *Essays on Social Organisation and Values* (London, 1964).

[79] *Ibid.*, p. 46.

[80] Fredrik Barth, *Models of Social Organisation* (Royal Anthropological Institute, Occasional Papers No. 23 [London, 1966]).

Neville Dyson–Hudson

re-thinking of the multiple components of role.[81] We have Goodenough's proposed technique for scaling various role attributes, which
may "allow us objectively to measure such things as anger, insult,
flattery, and the gravity of offences, and . . . help us to appreciate
the poetic justice of events in alien cultural contexts." [82] We have
Goode's formulation that individuals act in response to the strains
which they feel their various roles impose on them, and are continually
selecting among alternative role-response to reduce that strain.[83] We
have the theory developed by Coleman to demonstrate that collective
decisions may in fact be seen in terms of the action of individuals, and
that even social norms thus become the end product of individual behavior.[84] And we have, of course, Goffman, whose various concepts
(encounter, social order, and others based on a metaphor of theatrical
performance)[85] present perhaps the bravest attempt in recent years to
deal objectively with that "intersubjectivity" which Merleau-Ponty
considered to be the truly social, to discern the structure in apparently
unstructured situations.

Two recent anthropological field studies may also be cited as showing what is to be gained from attempting to treat individuals within
the framework of a social structure, even without a fully elaborated
set of concepts for doing so. Cunnison's study of the Baggara Arabs
achieves this by happy accident. I mean no offense by this: merely
that one has to seek in one source for the treatment of the individual [86]
and in another for the treatment of the structure.[87] Turner achieves it
by design in a single work, and has to elaborate a new notion, that of
the *social drama*, to do so.[88] There is not time here, unfortunately, to

[81] Levinson, "Role, Personality and Social Structure. . . ."
[82] Ward Goodenough, "Rethinking Status and Role," in M. Banton (ed.), *The
Relevance of Models for Social Anthropology* (London, 1965).
[83] William J. Goode, "A theory of role strain," *American Sociological Review*
25 (1960): 483–96.
[84] James S. Coleman, "Collective Decisions," *Social Inquiry* (Spring, 1964):
166–81; "Foundations for a theory of collective decisions," *American Journal of
Sociology* 71 (1966): 615–27.
[85] Erving Goffman, *The Presentation of Self in Everyday Life* (New York,
1959); *Encounters* (Indianapolis, 1961); *Behavior in Public Places* (Glencoe, 1963);
Interaction Ritual (New York, 1967).
[86] Ian Cunnison, "The Omda," in J. Casagrande (ed.), *In the Company of Man*
(New York, 1960).
[87] Ian Cunnison, *Baggara Arabs* (Oxford, 1966).
[88] Victor Turner, *Schism and Continuity in an African Society* (Manchester,
1957).

indicate how Turner (in considering Sandombu, a village headman of the Ndembu tribe) and how Cunnison (in considering Omda Hurgas of the Humr tribe) are able to bring individual and structural considerations to bear on each other. But they indicate the task can in some sense be accomplished even at this stage.

If you respond that this is a veritable rag bag of ideas, some of which may eventually cancel each other out, I will readily agree. Indeed, I will cheerfully agree, since I cannot feel blighted at a failure to present the solution to a problem which has in its time baffled so many, and has been effectively ignored by so many more (Radcliffe-Brown and Lévi-Strauss included). But I would add, in Durkheim's words: "It is true that we are double, that we are the realisation of an antinomy. . . . And, certainly, if this odd condition is one of the distinctive traits of humanity, the science of man must try to account for it." [89]

Let me make it quite clear that I am in no way suggesting that this notion of the individual is a proper and desirable substitute for that of structure, whether as proposed by Radcliffe-Brown or by Lévi-Strauss. tion the notion of *structure* needs the notion of *praxis*, then it seems to me equally true that the notion of *praxis* needs the notion of *structure*. The proposals of Radcliffe-Brown and Lévi-Strauss are, I have suggested, both only partial solutions. It may be that the only thing my proposal has in comparison with theirs is that mine also tries to offer a partial solution in an area I believe them both to ignore. But the sciences of man (like all sciences) can offer only partial solutions. I would hope, however, that such partial solutions, instead of vainly competing with each other, could be ranged alongside each other. And that we might perceive interconnections between the levels of (in Lacan's formula)[90] je/Moi: autre/Autre, of Individual/Person, of (for Lévi-Strauss and Radcliffe-Brown respectively) Social Structure and of Infrastructure. For all these pairs exhibit, it would seem, the intriguing opposition of interiority/exteriority at the different levels of human life to which they refer. In this way we might also be interpreting Merleau-Ponty's remark of twenty years ago, that "all knowledge of man by man . . . is the taking up by each, *as best he can*, of the acts of others." [91]

[89] Durkheim, in K. Wolff (ed.), *Essays on Sociology and Philosophy*, p. 330.
[90] Jacques Lacan, *The Language of the Self*, tr. A. Wilden (Baltimore, 1968).
[91] Merleau-Ponty, *Sense and Nonsense*, p. 93.

Comments

CARROLL PRATT: The disputes among anthropologists and sociologists, as outlined by Neville Dyson-Hudson, regarding the proper subject-matter of their disciplines are reminiscent of the bitter quarrels that divided American psychologists into opposing camps some thirty-five years ago. Classical psychologists looked upon consciousness as the unique and proper subject-matter for the study of the *mind*. The radical behaviorists would have nothing to do with consciousness and confined themselves to the study of stimulus and *response*. The classical psychologists said that behavior is a physical event and therefore does not belong in psychology, whereas the behaviorists insisted that consciousness, if there is such a thing, is too elusive and impalpable for scientific study. And so the battle lines were drawn and the warfare continued angrily for a decade or more. At last the sounds of conflict became faint, and at the present time they can rarely be heard. How did this change come about?

No science is capable of definition in terms of subject-matter, for the subject-matter of all sciences is the same. Some person, some scientist, makes a report on something he has observed. It may be the downward movement of a stone, a flash of light, the change of color in a liquid, the crossing of a line by a needle-point, the way an animal responds to various lights and sounds, the effect on a given area of color of changes in the surrounding colors, the length of time required to learn a list of words or for an animal to run a maze, the manner in which people are influenced by newspaper headlines, the speed with which a problem can be solved: the list of possible observations can obviously be run on indefinitely. Which observations are mental and which are physical? No satisfactory answer has ever been given, in spite of centuries of debate by philosophers. Mind and matter are indistinguishable as presentations at the level of initial observation, and so all disputes over which is which are idle and futile. What is mind? No matter. What is matter? Never mind. Disputes in psychology are now over concepts and theories, not over the ontological nature of given data. The subject-matter of all sciences comes from the same matrix of human experience. The divisions in science, such as astronomy, physics, anthropology, biology, psychology, etc., are merely divisions of labor. Their given data are neutral entities, as Bertrand Russell has called them.

WILLIAM BENZON: Dyson-Hudson's focus on the individual and the notion of *praxis* suggests a homology with structural linguistics: *parole:langue::praxis:structure.* Just as *langue* exists only through *parole* and *parole* is meaningful only as assimilated into *langue,* so structure is actualized only through *praxis* and *praxis* is meaningful only as it disappears into *structure.* The limitation of this homology is that the structural linguist studies *langue,* the system, and not *parole,* the individual acts through which the system is manifested, for to understand *parole* as an act of communication automatically assimilates it into *langue.* But the reason for introducing the notion of *praxis* is to provide a way of understanding the individual which doesn't result in his automatic absorption into *structure.*

This limitation arises because all individuals in a society possess the language of that society but none of the individuals possesses the society. Rather, each is a part of the society and each has a representation of that society in terms of the common language. When the object of study is language, reference to subjectivity and individuals is superfluous, as all individuals possess the language (more or less) equally. *Parole,* the product of the individual, can be assimilated into *langue* with *langue* being the object of study because the words are the possession of all and mean the same to all (the point where words do not mean the same to all is the point where *praxis* begins).

There is no *commonly held* immanent structure, however, to which all the individual representations of the society can be assimilated (though some masochistic anthropologist might wish to collate all these individual views into some fantastic meta-structure). Thus, as *praxis* is the path an individual cuts through the social space in terms of his perception of that space, there can be no structure into which *praxis* can be assimilated (lest it be the masochistic anthropologist's meta-structure) in the way *parole* is assimilated into *langue.* Rather, social structure is a process whereby individuals, through *praxis,* weave their various paths through the social space, acting through or out the complementarities and contradictions of their various perceptions of the society.

On this basis it seems best to regard infrastructure (Lévi-Strauss) as the *common base* of subjectivity which makes intersubjectivity meaningful, but without those differences of role and place in society which must be lived through rather than perceived. Infrastructure is the structure in terms of which the world is meaningfully perceived and is invisible because it is the instrument of perception—as the eye is invisible to the vision which emanates from it. It is this commonly held instrument which allows the differentiation and elaboration (through *praxis*) of a more complex reality than that embodied in the instrument; just as the myth is more complex than the categories on which it is built, and many very different myths can be built on the same categories, so the social interactions in society are more diverse and complex than those embedded in myth.

Similarly, social structure (Radcliffe-Brown) is that complex reality elaborated by individuals through *praxis*—a reality which transcends the individuals as the whole transcends the parts. Subjectivity is irrelevant to this transcendent order precisely because this order is based on the differences of individuals in the society (as the infrastructure is what they have in common) which are due to distinct differences of role (function) in society (as opposed to "merely" personality differences); this transcendent order is only concerned with the outsides of individuals, that aspect of the individual which escapes him to be assimilated into the society as a whole—which escapes from above—as infrastructure escapes from below.

Mediating between these two orders is *praxis*. Beneath *praxis* is infrastructure which is the perceptual instrument allowing individuals to represent their society and to act (*praxis*) on this representation. Above *praxis* is the social structure which arises from the interactions of individuals (*praxis*).

RICHARD MACKSEY: Since Mr. Benzon is a sometime jazz musician, I'm reminded that a ready example for his divertissement on the relationship of the two "structures" to *praxis* seems to exist in the classic form of jazz improvisation. The actual event mediates the almost formulaic harmonic pattern of the group's jazz tune and the improviser's spontaneous variations. This binary opposition is also doubled in the rhythmic treatment of traditional syncopation and, what some critics have called, the "polyrhythm" or "secondary rag." (As to the characteristic chromatic and cyclic progressions of the seventh-chords in the harmonization, I suppose that Lévi-Strauss could find some binary matrix behind the structure of the traditional accompanying instruments.)

My comment, however, relates to another sort of opposition. Given his fruitful comparison of French structuralism and British structuro-functionalism (with their common origin paradoxically in aspects of Durkheim's thought and "South West German" philosophy), I wonder if Dyson-Hudson could not extend the theoretical comparative approach to a confrontation of Lévi-Strauss and what Surtevant has called the "New Ethnography" in America? Certainly, both modes of approach have a common origin in the paradigmatic treatment of the linguistic model exported from Prague and both have some line of filiation from the early Kroeber. And both have given a new twist to the mentalism of what Pike styled the *emic* as opposed to the *etic* approach, a twist away from affective toward rationalist, "distinctive-feature" paradigms—though I doubt that they would agree on the precise character of the "actor's commitment" (as opposed to the "observer's evidence"), since they seem to have rather divergent ways of defining semantic and communication phenomena. But both demand an *emic* determination of the intersubjective criteria of similarity and difference; and one could, in fact, compare the Franco-British dispute about alliance theory vs. descent theory with the American civil unrest about status succession vs. lineage solidarity in the Crow and Omaha terminologies. Both the American ethnosemanticists and Lévi-Strauss seem to set a high priority on elegance and formal ingenuity in demonstration, and both surely prefer "mechanical" to "statistical" models. What would be most illuminating, however, would be precisely their significant differences; and these could perhaps be best elicited by a consideration of *praxis* and its operative insertion in their respective models. "Skewing rules" are, after all, of a different order of conceptualization from the transforms of *Mythologiques*, and the kind of componential analysis and cognitive calculus implicit in dealing with American kinship terminology can be posited on a different metaphysical basis from the camshaft ratios and speeds of the Lévi-Strauss jig-saw puzzle analogy. I suppose that the two schools may also differ even over the crucial protocols governing rules for breaking structural rules.

Finally, although the mechanical model has a special privilege in both cases, the order of evidence seems to be different and may possibly have a greater or lesser adhesion to what we laymen sometimes call reality—a possibility which reminds me of Peirce's bemused comment on Hegel's wonderful "anancastic" model: there seems to be everything in it save for one not so unimportant factor, namely, that it does not relate to what exists! (There is no rule, after all, that so beautiful a game as chess has to correspond with any exactness to the messier reality of war at any historic moment.)

Latterly, the invocation of *praxis* as a corrective, though, also reminds me that I'd someday like to understand what constitutes Lévi-

Comments

Straussian "Marxism," assuming that the eponym is not merely a pseudonym for Hegel? In the traditional academic slaughter of the father, one of the most popular, if confusing, variations seems to be the adoption of one or more surrogate "fathers" whose chastity in the alleged paternity seems beyond doubt.

Structure, Sign, and Play in the Discourse of the Human Sciences[1]

Jacques Derrida
Ecole Normale Supérieure

Perhaps something has occurred in the history of the concept of structure that could be called an "event," if this loaded word did not entail a meaning which it is precisely the function of structural—or structuralist—thought to reduce or to suspect. But let me use the term "event" anyway, employing it with caution and as if in quotation marks. In this sense, this event will have the exterior form of a *rupture* and a *redoubling*.

It would be easy enough to show that the concept of structure and even the word "structure" itself are as old as the *epistèmè*—that is to say, as old as western science and western philosophy—and that their roots thrust deep into the soil of ordinary language, into whose deepest recesses the *epistèmè* plunges to gather them together once more, making them part of itself in a metaphorical displacement. Nevertheless, up until the event which I wish to mark out and define, structure—or rather the structurality of structure—although it has always been involved, has always been neutralized or reduced, and this by a process of giving it a center or referring it to a point of presence, a fixed origin. The function of this center was not only to orient, balance, and organize the structure—one cannot in fact conceive of an unorganized structure—but above all to make sure that the organizing principle of the structure would limit what we might call the *free-*

[1] "La Structure, le signe et le jeu dans le discours des sciences humaines." The text which follows is a translation of the revised version of M. Derrida's communication. The word "jeu" is variously translated here as "play," "interplay," "game," and "stake," besides the normative translation "freeplay." All footnotes to this article are additions by the translator.

247

play of the structure. No doubt that by orienting and organizing the coherence of the system, the center of a structure permits the freeplay of its elements inside the total form. And even today the notion of a structure lacking any center represents the unthinkable itself.

Nevertheless, the center also closes off the freeplay it opens up and makes possible. *Qua* center, it is the point at which the substitution of contents, elements, or terms is no longer possible. At the center, the permutation or the transformation of elements (which may of course be structures enclosed within a structure) is forbidden. At least this permutation has always remained *interdicted* [2] (I use this word deliberately). Thus it has always been thought that the center, which is by definition unique, constituted that very thing within a structure which governs the structure, while escaping structurality. This is why classical thought concerning structure could say that the center is, paradoxically, *within* the structure and *outside* it. The center is at the center of the totality, and yet, since the center does not belong to the totality (is not part of the totality), the totality *has its center elsewhere.* The center is not the center. The concept of centered structure—although it represents coherence itself, the condition of the *epistèmè* as philosophy or science—is contradictorily coherent. And, as always, coherence in contradiction expresses the force of a desire. The concept of centered structure is in fact the concept of a freeplay based on a fundamental ground, a freeplay which is constituted upon a fundamental immobility and a reassuring certitude, which is itself beyond the reach of the freeplay. With this certitude anxiety can be mastered, for anxiety is invariably the result of a certain mode of being implicated in the game, of being caught by the game, of being as it were from the very beginning at stake in the game.[3] From the basis of what we therefore call the center (and which, because it can be either inside or outside, is as readily called the origin as the end, as readily *archè* as *telos*), the repetitions, the substitutions, the transformations, and the permutations are always *taken* from a history of meaning [*sens*]—that is, a history, period—whose origin may always be revealed or whose end may always be anticipated in the form of presence. This is why one could perhaps say that the movement of any archeology, like that of any eschatology, is an accomplice of this reduction of the structurality of structure and always attempts to conceive of structure from the basis of a full presence which is out of play.

[2] *Interdite:* "forbidden," "disconcerted," "confounded," "speechless."

[3] ". . . qui naît toujours d'une certaine manière d'être impliqué dans le jeu, d'être pris au jeu, d'être comme être d'entrée de jeu dans le jeu."

If this is so, the whole history of the concept of structure, before the rupture I spoke of, must be thought of as a series of substitutions of center for center, as a linked chain of determinations of the center. Successively, and in a regulated fashion, the center receives different forms or names. The history of metaphysics, like the history of the West, is the history of these metaphors and metonymies. Its matrix—if you will pardon me for demonstrating so little and for being so ellipitical in order to bring me more quickly to my principal theme—is the determination of being as *presence* in all the senses of this word. It would be possible to show that all the names related to fundamentals, to principles, or to the center have always designated the constant of a presence—*eidos, archè, telos, energeia, ousia* (essence, existence, substance, subject) *aletheia*, transcendentality, consciousness, or conscience, God, man, and so forth.

The event I called a rupture, the disruption I alluded to at the beginning of this paper, would presumably have come about when the structurality of structure had to begin to be thought, that is to say, repeated, and this is why I said that this disruption was repetition in all of the senses of this word. From then on it became necessary to think the law which governed, as it were, the desire for the center in the constitution of structure and the process of signification prescribing its displacements and its substitutions for this law of the central presence—but a central presence which was never itself, which has always already been transported outside itself in its surrogate. The surrogate does not substitute itself for anything which has somehow pre-existed it. From then on it was probably necessary to begin to think that there was no center, that the center could not be thought in the form of a being-present, that the center had no natural locus, that it was not a fixed locus but a function, a sort of non-locus in which an infinite number of sign-substitutions came into play. This moment was that in which language invaded the universal problematic; that in which, in the absence of a center or origin, everything became discourse—provided we can agree on this word—that is to say, when everything became a system where the central signified, the original or transcendental signified, is never absolutely present outside a system of differences. The absence of the transcendental signified extends the domain and the interplay of signification *ad infinitum*.

Where and how does this decentering, this notion of the structurality of structure, occur? It would be somewhat naïve to refer to an event, a doctrine, or an author in order to designate this occurrence. It is no doubt part of the totality of an era, our own, but still it has already begun to proclaim itself and begun to *work*. Nevertheless, if I wished to give some sort of indication by choosing one or two "names," and by recalling those authors in whose discourses this occurrence has most nearly maintained its most radical formulation, I would probably cite the Nietzschean critique of metaphysics, the critique of the concepts of being and truth, for which were substituted the concepts of play, interpretation, and sign (sign without truth present); the Freudian critique or self-presence, that is, the critique of consciousness, of the subject, of self-identity and of self-proximity or self-possession; and, more radically, the Heideggerean destruction of metaphysics, of onto-theology, of the determination of being as presence. But all these destructive discourses and all their analogues are trapped in a sort of circle. This circle is unique. It describes the form of the relationship between the history of metaphysics and the destruction of the history of metaphysics. *There is no sense* in doing without the concepts of metaphysics in order to attack metaphysics. We have no language—no syntax and no lexicon—which is alien to this history; we cannot utter a single destructive proposition which has not already slipped into the form, the logic, and the implicit postulations of precisely what it seeks to contest. To pick out one example from many: the metaphysics of presence is attacked with the help of the concept of the *sign*. But from the moment anyone wishes this to show, as I suggested a moment ago, that there is no transcendental or privileged signified and that the domain or the interplay of signification has, henceforth, no limit, he ought to extend his refusal to the concept and to the word sign itself—which is precisely what cannot be done. For the signification "sign" has always been comprehended and determined, in its sense, as sign-of, signifier referring to a signified, signifier different from its signified. If one erases the radical difference between signifier and signified, it is the word signifier itself which ought to be abandoned as a metaphysical concept. When Lèvi-Strauss says in the preface to *The Raw and the Cooked* [4] that he has "sought to transcend the opposition between the sensible and the intelligible by placing [himself] from the very beginning at the level of signs," the necessity, the force, and the legitimacy of his act cannot make us forget that the concept of the sign cannot in itself surpass or bypass this opposition between the sensible and the intelligible. The concept of the sign is determined by this opposition: through and throughout the totality of its history and by its system. But we cannot do without the concept of the sign, we cannot give up this metaphysical complicity without also giving up

[4] *Le cru et le cuit* (Paris: Plon, 1964).

the critique we are directing against this complicity, without the risk of erasing difference [altogether] in the self-identity of a signified reducing into itself its signifier, or, what amounts to the same thing, simply expelling it outside itself. For there are two heterogenous ways of erasing the difference between the signifier and the signified: one, the classic way, consists in reducing or deriving the signifier, that is to say, ultimately in *submitting* the sign to thought; the other, the one we are using here against the first one, consists in putting into question the system in which the preceding reduction functioned: first and foremost, the opposition between the sensible and the intelligible. The *paradox* is that the metaphysical reduction of the sign needed the opposition it was reducing. The opposition is part of the system, along with the reduction. And what I am saying here about the sign can be extended to all the concepts and all the sentences of metaphysics, in particular to the discourse on "structure." But there are many ways of being caught in this circle. They are all more or less naïve, more or less empirical, more or less systematic, more or less close to the formulation or even to the formalization of this circle. It is these differences which explain the multiplicity of destructive discourses and the disagreement between those who make them. It was within concepts inherited from metaphysics that Nietzsche, Freud, and Heidegger worked, for example. Since these concepts are not elements or atoms and since they are taken from a syntax and a system, every particular borrowing drags along with it the whole of metaphysics. This is what allows these destroyers to destroy each other reciprocally—for example, Heidegger considering Nietzsche, with as much lucidity and rigor as bad faith and misconstruction, as the last metaphysician, the last "Platonist." One could do the same for Heidegger himself, for Freud, or for a number of others. And today no exercise is more widespread.

What is the relevance of this formal schéma when we turn to what are called the "human sciences"? One of them perhaps occupies a privileged place—ethnology. One can in fact assume that ethnology could have been born as a science only at the moment when a de-centering had come about: at the moment when European culture—and, in consequence, the history of metaphysics and of its concepts—had been *dislocated*, driven from its locus, and forced to stop considering itself as the culture of reference. This moment is not first and foremost a moment of philosophical or scientific discourse, it is also a moment which is political, economic, technical, and so forth. One can say in total assurance that there is nothing fortuitous about the fact that the critique of ethnocentrism—the very condition of ethnology—should be systematically and historically contemporaneous with the destruction of the history of metaphysics. Both belong to a single and same era.

Ethnology—like any science—comes about within the element of discourse. And it is primarily a European science employing traditional concepts, however much it may struggle against them. Consequently, whether he wants to or not—and this does not depend on a decision on his part—the ethnologist accepts into his discourse the premises of ethnocentrism at the very moment when he is employed in denouncing them. This necessity is irreducible; it is not a historical contingency. We ought to consider very carefully all its implications. But if nobody can escape this necessity, and if no one is therefore responsible for giving in to it, however little, this does not mean that all the ways of giving in to it are of an equal pertinence. The quality and the fecundity of a discourse are perhaps measured by the critical rigor with which this relationship to the history of metaphysics and to inherited concepts is thought. Here it is a question of a critical relationship to the language of the human sciences and a question of a critical responsibility of the discourse. It is a question of putting expressly and systematically the problem of the status of a discourse which borrows from a heritage the resources necessary for the deconstruction of that heritage itself. A problem of *economy* and *strategy*.

If I now go on to employ an examination of the texts of Lévi-Strauss as an example, it is not only because of the privilege accorded to ethnology among the human sciences, nor yet because the thought of Lévi-Strauss weighs heavily on the contemporary theoretical situation. It is above all because a certain choice has made itself evident in the work of Lévi-Strauss and because a certain doctrine has been elaborated there, and precisely in a *more or less explicit manner*, in relation to this critique of language and to this critical language in the human sciences.

In order to follow this movement in the text of Lévi-Strauss, let me choose as one guiding thread among others the opposition between nature and culture. In spite of all its rejuvenations and its disguises, this opposition is congenital to philosophy. It is even older than Plato. It is at least as old as the Sophists. Since the statement of the opposition—*physis/nomos, physis/technè*—it has been passed on to us by a whole historical chain which opposes "nature" to the law, to education, to art, to technics—and also to liberty, to the arbitrary, to history, to society, to the mind, and so on. From the beginnings of his quest and from his first book, *The Elementary Structures of Kinship*,[5] Lévi-Strauss has felt at one and the same time the necessity of utilizing this opposition and the impossibility of making it acceptable. In the *Elementary Structures*, he begins from this axiom or definition: that belongs to nature which is *universal* and spontaneous, not depending on any particular culture or on any determinate norm. That belongs to culture, on the other hand, which depends on a system of *norms* regulating society and is therefore capable of *varying* from one social structure to another. These two definitions are of the traditional type. But, in the very first pages of the *Elementary Structures*, Lévi-Strauss, who has begun to give these concepts an acceptable standing, encounters what he calls a *scandal*, that is to say, something which no longer tolerates the nature/culture opposition he has accepted and which seems to require *at one and the same time* the predicates of nature and those of culture. This scandal is the *incest-prohibition*. The incest-prohibition is universal; in this sense one could call it natural. But it is also a prohibition, a system of norms and interdicts; in this sense one could call it cultural.

Let us assume therefore that everything universal in man derives from the order of nature and is characterized by spontaneity, that everything which is subject to a norm belongs to culture and presents the attributes of the relative and the particular. We then find ourselves confronted by a fact, or rather an ensemble of facts, which, in the light of the preceding definitions, is not far from appearing as a scandal: the prohibition of incest presents without the least equivocation, and indissolubly linked together, the two characteristics in which we recognized the contradictory attributes of two exclusive orders. The prohibition of incest constitutes a rule, but a rule, alone of all the social rules, which possesses at the same time a universal character (p. 9).

Obviously there is no scandal except in the *interior* of a system of concepts sanctioning the difference between nature and culture. In beginning his work with the *factum* of the incest-prohibition, Lévi-Strauss thus puts himself in a position entailing that this difference, which has always been assumed to be self-evident, becomes obliterated or disputed. For, from the moment that the incest-prohibition can no longer be conceived within the nature/culture opposition, it can no longer be said that it is a scandalous fact, a nucleus of opacity within a network of transparent significations. The incest-prohibition

[5] *Les structures élémentaires de la parenté* (Paris: Presses Universitaires de France, 1949).

is no longer a scandal one meets with or comes up against in the domain of traditional concepts; it is something which escapes these concepts and certainly precedes them—probably as the condition of their possibility. It could perhaps be said that the whole of philosophical conceptualization, systematically relating itself to the nature/culture opposition, is designed to leave in the domain of the unthinkable the very thing that makes this conceptualization possible: the origin of the prohibition of incest.

I have dealt too cursorily with this example, only one among so many others, but the example nevertheless reveals that language bears within itself the necessity of its own critique. This critique may be undertaken along two tracks, in two "manners." Once the limit of nature/culture opposition makes itself felt, one might want to question systematically and rigorously the history of these concepts. This is a first action. Such a systematic and historic questioning would be neither a philological nor a philosophical action in the classic sense of these words. Concerning oneself with the founding concepts of the whole history of philosophy, de-constituting them, is not to undertake the task of the philologist or of the classic historian of philosophy. In spite of appearances, it is probably the most daring way of making the beginnings of a step outside of philosophy. The step "outside philosophy" is much more difficult to conceive than is generally imagined by those who think they made it long ago with cavalier ease, and who are in general swallowed up in metaphysics by the whole body of the discourse that they claim to have disengaged from it.

In order to avoid the possibly sterilizing effect of the first way, the other choice—which I feel corresponds more nearly to the way chosen by Lévi-Strauss—consists in conserving in the field of empirical discovery all these old concepts, while at the same time exposing here and there their limits, treating them as tools which can still be of use. No longer is any truth-value attributed to them; there is a readiness to abandon them if necessary if other instruments should appear more useful. In the meantime, their relative efficacy is exploited, and they are employed to destroy the old machinery to which they belong and of which they themselves are pieces. Thus it is that the language of the human sciences criticizes *itself*. Lévi-Strauss thinks that in this way he can separate *method* from *truth*, the instruments of the method and the objective significations aimed at by it. One could almost say that this is the primary affirmation of Lévi-Strauss; in any event, the first words of the *Elementary Structures* are: "One begins to understand that the distinction between state of nature and state of society (we would be more apt to say today: state of nature and state of culture), while lacking any acceptable historical signification, presents a value which fully justifies its use by modern sociology: its value as a methodological instrument."

Lévi-Strauss will always remain faithful to this double intention: to preserve as an instrument that whose truth-value he criticizes.

On the one hand, he will continue in effect to contest the value of the nature/culture opposition. More than thirteen years after the *Elementary Structures, The Savage Mind* [6] faithfully echoes the text I have just quoted: "The opposition between nature and culture which I have previously insisted on seems today to offer a value which is above all methodological." And this methodological value is not affected by its "ontological" non-value (as could be said, if this notion were not suspect here): "It would not be enough to have absorbed particular humanities into a general humanity; this first enterprise prepares the way for others . . . which belong to the natural and exact sciences: to reintegrate culture into nature, and finally, to reintegrate life into the totality of its physiochemical conditions" (p. 327).

On the other hand, still in *The Savage Mind,* he presents as what he calls *bricolage*[7] what might be called the discourse of this method. The *bricoleur,* says Lévi-Strauss, is someone who uses "the means at hand," that is, the instruments he finds at his disposition around him, those which are already there, which had not been especially conceived with an eye to the operation for which they are to be used and to which one tries by trial and error to adapt them, not hesitating to change them whenever it appears necessary, or to try several of them at once, even if their form and their origin are heterogenous—and so forth. There is therefore a critique of language in the form of *bricolage,* and it has even been possible to say that *bricolage* is the critical language itself. I am thinking in particular of the article by G. Genette, "Structuralisme et Critique littéraire," published in homage to Lévi-Strauss in a special issue of *L'Arc* (no. 26, 1965), where it is stated that the analysis of *bricolage* could "be applied almost word for word" to criticism, and especially to "literary criticism." [8]

If one calls *bricolage* the necessity of borrowing one's concepts from the text of a heritage which is more or less coherent or ruined, it must be said that every discourse is *bricoleur.* The engineer, whom Lévi-

---

[6] *La pensée sauvage* (Paris: Plon, 1962).

[7] A *bricoleur* is a jack-of-all trades, someone who potters about with odds-and-ends, who puts things together out of bits and pieces.

[8] Reprinted in: G. Genette, *Figures* (Paris: Editions du Seuil, 1966), p. 145.

Strauss opposes to the *bricoleur*, should be the one to construct the totality of his language, syntax, and lexicon. In this sense the engineer is a myth. A subject who would supposedly be the absolute origin of his own discourse and would supposedly construct it "out of nothing," "out of whole cloth," would be the creator of the *verbe*, the *verbe* itself. The notion of the engineer who had supposedly broken with all forms of *bricolage* is therefore a theological idea; and since Lévi-Strauss tells us elsewhere that *bricolage* is mythopoetic, the odds are that the engineer is a myth produced by the *bricoleur*. From the moment that we cease to believe in such an engineer and in a discourse breaking with the received historical discourse, as soon as it is admitted that every finite discourse is bound by a certain *bricolage*, and that the engineer and the scientist are also species of *bricoleurs* then the very idea of *bricolage* is menaced and the difference in which it took on its meaning decomposes.

This brings out the second thread which might guide us in what is being unraveled here.

Lévi-Strauss describes *bricolage* not only as an intellectual activity but also as a mythopoetical activity. One reads in *The Savage Mind*, "Like *bricolage* on the technical level, mythical reflection can attain brilliant and unforeseen results on the intellectual level. Reciprocally, the mythopoetical character of *bricolage* has often been noted" (p. 26).

But the remarkable endeavor of Lévi-Strauss is not simply to put forward, notably in the most recent of his investigations, a structural science or knowledge of myths and of mythological activity. His endeavor also appears—I would say almost from the first—in the status which he accords to his own discourse on myths, to what he calls his "mythologicals." It is here that his discourse on the myth reflects on itself and criticizes itself. And this moment, this critical period, is evidently of concern to all the languages which share the field of the human sciences. What does Lévi-Strauss say of his "mythologicals"? It is here that we rediscover the mythopoetical virtue (power) of *bricolage*. In effect, what appears most fascinating in this critical search for a new status of the discourse is the stated abandonment of all reference to a *center*, to a *subject*, to a privileged *reference*, to an origin, or to an absolute *archè*. The theme of this decentering could be followed throughout the "Overture" to his last book, *The Raw and the Cooked*. I shall simply remark on a few key points.

1) From the very start, Lévi-Strauss recognizes that the Bororo myth which he employs in the book as the "reference-myth" does not

merit this name and this treatment. The name is specious and the use of the myth improper. This myth deserves no more than any other its referential privilege:

> In fact the Bororo myth which will from now on be designated by the name *reference-myth* is, as I shall try to show, nothing other than a more or less forced transformation of other myths originating either in the same society or in societies more or less far removed. It would therefore have been legitimate to choose as my point of departure any representative of the group whatsoever. From this point of view, the interest of the reference-myth does not depend on its typical character, but rather on its irregular position in the midst of a group (p. 10).

2) There is no unity or absolute source of the myth. The focus or the source of the myth are always shadows and virtualities which are elusive, unactualizable, and nonexistent in the first place. Everything begins with the structure, the configuration, the relationship. The discourse on this acentric structure, the myth, that is, cannot itself have an absolute subject or an absolute center. In order not to short change the form and the movement of the myth, that violence which consists in centering a language which is describing an acentric structure must be avoided. In this context, therefore it is necessary to forego scientific or philosophical discourse, to renounce the *epistèmè* which absolutely requires, which is the absolute requirement that we go back to the source, to the center, to the founding basis, to the principle, and so on. In opposition to *epistèmic* discourse, structural discourse on myths—*mythological* discourse—must itself be *mythomorphic*. It must have the form of that of which it speaks. This is what Lévi-Strauss says in *The Raw and the Cooked*, from which I would now like to quote a long and remarkable passage:

> In effect the study of myths poses a methodological problem by the fact that it cannot conform to the Cartesian principle of dividing the difficulty into as many parts as are necessary to resolve it. There exists no veritable end or term to mythical analysis, no secret unity which could be grasped at the end of the work of decomposition. The themes duplicate themselves to infinity. When we think we have disentangled them from each other and can hold them separate, it is only to realize that they are joining together again, in response to the attraction of unforeseen affinities. In consequence, the unity of the myth is only tendential and projective; it never reflects a state or a moment of the myth. An imaginary phenomenon implied by the endeavor to interpret, its role is to give a synthetic form to the myth and to impede its dissolution into the confusion of contraries. It could

Jacques Derrida

therefore be said that the science or knowledge of myths is an *anaclastic*, taking this ancient term in the widest sense authorized by its etymology, a science which admits into its definition the study of the reflected rays along with that of the broken ones. But, unlike philosophical reflection, which claims to go all the way back to its source, the reflections in question here concern rays without any other than a virtual focus. . . . In wanting to imitate the spontaneous movement of mythical thought, my enterprise, itself too brief and too long, has had to yield to its demands and respect its rhythm. Thus is this book, on myths itself and in its own way, a myth.

This statement is repeated a little farther on (p. 20): "Since myths themselves rest on second-order codes (the first-order codes being those in which language consists), this book thus offers the rough draft of a third-order code, destined to insure the reciprocal possibility of translation of several myths. This is why it would not be wrong to consider it a myth: the myth of mythology, as it were." It is by this absence of any real and fixed center of the mythical or mythological discourse that the musical model chosen by Lévi-Strauss for the composition of his book is apparently justified. The absence of a center is here the absence of a subject and the absence of an author: "The myth and the musical work thus appear as orchestra conductors whose listeners are the silent performers. If it be asked where the real focus of the work is to be found, it must be replied that its determination is impossible. Music and mythology bring man face to face with virtual objects whose shadow alone is actual. . . . Myths have no authors" (p. 25).

Thus it is at this point that ethnographic *bricolage* deliberately assumes its mythopoetic function. But by the same token, this function makes the philosophical or epistemological requirement of a center appear as mythological, that is to say, as a historical illusion.

Nevertheless, even if one yields to the necessity of what Lévi-Strauss has done, one cannot ignore its risks. If the mythological is mythomorphic, are all discourses on myths equivalent? Shall we have to abandon any epistemological requirement which permits us to distinguish between several qualities of discourse on the myth? A classic question, but inevitable. We cannot reply—and I do not believe Lévi-Strauss replies to it—as long as the problem of the relationships between the philosopheme or the theorem, on the one hand, and the mytheme or the mythopoem(e), on the other, has not been expressly posed. This is no small problem. For lack of expressly posing this problem, we condemn ourselves to transforming the claimed transgression of philosophy into an unperceived fault in the interior of the philosophical field. Empiricism would be the genus of which these faults would always be the species. Trans-philosophical concepts would be transformed into philosophical naïvetés. One could give many examples to demonstrate this risk: the concepts of sign, history, truth, and so forth. What I want to emphasize is simply that the passage beyond philosophy does not consist in turning the page of philosophy (which usually comes down to philosophizing badly), but in continuing to read philosophers *in a certain way*. The risk I am speaking of is always assumed by Lévi-Strauss and it is the very price of his endeavor. I have said that empiricism is the matrix of all the faults menacing a discourse which continues, as with Lévi-Strauss in particular, to elect to be scientific. If we wanted to pose the problem of empiricism and *bricolage* in depth, we would probably end up very quickly with a number of propositions absolutely contradictory in relation to the status of discourse in structural ethnography. On the one hand, structuralism justly claims to be the critique of empiricism. But at the same time there is not a single book or study by Lévi-Strauss which does not offer itself as an empirical essay which can always be completed or invalidated by new information. The structural schemata are always proposed as hypotheses resulting from a finite quantity of information and which are subjected to the proof of experience. Numerous texts could be used to demonstrate this double postulation. Let us turn once again to the "Overture" of *The Raw and the Cooked,* where it seems clear that if this postulation is double, it is because it is a question here of a language on language:

Critics who might take me to task for not having begun by making an exhaustive inventory of South American myths before analyzing them would be making a serious mistake about the nature and the role of these documents. The totality of the myths of a people is of the order of the discourse. Provided that this people does not become physically or morally extinct, this totality is never closed. Such a criticism would therefore be equivalent to reproaching a linguist with writing the grammar of a language without having recorded the totality of the words which have been uttered since that language came into existence and without knowing the verbal exchanges which will take place as long as the language continues to exist. Experience proves that an absurdly small number of sentences . . . allows the linguist to elaborate a grammar of the language he is studying. And even a partial grammar or an outline of a grammar represents valuable acquisitions in the case of unknown languages. Syntax does not wait until it has been possible to enumerate a theoretically unlimited series of events before becoming manifest, because syntax consists in the body of rules which presides over the generation of these events. And it is precisely a syntax of South American mythology that I wanted to outline. Should new texts appear to enrich the mythical discourse, then this will provide an opportunity to check or modify the way in which certain grammatical laws have been formulated, an opportunity to discard certain of them and an opportunity to discover new ones. But in no instance can the requirement of a total mythical discourse be raised as an objection. For we have just seen that such a requirement has no meaning (pp. 15–16).

Totalization is therefore defined at one time as *useless*, at another time as *impossible*. This is no doubt the result of the fact that there are two ways of conceiving the limit of totalization. And I assert once again that these two determinations coexist implicitly in the discourses of Lévi-Strauss. Totalization can be judged impossible in the classical style: one then refers to the empirical endeavor of a subject or of a finite discourse in a vain and breathless quest of an infinite richness which it can never master. There is too much, more than one can say. But nontotalization can also be determined in another way: not from the standpoint of the concept of finitude as assigning us to an empirical view, but from the standpoint of the concept of *freeplay*. If totalization no longer has any meaning, it is not because the infinity of a field cannot be covered by a finite glance or a finite discourse, but because the nature of the field—that is, language and a finite language —excludes totalization. This field is in fact that of *freeplay*, that is to say, a field of infinite substitutions in the closure of a finite ensemble. This field permits these infinite substitutions only because it is finite, that is to say, because instead of being an inexhaustible field, as in the classical hypothesis, instead of being too large, there is something missing from it: a center which arrests and founds the freeplay of substitutions. One could say—rigorously using that word whose scandalous signification is always obliterated in French—that this movement of the freeplay, permitted by the lack, the absence of a center or origin, is the movement of *supplementarity*. One cannot determine the center, the sign which *supplements*[9] it, which takes its place in its absence— because this sign adds itself, occurs in addition, over and above, comes as a *supplement*.[10] The movement of signification adds something, which results in the fact that there is always more, but this addition is a floating one because it comes to perform a vicarious function, to

[9] The point being that the word, both in English and French, means "to supply a deficiency," on the one hand, and "to supply something additional," on the other.

[10] ". . . ce signe s'ajoute, vient en sus, en *supplément*."

supplement a lack on the part of the signified. Although Lévi-Strauss in his use of the word supplementary never emphasizes as I am doing here the two directions of meaning which are so strangely compounded within it, it is not by chance that he uses this word twice in his "Introduction to the Work of Marcel Mauss," [11] at the point where he is speaking of the "superabundance of signifier, in relation to the signifieds to which this superabundance can refer":

In his endeavor to understand the world, man therefore always has at his disposition a surplus of signification (which he portions out amongst things according to the laws of symbolic thought—which it is the task of ethnologists and linguists to study). This distribution of a *supplementary* allowance [*ration* supplémentaire]—if it is permissible to put it that way—is absolutely necessary in order that on the whole the available signifier and the signified it aims at may remain in the relationship of complementarity which is the very condition of the use of symbolic thought (p. xlix).

(It could no doubt be demonstrated that this *ration supplémentaire* of signification is the origin of the *ratio* itself.) The word reappears a little farther on, after Lévi-Strauss has mentioned "this floating signifier, which is the servitude of all finite thought":

In other words—and taking as our guide Mauss's precept that all social phenomena can be assimilated to language—we see in *mana, Wakau, oranda* and other notions of the same type, the conscious expression of a semantic function, whose role it is to permit symbolic thought to operate in spite of the contradiction which is proper to it. In this way are explained the apparently insoluble antinomies attached to this notion. . . . At one and the same time force and action, quality and state, substantive and verb; abstract and concrete, omnipresent and localized—*mana* is in effect all these things. But is it not precisely because it is none of these things that *mana* is a simple form, or more exactly, a symbol in the pure state, and therefore capable of becoming charged with any sort of symbolic content whatever? In the system of symbols constituted by all cosmologies, *mana* would simply be a *valeur symbolique zéro*, that is to say, a sign marking the necessity of a symbolic content *supplementary* [my italics] to that with which the signified is already loaded, but which can take on any value required, provided only that this value still remains part of the available reserve and is not, as phonologists put it, a group-term.

Lévi-Strauss adds the note:

---

[11] "Introduction à l'oeuvre de Marcel Mauss," in: Marcel Mauss, *Sociologie et anthropologie* (Paris: Presses Universitaires de France, 1950).

Jacques Derrida

Linguists have already been led to formulate hypotheses of this type. For example: "A zero phoneme is opposed to all the other phonemes in French in that it entails no differential characters and no constant phonetic value. On the contrary, the proper function of the zero phoneme is to be opposed to phoneme absence." (R. Jakobson and J. Lutz, "Notes on the French Phonemic Pattern," *Word*, vol. 5, no. 2 [August, 1949], p. 155). Similarly, if we schematize the conception I am proposing here, it could almost be said that the function of notions like *mana* is to be opposed to the absence of signification, without entailing by itself any particular signification (p. 1 and note).

The *superabundance* of the signifier, its *supplementary* character, is thus the result of a finitude, that is to say, the result of a lack which must be *supplemented*.

It can now be understood why the concept of freeplay is important in Lévi-Strauss. His references to all sorts of games, notably to roulette, are very frequent, especially in his *Conversations*,[12] in *Race and History*,[13] and in *The Savage Mind*. This reference to the game or freeplay is always caught up in a tension.

It is in tension with history, first of all. This is a classical problem, objections to which are now well worn or used up. I shall simply indicate what seems to me the formality of the problem: by reducing history, Lévi-Strauss has treated as it deserves a concept which has always been in complicity with a teleological and eschatological metaphysics, in other words, paradoxically, in complicity with that philosophy of presence to which it was believed history could be opposed. The thematic of historicity, although it seems to be a somewhat late arrival in philosophy, has always been required by the determination of being as presence. With or without etymology, and in spite of the classic antagonism which opposes these significations throughout all of classical thought, it could be shown that the concept of *epistèmè* has always called forth that of *historia*, if history is always the unity of a becoming, as tradition of truth or development of science or knowledge oriented toward the appropriation of truth in presence and self-presence, toward knowledge in consciousness-of-self.[14] History has always been conceived as the movement of a resumption of history, a diversion between two presences. But if it is legitimate to sus-

---

[12] Presumably: G. Charbonnier, *Entretiens avec Claude Lévi-Strauss* (Paris: Plon-Julliard, 1961).

[13] *Race and History* (Paris: UNESCO Publications, 1958).

[14] ". . . l'unité d'un devenir, comme tradition de la vérité dans la présence et la présence à soi, vers le savoir dans la conscience de soi."

pect this concept of history, there is a risk, if it is reduced without an express statement of the problem I am indicating here, of falling back into an anhistoricism of a classical type, that is to say, in a determinate moment of the history of metaphysics. Such is the algebraic formality of the problem as I see it. More concretely, in the work of Lévi-Strauss it must be recognized that the respect for structurality, for the internal originality of the structure, compels a neutralization of time and history. For example, the appearance of a new structure, of an original system, always comes about—and this is the very condition of its structural specificity—by a rupture with its past, its origin, and its cause. One can therefore describe what is peculiar to the structural organization only by not taking into account, in the very moment of this description, its past conditions: by failing to pose the problem of the passage from one structure to another, by putting history into parentheses. In this "structuralist" moment, the concepts of chance and discontinuity are indispensable. And Lévi-Strauss does in fact often appeal to them as he does, for instance, for that structure of structures, language, of which he says in the "Introduction to the Work of Marcel Mauss" that it "could only have been born in one fell swoop":

Whatever may have been the moment and the circumstances of its appearance in the scale of animal life, language could only have been born in one fell swoop. Things could not have set about signifying progressively. Following a transformation the study of which is not the concern of the social sciences, but rather of biology and psychology, a crossing over came about from a stage where nothing had a meaning to another where everything possessed it (p. xlvi).

This standpoint does not prevent Lévi-Strauss from recognizing the slowness, the process of maturing, the continuous toil of factual transformations, history (for example, in *Race and History*). But, in accordance with an act which was also Rousseau's and Husserl's, he must "brush aside all the facts" at the moment when he wishes to recapture the specificity of a structure. Like Rousseau, he must always conceive of the origin of a new structure on the model of catastrophe—an overturning of nature in nature, a natural interruption of the natural sequence, a brushing aside *of* nature.

Besides the tension of freeplay with history, there is also the tension of freeplay with presence. Freeplay is the disruption of presence. The presence of an element is always a signifying and substitutive reference inscribed in a system of differences and the movement of a chain.

Jacques Derrida

Freeplay is always an interplay of absence and presence, but if it is to be radically conceived, freeplay must be conceived of before the alternative of presence and absence; being must be conceived of as presence or absence beginning with the possibility of freeplay and not the other way around. If Lévi-Strauss, better than any other, has brought to light the freeplay of repetition and the repetition of free-play, one no less perceives in his work a sort of ethic of presence, an ethic of nostalgia for origins, an ethic of archaic and natural inno-cence, of a purity of presence and self-presence in speech[15]—an ethic, nostalgia, and even remorse which he often presents as the motivation of the ethnological project when he moves toward archaic societies—exemplary societies in his eyes. These texts are well known.

As a turning toward the presence, lost or impossible, of the absent origin, this structuralist thematic of broken immediateness is thus the sad, *negative*, nostalgic, guilty, Rousseauist facet of the thinking of freeplay of which the Nietzschean *affirmation*—the joyous affirmation of the freeplay of the world and without truth, without origin, offered to an active interpretation—would be the other side. *This affirmation then determines the non-center otherwise than as loss of the center.* And it plays the game without security. For there is a *sure* freeplay: that which is limited to the *substitution* of *given and existing, present,* pieces. In absolute chance, affirmation also surrenders itself to *genetic* indetermination, to the *seminal* adventure of the trace.[16]

There are thus two interpretations of interpretation, of structure, of sign, of freeplay. The one seeks to decipher, dreams of decipher-ing, a truth or an origin which is free from freeplay and from the order of the sign, and lives like an exile the necessity of interpretation. The other, which is no longer turned toward the origin, affirms free-play and tries to pass beyond man and humanism, the name man being the name of that being who, throughout the history of metaphysics or of ontotheology—in other words, through the history of all of his

---

[15] ". . . de la présence à soi dans la parole."

[16] "Tournée vers la présence, perdue ou impossible, de l'origine absente, cette thématique structuraliste de l'immédiateté rompue est donc la face triste, *négative*, nostalgique, coupable, rousseauiste, de la pensée du jeu dont *l'affirmation* nietz-schéenne, l'affirmation joyeuse du jeu du monde et de l'innocence du devenir, l'affirmation d'un monde de signes sans faute, sans vérité, sans origine, offert à une interprétation active, serait l'autre face. *Cette affirmation détermine alors le* non-centre *autrement que comme perte du centre.* Et elle joue sans sécurité. Car il y a un jeu *sûr:* celui qui se limite à la *substitution* de pièces *données et ex-istantes, présentes.* Dans le hasard absolu, l'affirmation se livre aussi à l'indéter-mination *génétique,* à l'aventure *séminale* de la trace."

history—has dreamed of full presence, the reassuring foundation, the origin and the end of the game. The second interpretation of interpretation, to which Nietzsche showed us the way, does not seek in ethnography, as Lévi-Strauss wished, the "inspiration of a new humanism" (again from the "Introduction to the Work of Marcel Mauss").

There are more than enough indications today to suggest we might perceive that these two interpretations of interpretation—which are absolutely irreconcilable even if we live them simultaneously and reconcile them in an obscure economy—together share the field which we call, in such a problematic fashion, the human sciences.

For my part, although these two interpretations must acknowledge and accentuate their difference and define their irreducibility, I do not believe that today there is any question of *choosing*—in the first place because here we are in a region (let's say, provisionally, a region of historicity) where the category of choice seems particularly trivial; and in the second, because we must first try to conceive of the common ground, and the *différence* of this irreducible difference.[17] Here there is a sort of question, call it historical, of which we are only glimpsing today the *conception, the formation, the gestation, the labor.* I employ these words, I admit, with a glance toward the business of childbearing—but also with a glance toward those who, in a company from which I do not exclude myself, turn their eyes away in the face of the as yet unnameable which is proclaiming itself and which can do so, as is necessary whenever a birth is in the offing, only under the species of the non-species, in the formless, mute, infant, and terrifying form of monstrosity.

Discussion

JEAN HYPPOLITE: I should simply like to ask Derrida, whose presentation and discussion I have admired, for some explanation of what is, no doubt, the technical point of departure of the presentation. That is, a question of the concept of the center of structure, or what a center might mean. When I take, for example, the structure of certain

---

[17] From *différer,* in the sense of "to postpone," "put off," "defer." Elsewhere Derrida uses the word as a synonym for the German *Aufschub:* "postponement," and relates it to the central Freudian concepts of *Verspätung, Nachträglichkeit,* and to the "*détours* to death" of *Beyond the Pleasure Principle* by Sigmund Freud (Standard Edition, ed. James Strachey, vol. XIX, London, 1961), Chap. V.

algebraic constructions [ensembles], where is the center? Is the center the knowledge of general rules which, after a fashion, allow us to understand the interplay of the elements? Or is the center certain elements which enjoy a particular privilege within the ensemble?

My question is, I think, relevant since one cannot think of the structure without the center, and the center itself is "destructured," is it not?—the center is not structured. I think we have a great deal to learn as we study the sciences of man; we have much to learn from the natural sciences. They are like an image of the problems which we, in turn, put to ourselves. With Einstein, for example, we see the end of a kind of privilege of empiric evidence. And in that connection we see a constant appear, a constant which is a combination of space-time, which does not belong to any of the experimenters who live the experience, but which, in a way, dominates the whole construct; and this notion of the constant—is this the center? But natural science has gone much further. It no longer searches for the constant. It considers that there are events, somehow improbable, which bring about for a while a structure and an invariability. Is it that everything happens as though certain mutations, which don't come from any author or any hand, and which are, like the poor reading of a manuscript, realized [only] as a defect of a structure, simply exist as mutations? Is this the case? Is it a question of a structure which is in the nature of a genotype produced by chance from an improbable happening, of a meeting which involved a series of chemical molecules and which organized them in a certain way, creating a genotype which will be realized, and whose origin is lost in a mutation? Is that what you are tending toward? Because, for my part, I feel that I am going in that direction and that I find there the example—even when we are talking about a kind of end of history—of the integration of the historic; under the form of *event*, so long as it is improbable, at the very center of the realization of the structure, but a history which no longer has anything to do with eschatological history, a history which loses itself always in its own pursuit, since the origin is perpetually displaced. And you know that the language we are speaking today, *à propos* of language, is spoken about genotypes, and about information theory. Can this sign without sense, this perpetual turning back, be understood in the light of a kind of philosophy of nature in which nature will not only have realized a mutation, but will have realized a perpetual mutant: man? That is, a kind of error of transmission or of malformation would have created a being which is always malformed, whose adaptation is a perpetual aberration, and the problem of man would become part of a much larger field in which what you want to do, what you are in the process of doing, that is, the loss of the center—the fact that there is no privileged or original structure—could be seen under this very form to which man would be restored. Is this what you wanted to say, or were you getting at something else? That is my last question, and I apologize for having held the floor so long.

JACQUES DERRIDA: With the last part of your remarks, I can say that I agree fully—but you were asking a question. I was wondering myself if I know where I am going. So I would answer you by saying, first, that I am trying, precisely, to put myself at a point so that I do not know any longer where I am going. And, as to this loss of the center, I *refuse* to approach an idea of the "non-center" which would no longer be the tragedy of the loss of the center—this sadness is classical. And I don't mean to say that I thought of approaching an idea by which this loss of the center would be an affirmation.

As to what you said about the nature and the situation of man in the products of nature, I think that we have already discussed this together. I will assume entirely with you this partiality which you expressed—with the exception of your [choice of] words, and here the words are more than mere words, as always. That is to say, I cannot accept your precise formulation, although I am not prepared to offer a precise alternative. So, it being understood that I do not know where I am going, that the words which we are using do not satisfy me, with these reservations in mind, I am entirely in agreement with you.

Concerning the first part of your question, the Einsteinian constant is not a constant, is not a center. It is the very concept of variability —it is, finally, the concept of the game. In other words, it is not the concept of some*thing*—of a center starting from which an observer could master the field—but the very concept of the game which, after all, I was trying to elaborate.

HYPPOLITE: It is a constant in the game?

DERRIDA: It is *the* constant of the game . . .

HYPPOLITE: It is the rule of the game.

DERRIDA: It is a rule of the game which does not govern the game; it is a rule of the game which does not dominate the game. Now, when the rule of the game is displaced by the game itself, we must find something other than the word *rule*. In what concerns algebra, then,

I think that it is an example in which a group of significant figures, if you wish, or of signs, is deprived of a center. But we can consider algebra from two points of view. Either as the example or analogue of this absolutely de-centered game of which I have spoken; or we can try to consider algebra as a limited field of ideal objects, products in the Husserlian sense, beginning from a history, from a *Lebenswelt*, from a subject, etc., which constituted, created its ideal objects, and consequently we should always be able to make substitutions, by re-activating in it the origin—that of which the significants, seemingly lost, are the derivations. I think it is in this way that algebra was thought of classically. One could, perhaps, think of it otherwise as an image of the game. Or else one thinks of algebra as a field of ideal objects, produced by the activity of what we call a subject, or man, or history, and thus, we recover the possibility of algebra in the field of classical thought; or else we consider it as a disquieting mirror of a world which is algebraic through and through.

HYPPOLITE: What is a structure then? If I can't take the example of algebra anymore, how will you define a structure for me?—to see where the center is.

DERRIDA: The concept of structure itself—I say in passing—is no longer satisfactory to describe that game. How to define structure? Structure should be centered. But this center can be either thought, as it was classically, like a creator or being or a fixed and natural place; or also as a deficiency, let's say; or something which makes possible "free play," in the sense in which one speaks of the "jeu dans la machine," of the "jeu des pièces," and which receives—and this is what we call history—a series of determinations, of signifiers, which have no signifieds [*signifiés*] finally, which cannot become signifiers except as they begin from this deficiency. So, I think that what I have said can be understood as a criticism of structuralism, certainly.

RICHARD MACKSEY: I may be off-side [*hors jeu*] in trying to identify prematurely those players who can join your team in the critique of metaphysics represented by your tentative game-theory. Still, I was struck by the sympathy with which two contemporary figures might view that formidable prospect which you and Nietzsche invite us to contemplate. I am thinking, first, of the later career of Eugen Fink, a "reformed" phenomenologist with the peculiarly paradoxical relationship to Heidegger. Even as early as the colloquia at Krefeld and Royaumont he was prepared to argue the secondary status of the conceptual world, to see *Sein, Wahrheit,* and *Welt* as irreducibly part of a single, primal question. Certainly in his *Vor-Fragen* and in the last chapter of the Nietzsche book he advances a Zarathustrian notion of *game* as the step outside (or behind) philosophy. It is interesting to contrast his Nietzsche with Heidegger's; it seems to me that you would agree with him in reversing the latter's primacy of *Sein* over *Seiendes,* and thereby achieve some interesting consequences for the post-humanist critique of our announced topic, "les sciences *humaines.*" For surely, in *Spiel als Weltsymbol* the presiding Worldgame is profoundly anterior and anonymous, anterior to the Platonic division of being and appearance and dispossessed of a human, personal center.

The other figure is that writer who has made the shifting center of his fictional poetics the narrative game in "the *unanimous* night," that architect and prisoner of labyrinths, the creator of Pierre Menard.

DERRIDA: You are thinking, no doubt, of Jorge Luis Borges.

CHARLES MORAZÉ: Just a remark. Concerning the dialogue of the past twenty years with Lévi-Strauss on the possibility of a grammar other than that of language—I have a great deal of admiration for what Lévi-Strauss has done in the order of a grammar of mythologies. I would like to point out that there is also a grammar of the event— that one can make a grammar of the event. It is more difficult to establish. I think that in the coming months, in the coming years, we will begin to learn how this grammar or rather this set of grammars of events can be constituted. And [this grammar] leads to results, may I say, anyway with regard to my personal experience, which are a little less pessimistic than those you have indicated.

LUCIEN GOLDMANN: I would like to say that I find that Derrida, with whose conclusions I do not agree, has a catalytic function in French cultural life, and for that reason I pay him homage. I said once that he brings to my mind that memory of when I arrived in France in '34. At that time there was a very strong royalist movement among the students and suddenly a group appeared which was equally in defense of royalism, but which demanded a real Merovingian king!

In this movement of negation of the subject or of the center, if you like, which Derrida defines remarkably, he is in the process of saying to all the people who represent this position, "But you contradict yourself; you never carry through to the end. Finally, in criticizing mythologies, if you deny the position, the existence, of the critic and the necessity of saying anything, you contradict yourself, because you are still M. Lévi-Strauss who says something and if you make a new mythology. . . ." Well, the criticism was remarkable and it's not worth taking it up again. But if I have noted the few words which were added to the text and which were of a destructive character, we could discuss that on the level of semiology. But I would like to ask Derrida a question: "Let us suppose that instead of discussing on the basis of a series of postulates toward which all contemporary currents, irrationalist as well as formalist, are oriented, you have before you a very different position, say the dialectical position. Quite simply, you think that science is something that men make, that history is not an error, that what you call theology is something acceptable, an attempt not to say that the world is ordered, that it is theological, but that the human being is one who places his stake on the possibility of giving a meaning to a word which will eventually, at some point, resist this meaning. And the origin or the fundamental of that which is before a typical state of dichotomy of which you speak (or in grammatology the action which registers before there is a meaning) is something which we are studying today, but which we cannot, which we don't even want to, penetrate from the inside, because it can be penetrated from the inside only in silence, while we want to understand it according to the logic which we have elaborated, with which we try somehow or other to go farther, not to discover a meaning hidden by some god, but to give a meaning to a world in which that is the function of man (without knowing, moreover, where man comes from —we can't be entirely consistent, because if the question is clear, we know, if we say that man comes from God, then somebody will ask "Where does God come from?" and if we say that man comes from nature, somebody will ask "Where does nature come from?" and so on). But we are on the inside and we are in this situation. Is this position before you, then, still contradictory?

JAN KOTT: At one time this famous phrase of Mallarmé seemed to be very significant: "A throw of dice will never abolish chance." ["Un coup de dés n'abolira jamais le hasard."] After this lesson you have given us, isn't it possible to say that: "And chance will never abolish the throw of dice!" ["Et le hasard n'abolira jamais le coup de dés."]

DERRIDA: I say "Yes" immediately to Mr. Kott. As to what Mr. Goldmann has said to me, I feel that he has isolated, in what I said, the aspect that he calls destructive. I believe, however, that I was quite explicit about the fact that nothing of what I said had a destructive meaning. Here or there I have used the word *déconstruction,* which has nothing to do with destruction. That is to say, it is simply a question of (and this is a necessity of criticism in the classical sense of the word) being alert to the implications, to the historical sedimentation of the language which we use—and that is not destruction. I believe in the necessity of scientific work in the classical sense, I believe in the necessity of everything which is being done and even of what you are doing, but I don't see why I should renounce or why anyone should renounce the radicality of a critical work under the pretext that it risks the sterilization of science, humanity, progress, the origin of meaning, etc. I believe that the risk of sterility and of sterilization has always been the price of lucidity. Concerning the initial anecdote, I take it rather badly, because it defines me as an ultra-royalist, or an "ultra," as they said in my native country not so long ago, whereas I have a much more humble, modest, and classical conception of what I am doing.

Concerning Mr. Morazé's allusion to the grammar of the event, there I must return his question, because I don't know what a grammar of the event can be.

SERGE DOUBROVSKY: You always speak of a *non-center.* How can you, within your own perspective, explain or at least understand what a perception is? For a perception is precisely the manner in which the world appears *centered* to me. And language you represent as flat or level. Now language is something else again. It is, as Merleau-Ponty said, a corporeal intentionality. And starting from this utilization of language, in as much as there is an intention of language, I inevitably find a center again. For it is not "One" who speaks, but "I." And even if you reduce the I, you are obliged to come across once again the concept of intentionality, which I believe is at the base of a whole thought, which, moreover, you do not deny. Therefore I ask how you reconcile it with your present attempts?

DERRIDA: First of all, I didn't say that there was no center, that we could get along without the center. I believe that the center is a function, not a being—a reality, but a function. And this function is absolutely indispensable. The subject is absolutely indispensable. I don't destroy the subject; I situate it. That is to say, I believe that at a certain level both of experience and of philosophical and scientific discourse one cannot get along without the notion of subject. It is a question of knowing where it comes from and how it functions. Therefore I keep the concept of center, which I explained was indispensable, as well as that of subject, and the whole system of concepts to which you have referred.

Since you mentioned intentionality, I simply try to see those who are founding the movement of intentionality—which cannot be conceived in the term intentionality. As to perception, I should say that once I recognized it as a necessary conservation. I was extremely conservative. Now I don't know what perception is and I don't believe that anything like perception exists. Perception is precisely a concept, a concept of an intuition or of a given originating from the thing itself, present itself in its meaning, independently from language, from the system of reference. And I believe that perception is interdependent with the concept of origin and of center and consequently whatever strikes at the metaphysics of which I have spoken strikes also at the very concept of perception. I don't believe that there is any perception.

Greek Tragedy: Problems of Interpretation[1]

Jean-Pierre Vernant
Ecole Pratique
des Hautes Etudes

First of all, why Greek tragedy? Why any problem of interpretation? Like every other human work, a Greek tragedy is not directly readable. It is a message, a message which has to be deciphered. I would like to show you the series of problems posed by the deciphering of a text such as a Greek tragedy, emphasizing in particular the necessity for a study of the context, in a sense I shall define more precisely in a moment. It is not a social and psychological context nor is it an exterior context, alien to the meanings and internal structures of the tragedy. In my eyes the understanding of a Greek tragedy is not the painting of a historical picture of Greek or Athenian society, just because it is an Attic tragedy of the fifth century B.C.

I understand *context* in the following sense. If I say to you "What beautiful weather we're having today!" the meaning of my sentence and the stylistic devices I use differ according to whether you look out the window and see that the sun is shining or that it is pouring rain. In short, every message implies a necessary complicity between the interlocutor and his audience. That is what I call its *context*. Every message is based on a common body of knowledge which permits the use of allusion. Such is the case in Greek tragedy. Only in the case of tragedy, a work of literature, a message which subsists and be-

---

[1] "La Tragédie Grecque: problèmes d'interprétation." The text which follows is a translation and, in some instances, paraphrase of the tape-recording of M. Vernant's lecture. The French text of a supporting essay distributed at the Symposium is printed as an appendix to this volume. The notes and some citations to the English text have been supplied by the translator.

longs to human history, which is read by successive generations, the problem becomes more difficult for the following reasons.

I believe that the Greek tragedy has a meaning, that for the most part the tragic poet is saying what is expected by the people of Athens who come to sit in the theater and who want to hear about what they know, who know who is speaking, what he is speaking of, and how it concerns them. That is what I as a historian try to understand in restoring what I call the authentic sense of the Greek tragedy, of tragedy insofar as it is inseparable from a historical context as I have stated it; that is, tragedy as a particular historical moment.

But I am not unaware of the fact that this same Greek tragedy can be read by anybody at all, without preparation, by any non-Hellenist, and that the tragedy speaks even to him. Therefore the interpretation given by the historian of Greek thought and civilization—through all the by-ways of philology, religious, legal, social, and political history —must also permit us to explain why this tragedy still speaks to us today, and even to those who do not know the context.

Thus I must account not only for the sense of the tragedy but also for what I would be tempted to call its "counter-sense," for the fact that each of us has the right to read it in a different way, and to find in this tragedy itself the justification for reading it in a way different from the way in which the Greeks read it. That, it seems to me, is a fundamental problem, and the reason for my beginning with the question "Why Greek tragedy?" For, since Greek tragedy is a definite historical moment, we need to understand how we can still present it on our stages and how the audience can understand its message without knowing all that the Hellenist knows. There is the problem.

I have spoken of context and of allusions. The allusions are clear; they are found on many levels. Behind Greek tragedy there is a culture and there are historical situations. In the first place Greek tragedies are works which are involved in particular circumstances and current events. They are presented every year and they are heavily freighted with political allusions, so that a recent book was able to approach the problem of Euripides precisely from the point of view of his significance in relation to current political events. Forgive me for observing that no non-historical analysis—whether structural, mathematical, or psychoanalytical—can grasp those topical political events. Only the historian, by working very hard at it, can understand them. But these political allusions are of small account, even though, in certain cases, it is only through an understanding of the political allusion that one can understand exactly the sense of a passage of a tragic author. That is not the essential. What is essential, as you know, is the tragic poet's use of a certain language which he did not invent, which he found ready made, and which makes a philological study necessary for every term and every phrase, because the words carry a meaning which is not translatable. Especially when we are dealing with a very ancient culture, far removed from us, there is no possibility of exact translation.

There is for example one word which is heard throughout Greek tragedy, and that is the word *dikè*. I can translate it *justice*, but justice is not adequate for *dikè*. One has to have seen all the contexts in which *dikè* is used in a variety of situations, to understand the meaning through the message. And even this is not of primary importance for, beyond the studies of the uses of a term, there is something much more decisive, and that is what linguists today call "semantic fields." In different vocabularies, legal, religious, and political, such and such a term is associated with a constellation, which forms a definite pattern with a group of other terms. The tragic poets use these vocabularies of law, religion or politics, playing on the differences between semantic fields, contrasting them in order to emphasize the ambiguity of certain notions. Unless one knows these semantic fields beforehand, one cannot understand certain crucial elements. For example—and we shall take up a particular case shortly—*nomos, dikè, kratos, bia,* and *peitho* form constellations of notions whose inter-relationships shift with time, but whose meanings and configurations in the text of a tragedy must be understood. Here, for example, no study of the type based on mathematical statistics could be significant. Why? Well, it may happen that in a tragedy, at the moment when a character has just spoken of *peitho*, that is of persuasion, the chorus begins to speak of *kratos*, power, dominance. Because there is in this tragedy only this one case in which these words are associated, a statistical machine would consider the fact of absolutely no importance. On the contrary. For the Hellenist who knows the constellation in which *peitho* or *kratos* figures, this conjunction not only becomes pertinent but marks a decisive turning point in the tragedy.[2] Thus we cannot avoid the problems of meaning and all the difficulties associated with questions of meaning.

---

[2] Thus the ambiguities of *kratos* are well illustrated in *The Suppliants*, where the notion oscillates between two conflicting meanings. For King Pelasgos the word *kratos,* associated with *kuros,* designates a legitimate authority, the influence which a teacher rightfully exerts on his pupil. For the Danaïdes, the same word drawn into the semantic field of *bia,* designates brute force, the constraint of violence at the furthest remove from law and justice. So in 387ff., the King

Jean–Pierre Vernant

I take the example of another kind of context capable of illuminating a tragedy. A certain theme, a certain schema, mythic or ritualistic, may be used by the tragedy for its own ends, but it must be recognized, and this the non-Hellenist cannot do. Take the beginning of *Oedipus the King,* if you like. As you know, the situation at the beginning of *Oedipus the King* is that of catastrophe. We call it the plague, but it's not the plague; it's a *loimos,* a calamity, a defilement which has caused life to come to a halt, so that the world of human beings no longer communicates with the divine world. The smoke from sacrifices does not rise to heaven, women either do not give birth or give birth to monsters, the herds do not multiply, the earth is no longer fruitful. The human world is isolated in its foulness.

And the play opens on a *paian,* a paean, a joyous song of thanksgiving for some happy event, a joyous song, rapid in tempo. One wonders what a paean is doing here. But we have several clues that there is another sort of paean, sung at the change of seasons, at the passage from winter into summer, or at the entry of spring. For example in festivals of the type of the Athenian Thargelia, at the moment when

---

asks the Danaïdes if the sons of Aegyptos have, by the law of their country, power over them as their closest relations [Εἴ τοι κρατοῦσι]. The legal weight of this *kratos* is defined in the lines that follow. The King observes that, if this were the case, no one could stand in the way of the claims of the Aegyptiades over their cousins. It would be necessary for the latter to plead, inversely, that following the laws of their country, their cousins do not in reality have this power of guardianship [κῦρος] over them. The response of the Danaïdes is entirely beside the point. They see only the other aspect of *kratos* and the word, on their lips, takes a meaning opposite from that which Pelasgos lends it: it no longer designates the legal power of guardianship which their cousins might claim over them, but rather pure violence, the brutal force of the rough masculine domination to which women can only submit: "Ah, may I never be submitted to the power of males" [ὑποχείριος κράτεσιν ἀρσένων] (392–93). For this aspect of violence, cf. 820, 831, 863. To the *kratos* of man (951), the Danaïdes want to oppose the *kratos* of women (1069). If the sons of Aegyptos are wrong in trying to impose marriage on them, without convincing them by persuasion, but by violence (940–41, 943), the Danaïdes are no less at fault: in their hatred of the other sex, they will go as far as murder. King Pelasgos could reproach the Aegyptiades with wanting to take the girls against their will, without the agreement of their father, and outside of *Peitho's* sweet persuasion. But the daughters of Danaos also refuse to recognize *Peitho:* they reject Aphrodite, who is everywhere associated with *Peitho;* they do not let themselves be charmed or appeased by the seduction of *Peitho* (1041 and 1056). This semantic tension is expressed in a peculiarly striking way in the formula of line 315, whose ambiguity has been ably demonstrated by E. W. Whittle ("An Ambiguity in Aeschylus," *Classica et mediaevalia,* XXV, 1–2 (1964): 1–7).

the impurities of the past season are expelled at the entrance into a new season, there is, at Athens, the expulsion of one who is called the *pharmakos*. This paean, we are told, is characterized by its ambiguity. It is a joyous song, like a song of thanksgiving, and, at the same time, a song of terrible anguish with cries and lamentations. It is no accident that the tragic poet has placed this paean at the beginning of his tragedy. This paean gives us one of the fundamental oppositions in the structure of the work which enables us to understand it. If we compare this paean with what the chorus says at the moment when the tragedy, having reached its acme, takes an abrupt turn, the moment when Oedipus understands that he is damned, understands what he is, we find that the chorus intones a song which is equally astonishing, for it celebrates Oedipus from two points of view. It celebrates him as a savior of the City, as a king almost divine, while saying at the same time that "he is the most unfortunate and the foulest of men." [3] Thus we see that the tragedy is based on the idea that the same man is the divine king (and there we have a reminder of Greek history), on whom the prosperity of the earth, of the herds, and of the women depends, the king who bears the whole burden of the human group depending on him. And, seen from the perspective now shared by the audience and the poet, is at the same time considered to be something dreadfully dangerous, a sort of incarnation of *hubris*, which must be expelled. Into this opposition, of the divine king who is also an impurity, of the one who knows all but is blind, we can introduce as we must always in the act of interpretation, a whole series of meanings. But the fundamental, authentic Greek content is there: the idea that this divine king, who belongs to the Greek past, is at the same time superceded; and that, in a way, according to the scheme of the familiar ritual, he must be expelled as a *pharmakos*. (I might add that this link between the divine king and the *pharmakos* gets inverted, since in *Oedipus at Colonus* it is the *pharmakos* who becomes the savior of the City. But I shall not dwell on this point.) To indicate how deeply these ideas are rooted in social life, let me recall a Greek institution which is the sort we find in tragedy: ostracism. Ostracism is an institution which consists in the fact that at certain moments of the year, the assembly of the people may, for no reason, decide to expel as a *pharmakos* a person who has committed no crime, but who has risen too high, has too much good luck. The idea is that one who

[3] *Oedipus Tyrannus*, 1187–1221. The chorus stresses these contradictory aspects of the hero's career just before learning of the catastrophe while emphasizing the tension between appearance and reality, opinion and knowledge.

dominates from too great a height, who is too lucky, will bring on some calamity. So he is expelled and, remarkably, the institution specifies that no reason for the expulsion is to be given. Here we are not on the level of political procedure. We are rather on the level where men know that they are men, that the City is the City, and that when suddenly someone is discovered to have risen too high, to have controlled the City for too long, it may be necessary to expel him as an impurity, and bad luck along with him. (A procedure which might, after all, still have certain advantages.)

So much for the context. It is a historical context. I shall add a further word. When I talk of historical context, I have shown that even if I am making the examination from the outside—if I have to become a historian of law, religion, or institutions—the meanings which this context illuminates are internal.

When I say that I am a historian, that does not mean that I believe Greek tragedy can be explained (as many historical studies have tried to do) by referring to its antecedents, whatever they may be. Greek tragedy can be understood only when considered as an invention, in the full sense of the word, as a human invention under certain specific conditions, as something radically new in every respect. First of all it is an institution, and there the social aspect appears. The institution of tragedy was no small achievement! Between 534 and 530, contests in tragedy were instituted in Athens. I will not burden you with the details implied by this, but I would point out right away that it is no accident that at the end of the tragic contests, when the citizens, when the different tribes intervene, in a well regulated manner, this intervention is under the authority of the *archon eponymos* and not of the *archon basileus*—a detail which demonstrates the modernity of the institution. The only point which I would emphasize is the fact that the last act is a judgment, that the tribes have elected judges as they elect judges in popular tribunals, and that these judges will pass sentence by secret ballot at the end of the ceremony. A Greek tragedy is a tribunal. The institution of these tragic contests, with all of the practical organization implied, is but one institution and part of an institutional whole. Tragedy represents, specifically, a part of the establishment of a system of popular justice, a system of tribunals in which the City as City, with regard to individuals as individuals, now regulates what was formerly the object of a sort of contest among the *genè* of the noble families, a change resulting in the quite different system of arbitration. Tragedy is contemporaneous with the City and with its legal system. In this sense one can say that what tragedy is talking about is itself and the problems of law it is encountering. What is talking and what is talked about is the audience on the benches, but first of all it is the City: the City which puts itself on the stage and plays itself—explaining the reactions of the public, their violence, and, in certain cases, their refusal to hear a tragedy which touches them too closely, for example when it evokes Greek misfortune.[4] Not only does the tragedy enact itself on stage, but most important, it enacts its own problematics. It puts in question its own internal contradictions, revealing (through the medium of the technical legal vocabulary) that the true subject matter of tragedy is social thought and most especially juridical thought in the very process of elaboration. Tragedy poses the problems of law, and the question of what justice is. Greek law, which has just been formulated, unlike Roman law, is not systematized, not founded on axiomatic principles, but is made up tentatively of different levels, some of which call into question the great religious powers, the order of the world, Zeus, *dikè*, and at the other extreme raise the problems of human responsibility, such as the philosophers are already discussing. Between the nascent philosophical morality of Socrates and the old religious concepts, the law hardly knows its place. And from these shifts in the juridical vocabulary, Gernet has demonstrated, with his accustomed precision, that the use of a technical legal vocabulary can be shown in each tragedy.[5] The tragedy plays on this technical vocabulary by emphasizing the variations. For example one can say of tragedy what is said in the *Choëphoroe* (461) to show the meaning of the tragedy being played: Ἄρης Ἄρει ξυμβαλεῖ, Δίκᾳ Δίκα ["Ares shall struggle against Ares, and Right shall struggle against Right."] Or for example, in the *Choëphoroe* again (308) this formula, which is indeed extremely interesting:

$$\text{ἀλλ' ὦ μεγάλαι Μοῖραι Διόθεν}$$
$$\text{τῇδε τελευτᾶν,}$$
$$\text{ᾗ τὸ δίκαιον μεταβαίνει}$$

["Ye mighty Fates, through the power of Zeus, vouchsafe fulfilment

---

[4] The citizens are, of course, all male. Only men can be qualified representatives of the City; women are alien to political life. That is why the members of the chorus (not to speak of the actors) are always and exclusively males. Even when the chorus is supposed to represent a group of girls or women, which is the case in a whole series of plays, it is men, in disguise, who make up the chorus.

[5] Louis Gernet, *Recherches sur le développement de la pensée juridique et morale en Grèce* (Paris, 1917), p. 16: "La *dikè* hésiodique, elle [contrairement à la *dikè* homérique, plus homogène] est multiple et contradictoire parce qu'elle répond à un état nouveau et à un état critique de société . . ."

thus even as Justice now turneth."] The verb used, indicates that here (as indeed in every tragedy) we see the Right shifting, turning from one character to another. Thus Antigone can say for example (622) that for the man whose mind is deranged by divinity (which is the case of all the tragic heroes), evil (*kakon*) is taken for good. The tragic heroes are men who are placed at the crossroads of action in a world in which all legal values are ambiguous and elusive, and when these men choose the Good on their right hand then all of a sudden Good goes over to the other side and their choice of Good becomes criminal. This is one of the aspects of the tragic problem.[6]

Here is another example of this subtle play of vocabulary in which one can clearly see the errors of modern interpretation. This case occurs in *Antigone* where one of the essential elements of the whole organization of the work is a play on the relationship between *nomos* and *dikè*. The period of the tragedies is also the period of the development of Sophistry. *Nomos*, as you know, is traditionally opposed to nature (*phusis*)—that is, human laws, as men have developed them according to their own nature, opposed to the non-human. And on this level, the *nomoi* mean human laws instituted by the City. This is why Creon (verses 59, 213, 287) (and I shall summarize the quotations) says: "I shall issue *Nomoi* and consequently those who disobey go against the *Dikè*."[7] Now I would expect all the Greeks to say "Why, of course," but Antigone uses the same word, *nomos*, to express just the opposite. In verse 25 she says there are *nomoi* in harmony with the *mores* and linked with another image of the *dikè*—not the *dikè* of the tribunals which the City is establishing in its newness, but a *dikè* which, following certain traditions we may call orphic for the sake of simplicity, is represented as reigning below in Hades, the infernal *dikè*. This is why, at the moment when the drama is reaching a climax (449–61), Creon speaks to Antigone of the *nomoi* and Antigone replies in the name of the *dikè*, the one who inhabits the underworld, saying "This *Dikè* has established no such *Nomoi* as the ones you indicate." She opposes the unwritten laws of the gods [. . . agrapta . . . nomina] to Creon's laws which she refuses to call *nomoi* but which she calls simply *kèrugmata* [proclamations by the voice of a

---

[6] For a discussion of the place and function of ambiguity in the tragedians, cf. W. B. Stanford, *Ambiguity in Greek Literature: Studies in Theory and Practice* (Oxford, 1939), ch. X–XII.

[7] Cf. Antigone's question in verse 921. For a more extended discussion of the ambiguities of *dikè*, see M. Vernant's "Structures des mythes" in *Mythe et pensée chez les Grecs*, 2ᵉ éd. (Paris, 1966), pp. 17–47.

herald]. In verse 538 she solemnly affirms that *dikè* is with her, and I think that when you read this tragedy you agree with Antigone about unwritten laws. Unfortunately this interpretation is indefensible in the organization of the text, for in addition to the *nomoi* of Creon and the *nomoi* of Antigone, there is a text (613) where it is a question of yet another *nomos!* This is the *nomos* of Zeus of which the chorus says, "Throughout all eternity nothing will prevail against it." And this *nomos* is that "nothing good happens for humanity without some admixture of misfortune." To whom is this *nomos* of Zeus addressed? To Antigone, through the persona of the chorus. The chorus says: It looked as if everything were going to be all right for the descendants of Oedipus. Not at all. In reality the old demon is fiercely pursuing them. I see misfortune accumulating for the house of the Labdacidae. Hope is dying because of incautious words. The house of Oedipus is accused of committing faults. Of course the chorus, in predicting the misfortunes of Antigone, also senses vaguely that this applies to Creon. But when the chorus evokes the *nomos* of Zeus to condemn Antigone, it would be inexact to think either that it is really thinking of Creon or that it is mistaken in that it is Creon who will be punished; they will both be punished. Neither the *nomoi* of Creon nor the *nomoi* of Antigone are sufficient. They are both but aspects of the *nomos* of Zeus. I would point out right away, to indicate my disagreement with the Hegelian position, that this *nomos* of Zeus cannot be mediation because it is absolutely incomprehensible and impenetrable from the human viewpoint. This is why the same chorus will say to Antigone (in verse 821), contrary to modern interpretations: "You are Auto-Nomos," meaning "You think you are following the *nomoi* of *dikè*, whereas you are following *nomoi* which you have invented for yourself." Antigone has declared, "We have for our cause the *Dikè* who reigns below," and the chorus concludes, at the moment she is speaking (854): "Poor child. You have shown excessive audacity and you have flung yourself violently against the high throne of *Dikè*." Each protagonist invokes the *nomoi* and the *dikè*, and in the end, all of the human protagonists are similarly condemned because in their opposition they represent different rights. Of course Creon, as a chief of state, is right in not wanting to allow the burial of an enemy who is a traitor. "Why is he right?", one may ask. I would say "He is right from the Greek point of view" because he acts according to the laws of the Greek City-State. In Athens, the traitor or the sacrilege who dies or is executed must not have a tomb. One must know this in order to understand *Antigone*. When I say that the City calls itself into question,

I mean that Creon is right from the point of view of the City. Creon is doing what would be done in Athens; and yet, at the same time there is a questioning which results from the City's looking at itself objectively through the intermediary of heroic myths, the old legends which belong to the City's past. In the distance of objectivity afforded by these myths the City examines itself, seeking to determine what it has incorporated and what is alien to it. The City has its gods; it has its heroes in its civic and political religion; but there are peripheral gods like Dionysus which the City will try to incorporate, and there are the gods of the underworld. There are also all the problems of the family. And then there are the women, who are not political beings because they are not rational. It is extremely interesting, however, that the only characters in the tragedy (in the sense in which we say characters, and Aristotle says characters when he says that the tragedy is not concerned with the *ethos* or character) are women.

Let us take a character for instance in *The Seven Against Thebes*: Eteocles. What does Eteocles do? Eteocles is nothing other than an expression of the City's problems. In the beginning he is a rational man, a leader, a citizen, who commands. And what is contrasted with him? Women! Women who scream, wail, moan, while he keeps watch like a good helmsman. He places men at the gates of the City. For each enemy warrior he designates an adversary, and all the while the women are running in circles, tearing their hair, clinging to the temples and to the statues of the gods, lamenting. This is the opposition between the political man and the woman, who belongs to a different world. Then all of a sudden, Eteocles is told: "Your brother is at the last gate." Then this character, who has been a model of reason and poise, goes mad. He says: "My brother! Ah! Here it is! The old curse is coming back. You can see what will happen. We shall kill each other." There is no dissuading him. People have of course raised objections to this.[8] Some have said, "It is a very bad play; there is no psychological unity." Others have said "But on the contrary, even when Eteocles was rational, there was a hidden violence beneath his chilly concentration." But that is simply not the question, not what the tragedy is about. In Eteocles the tragedy is trying to present certain opposing structures, certain values and powers: social, religious, and

[8] Thus Wilamowitz has argued that the "character" of Eteocles does not appear to be drawn with a very firm hand: his behavior at the end of the drama is scarcely compatible with the portrait painted earlier. For Mazon, on the other hand, the same Eteocles counts as among the most beautiful figures in Greek drama; he incarnates with perfect coherence the type of the cursed hero.

psychological. Eteocles represents the City, and so long as he does, his behavior is civic. And then all of a sudden he ceases to be the City and becomes the hero of the old legends (the whole past which the City has rejected). Then it is hubris, madness, the old taint, which takes over and plunges him into misfortune. On the other hand, the women, who are outside of the City, are the only elements of ancient tragedy who already have something of the "character" about them. It is as if this lack of integration into the City were precisely what enabled the tragedy to give women a more completely developed psychological make-up.

Such then is the first point: the contradiction of the law with itself, with religious powers, with ethics. The second contradiction is the surprising fact, often pointed out, that there are more archaisms in Greek tragedy than, for example, in the epic. Greek tragedy puts on stage characters who are heroes, belonging to the Greek past. Even in Homer there is this sort of temporal distance, so that the Greeks already speak of the "first men," of "the men of a former time who were not like us." But, in the eyes of the Greeks of the City, the heroic world is one which has had to be rejected through a series of laws: sumptuary laws, laws regulating marriage, and laws rejecting the heroic ideal. The ideal of the City is for citizens to be equal, whereas the heroic ideal is to be always first. The heroic ideal is kept alive in the City in order to maintain a dialogue. The past is rejected as *hubris*. But it is a surprising paradox that there is no cult of the hero in Homer or Hesiod, the word "hero" simply designating a person of rank, as we might say "sir" or "gentleman." The cult of the hero is a civic cult, instituted by the City. The City is the frame of reference in which heroes, quite diverse characters or old vegetal spirits are gathered into a simple religious category, assigned to places in their Pantheon. These heroes and heroic legends, while they are relegated to the past, condemned, called into doubt, still do not cease to stimulate certain questions, precisely insofar as they represent mental attitudes, values, patterns of behavior, a religious thought, a human ideal which is opposed to that of the City.

Thus we have the following situation. The City is calling itself into question through dialogue with heroic characters, which continually produces a confrontation of two systems of values. This corresponds to the tragedy as a literary genre; for what characterizes tragedy is that the old *dithyramb*, which was simply a chorus, has been replaced by two elements. On the one hand there is the chorus, made up of citizens. Lots are drawn, by the ten tribes, to choose those who are to be magistrates and to officiate as *choreutai*. The chorus represents the presence of the City on the stage.[9] And, facing this chorus there is a masked character of another order who is precisely the hero whose legends are familiar to all Athenians. These two elements occupy the tragic stage and it is between them that the debate will take place. I call it a "debate" because there are two languages in tragedy. First of all, there is the lyric language of the chorus, which is sung and danced at the same time. Then there is the language spoken by the protagonists, the heroes, which, as Aristotle says, has been chosen as an approximation of everyday speech.[10] Therefore it is the heroes of another age who speak the most normal, the most prosaic language for Athenians of the period. This means that the heroes are not only enacted on the stage before the eyes of the public but also in the oral debates (and this is the novelty) which pit them against each other and against the chorus; they become something quite different from what they were for ancient lyric poetry, in which the hero was presented as the noble ideal, the model. The hero is called into question in the dialogue. He has become a problem for himself, for the protagonists and for the chorus. The dichotomy [*dédoublement*] of the chorus and the protagonists, the two types of language, the play between the community which officially represents the City as a magistracy, and a professional actor who is the incarnation of a hero from another age, the discussions—this whole form of tragedy was invented, so to speak, both to call the City into question within a well-defined context, and also (this is the third point of the invention) to call into question a certain image of man, and I would even say to indicate a change in man. You can imagine what this change is, and you can also imagine that it could be neither thought, lived, nor even expressed otherwise than through the form of tragedy. This change is contrary to the epic view where men are not seen considering the problem of their actions—except in one

[9] On the mooted question of the selection of the judges cf. Plutarch, *Kimon* 8, 7–9; Isocrates XVII, 33–34; Lysias IV, 3; Demosthenes, *Meidias* 17. For a general discussion of the selection and functions of the *choregoi*, judges, and chorus at the City Dionysia, see Arthur Pickard—Cambridge, *The Dramatic Festivals of Athens,* 2nd ed. (Oxford, 1968), ch. II and V. The number of the tragic chorus appears to have been twelve in the plays of Aeschylus, and fifteen in those of Sophocles and Euripides.

[10] Aristotle, *Poetics* iv, 18–19: ". . . when dialogue was introduced, Nature herself discovered the proper meter. The iambic [trimeter] is indeed the most conversational of the meters, and the proof is that in talking to each other we most often use iambic lines but very rarely hexameters and only when we rise above the ordinary pitch of conversation."

case, that of Hector, who asks himself whether he will go back inside the walls or stay outside.[11] When—like Achilles preparing to kill Agamemnon—he is about to act it is Athena who puts her hand on his shoulder; therefore it is a god who intervenes to keep him from acting.

What the tragedy will present is man faced with his action, at the crux of the action, reflecting on his action and no longer feeling that as a *man* he amounts to something or belongs to a world apart. Here we have rather the notion of human nature as developed by the Sophists of this period, or the notion clearly seen in a historian such as Thucydides: there is a sphere in which men are simply men. And thus the problem arises in the law of defining degrees of error, responsibility, and guilt. All the problems of responsibility, of degrees of intention, of the relationship between the human agent and his acts, the gods and the world are posed by tragedy, and it is only in the form of tragedy that they could be posed. We have here a language which corresponds to a given social state—the establishing of the law—and which corresponds even more deeply to a state of the inner man, at the moment when man discovers that he is not an agent (as we shall see that he is not), but rather discovers himself confronted with his action, as human action. It has been justly observed that the fundamental problem of tragedy is expressed in the *Choëphoroe* (899) when Orestes says: "What shall I do?" Πυλάδη, τί δράσω. This is an old Dorian verb, "*dran*," which is the equivalent of the Attic *prattein*, meaning "to act." Also in *The Suppliants* the problem is posed (380), not as by Hamlet's "To be or not to be" but when the king, Pelasgos, states it in this manner "To act or not to act." And there is the tragic problem.

When I say that man is presented as confronting his own action, I must add that one cannot understand this situation, or the tragic moment, except by referring here again to a past time. Just as the institution of the law is perpetually confronted with an anterior state, so is man in Greek tragedy perpetually confronted with old concepts of action, errors, and guilt—concepts which are disputed but which still weigh heavily on him. The central notion is no longer *dikè*, rather, it is now *hamartia*. That is, the verb which represents error and guilt in the form of what would be *errare* in Latin—a word which means at the same time that one has committed an error, made a mistake, and committed a crime.[12] What is *hamartia*? Hamartia means, in its proper

---

[11] This problematics of action does not occur, of course, in the lyric.

[12] The ambiguity of error or crime is compounded by the tension of the tragic hero's moral position between the ancient religious conception of the criminal taint, of the ἁμαρτία, as a mental or spiritual illness, a divinely caused insanity

sense, blindness. That is, something which surpasses man, which comes crashing down on him, which keeps him from seeing things as they are, so that he takes good for evil, commits a crime and is then punished by this crime. His blindness, his criminal act and the punishment are not separate realities. It is the same supernatural power—blindness, atè, madness, *hubris*—which takes on different aspects while remaining the same. It is like a cloud in which man is enveloped and which makes him blind, makes him criminal, and then punishes him. It is the same power. It is a notion (and I will not dwell on it since you are all familiar with this concept of *hamartia*) which is obviously still present, in a way, in tragedy. But if it were still entirely present in tragedy, there would be no tragic man. There is a tragic man because human action has become properly human. That is, the psychological motives of human action are now to be stressed. The problems of responsibility begin to appear. They are poorly formulated—you know that the world of ancient Greece never elaborated a vocabulary of the will. I would even say quite definitely that there is no category of will for the Greeks, and I would add (believing it can be demonstrated) that there cannot be any such category. The notion of free will, in the Kantian sense, has no meaning for the Greeks.

Thus, we have the problem of human action. But, on the other hand, human action has not attained so much autonomy that man can feel himself to be the unique, exclusive source of his action. There is the fundamental fact that the act takes on its meaning only when it has been detached from man and inserted into a religious, cosmic order which transcends man. So, I do what is good and then realize, afterward, that what I have done is not good but evil. For Kant the formula is "Do what you must, come what may." What comes of your act has no longer any connection with you. There may be destiny, but that does not concern you. For the Greek, this is not the case. If you do something, what comes of your act is what you have done. You know that you are a criminal because you are punished. This does not

---

which necessarily engenders crime, and the new conception according to which the guilty one, ἁμαρτών (and ἀδικῶν) is defined as one who, without being constrained, has deliberately chosen to transgress the law. In the formula that Aeschylus puts on the lips of the Choëphoroe (*Agamemnon* 1337-38) the two conceptions are to some extent superimposed or confused in the same words. In fact, in its ambiguity the phrase lends itself to a double interpretation: νῦν δ'εἰ προτέρων αἷμ' ἀποτείσῃ could mean: "And now if he must pay for the blood that he has spilled in the past." In the first case, Agamemnon is the victim of an ancestral curse: he pays for faults that he has not committed. In the second, he expiates the crimes for which he is responsible.

mean that you were not criminal, that you were not responsible; but you *understand* that you were criminal because you have been punished. This is to say that tragic man carries the weight and responsibility of his acts, and feels himself, in a sense, to be their cause; but at the same time cannot see them outside of a context of religious power. It is no accident that the semantic evolution of the word *hamartia*, this criminal aberration of which I have spoken, comes about in such a way as to make the verb *hamartanein* in the classic age imply both "voluntary crime" (*adikèma*) as well as "excusable, involuntary crime." Here again we find that instability of vocabulary which a study of Plato shows to be inevitable, as long as fault is considered in an intellectualist perspective as an error, involving the notion of constraint rather than will. This is why it would be quite wrong to consider tragedy solely (as we are wont to do) as a secular inquiry into human responsibility.

To take a famous example: in the scene of Agamemnon's return to his palace, his wife Clytemnestra spreads before him a purple carpet and says to him "Enter on this." Agamemnon is suspicious, being Greek, and says to her, "I am no oriental, and this purple carpet is reserved for the gods." (There is the ambiguity of the purple of the underworld and of the world of victory.) She insists. Agamemnon gives in and steps onto the carpet. The tragedian makes it perfectly clear that if Agamemnon walks on the carpet, it is, first of all, because he is a vain fool who is not, after all, unhappy to walk on purple, and secondly, because he is in a bad position to resist his wife because he is bringing home a concubine—Cassandra—and he is ill at ease. So, he gives in and enters. At that moment, from the point of view of tragic perspective, the tragedy is over. Why? Because, by walking on the purple carpet it is as though the king had signed his death warrant, from the Greek point of view. The tragic effect lies precisely in the intimate connection and the extraordinary distance between, on the one hand, the banal act of walking on a purple carpet, with the all too human motivation almost of bourgeois drama, and on the other hand, the religious forces which are by this act, in virtue of a symbolism on several levels, inexorably set in motion.[13]

[13] Past, present, and future merge in a single significant act, revealed and condensed in the symbolism of this act of impious *hubris*. Now the ultimate significance of Iphigenia is revealed: less obedience to the orders of Artemis, less the hard duty of a king who does not want to wrong his allies (cf. 213), than the guilty weakness of an ambitious man whose passion, in conspiracy with the divine *Tuchè*, has resolved to sacrifice his daughter; cf. 186: ἐμπαίοις τύχαισι συμπνέων.

Now we can understand that tragedy is, properly speaking, a moment. For tragedy to appear in Greece, there must first be a distance established between the heroic past, between the religious thought proper to an earlier epoch and the juridical and political thought which is that of the City performing the tragedy.[14] This distance must be great enough for the conflict of values to be painfully felt, but the distance must be small enough so that the heroic past is not liquidated, rejected, so that the confrontation does not cease. By the same token, for tragic man to appear, human action must have emerged as such, but the human agent must not have acquired too autonomous a status, the psychological category of the will must not be developed, and the distinction between voluntary and involuntary crime must not be clear enough for human action to be independent of the gods. This is the moment of tragedy.

And after tragedy, of course, something else will follow. Philosophy, with Aristotle, will attempt to take its place. Aristotle tells us, in 414 B.C.: "Euripides and Sophocles are dying. For us, tragedy is dead." All of the Attic tragedies that we have, date from a period of much less than a century. That is the flowering, the historical moment of tragedy. Aristotle, already, can no longer understand tragedy. He tells the story of a contemporary of Euripides, a younger man, Agathon, who also writes tragedies—for they continue to be written—but Aristotle tells us "He wrote tragedies in a new way; and in particular he invented his plots." [15] Tragedy no longer presents the old heroic myths; it is no longer tragedy because one no longer feels the need of a confrontation with a past which has vanished. In the same fashion, Aristotle will substitute for the tragic man in a certain number of texts in which he will distinguish degrees of will and degrees of intentionality. That is, he will try to make a philosophical analysis of the conditions of responsibility.

Tragedy appears then between these two moments. But, if it still has a meaning for us, it is because, in the themes which it organizes into a complicated architecture, there is a sort of formal structure, a frame which corresponds to the logic of this language. I shall describe briefly how things appear to me. Tragedy on this plane, in its formal

---

For commentary, see E. Fraenkel, Aeschylus *Agamemnon* (Oxford, 1950), II, p. 115.

[14] On the interpenetration of the two temporal orders, see P. Vidal-Naquet, "Temps des dieux et temps des hommes," *Revue de l'histoire des religions* (1950): 55–80.

[15] Aristotle, *Poetics* IX, 7.

logic on the most abstract level, is a passage between mythic thought and philosophic thought, between Hesiod and Aristotle. The logic of a writer, of a poet like Hesiod, is a logic of ambiguity. All of the notions are shifting. For example you have *Peitho*: there is a good one and a bad one. The same ambiguity is true of *Eris*. You have such and such a divinity, and there is a black one and a white one: and you cannot separate the black from the white. Notions form combinations through the play of complements, through logical, mythical oscillations of ambiguity, shifting meaning, and multiple meanings.

After Parmenides and the reflections of the philosophers, logic will be achieved which is a logic of identity, of the excluded third. A thing is either this or it is that. But the logic of tragedy is what I would like to call a logic of polarity. It is a logic of tension between opposites, between contrary forces as, in *Hippolytus*, between Artemis and Aphrodite or in the *Suppliants*, where all the themes are polarized. But note that along with polarity in Aeschylus there is sometimes an attempt at mediation, but one which can never succeed. The tension remains. The contradictions are not overcome and cannot be. This logic of polarity corresponds to the philosophical period of Sophistry. It is the logic of the Sophists. The Sophists, as you know, invented what are called the *dissoi-logoi*. The idea is that on any question tragedy considers, on any human problem, it is possible to compose two strictly contradictory arguments. Discourse implies polarity. There is not yet any Aristotelian logic because, for the Sophists, one discourse is as good as the other. The discourses are mutually exclusive. If I take up the one from the right I cannot take the one from the left. This is no longer Hesiod, where you had both at the same time. Now they are mutually exclusive, but you still cannot choose just one. Such are the *dissoi-logoi*. There is a polarity in every problem of human life. And later, with the great movement of classical philosophy, there will be truth and error, and, with truth and error, with true discourse and false discourse, we see the triumph of philosophy but the end of tragedy.

Discussion

RICHARD MACKSEY: I wonder if your persuasive analysis of tensions and ambiguities has sufficiently accounted for what is often called the "optimism" of Aeschylus? I am thinking specifically of the structure of the Aeschylean trilogy and the resolution of certain conflicts, clearly embedded in the language of the *Oresteia*, through the institution of the Court by Athena, a human tribunal. If each of the plays in the trilogy can be seen as a system of triangular tensions between the claims of family, state, and the old gods, culminating in a sacrifice, then the total structure of the trilogy could be analogized to M. Morazé's tetrahedron with the institution of the Athenian Court as its apex, the point which marks the end of the train of murder and revenge and the resolution of the conflicting claims on the hero of the Erinyes and of Apollo. The Court is precisely a *divinely* instituted *human* institution, which has become part of the City's veritable history. Characteristically, Euripides subjectivizes both the Erinyes and their ultimate catharsis, while Aeschylus sees his resolution within both the objective myth and the immanent social structure of Athens, the human tribunal which integrates the old gods and the old guilts.

JEAN-PIERRE VERNANT: You are surely right in characterizing Aeschylus as the most optimistic of the tragedians, but the exaltation of the civic ideal and the affirmation of its victory over all the forces of the past is less an achieved assurance than a hope and anguished appeal. At the end of the *Oresteia*, the founding of the human tribunal and the integration of the Erinyes into the new order of the City do not entirely dispense with the contradictions between the old and the new gods, between the heroic past of the noble *genè* and the present of fifth-century Athenian democracy. An equilibrium is established, but it is based on tensions. In the background the conflict between opposing forces continues. In this sense, tragic ambiguity is not resolved; ambivalence persists. To demonstrate, it will be sufficient to recall that the majority of human judges spoke against Orestes, for it is Athena who ties the voting (see line 735 and the scholium at line 746). This equality of the voices for and against avoids condemnation of the matricide in vengeance of the father; it absolves legally, by a procedural convention, the crime of murder, but it does not justify it or absolve it of guilt.

MACKSEY: Aristotle, when he gets around to questions of justice in the *Problems*, advances the argument that the defendant wins if the votes are equal because he is in a tactically weaker position—which is certainly true of Orestes in the present instance.

VERNANT: The vote and acquittal imply a sort of equilibrium between the ancient *dikè* of the Erinyes and the opposing *dikè* of the new gods like Apollo. Athena is therefore correct in assuring the

Daughters of Night: "You are not defeated; it is only an uncertain judgment that has come from the win"—ἰσόψηφοσ δίκη. Recalling their lot in the world of the gods at the beginning of the *Eumenides*, the Erinyes observed that, though they lived underground in a darkness cut off from the sun, they nonetheless have their *timè*, their share of honor. It is these ancient honors that Athena recognizes after the verdict of the tribunal: These are the same honors which Athena proclaims throughout the play. In fact, it is significant that in establishing the Areopagus, that is, in founding the City governed by law, Athena affirms the necessity of giving the sinister forces incarnated by the Erinyes their rightful place in the human community. *Philia*, mutual friendship, and *Peitho*, persuasion by reason, do not suffice to unite the citizens in a harmonious community. The City expects the intervention of powers of another nature, powers which act, not by sweetness and reason, but by constraint and terror. "These are cases," proclaimed the Erinyes in lines 516–18, "where dread(*tò deinòn*) is useful, and must sit permanently as a vigilant guardian of the heart." And when Athena establishes the Council of the Judges on the Areopagus, she repeats this theme, word for word. In establishing this rule as the imperative which her City must obey, the goddess emphasizes that the good is situated between two extremes, the City being based on a difficult accord between opposing powers which must find an equilibrium without destroying each other. Opposite the god of speech *Zeus agoraios*, and sweet Peitho, who has guided Athena's tongue, are seen the august Erinyes, instilling respect, fear and dread. And this power of terror, which emanates from the Erinyes, is institutionalized in the Areopagus to have a beneficent effect on the citizens, preventing them from committing crimes against one another. Athena can therefore say, in speaking of the monstrous aspect of the goddesses who have just agreed to reside in Attica: "I see a great advantage coming to the City from these terrifying faces." At the end of the tragedy, it is Athena herself who celebrates the power of the ancient goddesses among the Immortals as among the gods of the Underworld; she reminds the guardians of the City that these uncompromising divinities have the power "to determine everything among men." Finally, we must remember that in closely associating the Erinyes-Eumenides with the founding of the Areopagus, in placing this council, whose nocturnal and secret character has been twice underlined, under the sign not of the religious powers like Peitho which reign at the agora, but of those which inspire *Sebas* and *Phobos*, Aeschylus is in no way innovating; he is conforming to a mythical and cultural tradition that all Athenians recognize.

Discussion

JAN KOTT: Throughout this colloquium I have had the dizzy sensation that a world is collapsing, much as it must have felt during Bergson's time when there was the reaction against Comte and the old positivism. One speaks of the "structuration" of structure and of historicity which is history structuralized in a certain way. Most important to me, in speaking of language one no longer uses the word *code*, which requires an objective consciousness, but one says *Mark* which is will, meaning, and gesture. For me it was a relief listening to your talk and returning to the classical sphere of the historical interpretation of tragedy. Yet one is, after all, the child of his time, and I wonder if it is possible to analyze tragedy solely in its historical aspect. Can't we attempt an analysis of tragedy using the procedure that Lévi-Strauss applied to myth? On what level shall we interpret tragedy: the level of dialogue, content, or perhaps the levels that Lévi-Strauss established for myths? I think it is possible to interpret tragedy, as well as myth, according to its extra-historical value. To do so we could start from the notion of the situation, which I mean in a very concrete sense. The advantage of the term situation is that it includes both individuals (the actors) and persons (which are constituted by social content). The number of tragic situations seems to be limited. We might take a chance on the word *tragon* (as a parallel to Lévi-Strauss's term *mythème*), to designate structural unity based on a situation with a tragic opposition. It may be that the number of *tragons* does not exceed the number of five. For example there is the *tragon* of Orestes (the necessity to kill his mother in order to avenge his father); the *tragon* of Oedipus (one is responsible for his past, even when it exists only as a concrete given and not as personal reality—here we see the Freudian problematic); the *tragon* of Antigone (action versus non-action); the *tragon* of Ajax (the necessity of suicide when life has lost its value); and the fifth and most universal *tragon*, death which comes from outside, is foreseeable but is not felt by the individual as necessary or inevitable. These situations can always be explained historically and yet they can be seen in an anthropological, a universal perspective. The *tragon* of Orestes is seen again at another historical epoch in *Hamlet*. Thus we have both the historical and the extra-historical level. When we have established the anthropological perspective we can use the tools of anthropology in our analysis.

VERNANT: I had first intended to do an analysis of *The Suppliants*, but I didn't have time—I have already been too long. If I had made the analysis, I would have done it very exactly. There is a methodological problem in attempting to speak of unity and I don't think that the elements of opposition from which we can form the configuration of a tragedy are limited to the elements of situations. I will take the example of Lévi-Strauss's analysis of the Oedipus myth, with his own precaution that it is to be considered as an exercise of style and that a Hellenist would not agree—which is quite true. In analyses of myth we can take the situations within the narrative as unities, but I don't believe that that is the fundamental element in a tragedy, as I would have tried to show in my analysis. But I entirely agree with you that that can and must be done. We can include meaning here because we must deal with a play of opposites and, as I mentioned briefly, a logic of language and of tragic development. There are types of opposites with a particular meaning given to them by the fifth-century Greeks which can be modernized from the point of view of content and continue to function as opposites. The logic of tragedy is important. I think it could be shown that the same tragic framework is filled again in other historical conditions and in a different anthropological context. That is why I agree with Lévi-Strauss when he says that what the Freudians have to say about the Oedipus myth constitutes a new myth. I would say that there is no myth of Oedipus in Greek tragedy. The Oedipus in the tragedy may have complexes, but he doesn't have an Oedipus complex— that is obvious. Sophocles may have had an Oedipus complex, but Oedipus didn't, because Jocasta, the woman he married, is not his mother. He never had the relationship of a son to her, but to another woman who took him in when he was an infant. There is not a word in the text to indicate that he had any feeling at all for Jocasta. One might say that she is a mother substitute, but Oedipus doesn't have any filial sentiments toward her. You can say that since the Greeks invented the myth of Oedipus, they must have had an Oedipus complex, but you must show me other symptoms. Oedipus was abandoned at birth and taken in by the queen of a distant country. He lives with her as his mother until he is eighteen when he goes away, has several adventures, guesses the riddle which is a sign of royalty, and must thus marry Jocasta in order to become king of Thebes. If he had had an Oedipus complex it would have been in his relationship to his first mother. When I ask for proof you cite a few texts, which are cited by Dodds in his *The Greeks and the Irrational*. In the first text Oedipus (981 ff.) says it has been foretold that he would sleep with his mother and Jocasta replies that everybody dreams that—it is of no importance. That is not much of a censure. The second text is from the *Republic* (571) where Plato says that when a man is asleep and his *thumos* is no longer controlled by thought, he dreams terrible things, such as sleeping with his mother or committing an act of violence against his mother or some other man or animal. Here is the Oedipus text: "Don't be frightened at the thought of marriage with your mother. Many have already shared their mother's bed in dreams." Not much anguish there. In the third text (Herodotus VI, 107) a son of Pisistratus has returned to Attica where he hopes to come to power again. He has a dream that he sleeps with his mother which he interprets as a sign that he will become a sovereign. The only other text we have is from Artemidorus, who analyzes dreams, including that of sleeping with one's mother among many others, and who sometimes interprets this as a favorable dream and sometimes as an unfavorable dream. None of these texts can be seen as symptoms of an Oedipus complex unless you have already decided on it in advance. You cite the myth itself, but the myth has this meaning only because Freud labeled it a complex.

JACQUES DERRIDA: I admired your talk very much and now suddenly I am disappointed by what you have just said because you are proposing such a realistic reading of the play. That is, Oedipus always appears on the level of representation. The substitution is explained by the Oedipus complex. It is obvious that, if by *mother* one understands *real mother*, the Oedipus complex no longer has any meaning.

VERNANT: It is not a matter of a textual and factual reading but of discovering levels of meaning and tragic themes through the story, through what Oedipus represents. In order to do that I am ready to do a study of the text with you, if you like. We must read the text precisely and find proof in the written work itself. I have looked, but I haven't found any.

GUY ROSOLATO: M. Vernant, I agree with you. I don't believe we can say that Oedipus has an Oedipus complex. Freud himself said that the tragedy develops like an analysis. In order for there to be an Oedipus complex the subject must desire his mother unconsciously. I think that the pivotal point in the tragedy is the moment when Oedipus blinds himself. Before this point, the situation might be compared to the unconscious situation of a psychotic rather than a neurotic. The psychotic doesn't know what a mother is; he simply wants to sleep with this woman who is his mother. The neurotic, who does think about what his mother is, has an unconscious, unrealized desire, but no incest. So that in the play Oedipus passes from a psychotic situation to an absolutely abnormal situation where he has actually slept with his mother. There are actual human beings who have slept with their mothers, but they are generally psychotic.

VERNANT: I will not reply because the discussion could go on indefinitely. It is clear that we are reading the tragedy differently. It is just this type of reading which projects problems into the tragedy which do not really exist there.

Linguistics and Poetics[1]

Nicolas Ruwet
Fonds National Belge de
la Recherche Scientifique

I would like to make some remarks on the nature and limits of linguistic contributions to literary studies, particularly to poetics, and I shall speak of some of the difficulties that literary studies encounter when they are based on linguistic data.

To begin with, two observations. First of all, however one limits the object of linguistic theory, it is clear that this object will never completely coincide with that of literary studies. To take a simple example, linguists admit (cf. Bar-Hillel, 1964; Katz-Fodor, 1963)[2] that everything which arises from the "knowledge of the world" (which is not to be confused with the object of semantics) possessed by speakers is beyond the linguist's competence. Now, this knowledge of the world obviously plays an important role in literature, and literary studies, to take account of this role, will have to appeal to the separate sciences of linguistics, sociology, psychology, and so on.

In the second place, it would probably be desirable to forego baptizing our first efforts toward the rigorous study of poetry as "structural poetics." This term, in my view at least, underlines the dependence of poetics on structural linguistics too heavily. We are not only interested in carefully separating the object of poetics from that of linguistics; we must also remember that structural linguistics represents only a movement—now in the past, since the development of generative gram-

[1] "Linguistique et poétique." M. Ruwet helped with the English translation of his paper and made certain emendations in the final text.
[2] Cf. Bar-Hillel, Y., *Language and Information* (Reading, Mass., 1964), and Katz, J. J. and Fodor, Jerry A., "The Structure of a Semantic Theory," *Language,* 39 (April–June, 1963): 170–210.

mar[3]—in the history of linguistics. There would be little sense in binding the destiny of literary studies to what is merely a transitional stage of a neighboring discipline. I will add that there still exists, on a different level, a real danger, one which lies in the development of a "structuralist aesthetic." By this I mean the tendency, against which we should protect ourselves, to ascribe undue value to those few features—among all of the possible aspects of a work of art—which we are now able to describe with a certain rigor through terms drawn from the concepts of structural linguistics.

These distinctions once made, it seems to me that the status of linguistics, in relation to poetics and to literary studies in general, can only be that of an auxiliary discipline, whose role is roughly analogous to that played by phonetics with respect to the whole of linguistics. In other words, linguistics can bring a great body of materials to poetics, but it is incapable, working alone, of determining how pertinent these materials are from an aesthetic or poetic point of view. If linguistics has thus a rather modest role, it is no less indispensable, and each step in its progress is still capable of bringing something to poetics (even if the progress of poetics is not always determined by that of linguistics). This contribution results from the fact that linguistics describes with increasing precision certain of the materials belonging to poetics. A simple progress in the description of its materials can, in fact, permit poetics to ask new questions or, what is equally important, to perceive that certain questions which were asked formerly were only false problems.

I shall take a simple example which deals with the well-known question of the poetic role of sonorous elements. Let us take the famous line from Racine: "Le jour n'est pas plus pur que le fond de mon coeur." [The daylight is no less pure than the depths of my heart.] There has been much said of the second life led by this line, beyond its context, in the public memory, and, generally, an attempt has been made to explain this fact by a particular phonic structure. For example, some have noticed that this line is composed only of monosyllables, while others have noted the alliterations in *p* ("*pas plus pur*"), and so on. Modern linguistics alone is certainly not capable of explaining the beauty of this line, nor can it say why the line has assumed this sort of autonomy. But linguistics, here and now, can at least *describe* the phonic structure of the line with great precision. And, at the same

---

[3] Chomsky, Noam, *Current Issues in Linguistic Theory* (La Haye: Mouton and Co., 1964); *Aspects of the Theory of Syntax* (Cambridge, Mass.: M.I.T. Press, 1965).

Nicolas Ruwet

time, we can discredit certain hypotheses and put others into perspective. For instance, the monosyllabic hypothesis is immediately excluded by the observation (which is supported by certain considerations—syntactical, morphological, and phonological—which are too complex to be developed here) that such units as the article *le*, the preposition *de*, or the conjunction *que* (not to mention the negative particle *ne*) have only a very relative autonomy in French and cannot be accepted as monosyllabic "words" in the same sense as lexemes such as *jour* or *pur*.

Let us leave aside the syntactical structures of the line and its relationships (which are certainly pertinent) with the phonological and metrical structures. We will retain only two matters: (*a*) linguistic theory (that of Chomsky and Halle, evolving from that of Jakobson) clearly distinguishes lexical morphemes (lexemes) from grammatical morphemes; the description of the phonological structure of lexical morphemes is the object of a special part of grammar; this, then, authorizes us to consider separately the four units: *jour, pur, fond, coeur*; (*b*) linguistic theory[4] describes the phonological structure of lexemes in the form of a matrix of binary distinctive features.[5] In Figure 1,

[4] Jakobson, Roman, *Selected Writings. I. Phonological Studies* (La Haye: Mouton and Co., 1962). Halle, Morris, *The Sound Pattern of Russian* (La Haye: Mouton and Co., 1959).

[5] The following brief summary of phonological oppositions, after Jakobson and Halle, may be of some help to the general reader:

A. *Sonority features* (akin to prosodic force and quantity; sonority features utilize the amount and concentration of energy in the spectrum and in time).

  i. *Vocalic/non-vocalic:*
  accoustically—presence vs. absence of a sharply defined formant structure;
  genetically—primary or only excitation at the glottis together with a free passage through the vocal tract.

  ii. *Consonantal/non-consonantal:*
  accoustically—low (vs. high) total energy;
  genetically—presence vs. absence of an obstruction in the vocal tract. Vowels are vocalic and non-consonantal; consonants are consonantal and non-vocalic; liquids are vocalic and consonantal (with both free passage and obstruction in the oral cavity and the corresponding acoustic effect); glides are non-vocalic and non-consonantal.

  iii. *Compact-diffuse:*
  accoustically—higher (vs. lower) concentration of energy in a relatively narrow, central region of the spectrum, accompanied by an increase (vs. decrease) of the total amount of energy;
  genetically—forward-flanged vs. backward-flanged. The difference lies in the relation between the volume of the resonance chamber in front of the narrowest stricture and behind this stricture. The ratio of the

we give the matrices of the four lexemes *jour, pur, fond, coeur.* Each column corresponds to a segment (a phoneme), each row to a dis-

former to the latter is higher for the forward-flanged phonemes (wide vowels, and velar and palatal, including post-alveolar, consonants) than for the corresponding backward-flanged phonemes (narrow vowels, and labial and dental, including alveolar, consonants).

iv. *Tense/lax:*
accoustically—higher (vs. lower) total amount of energy in conjunction with a greater (vs. smaller) spread of the energy in the spectrum and in time;
genetically—greater (vs. smaller) deformation of the vocal tract—away from its rest position.

v. *Nasal/oral (nasalized/non-nasalized):*
accoustically—spreading the available energy over wider (vs. narrower) frequency regions by a reduction in the intensity of certain (primarily the first) formants and introduction of additional (nasal) formants;
genetically—mouth resonator supplemented by the nose cavity vs. the exclusion of the nasal resonator.

vi. *Discontinuous/continuant:*
accoustically—silence (at least in frequency range above vocal chord vibration) followed and/or preceded by spread of energy over a wide frequency region (either as a burst or as a rapid transition of vowel formants) vs. absence of abrupt transition between sound and such a silence;
genetically—rapid turning on or off of source either through a rapid closure and/or opening of the vocal tract that distinguishes plosives from constrictives or through one or more taps that differentiate the discontinuous liquids like a flap or trill/*r*/ from continuant liquids like the lateral /*l*/.

B. *Tonality features* (akin to prosodic pitch features; tonality features involve the ends of the frequency spectrum).

vii. *Grave/acute:*
accoustically—concentration of energy in the lower (vs. upper) frequencies of the spectrum;
genetically—peripheral vs. medial: peripheral phonemes (velar and labial) have an ampler and less compartmented resonator than the corresponding medial phonemes (palatal and dental).

viii. *Flat/non-flat:*
accoustically—flat phonemes in contradistinction to the corresponding plain ones are characterized by a downward shift or weakening of some of their upper frequency components;
genetically—the former (narrowed slit) phonemes in contradistinction to the latter (wider slit) phonemes are produced with a decreased back or front orifice of the mouth resonator, and a concomitant velarization expanding the mouth resonator. (Cf. rounded [labialized]/unrounded).

Jakobson, *Selected Writings*, I, pp. 484–86; the numbering of the features does not correspond to Jakobson and Halle's complete list of twelve binary oppositions. [Editor]

Nicolas Ruwet

tinctive feature. The presence of a zero indicates that the segment is not specified in relation to the relevant feature. Vertically, we have presented the distinctive features of French in an order which is not exactly the one in which they would be presented in a phonology of French, but our order is suitable for the discussion which we are pursuing here.

	3	U	r	P	y	r	F	5	K	œ	r
vocalic	−	+	+	−	+	+	−	+	−	+	r
consonantal	+	−	+	+	−	+	+	−	+	−	+
rounded	o	+	o	o	+	o	o	+	o	+	o
compact	+	−	o	−	−	o	−	−	+	−	o
continuant	+	o	−	−	o	−	+	o	−	o	−
diffuse	o	+	o	o	+	o	o	−	o	−	o
grave	o	+	o	+	−	o	+	+	o	−	o
nasal	−	−	o	−	−	o	−	+	−	−	o
tense	−	o	o	+	o	o	+	o	+	o	o

Figure 1.

If we examine Figure 1, we are led to make a certain number of observations. First of all, the matrices of our four lexemes have a certain number of common features: all are monosyllabic, composed of a consonant followed by a vowel, and in three out of four cases this vowel is followed by the liquid /r/. All of the vowels are rounded and non-compact (cf. the absence of /i/, /e/, /a/), and no consonant is acute (non-grave: cf. the absence of /t/ and so on), which probably contributes to the line's darkened tonality. Next, on this common basis, we perceive a systematic variation which concerns, among the consonants, the features compact/non-compact and continuous/discontinuous and, among the vowels, the features grave/non-grave and diffuse/non-diffuse (cf. the heavily outlined squares). In each of the two categories, consonantal and vocalic, the four possible combinations of two characteristics are all employed. It is probably this structure of correlations and oppositions which underlies Jean-Louis Barrault's remark commenting on this line: "One would say that the rela-

300

tionships between the sonorities of long (or accentuated) syllables are comparable to the perfect chords which one encounters in music." In spite of its more than approximate language, this remark rests on a correct intuition; there is indeed an analogy between the relations of equivalence and opposition which we have just isolated and the relations which link, through their common or differing tones, the successive chords of a tonal musical work.

If, in this way, linguistics permits us to describe a certain number of structural aspects of our line with precision, we cannot, however, say that it explains why this line is particularly "beautiful," "striking," and so on. Beyond the fact that it would be necessary to describe the relationships between the phonological structure of the line and its metric, syntactical, or semantic structures—which is in part already possible —it would also be necessary to command a theory of context, both linguistic and non-linguistic, which alone would be capable of explaining why this line leads an autonomous life outside of its context. Such a theory does not exist at the present time, and, furthermore, it would extend far beyond the framework of linguistics. It is clear, at any rate, that one could find a great many lines presenting a phonological structure quite analogous to that of Racine's line, yet which have never appeared to be particularly memorable.

After seeing us confine linguistics to an auxiliary role in poetics, one could object that it is nevertheless a linguist, Jakobson, who has brought forward a model which would give the key to what constitutes the specific difference between poetic language and other forms of language. As we know, this model is summed up in the principle that poetic language projects relationships of equivalence which usually occur on the *paradigmatic axis* (the axis of selection or substitutions) along the *syntagmatic axis* (the axis of combination or concatenations). The relations of equivalence brought to light in our phonological analysis of Racine's line are an illustration of this point. Without wanting to underestimate the importance of this model, which represents the first serious effort to formulate a general hypothesis concerning the structure of poetic language and one which unifies a great number of seemingly disparate characteristics under a single schema, it is nevertheless necessary to make some remarks which limit the model's range.

First of all, let us note that the link between this model and the aesthetic aspect of language is not clear. The existence of literary prose, on the one hand, and that of "prosaic" versification (rimed

Nicolas Ruwet

ends, and so on), on the other, indicates that the relation between this model and the aesthetic aspect is neither necessary nor sufficient.

Further, this model is connected directly to a classical structuralist theory, which reduces all relations between linguistic elements to two central types: relations of substitution (selection) and relations of concatenation (combination). Now, we know, since the development of the transformational model, that the theory of the two axes is not sufficient to account for the ensemble of linguistic facts in all of their complexity and that it is necessary to postulate the existence of other types of relations.

Third, the studies of the analysis of discourse[6] have shown that it was possible to describe the structure of all sorts of continuous texts —literary texts, but also conversations, newspaper articles, advertising texts, scientific articles—in the form of systems of equivalence, capable of being represented definitely by tables of two dimensions. The type of relationships of equivalence in play in poetry should then present a more specific character. For instance, while the analyses of Harris are situated essentially on the syntactical plane, one could imagine that poetic language requires the existence of systems of equivalence on at least two distinct planes: phonology and semantics, and/or syntax and semantics, and so on. This principle seems, moreover, to be implicit in Jakobson's studies of the question. Let us note, furthermore, that the privileged role of the study of relationships of equivalence—relationships conceived, what is more, in a rather simple form—in the diverse studies undertaken in the past (analyses of discourse by Harris, of poems by Jakobson, and of myths by Lévi-Strauss) derives perhaps solely from the limitations of structuralist models, models remaining too purely "taxonomical."[7] The survey of equivalent relationships probably only represents the most elementary aspect of the structure of texts, and a "syntagmatics of discourse" remains almost entirely still to be formulated.

Finally, while admitting that the projection of equivalent relationships along the syntagmatic chain plays a capital role in poetry—and, in any case, it is a hypothesis which requires some exploration in depth —a very serious theoretical problem arises, one which has not yet really been broached: which equivalences must be treated as pertinent? Jakobson draws a very exhaustive catalogue of all sorts of elements which, when associated by relationships of equivalance, *can* be perti-

[6] Harris, Z. S., "Discourse analysis," *Language* 28 (1952): 1–30; *Discourse Analysis Reprints* (La Haye: Mouton and Co., 1963).
[7] Cf. Chomsky, *Current Issues.*

302

nent from the poetic point of view.[8] But, up to the present time, we possess no criterion which might permit us to choose, among the multitude of possible equivalences, those which are really pertinent in a given poem, for a given author, or in a given style. As soon as one tries to outline relationships of equivalence, in a sonnet, for example, one discovers an infinite gradation of equivalences, beginning with some which are obvious (such as those which are codified, obligatory, as the phonic equivalences in rime) to others which are practically imperceptible. It seems reasonable to think that the existence of massive equivalences at certain points in the text might permit us to expose other equivalences which are less clear, at other points or at other levels, and which would pass unperceived, were the first equivalences absent. Perhaps one of the powers of poetic language—and one of the difficulties facing its analysis—depends on the fact that primary equivalences (of which some are rigorously codified) produce others, which are more subtle, and which, in turn, produce others even more tenuous than the latter, and so on, like those concentric circles produced by the fall of a pebble in water. But it seems impossible to formulate non-intuitive procedures allowing us to determine how far one has the right to go in the search for equivalences.

Lacking objective procedures, one can at least consider two different methods. One—which to a certain degree is that followed by Jakobson and Lévi-Strauss,[9] at least in the grammatical, non-semantic part of their analysis—consists in systematically recording all of the equivalences, taking each level separately. For example, we pass all of the grammatical categories in review (noun, verb, transitive verb, intransitive verb, gender, number, and so on), and all of the elements exhibiting the same category are considered equivalent; all of the animate nouns are equivalent and are opposed to all of the plural nouns; all of the singular nouns are opposed to all of the plural nouns, and so on. In this way we accumulate a mass of materials, a mass of equivalences, while hoping that certain *patterns* will finally appear. This method runs into at least one major difficulty, which is connected with the problem of the distinction between obligatory linguistic elements and those which are optional. At all levels, language includes a portion of obligatory machinery, represented by the grammatical rules which must be applied in order to obtain "correct" sentences; equally at all

---

[8] Jakobson, Roman, "Linguistics and poetics," in T. A. Sebeok, ed., *Style in Language* (New York: Wiley and Sons, 1960), pp. 350-77. See also Levin, S. R., *Linguistic Structures in Poetry* (La Haye: Mouton and Co., 1962).

[9] Jakobson, *Selected Writings.*

Nicolas Ruwet

levels, language presents certain possible choices, represented by those rules that one may or may not apply. Now, the presence at one point of another of a given category can be at times obligatory and at times optional. What complicates matters more is the fact that poetry is presently characterized by the violation of certain rules which are normally obligatory. We are therefore led to inquire into the equivalence between several elements, exhibiting the same category in such a way that their presence in this category results, in one case, from the application of an obligatory rule, in another from an optional choice, and in still another from the violation of an obligatory rule. In this way, many of Baudelaire's poems seem to use the opposition of singular and plural to poetic ends. But, in *L'Invitation au voyage*, for example, where one comes upon a great number of nominal syntagmas having the same internal structure (article plus substantive plus adjective), does one have the right to speak of an equivalence existing between *les riches plafonds, les miroirs profonds*—where the plural results from an option; *les soleils couchants*—where this results from a violation of a rule; and *la splendeur orientale*—where the singular stems from the application of an obligatory rule? It is certain that linguistic theory, in its present state, furnishes us with no means of evaluating these equivalences.

Another procedure would consist in choosing a determined level, in separating out the equivalences which are the most evident at this level, and in then using these to formulate hypotheses in relation to other possible equivalences which are less clear, at the same level or at different levels. One could then try to test the validity of these hypotheses by having recourse to other, non-linguistic approaches to the work, but this is a point which I will not discuss here.

I have chosen to sketch the analysis of a sonnet by Baudelaire, *La Géante*, beginning at the syntactical level. In principle, one could just as well begin at other levels—phonological, metrical, or semantic; the choice of the level of departure is largely a question of suitability. Nevertheless, the choice of the syntactical level has certain general justifications. On the one hand, according to the most recent linguistic conceptions,[10] syntax appears as the central part of grammar and, in a sense, the only "creative" part. On the other hand, as we have already stated, it is possible, here and now, at the syntactical level, to outline equivalences by means of purely formal procedures;[11] in our analysis

[10] Chomsky, *Theory of Syntax.*
[11] Cf. Harris, "Discourse analysis"; *Discourse Analysis Reprints.*

of *La Géante*, however, we shall not expose these procedures in detail, and we shall only give their results. While concentrating on the syntactical equivalences, we shall set apart equivalences on the prosodic and phonological levels (of which we shall say little here) and on the semantic plane.

Here is the text of the poem, quoted according to the edition of Crépet and Blin[12] (José Corti, 1950, pp. 22–23):

La Géante

Du temps que la Nature en sa verve puissante
Concevait chaque jour des enfants monstrueux,
J'eusse aimé vivre auprès d'une jeune géante,
Comme aux pieds d'une reine un chat voluptueux.

J'eusse aimé voir son corp fleurir avec son âme
Et grandir librement dans ses terribles jeux;
Deviner si son coeur couve une sombre flamme
Aux humides brouillards qui nagent dans ses yeux;

Parcourir à loisir ses magnifiques formes;
Ramper sur le versant de ses genoux énormes,
Et parfois en été, quand les soleils malsains,

Lasse, la font s'étendre à travers la campagne,
Dormir nonchalamment à l'ombre de ses seins,
Comme un hameau paisible au pied d'une montagne.

The Giantess[13]

In the times when Nature in her powerful zest
Conceived each day colossal children,
I would have liked to live close to a young giantess,
As at the feet of a queen, a voluptuous cat.

I would have liked to see her body bloom with her soul
And grow freely in her awesome games,
To divine whether her heart shelters a somber flame
With humid mists which swim in her eyes;

---

[12] (Jose Corti, 1950), pp. 22–23.

[13] The literal translation of *La Géante*, however awkward, attempts to retain as far as possible the order of the French and so may be of some help in following M. Ruwet's discussion of the original. No attempt has been made to suggest the historical ambiguities of words such as *ramper* nor the sexual overtones of phrases such as *vivre auprès d'une*. This translation was prepared by John Blegan.

> To rove at leisure across her magnificent forms;
> To crawl up the slope of her enormous knees,
> And sometimes in summer, when the fetid suns
>
> Make her stretch weary across the countryside,
> To sleep easily in the shadow of her breasts,
> Like a peaceful hamlet at the foot of a mountain.

The poem includes two complete sentences, P1 and P2, of unequal length—the first covers the first four lines, the second the ten others—but of parallel structure. Their *kernels* are equivalent and include an identical subject and verb plus one or several objects, which are all infinitive clauses:

> P1: J'eusse aimé vivre— I would have liked to live
> P2: J'eusse aimé voir— I would have liked to see
>   deviner—   to divine
>   parcourir—   to rove
>   ramper—   to crawl
>   dormir—   to sleep

The parallelism of the two *j'eusse aimé* groups is underlined by that of their prosodic positions (at the beginning of lines 3 and 5) and by the phonic similarity of the verbs which follow them immediately (3 *vivre*/5 *voir*). Let us note that if, from a methodological point of view, these phonic and prosodic equivalences can only be obtained by beginning with the syntactical equivalences (in the absence of the latter, there would be scarcely any reason to retain them), from the point of view of the poem's structure, their effect is to underline the syntactical and semantic equivalences. If one begins at the central syntactical level to separate both phonic and semantic equivalences, there is an asymmetry between these last: phonic equivalences, through the intermediary of syntax, serve to put the semantic structure into relief.

We can therefore say that the poem includes two parts, of which the second is an expansion of the first:

> P1: exposition — P2: development

In reality, this division includes another, which distinguishes a beginning (P1, or lines 1–4), a middle (5–10) and an end (11–14), which appears as the reprise of the beginning. Indeed, there is a very clear parallelism between the first and the last infinitive object clause:

vivre	auprès d'	une jeune géante
dormir nonchalamment	à l'ombre de	ses seins
comme un chat voluptueux (*)	aux pieds d'	une reine (*)
comme un hameau paisible	au pied d'	une montagne

The elements marked by an asterisk (*) are inverted in the text. We will return later to the possible significance of this relationship between an inverted order in line 4 and a straight order (or rather, to the degree to which it follows the inverse order, a "righted" order) in line 14.

The parallelisms isolated so far leave aside lines 1–2 and lines 11–12. Now, the elements which correspond in these instances are syntactically parallel to an equal extent: it is a question in both cases of "time adverbials," which, it is true, do not have the same place in the structure of P1 and of P2 (the first determines the entirety of the sentence, and the second only determines the subordinate clause, *dormir* . . .). Let us retain two things, that we might return to them later: first, these time adverbials have, by definition, a marginal place in the sentence, and, secondly, the massive parallelism of the other elements authorizes us to consider them parallel as well.

We will arbitrarily represent the time adverbials by *a*, the subject-plus-verb groups (*j'eusse aimé*) by *b*, the infinitive subordinates by *c*, and the objects of comparison (*comme* . . .) by *d*. We will indicate the relation of subordination by means of an arrow, going from the subordinate to that which subordinates it, and coordination by a period. We then obtain the following representation:

$$P_1: a \rightarrow (b \leftarrow (c \leftarrow d))$$
$$P_2: \quad b \leftarrow (c.c.c.c.(a \rightarrow (c \leftarrow d)))$$

Starting with this syntactical schema, we can now approach other aspects and see how the representation is supported by facts of a prosodic order—as it is by more abstruse grammatical data—and how it is used to construct a semantic structure.

In fact, this schema helps us to understand certain aspects of the poem's versification. In traditional terms, the poem must be considered an irregular sonnet. The rimes have the following distribution:

aBaB   cBcB   ddEfEf,

that is, six rimes instead of five, with the rimes of the quatrains alternating and not coupled. This distribution sets apart lines 9 and 10, which constitute a couplet with feminine rimes (it is the only case of a rimed couplet throughout the sonnet), inserted between the qua-

Nicolas Ruwet

trains. As for the relative distribution of feminine and masculine rimes, lines 11–14 present a structure which is the inverse of that of the first two quatrains. The feminine rimes, which open and close the sonnet and occur in the rimed couplet, are thus given prominence.

One could push the phonic analysis of rimes beyond the traditional limit; for example, we could take account of the phonemes which precede the last pronounced vowel and split the phonemes into distinctive features. One then perceives a kinship between the feminine rimes which first seemed disparate: in /ãtə/ (-ante), we find a compact nasal vowel followed by an oral consonant which is diffuse and acute; in /amə/, we find a compact oral vowel followed by a nasal consonant which is diffuse and grave. On the other hand, if one introduces the phonemes which precede the vowel of the masculine rimes, there is this time a divergence between the quatrains, a divergence neglected by the traditional point of view (cf. quatrain 1: . . . t(r)ueux vs. quatrain 2: jeux, yeux). The rimes of the second quatrain, then, present a variation on those of the first. Finally, in the feminine rimes of the final quatrain, one again finds a variation on those of the first two: /aɲə/ (-agne), a compact oral vowel plus a compact nasal consonant. The more complete schema of the system of rimes is the following:

1–4		5–8		9–10		11–14	
exposition		variation		transition		inverted reprise	
F	M	F	M	F	F	M	F

(where F and M designate feminine and masculine rimes)

Roman Jakobson has repeatedly insisted on the possible pertinence of the grammatical categories of the riming words. Our sonnet presents, in effect, a great unity from this point of view; all of the riming words are nominal syntagmas, either simple (article plus substantive) or complex (article plus adjective plus substantive, or article plus substantive plus adjective, the term article also including possessives). By this very fact, the verbs are thrown back into the first part of the line and, often, even as far as the beginning of the line, which accentuates the syntactical parallelism (cf. 7 *deviner*, 9 *parcourir*, 10 *ramper*, 13 *dormir*). Finally, only lines 1 and 4, 11 and 14, include no verb, and this particularity contributes in accentuating the parallelism between the first and the last quatrain which, both in concert, begin and conclude with objects.

Let us move to the semantic level. We again find two basic divisions which are themselves partially divided: one division opposes the first quatrain (P1) to the rest of the poem (P2), and the other distinguishes two exterior parts (the first and the last quatrains) from a central part which plays the role of transition.

From an elementary point of view, the last ten lines present a series of synecdoches of elements supplied by the first four: *son corps, son âme, son coeur, ses yeux, ses magnifiques formes, ses genoux énormes, ses seins*, are all synecdoches of *une jeune géante*, and, in a sense, all of the verbs (*voir, deviner, parcourir, ramper, dormir*) can be viewed as particular specifications of *vivre* (*auprès de*). I shall not insist here on the order in which the diverse elements of the central part (5–10) are given, nor on the degree of structural organization that one can find here; I shall only note the movement which goes from the general and the spiritual (*corps, âme, coeur*) to the particular and the physical (*genoux, seins*).

From the point of view of metaphorical relationships, the first and last quatrains are opposed to the central section—which presents its metaphors in an implicit form—by the presence of a metaphorical process which is explicit: the metaphors are developed in comparisons. We notice first that 13 *dormir* is not only a synecdoche of 3 *vivre*; between these two verbs there is an inverted relationship of equivalence: *vivre* is to *être mort* [to be dead] as *être éveillé* [to be awake] is to *dormir*.

Each comparison includes two place adverbials in parallel. Now, at the level of prepositional locutions (the equivalence of their environments authorizes us to put *auprès de* and *au(x) pied(s) de* or *à l'ombre de* on the same plane), one notices a lack of symmetry between the first terms of the two comparisons (*auprès de / à l'ombre de*) and, on the contrary, a symmetry between the second terms (*aux pieds de / au pied de*). The result of this is that, in the first comparison, the first term is opposed to the second as one being relatively less specific ((*vivre*) *auprès de* . . .) than the other ((*vivre*) *aux pieds de* . . .). The relationship is inverted in the second comparison: *à l'ombre de ses seins* is much more specific than *au pied d'une montagne*.

From the point of view of grammatical gender, lines 4 and 14 each oppose a masculine term (*chat, humain*) to a feminine term (*reine, montagne*). In line 4 this opposition is valid for animate beings, and the opposition of genders corresponds to that of the sexes. In line 14, however, the nouns designate inanimate beings, and the opposition of genders now has only a purely grammatical range. It would be tempting to connect this type of information (relating to the distinction between masculine and feminine rimes) to the central theme of the poem: the relation of the superior to the inferior, of dominant to dominated, which exists between the giantess, a feminine term, and the "I," a masculine term. The predominance of feminine rimes could be correlated with the dominance of the feminine term, and the fact that, at the end, the opposition of genders no longer corresponds to an opposition of sexes could be interpreted as expressing an attenuation or a reconciliation of this opposition of the sexes. There, however, we are dealing in speculations which I merely note, since I am unable to say if they are really pertinent.[14]

In lines 3–4 the second term of the comparison is borrowed from a semantic context which is different from that of the first term, and this context does not play a role in the rest of the sonnet. In lines 13–14, however, the context of the second term of the comparison is already implicit in that of the first; the metaphor is borrowed from the context. First, there is a link of contiguity between *campagne* and *hameau* or *montagne*. Next, the central section offers, by a series of metaphors which are at first implicit (the "exhausted" metaphor of 5 *fleurir*) and then, more and more explicit, a cosmic image of the giantess: the latter is identified with a mountain or a volcano (which "shelters a somber flame" and on whose "slope" one can "crawl"), with the earth itself, and, further, with the entire universe ("her eyes" are the sky in which the "humid mists . . . swim"). The second term only makes more explicit what was already given in the first term. It is even, one might say, redundant: both syntactically and semantically, the relationship of determination between *hameau* and *paisible* doubles that between *dormir* and *nonchalamment*, and, finally, the *hameau* is linked in a dual manner to the idea of *dormir*: the hamlet not only sleeps at the foot of the mountain but is also the place where one sleeps, the natural location of repose.

These observations—like that of the relationship between an inverted syntactical structure in line 4 and a "righted" structure in line 14—suggest that the first comparison introduces an element of tension and that the second brings a relaxation. The opposition is clearest between two terms which occupy exactly the same syntactical positions: *voluptueux* and *paisible* (one evoking the tension which precedes ecstasy, the other evoking the calm which follows?), but it is

[14] In line 4, the masculine gender of *chat* does not necessarily imply that it is a question of a male cat. Furthermore, as Lévi-Strauss and Jakobson have remarked, in Jakobson, *Selected Writings,* the cat is often sexually ambiguous in Baudelaire's work. This ambiguity is compounded with that implicit in the "dominated" position held by the masculine term in the poem. [Author's note.]

also quite evident throughout the context: *verve puissante, enfants monstrueux/lasse, s'étendre, nonchalamment.*

The first comparison puts a simple first term and a complex second term into relation, and the second comparison relates a complex first term and a simple second term. The *reine* and the *chat* can also be considered as being of a metaphorical nature: the queen, metaphor of the loved woman idealized, and the cat, a metaphor of the subjected lover. One can say the same thing in other terms by considering that line 4 condenses several expressions, such as:

> as at the feet of a queen, a prince (a page, a knight)
> as at the feet of a lady, a voluptuous lover
> as at the feet of a human being, a cat.

We could also say that the opposition between the queen and the cat brings several semantic dimensions into play: superior/inferior, feminine/masculine, human/animal.

Inversely, in the second comparison, it is the first term which condenses several dimensions or several themes (the breast, a partial object, the child in the lap of his mother, the lover asleep on the body of the beloved, the earth-mother, etc.), while in line 14 only one dimension comes into play. One can therefore condense the opposition of these two comparisons in the following schema:

	first term	second term
lines 3–4	"the word alone"	metaphorical language
lines 13–14	metaphorical language	"the word alone"

We have reserved the semantic interpretation of lines 1–2 and 11–12, having already said that one could consider them syntactically equivalent. Remaining on the syntactical level one could again outline a certain relationship of internal equivalence between these two segments, on the condition of dealing only with their kernels (subject–verb–object) and presenting these kernels in a "normalized form."[15]

| la Nature | concevait | des enfants monstrueux |
| les soleils malsains | font s'étendre | la (jeune géante) |

If we compare the structures of the groups which occupy the positions of the subject and of object, we notice a series of inversions. In the first sentence, the subject is a simple nominal syntagma in the

---

[15] Cf. Harris, *Discourse Analysis Reprints.*

feminine singular, and the object is a complex nominal syntagma in the masculine plural. In the second sentence, it is the subject which is a complex nominal syntagma in the masculine plural, while the object is a singular feminine pronoun (one could go even further and compare *en sa verve puissante*, which is linked again with *la Nature*, and *lasse*, which is linked with *la [jeune géante]*).

This parallelism permits us to see a synecdoche of *la Nature* in *les soleils malsains* (confirming the relation of the part to the whole which, in a general fashion, links the elements of P_2 to those of P_1) and, further, to glimpse a rather ambiguous relationship of equivalence between *la Nature* and *la géante*. At another point we have already spoken of the relationship of superior to inferior, of dominating to dominated, which binds the giantess to the "I." Now, on the condition of conceiving this relationship in a rather abstract form, one can say that it is found in the marginal segments of lines 1–2 and 11–12: *la Nature* "dominates" *les enfants monstrueux*, as *les soleils malsains* "dominates" *la jeune géante*. The latter thus occupies an ambiguous position, sometimes as a dominated term and sometimes as a term which dominates. This ambiguous position is accentuated by the fact that, at the end, having become a cosmic being, she is identified with Nature itself.

One could therefore represent the essentials of the semantic structure of the text by the following schema, where > signifies "dominates," where S represents the relations of the part to the whole (synecdoche), and M the relations of equivalence (metaphor):

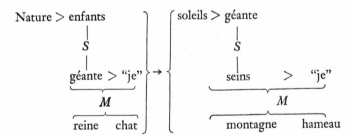

Only one term, *"je,"* occupies the same place in the two parts of the schema. We note that the relation of "dominance" between the giantess and *"je"* is only implicit in the first part. The central part (lines 5–10) appears to resemble a transition and section which has as its function—through more and more explicit synecdoche and metaphors—both to translate the giantess to a cosmic plane and to make more explicit the relation of dominance between the giantess and the "*je*."

On the whole, if one considers all of the relationships that we have briefly reviewed, the structure of the poem appears roughly analogous to the musical structure of the sonata movement, with an exposition which creates tension, a development of a fragmented character, and a reprise which transforms the tension into a release. One could even go to the point of connecting our analysis of the relation between the two comparisons (in lines 3–4 and 13–14) with the re-exposition of a sonata movement where two themes—one previously exposed in the tonic, the other in the dominant (whence a tension)—are both exposed in the tonic (whence a release).

Discussion

CHARLES MORAZÉ: I was very much moved by the modesty of your manner of presentation and by what was, in effect, a reminder to all of us of the need for modesty. You showed us that the things which are most modern in our eyes are already beginning to show signs of age and that we don't know where these paths will lead. The conclusion of this colloquium seems to invite us to hold another, perhaps in France, a few years hence in which Americans could bring us new elements for reflection.

In speaking of poetry you have alluded to some magnificent examples, such as: "Le jour n'est plus pur que le fond de mon coeur." This is Phèdre heralding her death, a death which will restore the purity of the day, that the pure heart bears its own crime which would disappear with it. Such is the poetry which you have evoked in speaking of extremely precise mechanical procedures.

You speak of a kind of poetics which I would call a "generalized particular" poetics, which, if applied to a given work as a whole—the work of Baudelaire, for example—would make it possible to produce all the possible poetry of Baudelaire, including some of what you judge to be bad poetry. To my mind such a procedure would give us not all the possible poetry of Baudelaire, not the prolegomena to a future, total Baudelaire, but a *general logic*. Who can say—since you say that it is still in the stages of imagination—that a generalized poetic or a generalized aesthetic would not be precisely a generalized logic. Once again I find this talk to be a striking conclusion because it brings both an element of criticism of everything which has been done and a great element of encouragement in suggesting everything which remains for us to do.

PETER CAWS: I think that many of us came to this colloquium hoping to find in structuralism the possibility of a methodological unity for what has come to be called in France "les sciences humaines." Here, however, we found that what has become primary in nearly all the discussions has been a metaphysical rather than a methodological question, principally the metaphysical question of the *subject* which has been considered to be a product of language, posterior to language. In this respect M. Vernant spoke about the impossibility of the vocabulary of the *will* among the Greeks and about the necessity of having linguistic formulation before one can speak in certain human terms. I think Michel Foucault, in his last work, has much the same point of view. Yet the discussion of a possible generative poetics seems to me to be a strong argument that language, in a creative sense, is posterior to the subject. I do not think that generative poetics is likely to produce any poems as good as those that Baudelaire wrote. There has been an attempt at generative music which has produced Mozart, but rather bad Mozart. I think there is a great deal of methodological work to be done before we can afford to indulge ourselves in the kind of metaphysics in which we have in fact indulged during the course of this colloquium. But the general reflection is that possibly metaphysics itself has been a product of our language.

RUWET: I only spoke of generative poetics in order to compare the stage we have reached in the study of poetry to the situation in linguistics. I certainly agree with you that the attempts to manufacture music have ended in very bad results, but the interesting thing here is to know exactly what one is doing in manufacturing synthetic music. When the result is so far from what we would call music, that tells us something about what we have yet to understand about music. In the same way in linguistics we can advance only by the progressive construction of grammars. These experiments allow us to measure the distance which still remains to be covered.

RICHARD MACKSEY: M. Ruwet has given us some welcome caveats for literary critics and at the same time has perhaps redefined the relationship of linguistics to poetics which was enunciated by Roman Jakobson in the justly famous paper at the Indiana stylistics conference. I could not agree more that one of the paradoxical excesses of American "formalism" was, at the level of phonology and syntax, often to dissolve the text into impressionistic fantasia. This was the result, I think, not merely of an attempt to install interpretation prematurely before an adequate description of the poetic act and its constituents, but of a more basic confusion about the very status of language and its proprieties in a text which the American critics wanted to insist was "autotelic" and "almost anonymous."

But I would like to observe that occasionally the literary critic in his attempt to understand his own act of interpretation has, in fact, *anticipated* some of the later insights and presiding concerns of linguistic analysis. Thus, your choice of the Baudelaire text inevitably suggests the tragic name of Walter Benjamin and his search for an adequate philosophy of language in essays like "Über die Sprache überhaupt und die Sprache der Menschen," the Goethe study, and "Probleme der Sprachsoziologie." His awareness of the coded, reciprocal relationships between objects, signs, and feeling ought to win him some sort of place in the structuralist pantheon of precursors. But I am thinking specifically of his extraordinary anticipation of Chomsky and a theory of universals and generative, transformational grammar in "Die Aufgabe des Übersetzers," dating, I believe, from the early 1920s, a generation before the American deep-meaning people rose to the challenge. In fact, Benjamin seemed to anticipate some of the divergent, ultimately ontological questions of "deep sense" which are at present dividing generative grammarians on critical and exciting issues which you know only too well. There is, of course, in Benjamin another aspect of his theory of language, the profound sense of what the jargon teaches us to call the *negative totalization* of the literary act, which would certainly distress some linguists, though it does, through his conception of, say, allegory, seem to give him that elusive prize of both critics and linguists—an emergent theory of context.

TZVETAN TODOROV: I am very concerned about Ruwet's skeptical account, especially since I am among those who hope to derive something from linguistics which may be of use in literary studies. And I should like to touch on a few points to which Ruwet has already alluded but which perhaps deserve a little further explication. Ruwet correctly remarked that all of us who have spoken of linguistics here have drawn on a few articles by Benveniste and not on the latest acquisitions in linguistics. I think that the explanation for this fact goes further than simple lack of information. Linguistics since Saussure has become a more and more intensive study of a more and more limited field, which might be called grammar and which is a very abstract code which engenders sentences. Literature, however, is a type of discourse, not a language. Benveniste, along with Jakobson, seems to be one of the rare linguists who has continued to be interested in the questions which serve to convert language into discourse, the "shifters" and so on. But I don't think that very complete results can be obtained from the direct application of linguistic methods to literary works. An analysis inspired by linguistics could describe the modalities and properties of literary discourse better than the concrete works. In each work such an analysis would discover only the manifestation of a property of literary discourse, which could obviously be grasped only in a work but which is itself the real object of this study. Literature is a system which remains to be described and I think that this type of literary study will be homologous not to linguistics but to other studies of other types of discourse. For example, we have heard here an inquiry into the properties of philosophic discourse based on a specific, concrete text of Hegel. And again, a study taking its inspiration from linguistics would address itself to the properties of literary discourse rather than to particular works.

RUWET: You seem to imply a progressive limitation of the field of study of linguistics. On the contrary, following a preliminary limitation which was absolutely necessary, there has been a new enrichment. One sees, for example, generative syntax now discovering many problems which had been completely abandoned since Saussure and which were the object of traditional grammars. I believe that in the years to come the field of semantics, for example, will be approached much more fruitfully. In regard to the "shifters," I agree, but I feel that that is one of the areas in semantics which can be most easily studied and that there are many others, much more complicated, about which we know very little and which it would be absolutely necessary to clarify in order to study literature.

ROLAND BARTHES: I would like to specify the relationship, as I see it, between literary semiotics and linguistics. I don't think it is right to assume linguistics, as it exists, and then to try to see what can be derived from it for literary analysis. In reality those who carry on literary analysis must sometimes demand a linguistics which does not exist. It is their role to determine, to a certain degree, the need for a linguistics which does not exist. That is why we have been led to rely, provisionally, on certain of Benveniste's formulations in contrast to what might be called *la linguistique du langage* from Saussure to Chomsky. There is also the need for what I would call *une linguistique des langues,* such as what I was seeking in my consideration of temporality and person etc. Literary analysis will need a change in linguistics. I insist on this kind of methodological relationship; literary semiotics cannot be considered as simply a follower and a parasite of linguistics.

RUWET: I think we are in complete agreement. It is simply a difference in point of view.

LUCIEN GOLDMANN: For me Ruwet was the great surprise in this colloquium. He seems to be the one who is closest, in the field of linguistics, to the project which I indicated in my talk of extending structuralist analysis to form, especially in his idea of pertinences coinciding on different levels. It seems to me that semantics is of the first importance here and that one must start from semantics in order to understand and show the coherence of form. I'd like to make a very hazardous attempt with the line that you quoted "Le jour n'est pas plus pur que le fond de mon coeur" [The day is no purer than the depth of my heart]. Thinking about this line for a few minutes I noticed that, as the line is heard, there is a definite harmony between what is said and the way in which it is said. What is said? First there are two levels: the high (day, *le jour*) and the depth [*le fond*]. Second, these two levels become homogeneous in the idea of purity. Third, the line establishes a relationship between these two different but homogeneous levels. In the first half of the line there are three *p*'s (*pas plus pur*) and three *u*'s (*jour . . . plus pur*), neither letter existing in the other half of the line. In the second half there are three *o*'s (*fond de mon coeur*). There are, thus, different, repetitive groups of sounds but they are linked by the fact that both groups end with an *r* (*pur, coeur*). I don't know if this exercise has any value, but it seems to me that for the listener there is a rigorous homology between what is said and the way in which it is said.

RUWET: I would say that this is a good example of what I don't want to do, because basically it is a sort of homology between two levels of impressionistic analysis. This is the sort of thing which could be said before the tools that I was speaking of were available, for example, the act of speaking in terms of unanalyzed phonemes. Undoubtedly certain things could be said in a fairly rigorous manner about semantics in relationship to this line. But to understand, for example, the question of why this line has a more or less dependent life, we would need more than the few elements of phonetics which I gave. We have certain givens but, in the end, we don't know how to interpret them. We would at least need a theory of context which would explain how sentences are attached to one another and how a sentence can be detached etc. As Chomsky said in a very recent text, we have absolutely nothing in the way of a theory of context which would be at all comparable in rigor to what is being done in other areas of linguistics. Certain very elementary things can be said, but, at the present, an attempt at comparing two levels could only be very impressionistic.

Concluding Remarks

RICHARD MACKSEY: It is formulaic in the closing moments of any such co-operative enterprise as this Symposium to speak of the project's success, to assess the common ground we have won, the critical positions we may have demystified. Without deliberately slighting this hallowed tradition, it may be more prudent to entrust such evaluations to the future and to recall, however briefly, that the phrase from Merleau-Ponty with which M. Hyppolite eloquently concluded his remarks could be adapted to our present purpose: "There is no Symposium without its shadow." Measured against the participants' original intentions, there have been, no doubt, a number of surprises, some shifts of emphasis, and a few clear lapses of programmatic aims. Further, there have been the topics which have acquired definition only through our reluctance or inability to address them directly.

The title under which the Symposium was conceived emphasized both the plurality of critical languages to be considered and the possibility of constituting as a frame for discussion the general methodology of the *sciences de l'homme*. In some respects the papers and debates only confirmed the first assumption and revealed the difficulties of achieving the latter. Many of the participants, while sharing certain crucial words in the critical vocabulary, clearly invested them with differing and even antithetical meanings. Yet these and other differences were debated and clarified —the first step toward any methodological review.

At the level of the discussions, some of you have observed that the announced concern for methodological and axiological questions was perhaps diverted by a recur-

319

rent preoccupation with a basically metaphysical question, namely, *the status of the subject* in the several disciplines before us. And yet this issue was clearly prolegomenous to any discussion of the constitutive discrepancy within intersubjective relationships, of the contest for priority between the sign [*signifiant*] and meaning [*signifié*], of the alleged privilege of any critical position whatever. At the opening of our sessions René Girard's reading of the hazards facing Tiresias as blind critic could serve as both warning and challenge.

Some observers may feel the equally important issues relating to values in the transfer of investigative models from one discipline to another have been also unfortunately slighted. Or, again, others may feel that although the great European architects of our labyrinth— Hegel, Marx, Nietzsche, Freud, and Saussure—have been given their due place in contemporary praxis, closer attention to the formative Anglo-American tradition of thought might have revealed important congruences and correctives, say in the work of Peirce and Dewey, of Kroeber, Lowie, and Sapir, of Harry Stack Sullivan, Mead, and Kenneth Burke. This bias no doubt reflects the distinctly Gallic flavor which our distinguished visitors have lent to the Symposium. It remains for the continuing seminars which these sessions have inaugurated to explore these other openings and possibly redress the balance.

The sessions have allowed us, however, not only to investigate some of the roots of the contemporary critical "crisis" but to assess some of the possible consequences for the humane sciences of new appropriations across disciplinary lines, to investigate contending interpretative models, and to consider such radical reappraisals of our assumptions as that advanced by M. Derrida on this final day.

Some of the vitality in the "structuralist adventure" as well as much of the confusion undoubtedly stems from the plurality of analytical languages and the internal divisions about status of the subject in the various disciplines. Yet we hope that the Symposium has demonstrated that this pluralism and these divisions were themselves susceptible to fruitful analysis. While dispelling any lingering dreams of a formalized and "pure" interpretative language which may have survived the philosophic onslaughts of the preceding generation, these sessions have, I think, renewed the urgency of Charles Peirce's isolated plea for the systematic study of methods and for the semiotic analysis of adjacent sign systems, in all their individuality, as keys to the understanding of the way in which communication and its paradoxes constitute the human community.

This is certainly not the moment to draw any systematic conclusions from what has transpired here, but in considering the language which men use to discuss their languages we might turn again to that tenet which Merleau-Ponty, in a late essay, derives from the familiar structural view of ordinary language's self-transcending power in the movement from the intention of the *signifiant* to the achieved expression of the *signifié*: "We who speak do not necessarily know what we express better than those who hear us." This insight clearly applies to any retrospective interpretation of these sessions and it was this creative sense which animated the debates and which, we hope, made, "Les Langages Critiques et les Sciences de l'Homme" more of an exploration of new perspectives than a consolidation of those already held.

RENÉ GIRARD: I can only concur with my colleague that there is not time at this hour to draw any summary conclusions from the Symposium. There remains much to be said, but this must be part of the dialogue commenced here, which will be continued as a supplement to our sessions—through the Ford Seminars planned for the next two years, through the articles which the week's topics will provoke, through the discussions and correspondence which will bind us together, and through the acts of the Symposium which will be published by The Johns Hopkins Press.

To conclude, in the name of the organizers of the Symposium, in the name of the new Humanities Center of The Johns Hopkins University and its Director, Charles Singleton, we wish to thank all our friends here for their collaboration, at once so active, so incisive, and so cordial. It was this cordial spirit of co-operation, so well defined by Professor Hyppolite, which we believe was essential to the success of the Symposium. We thank the participants, colloquists, and guests for their contributions to this dialogue and this spirit, for all that they have brought to Baltimore, and we resolve to keep open the lines of communication discovered here.

JEAN HYPPOLITE [on behalf of the European delegates to the Symposium]: I wish to say quite simply, on behalf of all my colleagues who have charged me to do so, how grateful we are for the warm welcome which has been accorded us at this University, by the Humanities Center, and by the support of the Ford Foundation.

And I wish to say—and I think that I speak for all those who together asked me to take the floor today—I wish to say how deeply we have been impressed, not only by the thoughtfulness in every physical arrangement, by the courtesy of the welcome, but especially by the rare atmosphere which has presided over this colloquium, where (despite the linguistic difficulties) we have felt so acutely how close this University is to those questions which have elsewhere concerned each of us, with what care and solicitude our problems have been anticipated, and how amply the discussion of the central topic has been opened and advanced. Finally, I want to thank you, M. Président, to thank the organizers, and to thank all those who have contributed to this fruitful encounter.

RICHARD MACKSEY: The eighth and final session of "The Languages of Criticism and the Sciences of Man" stands adjourned. We trust, however, that the critical exchanges and discussions have just begun.

Structure:
réalité humaine
et concept
méthodologique

Lucien Goldmann

I. *La structure comme réalité humaine*

1) Tout comportement humain (et même plus généralement tout comportement d'un être vivant d'une certaine complexité) est constitué par un ensemble de gestes (et chez l'homme de représentations, de concepts et d'affections) orienté vers un changement de la configuration sujet-monde ambiant dans un sens plus conforme à la survie et aux tendances (chez l'homme aussi aux besoins, aux désirs) du sujet.

2) Du point de vue de l'étude positive le comportement peut être considéré comme une tentative pour résoudre un problème ou pour répondre de manière pratique, théorique ou imaginaire à une question.

3) Deux concepts théoriques importants se dégagent de cette hypothèse.

a. Tout comportement humain (et probablement beaucoup de comportements animaux) a un caractère *significatif, ce terme se définissant par rapport aux tendances (désirs, besoins) du sujet et à la situation globale concrète dans laquelle il se trouve,* c'est-à-dire à l'existence d'une configuration traduisible en termes de problème et des possibilités de le résoudre sur le plan pratique, conceptuel, ou imaginaire.

b. Le caractère significatif d'un comportement n'existe pas dans chaque unité conceptuellement séparable de ce dernier mais seulement dans sa totalité (éléments et relations) au niveau de la réponse à un problème ou à un groupe de problèmes.

Par rapport à ce problème l'ensemble (nous préférons employer à partir de maintenant le terme de *totalité relative*) est tel que le changement d'un élément doit, pour conserver le caractère significatif (ou si l'on veut, adapté à la situation) du comportement, entrainer un certain nombre de changements correspondants des autres éléments et relations qui le constituent.

Nous désignons les ensembles pourvus de ces propriétés comme des *structures*, leur aptitude à résoudre un certain nombre de problèmes pratiques, théoriques ou imaginaires comme aptitude à remplir une ou plusieurs *fonctions*.

Structure, signification, fonction apparaissent ainsi comme trois concepts scientifiques à la fois complémentaires et inséparables.

La *structure* existe par son caractère significatif qui résulte de son aptitude à remplir une *fonction*. Les *fonctions* ne sauraient être remplies que par des *structures*, les structures sont *significatives* dans la mesure où elles sont aptes à remplir une fonction.

4) Les structures ont un caractère génétique, dans la mesure où lorsque le monde ambiant se transforme par l'action de facteurs endogènes ou exagènes à la configuration sujet-objet (qui est elle-même à son niveau une structure significative), elles ne sont plus aptes à remplir les fonctions qu'elles remplissaient auparavant et doivent être remplacées par des structures nouvelles adaptées aux nouvelles situations.

5) L'existence de structures significatives *n'est pas liée à celle d'un système symbolique et à la possibilité de communication*. De pareilles structures existent déjà au niveau du comportement animal avant tout langage (le comportement d'un chat qui poursuit une souris par exemple, constitue une *structure significative* et peut être traduit en termes de *solution d'un problème*) et continuent à exister chez l'homme comme structures biologiques qui intègrent le langage.

6) La différence entre les structures significatives à caractère *biologique prédominant* (nous parlerons chez l'homme de structures à caractère libidinal) et les structures significatives à caractère *social prédominant* réside en premier lieu dans le fait que le sujet des premières a un caractère *individuel* (tous les autres individus remplissant par rapport au comportement du sujet une fonction d'*objet*. Voir par exemple le cas de la mère et du père dans le complexe d'Oedipe décrit par Freud) alors que le sujet des secondes a un caractère *trans-individuel* (et cela dès le cas le plus simple, par exemple celui de deux hommes Jean et Jacques qui déplacent un meuble. Le sujet de l'action n'est dans ce cas ni Jean ni Jacques mais *Jean et Jacques*.)

J'ai proposé d'employer dans ce cas, pour désigner les relations entre les différents individus qui constituent le sujet de l'action le terme *relations intrasubjectives* (par opposition aux *relations intersubjectives* entre individus qui ne constituent pas le sujet d'une action commune).

7) La signification des structures et l'existence même de ces dernières peuvent se situer à trois niveaux différents que nous désignons par les termes d' *inconscient, non-conscient* et *conscient.*

Par le terme *inconscient* nous désignerons—suivant en cela un usage consacré par l'oeuvre de Freud—les significations des structures individuelles (libidinales) qui se trouvent en conflit avec les significations transindividuelles et peuvent à partir de ce conflit être refoulées ou avoir besoin de tourner un obstacle, la *censure*, pour pénétrer de manière déformée dans la conscience.

Nous appelerons *non-conscientes*, les significations et les structures qui ont sur le plan psychique un statut par certains côtés analogue à celui des structures physiologiques qui déterminent en grande mesure notre comportement sans pour cela être *ni conscientes ni inconscientes et refoulées.*

Il n'y a dans la structure psychique du sujet aucun obstacle à la prise de conscience de l'existence de ces structures et de leur signification. Elles n'ont besoin de tourner aucune censure pour pénétrer dans la conscience. Il faut cependant pour cela qu'elles soient mises en lumière et portées à la connaissance des individus par des recherches respectivement épistémologiques pour les structures psychiques et physiologiques pour les structures du corps.

Quant au *conscient,* il faut mentionner qu'il a presque toujours un caractère plus ou moins partiel et inadéquat (idéologie, fausse conscience) et ne correspond que très rarement à la signification réelle et totale de la structure psychique dont il fait partie.

8) Dans la réalité empirique ces quatres secteurs (ou niveaux) du comportement, de la pensée ou de l'imagination, à savoir:

Le libidinal inconscient (ou latent)
Le libidinal manifeste
Le transindividuel (ou social) nonconscient, et
Le transindividuel (ou social) conscient
sont toujours inextricablement mêlés.

Il est cependant essentiel pour la pensée scientifique *qui ne saurait étudier tels quels les mélanges,* de séparer conceptuellement ces secteurs pour pouvoir étudier par la suite soit l'aspect du comportement qui l'intéresse, soit éventuellement la nature de chaque mélange particulier (et nécessairement individuel).

9) Les deux types fondamentaux de structures significatives nous semblent se rattacher à deux groupes de tendances, à savoir:

a. Les structures à sujet individuel aux tendances libidinales pour lesquelles tout autre homme ne saurait être—à tous les niveaux conscient, non-conscient ou inconscient—qu'*objet* de désir, de répulsion ou d'indifférence.

Ces tendances *naturelles* subsistent bien entendu dans la vie sociale et culturelle et sont profondément modifiées par les systèmes symboliques auxquels elles s'intègrent et qu'elles intègrent en se modifiant et en les modifiant, *sans cependant perdre leur caractère de structures significatives à sujet individuel;* elles deviennent ainsi des faits à caractère fondamentalement biologique et subsidiairement culturel.

b. Les structures à sujet transindividuel (ou pluriel, collectif) correspondant aux tendances dont la satisfaction est liée à la maîtrise de la nature extérieure (faim, protection contre les dangers extérieurs de tout genre) et qui, tout en gardant un fondement naturel sont profondément et essentiellement modifiées dans leur nature même par l'apparition de la fonction symbolique qui rend possible la *division du travail* et avec elle la communication conceptuelle, le détour de la satisfaction par la technique et cela veut dire la société, l'histoire et la culture.

Toutes les structures du comportement correspondant à la satisfaction (de plus en plus médiatisée) de ces besoins, qui étaient à sujet individuel chez la plupart des animaux, deviennent chez l'homme des structures *à sujet transindividuel* et cela veut dire des structures à caractère *fondamentalement culturel et subsidiairement biologique.*

10) Il va de soi que les structures culturelles à sujet transindividuel peuvent avoir pour *objet* non seulement l'inanimé mais aussi des individus ou structures significatives. Il s'agit alors de relations *intersubjectives* par opposition aux relations *intrasubjectives.*

Pour éviter tout malentendu soulignons que ce sont là des distinctions à la fois nécessaires et relatives car deux groupes humains qui s'opposent sur un plan peuvent constituer *ensemble* le sujet d'un autre comportement dans lequel ils s'opposent à un groupe tiers, et ainsi de suite. A la limite, il existe même une certaine action de l'humanité tout entière sur la nature. Elle constitue le fondement de ces structures que sont aujourd'hui déjà les sciences physio-chimiques et biologiques.

11) Le développement de la vie sociale engendre bien entendu des conflits entre les deux groupes de structures significatives (à sujet individuel et transindividuel), conflits qui correspondent à ce que Freud a désigné comme *Malaise dans la culture* et dont une manifestation universelle (mais non pas unique) semble être—si Freud a raison —la prohibition de l'inceste, indispensable à la constitution et au dé-

veloppement de sociétés sufisamment vastes pour organiser, maintenir, et développer la division du travail.

12) Toute conscience individuelle apparaît ainsi à la fois comme un mélange de structures les plus diverses et un compromis plus ou moins original entre structures significatives correspondant aux tendances libidinales et structures correspondant aux tendances culturelles à sujet transindividuel.

Les innombrables compromis se situent sur une chaine dont les deux extrémités sont constituées par:

a. Les comportements pratiques, intellectuels et imaginaires dans lesquels les structures libidinales sont *entièrement* adaptées et subordonnées aux structures transindividuelles, de manière à ne modifier en rien ou presque l'agencement, la cohérence et le fonctionnement de celles-ci.

b. Les comportements pratiques, intellectuels ou imaginaires dans lesquels les structures libidinales se sont imposées à tel point aux structures transindividuelles et y ont provoqué des distorsions telles que ces comportements ne sauraient plus s'insérer dans la communication fondée sur les codes indispensables à la vie historique et culturelle (rêves, névroses, etc.).

Il va de soi que l'énorme majorité des consciences individuelles se situent quelque part entre les deux extrémités de l'aliénation ou du rêve et de la création des grandes oeuvres culturelles et des grandes réalisations biologiques.

II. Problèmes éspistémologiques

13) L'étude scientifique des faits humains ne saurait être ni purement subjective ni purement objective et cela pour une double raison:

a. Si tous les faits humains constituent des structures significatives qui se définissent par rapport à un sujet de la pensée et de l'action (individu ou groupe) et à l'objet de celles-ci (monde ambiant, situation), la pensée scientifique constitue elle-même une pareille structure qui ne saurait être comprise que par son caractère fonctionnel dans une situation *plus ou moins générale*, c'est-à-dire par sa double référence à un *sujet* et à un *objet*.

De plus en sciences de l'homme le lien entre les structures de la pensée scientifique et les caractères spécifiques et particuliers des valeurs du sujet est *encore* particulièrement accentué et insurmontable. C'est pourquoi alors que les sciences de la nature ont déjà atteint un stade où il existe un critère universel d'objectivité, les sciences humaines

structurées par des valeurs *spécifiques* et *particulières* sont loin de
posséder un pareil critère.

L'objectivité dans le sens de validité humaine universelle constitue
pour toute science l'idéal qu'il faut essayer d'approcher autant que
possible tout en restant conscient que l'on ne saurait jamais l'atteindre;
mais cette impossibilité est *encore* de nature différente en sciences
humaines et en sciences naturelles.

b. Les sciences humaines constituent un essai d'étudier des comportements humains, des créations et des expressions humaines à l'aide
d'instruments intellectuels qui sont eux-mêmes de telles créations et
expressions et parfois des créations et des expressions du *même sujet*
que les objets étudiés. Il y a là un facteur de distorsion dont la recherche
doit tenir compte et dont elle doit intégrer *l'action spécifique dans
chaque cas particulier.*

14) Ni les deux facteurs énumérés au point précédent, ni le cercle
constitutif de toute réflexion sur l'homme qui en résulte, n'impliquent
en aucune manière la nécessité pour une réflexion méthodologique
rigoureuse d'aboutir en sciences humaines au scepticisme, au relativisme
ou à l'historisme. L'action de ces facteurs ainsi que le cercle épistémo-
logique qu'ils engendrent peuvent parfaitement être intégrés à une
pensée scientifique et positive.

15) Les deux procédés intellectuels les plus importants pour l'étude
scientifique des faits humains sont la *compréhension* et l'*explication.* Ils
sont l'un et l'autre des procédés *purement conceptuels* et n'ont rien
en commun avec certaines attitudes affectives, notamment avec l'identification, l'empathie, la sympathie etc. auxquelles on rattache trop souvent le premier.

Ces attitudes affectives sont des circonstances *extérieures* à la pensée
qui peuvent, *comme toute circonstance extérieure* avoir une action
plus ou moins favorable ou défavorable sur la pensée en général et sur
la recherche scientifique en particulier.

La *compréhension* est constituée par la description conceptuelle
aussi rigoureuse que possible d'une structure significative dans sa totalité composée d'un certain nombre d'éléments et de relations unis
par une cohérence fonctionelle.

L'*explication* est la description d'une structure significative englo-
bante et de la genèse à l'intérieur de celle-ci de la structure significative
étudiée.

Il s'agit donc de deux procédés intellectuels *homologues* rapportés
respectivement dans le cas de la *compréhension* à la structure significa-

tive qu'on se propose d'étudier, dans le cas de l'*explication* à une structure significative qui englobe la structure étudiée.

16) Toute structure significative fait partie de plusieurs structures significatives plus vastes et de même tout élément d'une structure peut être en même temps élément d'autres structures. Cette situation est fondement de la *polysémie* de tout fait humain et de toute expression humaine, polysémie constatée par des chercheurs appartenant aux écoles les plus diverses.

17) Les trois types de recherche structuraliste génétique les plus développés jusqu'aujourd'hui sont l'épistémologie de Jean Piaget, la psychanalyse fondée sur l'insertion des faits humains dans des structures significatives *à sujet individuel*, et la sociologie structuraliste génétique qui essaye d'insérer ces faits dans des structures significatives *à sujet transindividuel*.

En tant que structuralisme génétique la psychanalyse et la sociologie structuraliste génétique ont un certain nombre de traits communs. Elles s'opposent néanmoins sur un certain nombre d'autres points.

Les traits communs sont:

a. l'hypothèse du caractère significatif, et à partir de là accessible à la compréhension de toute manifestation humaine.

b. la thèse que le sens du fait étudié ne saurait devenir visible que par son insertion dans une des structures significatives dont il fait partie.

c. la conception de ces structures significatives comme génétiques (biographiques pour la psychanalyse, historiques pour la sociologie).

L'opposition ne paraît résider dans le fait que la plupart des études psychanalytiques, et en tout cas celles de Freud, partent de l'idée que *toutes* les structures humaines ont un sujet *individuel* et à partir de là de l'idée que toutes les significations sont individuelles et intersubjectives, alors que la sociologie structuraliste génétique distingue les structures *à sujet individuel* et à fonction et signification libidinales des structures *à sujet transindividuel* et à signification et fonction historiques, sociales et culturelles.

18) Si l'on rapporte cette distinction aux deux procédés de recherche déjà mentionnés, la *compréhension* et l'*explication* on aboutit à une distinction particulièrement importante: psychanalyse et sociologie structuraliste génétique reconnaissent l'une et l'autre l'utilité et la nécessité de chacun de ces procédés dans l'étude positive des faits humains.

Seulement, comme dans les structures *à sujet individuel* les éléments conscients et manifestes ne constituent en aucune manière une struc-

Lucien Goldmann

ture significative relativement autonome et ne sauraient être séparés des pulsions du comportement et de l'affectivité sans par cela même perdre leur caractère significatif,* *l'explication et la compréhension s'avèrent non seulement complémentaires mais inséparables pour leur étude.*

On ne saurait *interpréter* un lapsus, un rêve, un symptome névrotique *uniquement* à partir d'éléments explicites ou manifestes sans recourir à leur caractère symbolique, à l'inconscient, et aux désirs refoulés, c'est-à-dire sans les expliquer.

La situation est par contre différente au niveau des structures significatives *à sujet transindividuel* pour lesquels la communication est un élément *intrasubjectif, constitutif du sujet comme tel* et qui ne sauraient se passer de système symbolique.

Sur ce plan les données explicites et manifestes tendent à constituer des structures cohérentes *relativement autonomes* et y parviennent sinon souvent du moins parfois et notamment dans un certain nombre de créations culturelles particulièrement importantes.

Dans ces derniers cas l'explication sociologique constitue sans doute un élément non seulement utile mais pratiquement indispensable de la recherche et de la mise en lumière du sens; une fois ces recherches suffisamment avancées, la structure peut cependant être décrite, la signification formulée et communiquée de manière *purement immanente* en se référant *uniquement* aux données explicites et manifestes sans aucun recours à l'explication c'est-à-dire à la psychologie ou à la sociologie.

On ne peut interpréter un rêve sans recourir à l'inconscient, au contenu latent, à la biographie et à *l'explication,* on peut et on doit en revanche *interpréter Bérénice* ou *Phèdre* sans aucun recours à un contenu latent, au caractère symbolique des énoncés, à la société française du XVIIe siècle ou à la morale janséniste, uniquement à partir du texte sans rien lui ajouter et sans rien lui ôter.

Cela ne met bien entendu nullement en cause l'utilité de la recherche historique ou sociologique pour parvenir à trouver cette signification immanente puisque cette recherche permet seule de mettre en lumière *la genèse, la nature et le caractère fonctionnel* des structures mentales, (nous les avons appelées *visions du monde*) qui créent l'unité et la

---

* Peut-être le comprendra-t-on plus aisément si l'on se rappelle que pour ces structures significatives la conscience est un élément adventice et secondaire; le comportement animal (celui déjà mentionné du chat qui poursuit une souris par exemple) constitue le plus souvent une telle structure significative à sujet individuel sans qu'il y ait ni conscience, ni système symbolique.

cohérence de l'univers de chaque tragédie (et doivent *en principe* rendre compte même de ses caractères formels dans le sens le plus étroit du mot).

Il reste qu'il n'y a *dans la pièce* qu'un univers rigoureusement co-hérent de personnages individuels, de relations concrètes, de situations et de comportements pratiques et surtout verbaux et qu'on n'y trouve ni l'inconscient ou la biographie de Racine puisque celui-ci ne s'y est pas introduit de manière *explicite,* ni jansénisme, ni société française puisque l'action se passe à Trézène.

En revanche, la structure sociale française XVIIe siècle, la morale et la théologie janséniste sont des données indispensables pour *trouver* la signification unitaire et cohérente de *Bérénice* ou de *Phèdre* et pour expliquer pourquoi elles ont pu être écrites, de même que l'inconscient de Racine (et non pas ceux de Bérénice ou de Phèdre, qui ne sauraient exister) peut nous expliquer pourquoi *c'est précisément lui* qui les a imaginées et réalisées.

III. Statut de la sociologie structuraliste génétique de la littérature
19) La sociologie littéraire traditionelle (qui continue d'ailleurs à dominer dans une très grande mesure la recherche et l'enseignement uni-versitaires) s'efforçait à établir des relations entre *le contenu* de l'oeuvre littéraire et *le contenu* de la conscience collective, c'est-à-dire les manières de penser et de se comporter des hommes dans la vie quo-tidienne. Dans cette perspective elle aboutissait naturellement aux ré-sultats que ces rapports étaient d'autant plus nombreux et la sociologie littéraire d'autant plus efficace que l'auteur des écrits étudiés avait fait preuve de moins d'imagination créatrice et s'était contenté de ra-conter ses expériences en les transposant le moins possible. De plus, ce type d'étude devait par sa méthode même briser l'unité de l'oeuvre en s'intéressant surtout à ce qui, en elle n'était que reproduction de la réalité empirique et de la vie quotidienne. En bref, cette sociologie était d'autant plus féconde que les oeuvres étudiées étaient plus médio-cres. De surcroît elle recherchait dans les oeuvres plus le document que la littérature.

Rien d'étonnant, dans ces conditions que la grande majorité parmi ceux qui s'intéressent à la littérature considèrent ce genre de recherches, dans le meilleur des cas comme des travaux auxiliaires plus ou moins utiles, lorsqu'il ne les refusent pas entièrement. La sociologie struc-turaliste génétique part de prémisses non seulement différentes, mais même opposées dont nous voudrions mentionner ici cinq parmi les plus importantes:

Lucien Goldmann

a. La relation essentielle entre la vie sociale et la création littéraire ne concerne pas selon elle le contenu de ces deux secteurs de la réalité humaine, mais seulement *les structures mentales*, ce qu'on pourrait appeler les catégories qui organisent à la fois la conscience empirique d'un certain groupe social et l'univers imaginaire créé par l'écrivain.

b. L'expérience d'un seul individu est beaucoup trop brève et trop limitée pour pouvoir créer une pareille structure mentale; celle-ci ne peut être que le résultat de l'activité conjointe d'un nombre important d'individus se trouvant dans une situation analogue, c'est-à-dire constituant un groupe social privilégié, individus ayant vécu longtemps et d'une manière intensive un ensemble de problèmes et s'étant efforcé de leur trouver une solution significative. C'est-à-dire que les structures mentales ou, pour employer un terme plus abstrait, les structures catégorielles significatives ne sont pas des phénomènes individuels mais des phénomènes sociaux.

c. La relation déjà mentionnée entre la structure de la conscience empirique d'un groupe social et celle qui régit l'univers de l'oeuvre constitue, dans les cas les plus favorables, pour le chercheur, une homologie plus ou moins rigoureuse, mais souvent aussi une simple relation significative.

Il peut donc arriver, dans cette perspective, et il arrive même le plus souvent, que des contenus entièrement hétérogènes et même opposées, soient sur le plan des structures catégorielles. Un univers imaginaire, tout à fait étranger en apparence à l'expérience empirique, celui d'un conte de fées par exemple, peut être rigoureusement homologue, *dans sa structure*, à l'expérience d'un groupe social particulier ou, tout au moins, relié à elle d'une manière significative. Il n'y a plus aucune contradiction entre l'existence d'une relation étroite de la création littéraire avec la réalité sociale et historique, et l'imagination créatrice la plus puissante.

d. Les sommets de la création littéraire peuvent non seulement être étudiés, dans une telle perspective sociologique, tout aussi bien que les oeuvres moyennes, ils se révèlent même particulièrement accessibles à une pareille recherche. D'autre part, les structures catégorielles sur lesquelles porte ce genre de sociologie littéraire constituent précisément ce qui confère à l'oeuvre son unité, son caractère spécifiquement esthétique et, dans le cas qui nous intéresse, sa qualité proprement littéraire.

e. Les structures catégorielles qui régissent la conscience collective et sont transposées dans l'univers imaginaire créé par l'artiste ne sont ni conscientes ni inconscientes, dans le sens freudien du mot qui suppose un refoulement, mais des processus non-conscients.

C'est pourquoi, dans la plupart des cas, la mise en lumière de ces structures n'est accessible ni à une étude littéraire immanente, ni à une étude orientée vers les intentions conscientes de l'écrivain ou vers la psychologie des profondeurs, mais seulement à une recherche de type structuraliste et sociologique.

Remarques finales

Si tous les faits humains constituent des structures significatives et si les faits sociaux, historiques et culturels constituent de telles structures à *sujet transindividuel* il en résulte:

a. qu'on ne peut les comprendre et les rendre intelligibles dans leur ensemble qu'en les rapportant respectivement au *sujet individuel* pour les structures *libidinales* et au sujet collectif pour les structures historiques, sociales et culturelles.

b. qu'on ne saurait étudier scientifiquement ces faits avec des méthodes positivistes en partant—de manière purement analytique—d'éléments partiels et immédiats car les significations de ces éléments dépendent en premier lieu de leur insertion dans une ou plusieurs structures.

c. que les significations individuelles et transindividuelles inter-subjectives et intrasubjectives étant inextricablement mêlées dans la réalité concrète on ne saurait pas non plus les étudier de manière synthétique et dialectique *à partir du donné immédiat* sans séparer analytiquement sur le plan conceptuel les différents secteurs d'un mélange impossible à atteindre tel que par la recherche positive.

d. qu'on ne saurait comprendre le caractère significatif essentiel à tous les faits humains en morcelant les structures en éléments communs et en essayant d'établir les lois générales des transformations de leurs combinaisons.

La signification concrète de tout élément dépend de *son insertion dans une structure significative particulière et du rattachement de celle-ci à un groupe de situations et à une fonction.*

Les lois générales qui régissent les combinaisons des éléments ne sauraient aborder les significations elles-mêmes mais seulement la nature des matériaux à travers lesquels elles s'expriment (réflexes, langage, etc.) et éventuellement certains aspects de la relation entre ces matériaux et la signification.

e. qu'on ne saurait étudier les faits sociaux et culturels en les rapportant à un sujet individuel (une oeuvre littéraire à son auteur, par exemple) sans d'une part briser leur unité, les morceler, et d'autre part,

Lucien Goldmann

éliminer pour des raisons méthodologiques leur signification spécifiquement historique et culturelle.

(L'explication psychanalytique même la plus réussie d'une oeuvre
littéraire ne saurait presque jamais rendre compte de l'*ensemble* de
cette oeuvre et surtout ne saurait pour des raisons méthodologiques
rendre compte de ce qui dans cette oeuvre est spécifiquement littéraire
et la sépare de l'écrit d'un aliéné qui aurait dans un contexte psychique
et biographique analogue une signification apparentée.)

f. Enfin que la genèse ne se confondant pas avec le sens et l'essence, toute étude structuraliste génétique doit à tout prix éviter la
réduction des faits étudiés à leur origine.

Un rêve ou un fantasme est autre chose que la pulsion qui les a
engendrés, un ouvrage littéraire ne se confond pas avec les structures
qui l'organisent et encore moins avec la conscience des groupes au sein
desquels ont été élaborées ses structures.

Bien qu'elle soit née à partir d'une certaine situation, l'oeuvre ne se
réduit pas à cette situation et loin d'être un simple *reflet* de celle-ci ou
d'une conscience collective, elle constitue l'expression *à un degré particulier d'unité et de cohérence* des tendances, des aspirations d'un
groupe privilégié.

Ecrite par un individu elle révèle aux membres du groupe ce vers
quoi ils tendaient sans en être conscients, ce qu'ils sentaient et pensaient
"sans le savoir" et constitue la rencontre du "je" et du "nous," du per-
sonnel et du collectif au niveau le plus élévé de structuration significative.

Appendix II

Structure du langage philosophique d'après la "Préface de la Phénoménologie de l'esprit" de Hegel

Jean Hyppolite

I

N'est-il pas trop tard pour parler encore de Hegel? Notre temps n'est-il pas celui des sciences positives qui non seulement ont su conquérir des vérités dans leurs domaines respectifs, mais encore ont su apprécier et fonder elles-mêmes ces vérités dans le champ de leur savoir, sans avoir besoin du secours du métaphysicien? L'épistémologie contemporaine et l'histoire des sciences et des techniques sont des disciplines positives. Enfin les sciences humaines, et la première d'entre elles, la linguistique, sont, du moins elles le croient, parvenues à se libérer des hypothèses philosophiques. Reste-t-il encore une place disponible pour la spéculation philosophique? Dans ce cas y a-t-il un style, un caractère propre d'une exposition ou d'une présentation philosophique, comme il y a un style et un caractère propre des grandes oeuvres littéraires?

On a souvent dit de Hegel qu'il était le dernier philosophe classique. Avec lui peut-être, après lui à coup sûr commence le déclin de la métaphysique. Des chercheurs audacieux ont frayé des voies nouvelles, Nietzsche, Marx, Freud, sont-ils encore des philosophes? Ou sont-ils seulement les critiques des métaphysiques du passé? Que signifie alors cette pensée qui n'appartient ni à la science positive, ni à l'ontologie classique? C'est justement parce que Hegel est le dernier des grands métaphysiciens, et parce qu'il en a eu une claire conscience, que sa pensée nous intéresse. Nous sommes un peu, par rapport à lui, ce que fut le moyen âge par rapport à Aristote. Sa grande ombre couvre tous les essais philosophiques qui se firent jouer pour ou contre lui. Hier encore il était considéré comme l'inspirateur de toutes les recherches génétiques et historiques—l'histoire de la philosophie devenant elle-même une philosophie, ou l'histoire humaine surmontant l'aliénation. Maintenant depuis la nouvelle découverte de la *Phénoménologie de l'esprit*, on a considéré Hegel comme une des sources de la pensée contemporaine et de l'existentialisme. Cependant la pensée la plus moderne se détourne des genèses pour s'attacher aux structures, aux systèmes formels, aux correspondances et aux analogies. Ici c'est plutôt Leibniz qui est considéré comme le grand ancêtre. Pourtant Hegel aussi a pensé structures et systèmes, non pas seulement genèse et histoire, mais Leibniz a aperçu la fécondité de la pensée formelle, la systématicité des systèmes, tandis que Hegel a toujours condamné le formalisme. C'est lui qui a dit: "En Art comme en tout autre domaine, c'est le Contenu qui compte." Cependant la pensée formelle de Leibniz est si riche, et la pensée du contenu chez Hegel si systématique, que le rapprochement de ces deux philosophes s'imposera peut-être un jour.

Mais revenons à notre question préalable. N'est-il pas trop tard pour s'occuper encore de Hegel? Que pouvons-nous apprendre de lui, qu'avons-nous à lui demander? Certes il ne s'agit pas de faire revivre un système condamné, il ne s'agit même pas d'être encore hégélien en un sens quelconque. Mais l'oeuvre de Hegel, particulièrement la *Phénoménologie de l'esprit*, et la *Science de la Logique* sont comme des modèles d'une présentation, d'un *discours philosophique*. Comme la *Divine Comédie* de Dante, ou le *Don Quichotte* de Cervantes, ou la *Comédie humaine* de Balzac, sont des oeuvres dont nous pouvons étudier la structure, l'organisation du Discours, ainsi pouvons nous considérer, dans ces oeuvres philosophiques de Hegel, le discours philosophique comme tel. La comparaison avec les oeuvres littéraires s'impose d'autant plus que Hegel l'a faite lui-même, mais la différence est non moins importante. Le discours philosophique ne veut pas être une spéculation imaginaire, il engage une norme de vérité, enfin il contient en lui-même sa méthode et sa critique, il parle et il parle encore sur sa propre parole.

II

C'est à ce titre qu'il est intéressant d'étudier la préface de la *Phénoménologie de 1807*. Hegel l'a écrite après coup. Il vient d'achever cet étonnant roman de culture qu'est la *Phénoménologie*, plus proche de certaines grandes oeuvres littéraires que de l'Ethique de Spinoza. Il a tenté de repenser la culture de l'individu à la lumière des étapes de l'histoire de l'esprit du monde. Il prend alors une claire conscience de son projet philosophique. Il envisage une Logique spéculative qui remplacera la métaphysique dogmatique d'autrefois. Il y présentera le développement des catégories ou des déterminations de pensées qui constituent le Logos de l'Etre et qui correspondent, dans l'ensemble, aux systèmes philosophiques du passé. C'est entre cette *Phénoménologie* et cette *Logique* que se situe cette préface de la *Phénoménologie*. Elle dit le projet hégélien, elle l'oppose au mythe et à la représentation religieuse, comme aux représentations esthétiques. Elle l'oppose aussi au langage formel des mathématiques, elle situe enfin ce projet de discours philosophique par rapport à la pensée commune, ou au savoir positif. C'est pourquoi Hegel traite dans cette préface du discours et du langage philosophique comme tel, du mode de développement des propositions philosophiques, et si l'on ose ainsi s'exprimer, de leur style propre. On peut se demander pourquoi j'insiste ici sur ces termes de *langage,* de *discours* et même de *style,* pourquoi je ne me suis pas contenté de parler de la pensée philosophique en l'opposant aux autres formes de pensée. C'est que la philosophie de Hegel est dominée par le problème du langage qui est pour lui *"l'enfant et l'instrument de l'intelligence";* l'enfant parce que le langage est pour lui consubstantiel à la pensée, qu'il est notre milieu originel, et qu'il ne saurait se séparer d'elle, comme elle de lui; l'instrument, parce qu'il est aussi le moyen de la signification et de la communication, mais un moyen qui n'a jamais l'objectivité complète de l'outil. Le langage est le *sujet-objet.* C'est dans le langage seulement que la pensée existe. Dans toute autre extériorisation, elle se perd et s'égare, si elle n'est pas confirmée par un langage. Dans le langage le Moi, ce Moi-ci, est en même temps pour autrui, il est universel et singulier à la fois. Le langage est cet objet qui est en même temps réfléchi en soi-même, c'est dans le langage que le monde se signifie, et que la pensée est pour elle-même sujet et objet. Le milieu du langage est la conscience de soi universelle de l'Etre. Toute la *Phénoménologie* développe cette thèse sur le langage et la répète à différents niveaux. La Connaissance est possible parce que dès la certitude sensible, jouent ces pronoms personnels—*je, tu*—et ces déterminations originales du *ceci,* de l'*ici* et du *maintenant,* qui disent à leur façon l'universel dans la visée singulière. C'est à partir d'eux que le dialogue et la détermination deviennent effectifs. La conscience commune ne sait pas toujours ce qu'elle dit ni qui parle en elle mais elle le dit et elle parle, une autre conscience pourra l'entendre. C'est dans le langage et dans son exercice que l'esprit existe. Il est le sujet universel qui est en même temps objet; et s'il y a une diversité de langues, comme il y a une intersubjectivité, cette diversité est contenue dialectiquement dans l'uni-

Jean Hyppolite

versalité du langage humain. Certes nous regrettons que Hegel n'ait pas poussé plus loin encore sa réflexion sur le langage, et sur les langages; nous ne pouvons que tenter de prolonger sa pensée jusqu'à la nôtre.

Dans toute la *Phénoménologie* le langage apparaît bien comme cet élément, ce milieu de l'universel concret que Hegel a voulu présenter. Si dès la certitude sensible, le langage nous situe dans l'universel pour pouvoir atteindre les objets singuliers du monde, et nous manifeste que c'est à travers les significations seulement que nous pouvons nous référer au monde, et ainsi voir, manier et comprendre les choses, il est aussi l'expression des moments successifs, des thèmes de la culture. Il y a le langage du commandement dans la vie éthique, l'impératif de l'ordre, le langage qui agit par sa seule forme de langage dans le serment, il y a enfin le langage d'une culture particulière, le langage de l'honneur ou de la flatterie, le langage du déchirement tel qu'il apparaît dans *Le Neveu de Rameau*, l'oeuvre de Diderot analysée par Hegel dans la *Phénoménologie*. A la fin de la *Phénoménologie*, quand il traite de la religion, Hegel parle de l'oeuvre spirituelle, il montre comment le monde est dit dans l'épopée, comment la subjectivité s'exprime dans la fluidité de l'oeuvre lyrique, comment enfin le théâtre, tragédie et comédie, concilie la subjectivité du Moi et l'objectivité du monde, la nécessité et le destin. Avec la religion, avec ces expressions esthétiques dont Hegel montrera plus tard qu'elles aboutissent à l'oeuvre poétique, comme à leur fin, nous sommes proches du Discours philosophique; mais pour Hegel ce discours n'est plus celui de la représentation, mais du concept, il est, pourrait-on dire, l'essence même du langage, des significations comme telles et de leurs médiations.

Dans la *Préface* de la *Phénoménologie*, Hegel tente de caractériser le langage et le discours philosophique, en l'opposant aux autres formes de langage; il critique d'ailleurs la possibilité de traiter cette question dans une préface qui ne peut être qu'une indication, un schéma formel. Pour lui la philosophie ne se sépare pas de sa présentation effective. Il n'y a pas de méthode préalable, d'instrument séparable de son usage. On a souvent reproché à Hegel un mécanisme formel procédant par thèses, antithèses, et synthèses, et se répétant avec monotonie. Pourtant il a lui-même condamné ce schématisme. Le contenu et la forme sont pour lui inséparables dans le message philosophique. Le message est à la fois contenu et forme, il est le message et le message sur ce message. Cependant Hegel a écrit cette préface sur l'oeuvre, son discours de la méthode, et nous y sommes aujourd'hui plus sensibles encore qu'à l'oeuvre elle-même. Si nous admirons, comme elles le méritent, la *Phénoménologie*, science originale de la pensée commune et du langage quotidien—

et la *Logique*, science des catégories qui sous-tendent et articulent toute l'expression de la pensée, nous ne pouvons cependant les considérer que comme des essais; elles valent pour nous comme des exemples d'une présentation philosophique, nous ne croyons pas comme Hegel qu'elles embrassent la totalité; mais le projet qui les anime et qui est un projet de totalisation est aussi le nôtre, dans la mesure où nous essayons encore de dire et de communiquer le savoir lui-même. Même si des divergences essentielles nous séparent de Hegel, nous ne pouvons pas être insensibles à cette réflexion sur le langage et le discours philosophique.

III

Nous comprendrons mieux Hegel si nous nous représentons ce que furent ses travaux de jeunesse, et les premières manifestations de sa pensée. Il ne fut pas d'abord un philosophe au sens technique du terme, mais il étudia par exemple Montesquieu et Lessing, Rousseau, etc. Il s'est nourri de toute la pensée française du XVIIIe siècle. Il a été formé par l' "Aufklärung." Il semble bien que la pensée philosophique devint pour lui l'expression de la vie et de la culture humaine, prenant la place de la religion. C'est ainsi du moins qu'il la présente dans sa première oeuvre philosophique sur la *différence des systèmes de Fichte et de Schelling* en 1801. A l'époque de la *Phénoménologie*, en 1807, il s'agissait pour lui de caractériser la philosophie par rapport à la pensée commune. Par une sorte de paradoxe la *Phénoménologie de l'esprit* qui nous paraît si difficile, est une réflexion sur la conscience commune, nous dirions aujourd'hui sur le langage quotidien. A la fin de sa préface Hegel dit qu'on la comprendra bientôt, mais ce n'est qu'aujourd'hui que l'originalité et la portée de la *Phénoménologie de l'esprit* nous apparaissent. Il s'agit en effet d'une science de l'expérience commune, et nous savons que le langage quotidien est le plus difficile à penser. Dans sa préface Hegel nous dit que la Science, si elle est en dehors de la conscience de soi commune, reste ineffective. Elle doit donc montrer elle-même son rapport à la conscience et à l'expérience commune. Celle-ci doit de son côté découvrir en elle l'apparition de la Science; ainsi elle surmontera son inconscience profonde, car elle se méconnaît elle-même, elle ne sait pas ce qu'elle dit ou fait; pourtant le philosophe ne doit pas se substituer à elle, mais la suivre dans ses expériences théoriques et pratiques, les recueillir dans l'élément du savoir (Hegel dit l'élément comme nous disons l'élément marin), jusqu'au moment où, dans le *savoir absolu*, la conscience commune pourra se reconnaître dans la conscience philosophique; et celle-ci à son tour dans celle-là. Il en est un peu comme dans une psychanalyse, où le patient peut dire à la fin de la cure "je l'avais toujours su." Car, ce qui est remarquable dans cette histoire de la conscience commune et de son langage, c'est qu'elle est toujours un *dialogue humain*, et que l'élément du dialogue accompagne l'élément cognitif. Le savoir passe par la communication et d'abord par l'inégalité des consciences avant la reconnaissance effective.

Cette tentative de présenter la conscience commune, d'en suivre l'histoire, de voir germer en elle un savoir de soi plus profond qu'il ne lui semblait, est certainement une acquisition définitive de notre pensée. Nous pouvons trouver que Hegel n'a pas résolu la question qu'il a posée, qu'il n'a pas tenu compte (comment l'aurait-il pu à cette date?) du développement des sciences positives et donc de leur relation à la conscience commune, problème pour nous si important et que Husserl a abordé pour sa part dans ses dernières oeuvres, mais nous ne pouvons méconnaître la portée d'une relation du savoir scientifique au savoir commun, du langage scientifique au langage quotidien. Si l'oeuvre littéraire, les romans de culture, auxquels Hegel se réfère explicitement, sont une présentation imaginaire d'une vie exemplaire, que sera donc l'oeuvre philosophique dans la mesure où elle présentera la conscience commune. Quel sera le caractère de cette présentation? A quelles conditions le Discours commun deviendra-t-il discours proprement philosophique? Dans la préface de la *Phénoménologie*, Hegel oppose le discours philosophique aussi bien au bavardage et à la conversation, ou à l'oeuvre littéraire, qu'à la science dogmatique et plus spécialement au savoir formel des mathématiques. Il s'oppose à un savoir qui ne serait qu'un catalogue ou une nomenclature; le langage dans sa profondeur est pour lui bien autre chose. Il tente de caractériser le discours philosophique par sa nécessité interne, par son développement intérieur qui, moins lâche qu'un récit ou qu'une histoire événementielle n'a pourtant pas recours à des démonstrations extrinsèques. Ce qu'il condamne dans le savoir formel, ou dans le savoir dogmatique, c'est la séparation de la forme et du contenu; des démarches du savoir et de leur résultat. Le discours philosophique sera le seul dans lequel le *Soi du savoir* et le *Soi du contenu* s'identifieront. Ce langage ne sera pas un langage *sur* quelque chose qui viendrait du dehors, ou un langage formel qui servirait seulement de cadre à un contenu absent, il sera le *dit de* l'Etre qui est son propre savoir, et le savoir de sa différence. Comment l'expérience peut-elle ainsi se signifier et se dire, comment peut-elle—et ce sera le sens de la *Logique*—présenter ses déterminations et ses articulations fondamentales, aussi bien dans leur fixation que dans leur mouvement? La logique hégélienne s'efforcera de réconcilier la fixation de l'écriture avec la vitalité de la parole vivante.

Hegel oppose le discours philosophique à la pensée dogmatique et à la pensée critique. Dans un cas la vérité se manifeste sous l'aspect d'une proposition fixe, d'un résultat. Les preuves sont seulement un instrument de la connaissance qui ont servi à établir la proposition, mais elles n'appartiennent pas au vrai lui-même. Hegel critique le formalisme mathématique; il considère que les démonstrations mathématiques sont des moyens de la connaissance, une argumentation comme le langage d'Euclide le manifeste déjà: axiomes, postulats, etc. Elles n'expriment pas le devenir de la Chose elle-même. C'est au contraire ce devenir que doit présenter le discours philosophique. Dans la pensée critique qui inclut toutes ces formes d'argumentations et de polémiques, le savoir se replie toujours sur soi. Il sait montrer ce que la Chose n'est pas, mais il ne peut aller au-delà de sa critique, il doit attendre qu'un nouveau contenu s'offre à lui du dehors, pour en faire à nouveau le thème de sa critique. C'est ici que Hegel définit la pensée philosophique comme celle qui concilie en elle la pensée dogmatique et la pensée critique. La critique ne vient pas du dehors, elle appartient au développement même de la Chose, elle est son mouvement et son devenir, inversement la proposition vraie n'a plus le caractère d'une affirmation séparable en droit des moyens qui ont servi à l'établir. Le Vrai dit Hegel est sujet, il est le délire bachique, dont tous les membres sont ivres et qui résout aussi bien tout ce qui tend à se séparer. C'est pourquoi il est à la fois le mouvement et le repos. Dans la pensée représentative, le sujet dont on parle, et le sujet du savoir, celui qui parle, sont différents. Il y a un support, une base fixe à laquelle les prédicats sont attachés. La proposition commune comporte ce lien extérieur du prédicat au sujet. C'est pourquoi elle oscille entre un noyau inconnaissable, une chose en soi, d'où lui viendrait son objectivité, et des prédicats qui sont attribués à ce noyau, mais dont le lien résulte d'une argumentation propre au sujet connaissant. Ainsi la pensée représentative a besoin de cette référence à une chose extérieure, pour se donner un contenu, mais en même temps elle réfléchit dans le sujet connaissant toutes les démarches du savoir. C'est cette séparation des deux sujets, celui de la chose même et celui du savoir, qui oppose la pensée représentative à la pensée philosophique. Cette opposition se traduit dans le langage et dans le discours lui-même. Le savoir non philosophique va d'un de ces sujets à l'autre, il n'est pas capable de s'oublier lui-même dans le contenu, il y a donc d'un côté l'argumentation et le savoir, de l'autre le

Jean Hyppolite

support fixe, d'un côté la réflexion, de l'autre la Chose, d'un côté une pensée subjective, de l'autre l'objectivité. C'est ce que traduisent la structure ordinaire du discours, et l'extériorité de la médiation par rapport aux termes. Le style de la pensée philosophique—que Hegel nomme la *dialectique*—apparaît dans un discours dans lequel la médiation est la Chose même, un discours qui est celui d'un sujet impersonnel comme c'est après tout le langage lui-même. L'Idéalisme hégélien est le contraire d'un subjectivisme ou d'un criticisme, au sens kantien du terme. Si le vrai est sujet, cela ne signifie pas qu'il est la subjectivité humaine, celle de l'individu singulier ou d'un sujet du savoir séparable de l'univers. Il y a bien une pensée représentative, une pensée subjective mais ce sont là seulement des moments, et le sens de la *Phénoménologie* est de reconduire ces moments au savoir philosophique, au savoir absolu, qui est la dialectique des Choses et non la dialectique d'un savoir qui en serait séparable.

Le discours philosophique bouleverse la manière commune d'entendre la proposition et le lien des propositions entre elles. C'est la distinction du sujet et du prédicat qui est dépassée. Le sujet n'est plus la base immobile, la référence constante et le prédicat n'est plus un attribut extérieur. Le sujet passe dans ce qu'on nommait le prédicat, mais celui-ci à son tour devient sujet. L'essence, la détermination, la spécification sont des moments d'un développement et c'est ce développement qui est devenu le sujet même. Il n'y a pas d'originaire, de terme premier, c'est le devenir et la médiation qui sont à la fois le sujet du contenu et le sujet du savoir. La présentation philosophique ne sera pas une représentation subjective des choses, mais l'expression, le sens des choses elles-mêmes. La négation n'est pas isolable de ce qu'elle nie, comme si elle appartenait seulement au sujet du savoir, elle est dans les choses elles-mêmes sous l'aspect de leur détermination et de leur fixation, et du mouvement qui dépasse cette division. L'analyse des représentations, la décomposition qui est la puissance même de l'entendement, puissance qui paraît si étrange à la conscience qui s'était arrêtée aux représentations familières et soi-disant bien connues, est un moment essentiel, aussi bien que la médiation; le système qui reconstitue le Tout dans son mouvement. Ces caractères du discours philosophique en font la difficulté dont on se plaint toujours, car la référence, le de quoi on parle et le qui parle échappent sans cesse. C'est le *devenir* qui est sujet.

IV

Au terme de cette réflexion sur le Discours philosophique je voudrais seulement insister sur ce qui me paraît encore valable dans cette pensée hégélienne. Nous devons à Hegel ce double projet qu'il a tenté de réaliser dans la *Phénoménologie de l'esprit* et dans la *Logique,* celui d'une science de l'expérience commune, du langage quotidien, et celui d'un système des déterminations de pensée. Toutes les formes modernes de *Phénoménologie* reprennent le premier projet. Les résultats des sciences et des langages techniques doivent pouvoir à leur tour se traduire dans le langage quotidien. Ils parlent de lui, et doivent y retrouver leur sens. Mais d'autre part la recherche de toutes les déterminations de pensée, de toutes les articulations du langage humain en général à travers lequel passe inconsciemment notre rapport fondamental au monde sont aussi au centre des recherches contemporaines. Il nous faut bien reconnaître que ces deux projets ne sont pas envisagés aujourd'hui, comme pouvait les envisager Hegel, mais nous devons pourtant nous référer à lui pour mieux évaluer leur portée et les limites de leurs réalisations possibles.

Enfin il me semble que s'il reste bien un domaine philosophique, dans lequel seront étudiés le rapport de la conscience commune aux sciences et le système du langage, le style philosophique dans ce qu'il a d'original devra être considéré pour lui-même. Il faudra voir comment il n'a ni le caractère dogmatique des sciences positives, ni le caractère subjectif des examens critiques. La présentation est quasi impersonnelle, elle n'est plus celle d'une confession ou d'un récit, et pourtant, elle est la présentation d'un sujet qui coincide avec son devenir. Qui parle? La réponse n'est ni le *on* ni le *ça,* ni tout à fait le *je* ou le *nous.* Ce nom de *dialectique* que Hegel a repris pour le caractériser et qui désigne une dialectique des choses elles-mêmes, et non un instrument du savoir, est lui-même au centre de ce problème. Qu'est-ce qu'une présentation philosophique et quelle est sa structure? Il est remarquable que Hegel, en tentant de présenter le système des articulations et des déterminations de pensée, a vu à la fois leur objectivité—elles sont une conscience universelle de l'Etre—et ce qui les oppose à l'étant lui-même, à la Nature. Le logos dit aussi la différence absolue, mais il n'est pas lui-même la différence absolue car cette différence appartient encore au logos. Le Savoir universel sait donc aussi sa propre limite, il mesure les limites de la signification ou du sens, la part du *non-sens* qui investit encore la signification, ce que Hegel envisageait comme le rapport du Logos et de la Nature le jeu de leur identité et leur différence. Pour Hegel il ne s'agissait pas là d'une théologie négative, d'un sens si l'on peut dire au-delà du sens, mais d'une finitude irrémédiable, d'un sens perdu (comme on dit une cause perdue) et qui n'est jamais totalement récupérable. Le Discours philosophique doit reconnaître cette finitude, peut-être plus encore que ne l'a fait Hegel, sans se replier pour autant dans un subjectivisme critique. Enfin n'y a-t-il pas entre la présentation génétique et la systématicité un antagonisme latent que Hegel n'a pu réussir à faire disparaître? Genèse et structure s'accordent-elles dans la présentation philosophique?

*Le Moment
historique
de la tragédie
en Grèce—essai
d'interprétation*

Jean-Pierre Vernant

Au cours du dernier demi siècle les hellé-
nistes se sont surtout interrogés sur les
origines de la tragédie. Si même ils avaient
apporté sur ce point une réponse con-
cluante, le problème de la tragédie ne s'en
trouverait pas pour autant résolu. Il resterait
à comprendre l'essentiel: les innovations que
la tragédie attique a apportées et qui font
d'elle, sur le plan des institutions sociales, des
formes d'art, de la psychologie humaine,
une invention. Genre littéraire original pos-
sédant ses règles et ses caractéristiques pro-
pres, la tragédie instaure, dans le système
des fêtes publiques de la cité, un nouveau
type de spectacle; de plus, elle traduit,
comme forme d'expression spécifique, des
aspects jusqu'alors méconnus de l'expérience humaine; elle marque une étape dans
la formation de l'homme intérieur, du sujet
responsable. Concours tragiques, genre
tragique, homme tragique: sous ses trois
aspects le phénomène apparaît avec des
caractères irréductibles.

Le problème des origines est donc, en un
certain sens, un faux problème. Mieux vau-
drait parler d'antécédents. Encore devrait-
on noter qu'ils se situent à un tout autre
niveau que le fait à expliquer. Ils ne sont pas
à sa mesure; ils ne peuvent rendre raison du
tragique comme tel. Un exemple: le masque
soulignerait la parenté de la tragédie avec
les mascarades rituelles. Mais, par sa nature,
par sa fonction, le masque tragique est tout
autre chose qu'un travestissement religieux.
C'est un masque humain, non un déguise-
ment animal. Son rôle est esthétique, non
plus rituel. Le masque peut, entre autres,
servir à souligner la distance, la différen-
ciation entre les deux éléments qui occupent

Jean–Pierre Vernant

la scène tragique, éléments opposés mais en même temps étroitement solidaires. D'une part le choeur, dans le principe non masqué mais seulement déguisé, personnage collectif, incarné par un collège officiel de citoyens; d'autre part le personnage tragique, joué par un acteur professionnel, et que son masque individualise par rapport au groupe anonyme du choeur. Cette individualisation ne fait nullement du porteur de masque un sujet psychologique, une "personne" individuelle. Au contraire le masque intègre le personnage tragique dans une catégorie religieuse très définie: celle des héros. Il en fait l'incarnation d'un de ces êtres exceptionnels dont la légende, fixée dans la tradition héroïque que chantent les poètes, constitue pour les Grecs du Ve siècle une des dimensions de leur passé—passé lointain et révolu—qui fait contraste avec l'ordre de la Cité, mais qui reste cependant encore vivant dans la religion civique où le culte des héros, ignoré d'Homère et d'Hésiode, occupe une place de choix. Polarité donc, dans la technique tragique, entre deux éléments: le choeur, être collectif et anonyme, dont le rôle consiste à exprimer dans ses craintes, ses espoirs et ses jugements, les sentiments des spectateurs qui composent la communauté civique; le personnage individualisé, dont l'action forme le centre du drame et qui a figure de héros d'un autre âge, toujours plus ou moins étranger à la condition ordinaire du citoyen.

A ce dédoublement du choeur et du héros tragiques correspond, dans la langue même de la tragédie, une dualité: d'une part le lyrisme choral, d'autre part, chez les protagonistes du drame, une forme dialoguée dont la métrique est plus voisine de la prose. Les personnages héroïques, rapprochés par leur langage de l'homme ordinaire, ne sont pas seulement rendus présents sur la scène aux yeux de tous les spectateurs, mais à travers les discussions qui les opposent aux choristes ou les uns aux autres ils deviennent l'objet d'un débat; ils sont en quelque sorte mis en question devant le public. De son côté le choeur, dans les parties chantées, exalte moins les vertus exemplaires du héros, comme dans la tradition lyrique de Simonide ou de Pindare, qu'il ne s'inquiète et ne s'interroge à son sujet. Dans le cadre nouveau de jeu tragique le héros a donc cessé d'être un modèle; il est devenu, pour lui-même et pour les autres, un problème.

Ces remarques préliminaires permettent, nous semble-t-il, de mieux cerner les termes dans lesquels se pose le problème de la tragédie. La tragédie grecque apparaît comme un moment historique très précisément circonscrit et daté. On la voit naître, à Athènes, s'y épanouir et disparaître presque en l'espace d'un siècle. Pourquoi? Il ne suffit pas de noter que le tragique traduit une conscience déchirée, le sentiment des contradictions qui divisent l'homme contre lui-même, il faut rechercher sur quel plan se situent en Grèce les oppositions tragiques, quel est leur contenu, dans quelles conditions elles sont venues au jour.

C'est ce que Louis Gernet avait entrepris par une analyse du vocabulaire et des structures de chaque oeuvre tragique. Il avait pu montrer ainsi que la matière véritable de la tragédie, c'est la pensée sociale propre à la Cité, spécialement la pensée juridique en plein travail d'élaboration. La présence d'un vocabulaire technique du Droit chez les Tragiques souligne les affinités entre les thèmes de prédilection de la tragédie et certains cas relevants de la compétence des tribunaux, ces tribunaux dont l'institution est assez récente pour que soit encore pleinement sentie la nouveauté des valeurs qui en ont commandé la fondation et qui en règlent le fonctionnement. Les poètes tragiques utilisent ce vocabulaire de Droit en jouant délibérément de ses incertitudes, de ses flottements, de son inachèvement: imprécision des termes, glissements de sens, incohérences et oppositions, qui révèlent des discordances au sein de la pensée juridique elle-même, qui traduisent également ses conflits avec une tradition religieuse, une réflexion morale dont le Droit est déjà distinct mais dont les domaines ne sont pas clairement délimités par rapport au sien.

C'est que le Droit n'est pas une construction logique; il s'est constitué historiquement à partir de procédures "préjuridiques" dont il s'est dégagé, auxquelles il s'oppose mais dont il reste en partie solidaire. Les Grecs n'ont pas l'idée d'un Droit absolu, fondé sur des principes, s'organisant en système cohérent. Il y a pour eux comme des degrés de droit. A un pôle, le Droit s'appuie sur l'autorité de fait, sur la contrainte; à l'autre, il met en jeu des puissances sacrées: l'ordre du monde, la justice de Zeus. Il pose aussi des problèmes moraux touchant la responsabilité de l'homme. De ce point de vue la *Dikè* divine elle-même peut apparaître opaque et incompréhensible: elle comporte, pour les humains, un élément irrationnel de puissance brute. Aussi voit-on dans *Les Suppliantes* la notion de *kratos* osciller entre deux acceptions contraires: tantôt elle désigne l'autorité légitime, une mainmise juridiquement fondée, tantôt la force brutale dans son aspect de violence le plus opposé au droit et à la justice. De même, dans *Antigone*, le mot *nomos* peut être invoqué avec des valeurs exactement inverses par les différents protagonistes. Ce que montre la tragédie, c'est une *dikè* en lutte contre une autre *dikè*, un droit qui n'est pas fixé, qui se déplace et se transforme en son contraire. Bien entendu la tragédie est tout autre chose qu'un débat juridique. Elle prend pour objet l'homme vivant lui-même ce débat, contraint de faire un choix décisif, d'orienter son action dans un univers de valeurs ambigües, où rien jamais n'est stable ni univoque.

Jean–Pierre Vernant

Tel est, dans la matière tragique, le premier aspect de conflit. Il y en a un second étroitement associé au précédent. Nous avons vu que la tragédie, tant qu'elle demeure vivante, puise ses thèmes dans les légendes de héros. Cet enracinement dans une tradition de récits mythiques explique qu'on trouve, à bien des égards, plus d'archaïsme religieux chez les grands Tragiques que dans Homère. Cependant la tragédie prend ses distances par rapport aux mythes de héros dont elle s'inspire et qu'elle transpose très librement. Elle les met en question. Elle confronte les valeurs héroïques, les représentations religieuses anciennes, avec les modes de pensée nouveaux qui marquent l'avènement du Droit dans le cadre de la Cité. Les légendes de héros se rattachent en effet à des lignées royales, des *génè* nobles qui, sur le plan des valeurs, des pratiques sociales, des formes de religiosité, des comportements humains, représentent pour la Cité cela même qu'elle a dû condamner et rejeter, ce contre quoi il lui a fallu lutter pour s'établir, mais aussi ce à partir de quoi elle s'est constituée et dont elle reste très profondément solidaire.

Le moment tragique est donc celui où une distance s'est creusée au coeur de l'expérience sociale, assez grande pour qu'entre la pensée juridique et politique d'une part, les traditions mythiques et héroïques de l'autre, les oppositions se dessinent clairement, assez courte cependant pour que les conflits de valeur soient encore douloureusement ressentis et que la confrontation ne cesse pas de s'effectuer. La situation est la même en ce qui concerne les problèmes de la responsabilité humaine tels qu'ils se posent à travers les progrès tâtonnants du Droit. Il y a une conscience tragique de la responsabilité quand les plans humains et divins sont assez distincts pour s'opposer sans cesser pourtant d'apparaître inséparables. Le sens tragique de la responsabilité surgit lorsque l'action humaine fait l'objet d'une réflexion, d'un débat, mais qu'elle n'a pas acquit un statut assez autonome pour se suffire pleinement à elle-même. Le domaine propre de la tragédie se situe à cette zone frontière où les actes humains proviennent s'articuler avec les puissances divines, où ils révèlent leur sens véritable, ignoré de ceux-là même qui en ont pris l'initiative et en portent la responsabilité, en s'insérant dans un ordre qui dépasse l'homme et lui échappe.

Toute tragédie joue donc nécessairement sur deux plans. Son aspect d'enquête profane sur l'homme, comme agent responsable, a seulement valeur de contre-point par rapport au thème central. On se tromperait donc en braquant sur l'élément psychologique l'éclairage. Dans la scène fameuse du tapis de l'*Agamemnon*, la décision fatale du souverain tient sans nul doute à sa pauvre vanité d'homme, aussi peut-être à la mauvaise conscience d'un mari d'autant plus enclin à céder aux prières de sa femme qu'il lui ramène une concubine à la maison. Mais l'essentiel n'est pas là. L'effet proprement tragique provient du rapport intime en même temps que de l'extraordinaire distance entre l'acte banal de marcher sur un tapis de pourpre, avec ses motivations trop humaines, et les forces religieuses qui se trouvent par lui inexorablement déclenchées.

On comprend mieux alors que la tragédie soit un *moment*, et qu'on puisse fixer sa floraison entre deux dates, qui définissent deux attitudes à l'égard du spectacle tragique. Au départ, la colère d'un Solon, quittant indigné une des premières représentations théâtrales, avant même l'institution des concours tragiques, à Thespis, plaidant qu'il ne s'agissait après tout que d'un jeu, le vieux nomothète, inquiet des ambitions grandissantes de Pisistrate, répliqua, selon Plutarque, qu'on ne tarderait pas à voir les conséquences de telles fictions sur les rapports entre les citoyens. Pour le Sage, moraliste et homme d'état, qui s'est donné pour tâche de fonder l'ordre de la Cité sur la modération et le contrat, qui a dû briser l'orgueil des nobles et cherche à éviter à sa patrie l'*Hybris* du tyran, le passé "héroïque" apparaît trop vivant pour qu'on puisse sans péril le donner en spectacle sur la scène. Au terme de l'évolution, on placerait l'indication d'Aristote concernant Agathon, jeune contemporain d'Euripide et qui écrivait des tragédies dont l'intrigue était tout entière de son cru. Le lien avec la tradition légendaire est désormais si distendu qu'on ne sent plus la nécessité d'un débat avec le passé "héroïque." L'homme de théâtre peut bien continuer d'écrire des pièces, en inventer lui-même la trame suivant un modèle qu'il croit conforme aux oeuvres de ses grands devanciers. Chez lui, dans son public, dans toute la culture grecque, le ressort tragique est brisé.

About the
Participants

Roland Barthes

Roland Barthes is at present Directeur d'Études in the VIe Section of the École Pratique des Hautes Études, where he conducts seminars on "semio-criticism and the sociology of signs, symbols, and collective representations." His early essays in *Combat* were published in *Le Degré zero de l'écriture*, a landmark in contemporary criticism. He was also one of the founders of Théâtre Populaire and an early champion of Brecht in France. During the first term of 1967–68, he was a visiting professor at The Johns Hopkins University. He also participated in the Continuing Seminars under the Ford Grant. His publications include:

Le Degré zero de l'écriture. Paris: Editions du Seuil, 1953. [*Writing Degree Zero*. London: J. Cape, 1967.]

Michelet par lui-même. Paris: Editions du Seuil, 1954.

Mythologies. Paris: Editions du Seuil, 1957.

Sur Racine. Paris: Editions du Seuil, 1963. [*On Racine* (tr. Richard Howard). New York: Hill and Wang, 1964.]

La Bruyère, du mythe à l'écriture. Paris: Union Générale d'Éditions, 1963.

Essais critiques. Paris: Editions du Seuil, 1964.

La Tour Eiffel (Barthes et André Martin). Paris: Delpire, 1964.

La Voyageuse de nuit. Paris: Union Générale d'Éditions, 1965.

Eléments de sémiologie. Paris: Editions Gonthier, 1965. [*Elements of Semiology*. London: Jonathan Cape, 1967.]

Critique et vérité. Paris: Editions du Seuil, 1966.

Système de la mode. Paris: Editions du Seuil, 1967

Jacques Derrida Jacques Derrida of the École Normale Supérieure did work on Edmund Husserl and has recently published remarkably influential essays on contemporary questions in methodology. He has recently joined The Johns Hopkins faculty. His publications include:
Edmund Husserl. *L'Origine de la géométrie.*
 Paris: Presses Universitaires de France, 1962.
De la grammatologie. Paris: Editions de
 Minuit, 1967.
L'Écriture et la différence. Paris: Editions du
 Seuil, 1967.
La Voix et le phénomène: introduction au
 problème du signe dans la phénoménologie
 de Husserl. Paris: Presses Universitaires de
 France, 1967.

Eugenio Donato Eugenio Donato, one of the organizers of the Symposium, has recently joined the faculty of the State University of New York in Buffalo. His training was in mathematics and Romance philology. He has published essays on Italian and French literature and on the methodology of the *sciences de l'homme.*

Neville Dyson–Hudson Neville Dyson–Hudson is a faculty member of The Johns Hopkins University. He studied at Oxford under Evans–Pritchard. His publications include:
Karimojong Politics. Oxford: Clarendon Press,
 1966.

René Girard René Girard is the former chairman of the Department of Romance Languages at The Johns Hopkins University and one of the organizers of the Symposium. He has written widely on topics in French literature and is currently concerned with the psychological and philosophical implications of the Oedipus myth. His publications include:
Mensonge romantique et vérité romanesque.
 Paris: Grasset, 1961. [*Deceit, Desire, and the*
 Novel: Self and Other in Literary Structure
 (tr. Yvonne Freccero). Baltimore: The
 Johns Hopkins Press, 1965.]

> *Proust: Twentieth Century Views* (ed. R. Girard). Englewood Cliffs: Prentice-Hall, 1962.
> *Dostoievski: du double à l'unité.* Paris: Plon, 1963

Lucien Goldmann   Lucien Goldmann, Directeur d'Études in the VIᵉ Section of the École Pratique des Hautes Études, and a member of the Institut de Sociologie (Brussels), is the author of *Le Dieu caché,* a crucial book in developing his "structuralisme génétique." He was a visiting professor at Hopkins the first term of 1966–67. His publications include:

> *La communauté humaine et l'univers chez Kant.* Paris: Presses Universitaires de France, 1948.
> *Etudes sur la pensée dialectique et son histoire.* Paris: 1948.
> *Sciences humaines et philosophie.* Paris: Presses Universitaires de France, 1952.
> *Le Dieu caché; étude sur la vision tragique dans les Pensées de Pascal et dans le théâtre de Racine.* Paris: Gallimard, 1955. [*The Hidden God* (tr. Philip Thody). London: Routledge and K. Paul, 1964.]
> *Correspondance de Martin de Barcos, abbé de St.-Cyran, avec les abbesses de Port-Royal et les principaux personnages du groupe janséniste.* Paris: Presses Universitaires de France, 1956.
> *Jean Racine, dramaturge.* Paris: L'Arche, 1956.
> *Recherches dialectiques.* Paris: Gallimard, 1958.
> *Pour une sociologie du roman.* Paris: Gallimard, 1964.
> *Entretiens sur les notions de genèse et de structure,* sous la direction de Maurice de Gandillac, Lucien Goldmann et Jean Piaget. Paris: Mouton, 1965

Jean Hyppolite   Jean Hyppolite was professor of the History of Philosophy at the Collège de France and former Director of the École Normale Supérieure. His publications include:

G. W. F. Hegel. *La phénoménologie de
l'esprit* (traduction de Jean Hyppolite)
Paris: Aubier, Editions Montaigne, 1939–
1941.
*Genèse et structure de la phénoménologie de
l'esprit de Hegel*. Paris: Aubier, Editions
Montaigne, 1946.
*Introduction à la philosophie de l'histoire de
Hegel*. Paris: Librairie M. Rivière et cie.,
1948.
*Logique et existence, essai sur la logique de
Hegel*. Paris: Presses Universitaires de
France, 1952.
Etudes sur Marx et Hegel. Paris: M. Rivière,
1955 [revised ed., 1965]. [*Studies on Marx
and Hegel* (tr. John O'Neill) New York:
Basic Books, 1969.]
*Sens et existence, dans la philosophie de
Maurice Merleau-Ponty*. Oxford: Clarendon
Press, 1963.
G. W. F. Hegel. *Préface à la Phénoménologie
de l'Esprit*. [Bilingual edition with
commentary by Jean Hyppolite] Paris:
Aubier, Editions Montaigne, 1966.

Jacques Lacan   Jacques Lacan, the founder of l'École Freud-
ienne de Paris, is one of the most seminal and
controversial figures in contemporary French
intellectual life. During his visit to Baltimore,
he also lectured at the Sheppard and Enoch
Pratt Hospital.
*De la psychose paranoiaque dans ses rapports
avec la personnalité*. Paris: Le François, 1932.
Écrits. Paris: Éditions du Seuil, 1966.
*The Language of the Self: The Function of
Language in Psychoanalysis*, translated with
Notes and Commentary by Anthony
Wilden. Baltimore: The Johns Hopkins
Press, 1968 [includes a complete
bibliography].

Richard Macksey   Richard Macksey is the Acting Director of
the Humanities Center and has published work
in number theory, intellectual history, and

hermeneutics, as well as poems and translations. He has been involved in film-making and has written on the semiotics of the film, music and critical studies of Sterne, Darwin, Henry James, Rilke, Proust, Wallace Stevens, William Carlos Williams, and Robbe-Grillet.

Charles Morazé   Secretary of the École Pratique des Hautes Études, Charles Morazé is one of the founders of the VIᵉ Section. He participated in the Ford Continuing Seminars, exploring questions raised at the Symposium. His publications include:

La France bourgeoise, XVIIᵉ–XXᵉ siècles. Paris: A. Colin, 1946.

Études de sociologie électorale. Paris: A. Colin, 1947.

Trois essais sur histoire et culture. Paris: A. Colin, 1948.

Introduction à l'histoire économique. Paris: A. Colin, 1948.

Les Trois ages du Brésil: essai de politique. Paris: A. Colin, 1954.

Les Français et la république. Paris: A. Colin, 1956. [*The French and the Republic* (tr. by Jean-Jacques Demorest) Ithaca, N.Y.: Cornell University Press, 1958.]

Les Bourgeois conquérants, XIX siécle. Paris: A. Colin, 1957. [*The Triumph of the Middle Classes: A Study of European Values in the 19th Century.* Cleveland: World Publishing Co., 1967.]

La Logique de l'histoire. Paris: Gallimard, 1967.

Also numerous titles in collaboration with Philippe Wolff *et al.*

Georges Poulet   Georges Poulet, former chairman of Romance Languages at Johns Hopkins, was until recently the Director of the Romanisches Seminar at the Universität Zürich; he has just assumed the Chair at the Université de Nice. His publications include:

Études sur le temps humain [I]. Edinburgh: University Press, 1949. [*Studies in Human*

Time (tr. Elliott Coleman) Baltimore: The
Johns Hopkins Press, 1956.]
*Études sur le temps humain: [II]: La
Distance intérieure.* Paris: Plon, 1952. [*The
Interior Distance* (tr. Elliott Coleman)
Baltimore: The Johns Hopkins Press, 1959.]
Les Métamorphoses du cercle. Paris: Plon,
1961. [*The Metamorphoses of the Circle* (tr.
Carley Dawson and Elliott Coleman in
collaboration with the author) Baltimore:
The Johns Hopkins Press, 1966.]
L'Espace proustien. Paris: Gallimard, 1963.
*Études sur le temps humain: [III]: Le Point de
départ.* Paris: Plon, 1964.
Trois essais de mythologie romantique. Paris:
Corti, 1966.
Joseph Joubert. *Pensées;* choix et introduction
par Georges Poulet. Paris: Union Générale
d'Éditions, 1966.
Benjamin Constant par lui-même. Paris:
Editions du Seuil, 1968.
*Études sur le temps humain: [IV]: Mesure de
l'instant.* Paris: Plon, 1968.
Chemins actuels de la critique (ed. G. Poulet).
Paris: Union Generale d'Editions, 1968.

Guy Rosolato   Guy Rosolato of the Clinique Delay, Paris, is
a practicing psychoanalyst who has published
widely both in psychoanalytical and literary
journals. He is a contributor to numerous volumes of *La Psychanalyse.* He also participated
in the Ford Continuing Seminars.

Nicolas Ruwet   Nicolas Ruwet of the Fonds National Belge
de la Recherche Scientifique is the French
translator of Roman Jakobson. He has contributed important synthetic articles on structural linguistics, its methods, problems, and
possible application to musicology. He was a
visiting professor at the Massachusetts Institute of Technology in 1967–68 and participated in the Ford Continuing Seminars. He
will join The Johns Hopkins faculty in 1970.
His publications include:
Roman Jakobson. *Essais de linguistique*

générale (traduction de Nicolas Ruwet).
Paris: Gallimard, 1963.
Introduction à la grammaire générative.
Nouvelle édition. Paris: Plon, 1968.

Tzvetan Todorov

Tzvetan Todorov of the École Pratique des
Hautes Études, participated in the Ford Continuing Seminars exploring questions raised at
the symposium. His publications include:
*Théorie de la littérature: textes des formalistes
russes réunis.* Paris: Editions du Seuil,
1965.
Littérature et signification. Paris: Larousse,
1967.
*Analyse sémiologique des "Liaisons
Dangereuses": contribution à l'étude du
sens.* [Thèse dact., Nanterre, 1968]
"La Poétique," in *Qu'est-ce que le structuralisme?* Paris: Editions du Seuil, 1968.

Jean-Pierre Vernant

Jean-Pierre Vernant is Directeur d'Études in
the VIᵉ Section of the École Pratique des
Hautes Études. During 1967–68 he participated
in the Johns Hopkins Humanities Seminars
(Interpretation: Theory and Practice) both in
Baltimore and in Zürich. His publications in-
clude:
*Mythe et pensée chez les grecs: études de
psychologie historique.* Paris: François
Maspero, 1966.
Les Origines de la pensée grecque. Paris:
Presses Universitaires de France, 1962.
Problèmes de la en Grèce ancienne (ed.
J.-P. Vernant). Paris: Mouton, 1968.

Colloquists

Henry David Aiken
Brandeis University

Hume, David. *Moral and Political Philosophy*
(ed. Aiken). New York: Hafner
Publishing Co., 1948.
*The Age of Ideology: The Nineteenth
Century Philosophers, Selected with
Introduction and Interpretive Commentary.*
Boston: Houghton Mifflin, 1957.
Philosophy and Education: Modern Readings
[by] H. D. Aiken [and others]
(Scheffler, Israel, ed.). Boston: Allyn
and Bacon, 1958.
Hume, David. *Dialogues concerning Natural
Religion* (edited with introduction by
Henry D. Aiken). New York: Hafner
Publishing Co., 1960.
*Reason and Conduct: New Bearings in Moral
Philosophy.* New York: Knopf, 1962.

Peter Caws
Hunter College

*The Philosophy of Science, A Systematic
Account.* Princeton, N.J.: Van Nostrand,
1965.
Science and the Theory of Value. New
York: Random House, 1967.
*A Critical Survey of Contemporary
Structuralist Thought* [to be published
by The University of Chicago Press
in 1970].

Albert Cook
SUNY—Buffalo

*The Dark Voyage and the Golden Mean:
A Philosophy of Comedy.* Cambridge:
Harvard University Press, 1949.
The Meaning of Fiction. Detroit: Wayne
State University, 1960.
Oedipus Rex: A Mirror for Greek Drama.
San Francisco: Wadsworth, 1963.
Progressions and Other Poems. Tucson:
University of Arizona, 1963.
The Classic Line: A Study in Epic Poetry.
Bloomington: Indiana University Press,
1966.
Prisms: Studies in Modern Literature.

357

Bloomington: Indiana University Press, 1967.
Homer. *The Odyssey: A New Verse Translation.* New York: Norton, 1967.

Serge Doubrovsky
New York University

Corneille et la dialectique du héros. Paris: Gallimard, 1963.
Le Jour S. Paris: Mercure de France, 1963.
Pourquoi la nouvelle critique: critique et objectivité. Paris: Mercure de France, 1966.

James M. Edie
Northwestern University

Thévenaz, Pierre. *What is Phenomenology?* (ed. with an introduction by James M. Edie). Chicago: Quadrangle Books, 1962.
Christianity and Existentialism, essays by William Earle, James M. Edie [and] John Wild. Evanston, Ill.: Northwestern University Press, 1963.
Merleau-Ponty, Maurice. *In Praise of Philosophy* (tr. with a preface by John Wild and James M. Edie). Evanston, Ill.: Northwestern University Press, 1963.
Merleau-Ponty, Maurice. *The Primacy of Perception, and other essays on phenomenological psychology, the philosophy of art, history and politics* (ed. James M. Edie). Evanston, Ill.: Northwestern University Press, 1964.
An Invitation to Phenomenology: Studies in the Philosophy of Experience (ed. James M. Edie). Chicago: Quadrangle Books, 1965.
Russian Philosophy (eds. James M. Edie, James P. Scanlan [and] Mary-Barbara Zeldin, with the collaboration of George L. Kline). Chicago: Quadrangle Books, 1965.
Phenomenology in America: Studies in the Philosophy of Experience (ed. James M. Edie). Chicago: Quadrangle Books, 1967.
New Essays in Phenomenology: Studies in the Philosophy of Experience (ed. James

M. Edie). Chicago: Quadrangle Books, 1969.

Jacques Ehrmann
Yale University

Un Paradis désespéré, l'amour et l'illusion dans l'Astrée. New Haven: Yale University Press, 1963.
Structuralism. Yale French Studies, 36–37 (ed. J. Ehrmann). New Haven: Yale French Studies, 1966.
Literature and Revolution. Yale French Studies, 39 (ed. J. Ehrmann). New Haven: Yale French Studies, 1967.
Game, Play, Literature. Yale French Studies, 41 (ed. J. Ehrmann). New Haven: Yale French Studies, 1968.

Norman N. Holland
SUNY—Buffalo

The First Modern Comedies: The Significance of Etherage, Wycherley, and Congreve. Cambridge, Mass.: Harvard University Press, 1959.
The Shakespearean Imagination. New York: Macmillan, 1964.
Psychoanalysis and Shakespeare. New York: McGraw–Hill, 1966.
The Dynamics of Literary Response. New York: Oxford University Press, 1968.

Roman Jakobson
Harvard University and Massachusetts Institute of Technology

A bibliography of his publications (in general linguistics and poetics; Slavic philology, literary history, and folklore; and Paleosiberian languages) appeared in *For Roman Jakobson* (1956). Professor Jakobson's *Selected Writings* are being published in seven volumes by Mouton (1962–   ).

Roger Kempf
Universität Zürich

Diderot et le roman ou le démon de la présence. Paris: Editions du Seuil, 1964.
Sur le corps romanesque. Paris: Editions du Seuil, 1968.

Jan Kott
University of Warsaw and SUNY— Stony Brook

Warszawa wieku oświecenia (ed. Jan Kott, with Stanislaw Lorentz). Warszawa: P.I.W., 1954.
Szkola klasyków. [Warszawa]: Czytelnik, 1955

Postep i gtupstwo. Warszawa: P.I.W., 1956.
Szkice o Szekspirze. Warszawa: P.I.W., 1961.
[Shakespeare, Our Contemporary (tr.
Boleslaw Taborski), Garden City, N.Y.:
Doubleday, 1964.]
Jak wam sie podoba. Warszawa: P.I.W.,
[1965].
Szekspir wspotczezesny. Warszawa: P.I.W.,
1965.
Teatr Narodowy: 1765–1794. Warszawa:
P.I.W., 1967.
Theatre Notebook: 1947–1967. Garden
City: Doubleday, 1968.

Jacob Loewenberg
*University of California
at Berkeley*

*Hegels Entwürfe zur enzyklopädie und
propädeutik nach den handschriften der
Harvard-Universität,* mit einer
handschriftenprobe, herausgegeben von
Dr. J. Loewenberg. Leipzig, 1912.
Josiah Royce. *Lectures on Modern Idealism*
(ed. J. Loewenberg). New Haven: Yale
University Press, 1919.
Fugitive Essays by Josiah Royce (introduction
by J. Loewenberg). Cambridge: Harvard
University Press, 1920.
Dialogues from Delphi. Berkeley: University
of California Press, 1949.
*Reason and the Nature of Things: Reflections
on the Cognitive Function of Philosophy.*
La Salle, Ill.: Open Court Publishing Co.,
1959.
Hegel . . . Selections (ed. J. Loewenberg).
New York: Charles Scribner's Sons, 1965.
*Hegel's Phenomenology: Dialogues on the
Life of the Mind.* La Salle, Ill.: Open
Court Publishing Company, 1965.
*Thrice-Born: Selected Memories of an
Immigrant.* New York: Hobbs,
Dorman, 1968.

Paul de Man
Zürich—Johns Hopkins

Editor. Gustave Flaubert. *Madame Bovary.*
New York: Norton Critical Editions,
1965.
Editor. *The Poetry of John Keats.* New
York: New American Library, 1966.

Blindness and Insight in Contemporary
Criticism. New York: Oxford, 1970.

Carroll C. Pratt
Princeton University

*The Meaning of Music: A Study in
Psychological Aesthetics.* New York and
London: McGraw-Hill, 1931.
The Logic of Modern Psychology. New
York: The Macmillan Company, 1939.
Military Psychology (ed. C. C. Pratt).
Evanston, Illinois: American Psychological
Association, 1941.
*Psychology: The Third Dimension of the
War.* New York: Columbia University
Press, 1942.
Music as the Language of Emotion.
Washington, D.C.: U.S. Government
Printing Office, 1952.
Some Aspects of Musicology. [Princeton],
1957.

Pietro Pucci
Cornell University

*Aristofane ed Euripide: ricerche metriche
e stilistiche.* Rome: Accademia Nazionale
dei Lincei, 1961.

David M. Schneider
University of Chicago

*Marriage, Authority, and Final Causes: A
Study of Unilateral Cross-Cousin Marriage*
(with George C. Homans). Glencoe, Ill.:
Free Press, 1955.
Zuñi Kin Terms. Lincoln: University of
Nebraska, 1956.
Matrilineal Kinship (with Kathleen Gough).
Berkeley: University of California, 1961.

Johns Hopkins University Sponsoring Committee	James E. Deese
	Eugenio Donato
	Neville Dyson—Hudson
	René Girard
	J. Lionel Gossman
	Edward N. Lee
	Richard Macksey
	J. Hillis Miller
	Paul R. Olson
	Elias Rivers
	Eduardo Saccone
	Charles S. Singleton
	Bernard Vannier
	Harry Woolf
Seminars— Publications Advisory Committee	Roland Barthes
	Eugenio Donato
	René Girard
	Jean Hyppolite
	Richard Macksey
	J. Hillis Miller
Student Reception Committee	John C. Blegen
	Jonathan Botelho
	David Carroll
	Robert Carroll
	Murray Cohen
	John Foran
	Josue Harari
	Michael Koppisch
	Margaret Meyer
	Anthony G. Wilden